childhood

childhood

MELVIN KONNER

LITTLE, BROWN AND COMPANY
Boston • Toronto • London

FIRST EDITION

The "Childhood" series is a production of Thirteen/WNET and The
Childhood Project, Inc., in association with Channel Four television
and Antelope Films, Ltd.

Permissions for copyrighted material quoted in the text and credits
for illustrations appear on pages 437–442.

Library of Congress Cataloging-in-Publication Data

Konner, Melvin.
    Childhood / Melvin Konner. — 1st ed.
        p.   cm.
    Includes bibliographical references and index.
    ISBN 0-316-50184-0
    1. Children.   I. Title.
HQ781.K66   1991
305.23—dc20   91-26458

        10   9   8   7   6   5   4   3   2   1

RRD-OH

Designed by Jeanne Abboud

*Published simultaneously in Canada
by Little, Brown & Company (Canada) Limited*

PRINTED IN THE UNITED STATES OF AMERICA

HANNAH KONNER
1910—1990

"Her children arise up, and call her blessed . . ."
— PROVERBS 31:28

Contents

PREFACE xiii

ONE: *Great Expectations* 3

TWO: *Love's Labors* 31

THREE: *Love, Separation, and the Sense of Self* 81

FOUR: *Language in Play and Imagination* 135

FIVE: *Risk and Resilience* 189

SIX: *Life's Lessons* 237

SEVEN: *Marbles and Morals* 289

EIGHT: *Metamorphosis* 341

EPILOGUE: *The House of Tomorrow* 399

BIBLIOGRAPHY/READING LIST 429

TEXT AND ILLUSTRATION CREDITS 437

INDEX 443

In childhood, everything was more vivid — the sun brighter, the smell of the fields sharper, the thunder louder, the rain more abundant and the grass taller.

— Constantin Paustovsky

A child is like a precious stone, but also a heavy burden.

— African (Swahili) proverb

Preface

T H I S   B O O K has the good fortune to be tied to the public television series "Childhood," and while it is different from the series in important ways, it is also greatly enhanced by the tie. The book came about when I was contacted by David Wolff, the then-new publishing director for Thirteen–WNET New York, and Geoffrey Haines-Stiles, executive producer for the series. They wanted a book that would be as unusual as the series: not a child psychology text, not a how-to of baby-and-child care for parents, and not another critique of how our institutions take care of children. They wanted all this and more — in essence, a book about the total experience of childhood. They wanted my training and "expertise," but they also wanted something much more personal: how I view childhood from the perspective of the parent I am and the child I once was.

The excitement of this project was apparent to me immediately. I soon found out that it stemmed most centrally from Geoffrey's commitment, enthusiasm, and prodigious energy. We have a couple of strong egos, he and I, and I suspect we gave each other a few new gray hairs. But I and my book have gained enormously from contact with him. He generously admitted me to extensive consultations with expert advisers to the series, to early viewings of raw footage and rough-cuts of the episodes, to a large library of material about childhood, to compelling visual images of tremendous variety, to his particular expertise in the history of childhood, and to his valuable opinions on everything from the proper form of Japanese children's nicknames, through nursery rhymes, to the nature-nurture controversy. He had been working on this project for at least three years before I was brought in, and this book reflects much that he learned and did in those years. In the most hectic phase of television production he somehow found time to read the entire manuscript three times and to provide comments, corrections, and suggestions at a level of detail that amazed me. And on top of all this he managed to get me on camera more than once with a deft directorial touch that prevented me from seeming too ridiculous. I am deeply grateful to him for all this and more.

Sadly, his partner as executive producer, David Loxton, died of pancreatic cancer early in my collaboration with the series. He had contributed a great deal to the development of the series. I knew that he had a deadly illness, but not because he told me. He was a brave man of evident talent and vision, both of which have indirectly influenced this book. Another executive producer, Peter Montagnon, coordinated the "families" filming outside America and also represented Channel 4 in Britain, and we have had many very helpful and pleasant interactions. His gentle manner belies his life as an aggressive director and producer with a wonderful eye, and it was a privilege for me to know him.

Gene Marner and Erna Akuginow directed two episodes each, and I enjoyed working with both of them. Gene took me to Israel for the Kibbutz Bar Am childhood sequence, and Erna arranged for the shooting at P.S. 152, my own old elementary school, and at the Bronx Zoo, although illness prevented her from doing the actual shooting. Both directors made very helpful comments on drafts of certain chapters. I especially thank Erna for her constructive comments on chapter 6, "Life's Lessons."

For me, one of the most important aspects of the collaboration has been the chance to work with some of the leading authorities in the field of child development. Five of these serve as observers for the series; that means they appear on camera on location offering insights into some aspect of childhood we are seeing. These five are Urie Bronfenbrenner, Professor of Human Development and Family Studies at Cornell University; Sandra Scarr, Professor of Psychology at the University of Virginia; Robert Hinde, Royal Society Research Professor and Master of St. John's

College, Cambridge University; Jerome Kagan, Professor of Developmental Psychology at Harvard University; and Marian Wright Edelman — attorney, tireless child advocate, and president of the Children's Defense Fund.

With the exception of Edelman, with whom I had not had the privilege of working before, all had influenced me markedly through their research and writing beginning a quarter of a century ago. But I had only worked directly with Kagan; it was a superb experience to work with him again, and also to work directly with Bronfenbrenner, Scarr, and Hinde. In addition, we had consultations at WNET with Alvin Poussaint, Associate Professor of Psychiatry at Harvard; Lewis Lipsitt, Director, Child Study Center, Brown University; Ray Hiner, Professor of History and Education at the University of Kansas; Robert Wozniak, Professor of Human Development at Bryn Mawr; Linda Pollock of Churchill College, Cambridge University and now at Tulane; and John Demos, Professor of History at Yale University.

All of these authorities have been generous with their time and expertise. In the case of observers Hinde, Scarr, and Kagan, they have gone through most of one or another draft of the manuscript, making remarkably detailed comments on content and style. It was intimidating for me to have some of my intellectual heroes looking over my shoulder while I tried to say what I thought about childhood.

But here is a very important message: None of these scientists and scholars, leaders in their fields, supports every conclusion or interpretation in this book. They may be responsible for a good deal of my knowledge, but they are not responsible for my opinions, or for my use and abuse of that knowledge. This is a rapidly moving field filled with lively controversy. Sometimes the observers contradicted each other; more often they only contradicted me. I have tried hard to get the story straight on matters of fact and to make good judgments about areas open to legitimate question. In almost all cases, I could find at least one expert in the panel of advisers who would agree with my opinion. Others might well disagree. Most have written their own very different good books, and these are included in the suggested readings.

Ann Cale Kruger, then on the psychology faculty at Emory University, helped lay the foundation for the whole of the book, by providing a

sweeping professional view of the best research in the field of child development. Her wisdom and judgment in selecting research and in giving
me advice about how to interpret it led me off the wrong track over and
over again. She resisted my biologizing fiercely, and would not support
many of my opinions. Yet without her help this book would be a pale
shadow of its present form. Victor Balaban, a research associate based at
the "Childhood" series, also provided many important references, and
helped to prepare the list of suggested readings. He also led me to several
of the epigraphs. Melissa Walker provided important help in some of the
literary references.

David Wolff has been a constant source of support to me and an immensely helpful liaison to the people involved in production. He and Licia
Hurst, with the help of photo researchers Laura Resen, Mia Gallison, and
David Reisman, spent countless hours working with me (and more without me) on the selection of the illustrations. Others at WNET who helped
facilitate my work include Anne Troise, Myra Setzer, Pam Loxton, Har-
riet Reisen, and Meg Kruizinga. Eli Regev, a resident psychologist and
researcher at Kibbutz Bar Am, not only guided me and a film crew
through the world of his community, but also lent his knowledge to help
me interpret the effects of how they care for children in that community.
Louis Lissak, M.D., the obstetrician who delivered Michelle Kaufman,
put up with the intrusion of a film crew and a so-called expert observer,
and brought Michelle into the world with complete professional aplomb.
I also thank Lester Kostick, Principal of P.S. 152 in Brooklyn, who guided
me gently on a very nostalgic journey.

It is a great pleasure to thank all the real people in real families
throughout the world, caring for their children, doing the best they can,
struggling and adapting as we all try to do — yet willing to let us in on
their struggles. All who watch "Childhood" will be struck by shock after
shock of recognition and experience the sense of looking in a mirror that
reflects stunning images from all around the world. They will also feel,
as I do, a profound debt of gratitude to these people who have en-
lightened so many strangers by inviting all of us into their lives:

- Deni and Likano, the mother and father of Yeye, eight, Ali, four,
  and Kamala, newly born — a family among the Baka, hunters,

gatherers, and traders in the southeastern rain forest of Cameroon in Africa;

- Maria Oliveira, a seamstress, her husband, Manoel, a welder, and their six children — Sandra (the oldest at sixteen), Simone, Sylvia, Sergio, Suellen, and newborn Sydney — migrants from rural northeastern Brazil, who somehow thrive in the urban crush of one of the poorest sections of São Paulo;

- Barbara Kaufman, a Manhattan architect, her husband, David, a urologist, and their first baby, Michelle, like Sydney Oliveira, born on camera;

- Larissa Popov, an ex–obstetrics nurse, her husband, Mikhail ("Misha"), an Afghan war veteran and auto-body press operator, and their children Stas, three, a tiny but tireless gymnast, and Vitaly, whom we follow from shortly after birth;

- Natasha Kalugin, a part-time cleaner, her husband, Aleksander, a Moscow subway supervisor and maintenance worker, and their children (all under six) Roman, Nadia, Katya, and baby Vera;

- Raisa Krilov, a patent engineer, who at one point seemed headed for divorce from her husband, Igor, an auto prototype–model maker, and the children — Anya, Raisa's child by a previous marriage, who is going through puberty, and her little brother, Sasha;

- Nadia Shlyapnikov, a librarian, her husband, Zhenya, an auto mechanic (and Raisa Krilov's brother), and their children Igor, thirteen, and Seryozha, seven;

- Anita Gholston, a college counselor, her husband, Felton, who repairs photocopiers, and their three children, Benjamin, six, Malcolm, five, and two-year-old sister Avery — a black family living in white America;

- Nancy and Michael Kirkpatrick, who work together in the family-owned swimming pool business, and their three children: Shannon, twelve, Michael Jr., ten, and Kelly Ann, eight — like the Gholstons, suburban New Yorkers;

- Shizue Hijikata, a full-time mother and homemaker, her husband, Yoshinori, a city councillor in the Tokyo suburb of Hino, and their daughters Megumi, twelve, and Naomi, ten, and son Toshiyuki, eight;

- Sumiko Nakayama, also a full-time homemaker, her husband Takasuke, a graphic designer, and their daughters Karuna, thirteen, and Chizuka, six;
- Mikiko Nouhata, a former nurse, her husband, Yushiro, a sales manager, and their three under-five children, Koichiro, Yojiro, and baby Kenzaburo.

I also would like to thank the generosity of those whose funding made the "Childhood" project possible: the National Science Foundation, the National Institute of Mental Health, the National Institute of Child Health and Human Development, PBS, CPB, and Nabisco.

I have also had the privilege of working with Bill Phillips, Vice President and Editor in Chief at Little, Brown. His enthusiasm kept me going when my own was flagging, and he provided an unfailingly intelligent literary eye. His contributions in writing and in person helped shape the book, and I wish all writers editors like him. Karen Dane, also a Little, Brown editor, lent a sensitive and helpful editorial hand, a resonance with my style, and even an episode from her own childhood. Michael Mattil copyedited the manuscript with a professional eye and a gentle but decisive hand. Megan Gray, Bill Phillips's assistant, helped facilitate all aspects of the editorial work. The project was brought to a full stop for six weeks by my recovery from surgery, a delay that made life much more difficult for everyone at Little, Brown. They shouldered this burden with grace, kindness, and humor.

Elaine Markson, my agent, has stuck with me through thick and thin, mostly thin, with a warm, supportive friendship and a great sense of humor. I hope the muses reward her for all she has done for me.

Peter Brown, the head of my department at Emory University, made this work possible by helping to release me from many teaching and administrative duties. Filling in required exceptional effort, especially when I became seriously ill in midsemester. He has been more than a facilitator; he has been a sympathetic friend. I am also grateful to other members of the faculty of anthropology; to President James T. Laney and Vice Presidents David Minter, Bill Frye, and George Jones; and to the staff of the Department of Anthropology, especially Paul Weimer, Judy Robertson, and Carey Hardwick.

The following are people who, either formally or informally, have contributed greatly to my understanding of childhood over the years, outside the context of the "Childhood" series. Alas for me, none of them can be held responsible for views in this book, unless specifically attributed to them. Nevertheless I am very grateful: Lauren Adamson, Roger Bakeman, Ronald Barr, Paul Bianchi, Hans Bode, Jane Borden, Nicholas Blurton Jones, T. Berry Brazelton, Sidney Briebart, Thomas Considine, Victor Denenberg, Irven DeVore, Irenäus Eibl-Eibesfeldt, Marjorie Elias, Susan Goldberg, Edward Gross, Elizabeth Gude, Gerald Henderson, Jerome Kagan, Hans Kalverboer, Jane Lancaster, P. Herbert Leiderman, Myrtle McGraw, James McKenna, Ulric Neisser, Paul Pavel, Heinz Prechtl, Howard Rollins, Alice Rossi, Wulf Schiefenhövel, Stefan Stein, Daniel Stern, Charles Super, James Tanner, Michael Tomasello, Robert Trivers, Edward Tronick, Steven Tulkin, George Vaillant, Eric Wanner, Neil Warren, Beatrice Whiting, John Whiting, and Carol Worthman.

Dr. Julian Gomez and Dr. Boyd Eaton helped me through a major illness during the writing of the book, and supported me with their friendship and advice from the inception of the project. Joseph Beck and Dr. John Stone have been important friends throughout, and Dudley Clendinen has helped me through some rough seas recently. Kathy Mote has been a fiercely loyal friend who has helped me to understand my children and myself. Becky Perry, my "extra daughter," has let me look in on her own adolescence and helped me to understand childhood.

To my children, Susanna, Adam, and Sarah, I owe an enormous debt for teaching me so much of what I know about childhood. I must also thank them for providing, and then giving me permission to use, the bits and pieces of their lives that appear in this book. I have referred only to minor problems, or to things that are cute or touching and that illustrate some point in a theory or process I am trying to make clear — usually because the events in question helped make the theories clear to me. I don't mean to make my children seem perfect. Like most children, they do have significant problems, but those belong exclusively to them. I am aware of the limits of children's informed consent, and if I have set anything down here that offends them in the future, I ask their forgiveness.

To my wife, their mother, Marjorie Shostak, I owe a much more complex debt: for accompanying and sometimes guiding me through the maze of their childhood; for teaching me much about how hunter-gatherers like the !Kung grapple with the problems of growing up in their challenging world; for helping me through my mother's terminal illness and my own recovery from surgery, either of which could otherwise have derailed this book; and for supporting a creative process that is sometimes very burdensome for those who must stay close to it.

My brother, Lawrence Konner, started life younger than me, but has often been the older brother recently. That is one of the paradoxes of an enduring sibling bond — the most foolishly maligned and egregiously underestimated of all human relationships. He has helped me to understand my children, has given freely of his knowledge of his own, and has applied his fine blend of wisdom and common sense to almost all the problems of my life. He shepherded me personally through a chapter and a half of this book, and generously took care of me when I was ill. It's a dreadful cliché, but I sometimes find it hard to know where he ends and I begin.

And of course, I thank my parents for giving me my childhood, for struggling bravely against their hearing impairment every day, for doing the best they could to help me grow up, and for forgiving all the things I did in earlier life stages that unquestionably hurt or confused them. My mother, Hannah Konner, died during the writing of this book, at the age of eighty. I still remember vividly the warm feeling I got when she talked to me about my first childish poems and essays — the feeling that she, at least, believed I would amount to something. Fortunately for me, she always felt, later on, that I did. She was truly a woman of valor in the sense of Proverbs 31, and "her children arise up, and call her blessed."

[xx]

childhood

ONE

Great Expectations

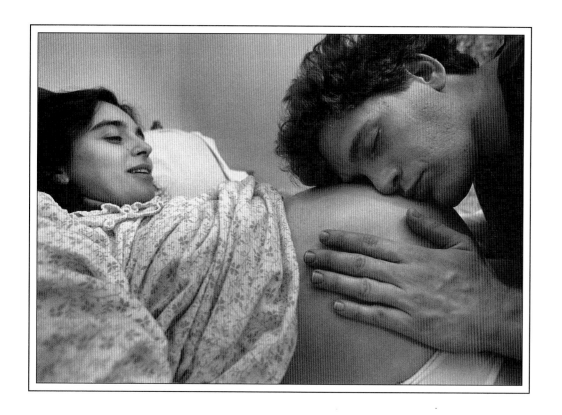

Every time a child is born it brings with it the
hope that God is not yet disappointed with man.

— RABINDRANATH TAGORE

THE EXCITEMENT, the conflict, the pleasure of childhood: the grin that breaks across a woman's face when, after an exhausting night of labor, she greets her first child for the first time in the dawn light; the waddle of a thirteen-month-old boy stumbling across a room, coming out with the sounds that — his father can finally tell himself — correspond more or less to the word "Daddy"; two eight-year-old girls so engrossed in a mathematical game that parental bedtime urgings don't even dent their consciousness; a teenage boy's agitated embarrassment over a wet dream, and his classmate's equally private awe at her own first menstrual blood; and then, for every parent, that moment: a voice in the choir, a rush on the football field, a turn of phrase in a debate, a computer puzzle solved, a way of holding a baby, or even just a firm handshake and a really convincing smile — the small thing that stuns you into stepping back for a moment and visualizing the person this child may someday be.

It has been happening, unfolding, since the dawn of the human species, in every epoch, in every place on earth. This drama of metamorphosis — for that is really what it is — is being played out right now, in a farming village in northeastern Brazil, among hunters in the heart of the Cameroon rain forest, on the thirtieth floor of high-rise public housing in Cincinnati, and in a villa on the Italian Riviera with an unbelievable view of the Mediterranean. Growth and learning, need and challenge, discipline and freedom, male and female, love and jealousy, anger and forgiveness — these are some of the themes that clash on the stage of every family, in every culture, in every generation.

The main character — a partially formed person unknowingly bearing the burden of our hopes and dreams — is always the same, and yet always different. Those of us who read (or write) books like this one spend much of our lives in the thrall of such creatures. But, of course, they aren't just our children — diminutive reflections of ourselves, to watch, to teach, to learn from, to puzzle out, to bank much of the future on . . . to love.

The figures we dimly perceive when we think about childhood are also we ourselves, and not just the doted-upon reflections. We were once such creatures, every bit as oblivious to the complexities of life, guarded as closely by our own personal grown-ups, struggling across obstacles to try to reach the future. So this book is not just about *them,* our charges, the ones we care so keenly for, and sometimes despair of, as we guide them through the maze of growth. It is also about our former selves, those shadowy, miniature versions of us that move darkly across the screen of memory. The unexamined life is not worth living, said Socrates. I'm not sure that he was right universally; but for some of us, the examination is half of what makes it interesting. So a study of childhood has to be a study of ourselves: why we are what we are, as seen from what we were, and how we came to be.

The great Welsh poet Dylan Thomas once wrote:

> *The force that through the green fuse drives the flower*
> *Drives my green age . . .*

The force of life, he meant; the force of growth. Whatever magic wells up irrepressibly through the stem and then slowly breaks a blossom out of the bud, also presses the man up through the body and mind of the boy, the woman through the small frame of the girl. Thomas wrote, too, of a boy his age who'd moved into his neighborhood. They saw each other, and immediately were fighting. Then, having thrashed one another soundly, they strode off, arms around each other's shoulders, friends for life — love at first fight. Such a moment is charged with the mystery of development, with the strange wild incomprehensible independence of childhood: *the force that through the green fuse drives the flower.*

And yet we say, too, "As the twig is bent, so grows the tree," which seems to mean that we can make a child in our image, that we can gain complete control of the same growth forces. Or even more arrogantly in our grown-up delusion of power, "Give me a child till he's ten and he'll be mine forever" — in one form or another, a cherished belief of ideologues from the Jesuits to the Bolsheviks. The image is one of training, drill, reward, punishment, setting examples, molding, shaping moist clay in our hands. In this view the life force seems almost incidental — something like, say, the consistency of the clay. So which vision of childhood is the right one?

Neither, of course — and both. That is the other part of the mystery — the unknown; which, increasingly, we are justified in calling the partly known. It is the vast unexplored sea of *potential* knowledge of just how children change and grow. It is the "science" part. For about a century we have been systematically studying child development with increasingly sophisticated methods. Although much of this research has been in the framework of child psychology, it is now deriving from a surprising array of other disciplines: neuropsychology, sociobiology, cognitive science, molecular genetics, psychological anthropology, computer-based training, behavioral pediatrics, neonatology, adolescent psychiatry, evolutionary biology, pediatric endocrinology, physical anthropology, behavior modification, psychopharmacology. . . . We could go on, but we needn't detain ourselves with such jargon. The point is knowledge, new knowledge, based on really superb research. And drawing on the methods, traditions, and wisdom of fields of science so fast moving and different that it's difficult to keep watch on them, even in their outlines.

The secret in making use of them is knowing that *as distinct disciplines* they matter less and less. What matters is the developing child and the light that these fields of science shed on her. (I don't mean to slight boys, this is about them too, but they've had more than their share of precedence over the centuries.) The question of how she gets to be the person she will be — or more precisely, the person she will, always, be *becoming* — is now being addressed with an almost astounding rigor. The parent who wants to learn more about childhood will not, of course, be able to master all these sciences — who could, when even those who devote their lives to them have constant trouble keeping up? The best any of us can do is master a few basic facts, a few fundamental concepts, keeping in mind that we are setting out in a rocking little boat on an immense, poorly charted ocean.

Consider, for example, a parent who is facing the problem of childhood hyperactivity. She begins paying attention to certain television shows, reading certain articles in magazines and newspapers, maybe even consulting a book or two. She soon learns that it is usually first identified by teachers, since it can cause school failure; that it affects at least four times as many boys as girls; that it sometimes, though not always, runs in families; and that certain prescription drugs resembling amphetamines, or "speed," have the paradoxical effect of settling the child down. But she also learns that the long-term value of the drugs remains uncertain; that some people who claim to be experts oppose their use, advocating the methods of child psychology instead; and that some even view heightened activity as a part of the normal range of children's temperament, made to seem abnormal because of a failure of teaching or a poorly designed educational environment.

Now, our parent is the kind of person who doesn't jump to conclusions. For reasons buried in her own childhood, she is more than usually skeptical. Naturally curious, she reads more articles, until they begin to blur before her eyes. She talks to friends, relatives, teachers, doctors. Many cultures, says one article, don't even identify hyperactivity; without schools where you have to sit still to learn, some kinds of hyperactivity may be no disadvantage or even an advantage. Another points out the enormous hormonal differences between boys and girls as they grow; perhaps the sex difference in hyperactivity points toward an underlying difference in chemistry. One day she sees a program about the "open classroom": some educators, it seems, think children were not meant to study at fixed desks, but rather should be allowed to move from place to place in a classroom full of opportunities; but their critics think they are just knuckling under to falling standards. In a magazine for parents she finds an article about one expert who claims that food additives can cause hyperactivity; but it seems implausible to her, and some other experts say it isn't true.

She remains confused. Yet one night, settling down perhaps with a cup of tea, she must make a decision about her own child. The experts may continue to debate one another, but she alone in her quiet house must come to a decision. No one else will make the decision for her. And it has to be made now.

Try, if you like, to find a religious, or philosophic, or political program that will lead her in some way to the one right answer. There isn't one.

There is just the desire to help, and to do something complex enough to reflect her child's reality, yet simple enough to yield some kind of solution. And there is the love, of course. But she has long since made the discovery that love is not enough.

• • •

Not too many decades ago, in the bad old days before women began to demand equal rights, the field of child development was more or less a branch of home economics or (at its most sophisticated) of teacher education. It was a subject that experts (often male) taught to students (mostly female) in an effort to make them "better" parents and educators. This did not mean that nothing was known — we "knew" a lot. But, unfortunately, a lot of what we thought we knew was wrong. It was folklore, it was casual observation, it was "professional experience," it was dogma — religious or medical or scientific, dogma is dogma — and, to be fair, it was also to some extent knowledge based in research.

But this last category is now expanding exponentially, edging out dogma left and right. Consider a few things we have learned in the 1980s alone:

- Exposure of a fetus to even small amounts of alcohol, as delivered by a pregnant woman who drinks, may cause permanent damage to the infant's brain.
- Infants, including the very youngest infants, are as sensitive to pain as are adults, and possibly more so, despite myths to the contrary that have surrounded medical procedures in the past.
- Having a need for dependency indulged early in life has remarkably little impact, either way, on the likelihood of being overdependent later on.
- Empathy, the vicarious sharing of another person's suffering, appears in the first year of life — much earlier than we formerly thought — and is almost certainly unlearned.
- High-quality day-care centers are, psychologically as well as medically, a perfectly adequate way to look after infants and young children.
- A subgroup of infants and toddlers, identifiable early in life, show persistent timidity, almost certainly because of distinctive genes.
- Remarkably little of the similarity between siblings in personality is

because they have shared the same home environment; identical twins, for instance, are no more alike in personality — and may be more different — if they are reared together than if they are reared apart.

- Boys who are *extremely* interested in acting and dressing like girls — so much so that their parents obtain psychiatric advice — are likely to grow up to be homosexual or bisexual; yet these boys make up only a small proportion of male homosexuals.

- Child abusers are highly likely to have been abused as children themselves; but, all else being equal, nonrelatives are much more likely than relatives are to commit severe abuse.

- Many kids have persistent turmoil following puberty, but at least as many apparently do not; instead, they experience transient difficulties — depression, for instance, or irritability or "acting out" — that fade from view in two or three years as they grow, learn, and adjust to surging hormones and changing bodies.

These are only scattered highlights — a handful among hundreds of new research findings. This book, as far as it can, will describe some of the new knowledge and consider its human implications. But there will be much more to consider than research. There will be real families and children, including the families followed by "Childhood" — one among the Baka of Cameroon, three in Japan, three in the United States, four in the Soviet Union, and one in Brazil.

With great generosity, these families have allowed us to peek in on and even film some intimacies of their lives — twelve families on five continents, for up to a year and a half — especially the parents' relationships with their children. We see those children change, grow, and experience some great events: Michelle Kaufman and Sydney Oliveira are born; Vera Popov, Kenzaburo Nouhata, and Baka baby Kamala move through the great changes of infancy, while their apprehensive older siblings adjust; Avery Gholston learns to talk; Chizuka Nakayama and Benji Gholston start school; father Likano teaches Ali about termites; Shannon Kirkpatrick goes on her first overnight class trip; and Anya Krilov roams around with other adolescent girls, hanging out Moscow-style. These growing children give life to academic and medical facts about childhood. What they have to teach us about it, and about ourselves is often familiar, sometimes chastening, frequently funny, but almost always enriching and inspiring; it is the daily drama of human growth and development in the family.

But I've done more than thank these families for their generosity; I've volunteered my own family. Susanna, twelve, Adam, nine, and Sarah, four, were not being filmed, but they were being watched by me, and by their mother, Marjorie Shostak, a writer-anthropologist. Unlike some scientists of the past — Charles Darwin and Jean Piaget, for example, to whom I would not relish being compared — I have not tried to use my children as data to establish new hypotheses of the science of childhood. Rather, I refer to them the way I refer to the families filmed all over the world: as illustrations of what the science of childhood has learned. For me, of course, they are uniquely vivid illustrations.

Other cultural settings extend the breadth of the series even farther. In particular, cultures I have lived in and with, studied, or at least visited for a time — especially the !Kung San, or Bushmen, hunters and gatherers of Africa's Kalahari Desert (made famous by the film *The Gods Must Be Crazy*); the most traditional, hogan-dwelling, Navajo sheep farmers of the Four Corners region of the American Southwest, where I was the guest of anthropologist James Chisholm; the traditionally religious Jewish community in Brooklyn, New York, where I grew up; and members of La Leche League in suburban Boston — subjects of a study I participated in with Marjorie Elias — who believe in and practice an ideal of extremely indulgent baby and child care, including breast-feeding at least once an hour until age two, sleeping with infants, and keeping mother-infant separations to a minimum, but who otherwise closely resemble suburban mothers throughout the United States.

Discussions of childhood past are here, too. They evoke the schoolchildren of ancient Athens and the family of colonial Williamsburg, the first alphabet lessons of five-year-old traditional Jewish scholars and the difficult but often positive experience of farm children sharing chores, an ancient Mesopotamian scribe's complaints about schoolwork, and a "wild child" in France adopted and "tamed" by a dedicated eighteenth-century physician; these and other historical examples show the impact of nature and nurture on growing children, what has been tried and how well it has worked, and where our culture's current practice, with all its successes and failures, originated.

Yet there is older and deeper history that can be approached through the voluminous recent research on the evolution of childhood. A five-thousand-year-old burial of a mother and child together in a bog in Denmark, and mother-child figurines from the ancient Near East might seem to begin the story, but really do not take us back very far. Modern studies of childhood in hunting-and-gathering societies, in which I was lucky to play a small part — the Baka and the !Kung San are only two examples — allow some plausible inferences about the basic nature of human childhood — what childhood may have been like in the conditions in which we evolved. This is not quite like the other uses of cross-cultural material in the book; it goes further, to ideas about the origins of childhood and parenting. And these origins are in turn given greater depth by references to parent-offspring relations among our nonhuman relatives. We can draw not only on facts but on images of surprisingly tender and complex animal families. For example, marmosets — small monkeys of South America — have strong male-female bonds with fathers who carry the infant twins day and night; while chimpanzees, with much longer and more complex childhoods, have been known to show violence to unprotected mother-infant pairs. These kinds of examples are not just interesting nature stories, but case studies that test new theories of the evolution of childhood.

At another extreme, far from data and theory per se, human memory in literary and autobiographical narrative gives us access to a different kind of truth — and sometimes to fiction passing as truth. Excerpts from autobiographical accounts of people famous or obscure reveal experience, or at least imagined experience, not only vivid enough to live indelibly in memory, but powerful enough to illustrate the discoveries of modern developmental science. As "Childhood" observer Urie Bronfenbrenner, a child psychologist at Cornell University, has put it, "All of us partly see the world through the eyes of the child we once were."

• • •

The book, like the series, tries to show as well as say what we know: how the boundaries between disciplines break down as they try to encompass the complexity of childhood, and how research is beginning to answer the great timeless questions of how we should treat our children and how we ourselves became who we are. The book follows the simple outline of human development, beginning before birth and proceeding through puberty.

For example, a quiet revolution has taken place in the way life begins in our culture; and strangely, it harks back to the way life began throughout much of human history. The event is full of risk, it is true, and more than a little pain; but it is also full of love, and spontaneity, and joy. This coming into the world was a "rite of passage" in most cultures, charged with emotional and spiritual meaning. Yet in ours, by the 1960s, technology had nearly eliminated all that — while, admittedly, making the process safer than it had ever been. But then mothers and fathers, acting from impulses fundamental to human nature, began to take the process back, and they made a revolution that we call natural childbirth.

We also know that despite individual differences, infants in all cultures start out with much of the same basic biological equipment. At the time of manufacture, so to speak, human cultures have somewhat interchangeable parts — newborn babies. True, genes set them going toward subtle biological uniqueness. But we are beginning to understand how the wide variations in the treatment of infants start them down the road of *cultural* difference — and ultimately, of a fully realized individuality.

Yet culture is not all there is to individuality. In the midst of the extreme environmental and cultural determinism of the American social sciences, a few professional voices were raised in favor of another kind of determinant. Arnold Gesell and Myrtle McGraw, for example, writing in the 1930s and 1940s, kept reminding parents that much of the child's behavior simply — or maybe not so simply — unfolds as the child grows. In recent years that message of maturation has been decisively confirmed. It has also been extended to broad realms of children's thought and feeling, which also change predictably as birthdays go by. Many things the mind does are not really learned — they just grow. Language, for instance, seems at first glance as if it must be purely cultural, because it is so varied. Yet the fundamental mental and social functions performed by language are remarkably universal, emerging in a similar way with similar milestones in children of all cultures.

In the 1980s, neuropsychology has come into play, extending this analysis deep into the brain. Increasingly, we can show that universal features of children's behavior and mental life mature more or less the way walking does — the result more of brain maturation than cultural training. Even emotions mature with a certain universality that may be attributable to the growth of the brain.

But universal sequences are only half the maturational story. New research has also focused on individual differences. We parents, in our arrogance of power, tend to be cultural determinists until our second child is born. It is only then that we are forced to realize that we have had two quite different human beings right (as it were) from the starting gate. Even by the 1960s it was shown that infants have stable temperaments — budding personalities — from the early months of life. The 1980s have seen this basic fact confirmed beyond dispute. It doesn't mean that temperaments don't change, or that the environment has no effect, or that all emotional characteristics are stable. It just means that certain features of temperament — timidity, for instance — are characteristics the infant brings into the world, relatively resistant to environmental molding. We are fearful of this insight, because we think it impinges upon our sense of freedom. But to deny it is not far from denying human individuality.

Few questions trouble parents in our culture more than how to balance love and discipline. In China, the Soviet Union, and even modern Japan, parents have decided much more in favor of discipline than most Americans have. It is their tradition, and they seem to be at peace with it. They think that children are comforted by discipline, and that it does not interfere with self-reliance; the Japanese, at any rate, are doing very well without the sort of childhood that *we* think promotes independent achievement. What are the long-term consequences of discipline or "spoiling"? The book reviews new research that is directed at giving answers to this and related questions.

Fortunately, childhood almost always unfolds in the context of some type of family. The family has been rightly called a "haven in a heartless world," and there is no doubt that it is now under siege. Yet recent historical and anthropological studies have suggested basic resiliencies that most pessimists could not have imagined. The African-American family, for instance, was certainly hurt by slavery, and many psychiatrists and sociologists see evidence of that damage even now. But, facing some of the worst conditions ever endured by the human family, it resisted dissolution.

What accounts for the family's tenacity in the face of such pressures? Some anthropologists say that when you look at some of the world's cultures, all bets about the family are off. Most of these cases have validity and interest, but the implied degrees of freedom are much fewer than they seem. So we are still looking at variations in the family, albeit an extended one. During the 1980s, sociobiologists, along with some anthropologists, have organized the worldwide data on the family in such a way as to give it a new scientific foundation. We need to take seriously their intriguing new view, which explains the family's resilience by reference to human nature — and suggests, optimistically, that the family will always be around.

School is something we take for granted. But, of course, most of the people who have ever lived have not had it — nor even been literate. Yet obviously some sort of evolutionary preparation must have taken place in order for so many millions of children to engage in such an "unnatural" activity. Every child in every human culture must learn vastly more than our most intelligent relative, the wild chimpanzee. Not that the chimp is a sluggard or a dolt; as animals go, he is quite the philosopher. And we are only one or two percent different genetically. Yet that small advance has somehow enabled us to store more information by age eight than an adult chimpanzee could ever grapple with. Information about plants, animals, tool-using and tool-making, dozens of relatives, thousands of words, a grammar, religious symbols, a personal and family and tribal history — all this in a culture (like the Baka or the !Kung) where reading, writing, and 'rithmetic do not even play a role.

The evolutionary fact is that human children are vessels for the passing on of culture. They soak it up, find it impossible to avoid. But on the average, they begin to be especially good at receiving and storing information after the age of seven or so. And what of the demands they face? Comparisons among different schooling tactics are instructive, and we will consider some patterns of schooling in detail. American schools concentrate on language arts, but Soviet children far exceed Americans in their mastery of their own country's literature. And in Japan — where parents light votive candles to pray for their children's grades — superior mathematical training produces vastly superior ability. We think of American homes as light on chores for children, but actually we assign more of them than the Japanese, while the latter spend much more time on homework.

Such cultural differences result in different performance. Yet we only have to review the careers of prodigies in music or math to realize that some children just have special brains. As for the nonprodigies, are their brains all the same? Can each, sufficiently motivated, be anything he or she wants to be? Does the expectation that all can be equally successful if sufficiently motivated achieve its goal of providing equal opportunity, or does it merely place an intolerable burden of pressure, not only on schools but on most children? New research has begun to provide some answers that will enable us to fit the child's mind — each special in some way — to an educational plan that will maximize freedom of choice and opportunity while minimizing the anguish of disappointment.

But school is just one facet of learning. Everything we know about children suggests that play with peers is critical — as important, perhaps, as the crucible of the family. Yet what psychotherapist asks as carefully about peers as about, say, an allegedly seductive or domineering mother? In every culture throughout the world play groups are important. And even experiments with monkeys — the now-classic work of Harry Harlow — show that young monkeys deprived of peer play will grow up with emotional and sexual abnormalities that would be devastating if they occurred in the wild. In some ways, monkeys deprived of mothers but given peer play were better off as adults than monkeys with the opposite deprivation.

What then of the famous violence of the shipwrecked boys in William Golding's novel *Lord of the Flies?* It, too, has a piece of the truth; it shows — albeit fictionally — that human biological nature can unfold in terrible ways under certain conditions. But it is fact, not fiction, that most children in most cultures throughout the world have played in groups of mixed age and sex — same-sex, same-age *peer* groups in the strict sense have been a demographic impossibility in many cultures, and we will consider the implications of the change.

As for the cultural materials of play — the games, rhymes, riddles, songs, and chants — some have been traced to sources separated by thousands of miles and thousands of years. These creative achievements of child culture, which ordinarily exist only on the periphery of adult consciousness, convey concepts like fairness, rebellion, gender identity, power, and rights. To study them is to study childhood from the view-point of children themselves. And the study shows how much they are alike in every corner of the world.

After infancy, the most stunningly *biological* phase of childhood is puberty. It is now that the steamroller of real adulthood begins to bear down on the child's hopes and dreams, and the child must not merely get out of the way but somehow scramble up into the driver's seat. Now, too, the child's suspicion that boys and girls have somewhat different destinies begins to be confirmed by transformations of the body. Girls take the lead, as they have before in the course of development; if a boy knew of it, the appearance of a breast bud — a nubbin of new tissue behind a nipple — under one of his classmate's T-shirts would be, for him too, the first herald of his age-group's coming collective change.

Needless to say, these transformations are not just physical. New research has shown that the way pubescent children respond to the command "Draw a person" is determined not by age but by where they stand in the pubertal metamorphosis. *Self-concept* is drastically changing. And the relative pace at which children go through the process, in a given group or class or school, can help determine their social status and opportunities for years — often life-determining years. It is also an age when boys and girls diverge decisively in one realm: aggression. With current research on hormones and behavior, there is less and less reason to think that this difference is attributable solely, or mainly, to culture.

Yet girls run their own risks — and the main one, in America today, is still school-age pregnancy. There are many complex causes of this problem, but the way for it was prepared by one of the greatest and least appreciated biological processes in recent human history: the "secular trend," an increase in height and weight and an acceleration of growth that has affected populations throughout the world. Estimates suggest that the age of puberty has dropped between two and four years over the past two centuries in the United States and Europe. The book will consider some implications of the fact that bodies and minds are mismatched in a new way.

• • •

Yet despite dealing with all this information, this is not a textbook of child development, and certainly not a textbook of developmental psychology. It is not any kind of a textbook, and its subject is childhood —

something much larger than the science of child development. It scans a much larger field of view, sometimes more subjective, sometimes more rigorous, but often focused on experience rather than data. I have had to be more selective than a textbook is; important contributions of many experiments and theorists have had to be omitted in order to tell a coherent, accessible story. I have tried to be fair, but I have also had to make judgments; in many places my biases are at play.

Still, it can't be made simple, this strange dynamic of being a child. But at the very least it should be promising and joyful. It seems that adults, with all our power — children, after all, are pretty powerless — might manage to protect them, or at least to avoid hurting them. But consider: Throughout the developing world, and in portions of the industrial world, there are millions of children who are hungry; living on the streets; physically and sexually abused; exposed to alcohol and drugs; pregnant; deprived of schooling; dying of easily preventable or curable diseases; killed by accidents caused by negligence; or robbed of their childhood by war, bigotry, or poverty.

Can we really continue to live with ourselves and our consciences without doing more for these children — without taking better care of them? Even if the answer to that is yes, we can't continue to ignore our own self-interest, which tells us that the world is growing smaller every day and that sooner or later those hurt children will be adults that we will have to live with. Given what we know now about how children grow and what they need — even given merely the knowledge between the covers of this book — can we go on failing them so greatly?

As for children in relatively nurturing circumstances, we need to apply the enormous advances in knowledge that have come to us in recent years. This powerful new research has destroyed myth after myth about how children change and grow, what their emotional needs are, how and what they learn, and why they (and we) get to be the people we become. Does this mean that the "old masters" of the field of child psychology — Sigmund Freud, John Dewey, Jean Piaget, Erik Erikson, B. F. Skinner, Benjamin Spock, Bruno Bettelheim, John Bowlby, and others living and dead — have been completely superseded, that their voluminous writings have nothing further to offer us? Certainly not. Each of them had a piece of the truth — the ones mentioned, a sizable piece. And the more I learn — not just from new research but from watching my own and other people's children, and even because of my own childhood memories — the more reason I see to be grateful to them.

But I also realize that they all pulled their pants on one leg at a time. They had troubles, fears, aches and pains, families, children of their own, educations, religions, cultural backgrounds, indoctrinations, theories. They wanted desperately to think they had solved puzzles that no one has solved even now. And, above all, they had childhoods; childhoods to justify, to heal from, to remember, to laugh or cry or rage at, to relive a thousand times, to — at all cost — comprehend. The grand theorists have taught us much, and have pointed the way forward. But they have also left a legacy of problems. They have left us divided into intellectual camps contending for supremacy and prematurely asserting things that no one can yet know.

Erik Erikson, perhaps the most modest grand theorist, once said wisely: "The trouble with followers is, they repeat what the leader said fifty years ago and they think they are following him, but they are not following him any more." He meant, of course, that the leader would have moved, as he always did while he was living and thinking. To repeat without modification what he said long ago is unfairly to fossilize that thought, and to restrict our own freedom to discover what is true. Early in my career — not long, in fact, after the lecture in which I heard Erikson say that — I promised myself that I would neither subscribe to a single, over-arching grand theory nor try to invent a new one.

It was not in the nature of my chosen subject matter — how the human mind and human behavior change and grow, or how they don't — to lend itself truthfully to simplifying theories. I thought that Western theorists had ignored whole worlds of childhood that were essential to understanding who we are as human beings. So I followed my dream to the Kalahari Desert of Botswana, where I saw a "primitive" hunting-and-gathering culture that in some ways turned my idea of childhood upside down; and never since have I underestimated the importance of taking off our cultural blinders — seeking insights in exotic corners of the world and remote moments of history. Without this kind of test, theories are not about children, they are only about theories — self-fulfilling prophecies.

At the same time, there were certain cross-cultural constancies in the nature of the child, and some of my teachers — Irven DeVore, Jerome Kagan, Beatrice and John Whiting, and T. Berry Brazelton, among others — increasingly recognized such constancies. In my own view, human childhood had come from somewhere — it had evolved for some ·purpose — and in this remote past were some keys to figuring out the universals. But the keys were also under the skin — the hormones and other chemicals circulating in the womb, the state of the brain at birth, its rapid growth in the first few years, the transformations of puberty: these unified the children in cultures throughout the world, and helped to explain their similarities.

Some years later my own process of adult development, and my restlessness, dragged me from anthropology into medicine. My life had begun to feel too academic. I wanted to help in a way more immediate and practical. I wanted to dirty my hands again, as I once had wanted to sleep in the sand in Africa. Soon enough my hands were steeped in blood — and other bodily fluids. I delivered thirty-five babies — one of the greatest thrills of my life — and encountered children of all ages (and their parents) in health and sickness, in hope and pain, in healing and dying. I am back now in the academic world, but I will never be the same again. I no longer think only abstractly about childhood. And when I interact, day by day, with my own three children, my mind flashes with images — exhilarating, terrible, or merely mundane and real — of the hospital as well as the African bush.

After I had taught for years about human development, my own first child was born, and I soon realized that she was going to give me a different kind of education. So began a roller-coaster ride I am still on — with a seat belt woven of one part research, three parts love, and two parts common sense. I am holding on for dear life, but I and my children are having fun, and I learn something new about my ignorance every day.

I, too, am impatient for the results of research on childhood — at least as much as anyone else. I, too, watch my children grow from the perspective of my own confusion about the consequences of what I do, about what the right thing is. I am at or near the frontier of knowledge, but I still feel I know only a little bit. All I can say is, I am convinced that to recognize our ignorance is much better than to pretend — as many have done for a long time — that we know most of what we need to know already. We have to be patient; we are finding out new things just as fast as we know how. And if anyone gives you the impression that he has the answers *now* to the great timeless questions about childhood, you can smile and listen politely or you can turn your back and walk away, but in any case don't believe him.

If there is one theme among all the ambiguities, it is that for generations we have underestimated the role played by biology in explaining the experience and development of children. This book is in part an attempt to rectify that imbalance. But there is no implication that cultural and other environmental effects are therefore weak. What is implied is that the more we find out about the "nature" side of the nature-nurture equation, the more we can tailor our understanding and our interventions — to each individual child, at the right age, in the right way. Every parent wants to know how much childhood owes to nature, and how much to nurture — to culture.

In the blur of my own almost continual parental confusion, this knowledge has helped me to understand my children. It has made me more patient with an emotionally unrewarding newborn and a sometimes downright punitive adolescent. It has guided me in whatever teaching and shaping I try to do, helping to rid me of both unrealistic expectations and gross underestimates of what a given child of a given age can do. It has protected me from many passing child-care fads and quackeries, and even from some expert advice when that has been biased or narrow. And best of all, perhaps, it has prevented me from shouldering the burden of a false belief that I must take responsibility — or, for that matter, credit — for every mood, tendency, competence, for every bump or wrinkle in my children's adaptation to life.

In another couple of decades I hope to be around to watch those same children when the possibility of parenthood begins to dawn on them, as it dawned long before on their mother and father. At that moment, the gleam in their eyes will not be only lust, if they are lucky, but a strange and durable alloy of lust, love, and dreams of the future. In those dreams begin great responsibilities. And I like to think that I might be able to help a bit — wishful, perhaps, but pleasant thinking; we *will* at least know more by then — as they press those strange responsibilities into being, and a new generation embarks on the immense, unpredictable, magnificent adventure of childhood.

1.

2.

3.

4.

1. Vessel crafted between the years 200 and 700 by the Moche people of Peru depicts a birth scene, with laboring mother, assistant, and midwife.

2. The oldest type of fertility symbol is a depiction of an ample, probably gravid woman; these go back at least twenty thousand years. This one is from Willendorf, Austria.

3. Rebecca giving birth to Jacob, from an eleventh-century Old Testament.

4. Mythologies surrounding birth have always been powerful. This Balinese wood sculpture depicts a woman in childbirth, with her husband and toddler. The demon poised to devour the new baby symbolizes the risks of being born.

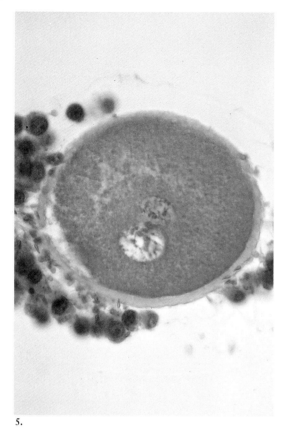

5.

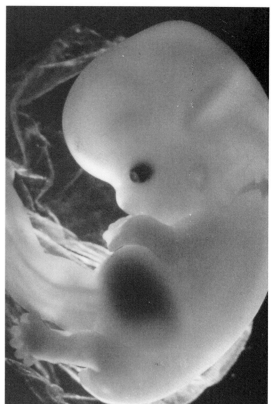

6.

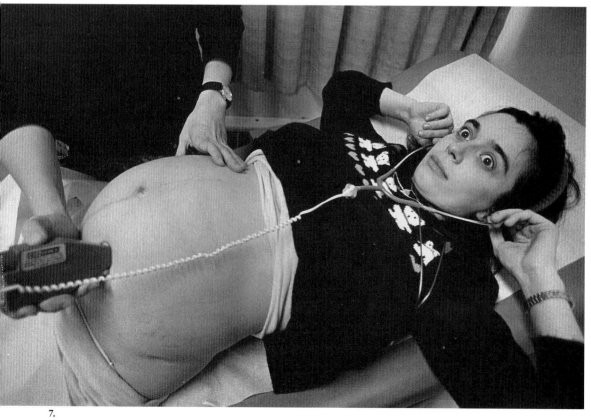

7.

5. Sperm cells crowd the egg; only one will penetrate.

6. At seven weeks of gestation, most organs are actively being formed.

7, 9. A woman hears her baby-to-be's heartbeat through ultrasound. Fathers, too, can "bond" with their infants before birth.

8. Hand-to-mouth activity, as in this five-month-old fetus, is one of many in-the-womb actions given to children by nature rather than culture.

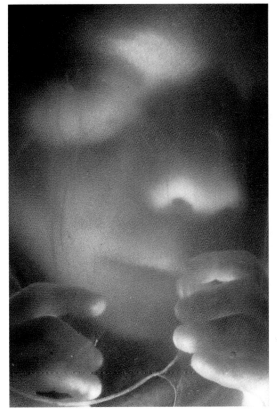

8.

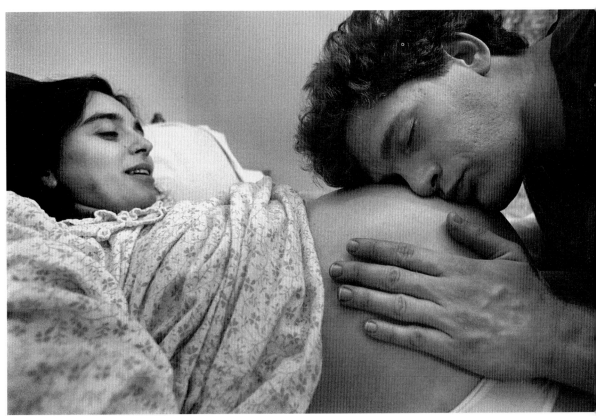

9.

10.

Reclining with the feet up ("the lithotomy position") is the typical birth position in our culture today. But leaning on another person, squatting, or even hands-and-knees crouching are workable — and, some would argue, possibly better. In some times and places, modesty took precedence over safety.

10. From a manual for midwives published in 1513.

11. Watching in a mirror the birth of their first child, a girl.

12. An American pioneer birth scene.

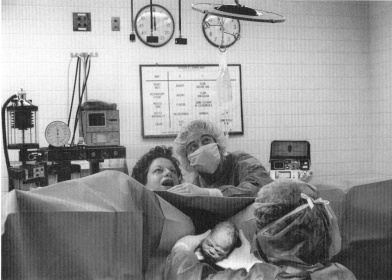

11.

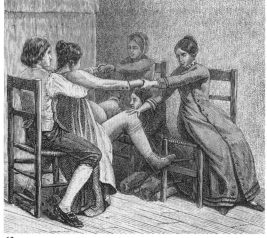

12.

13. From an eighteenth-century Japanese birthing manual. Genesis 30:3 suggests this may also have been a position in biblical times. A barren Rachel gives her maid to her husband, Jacob, saying, "Go in unto her, that she may bear upon my knees, and I also may be builded up through her."

14.

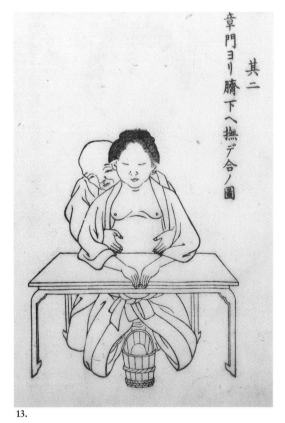

13.

A !Kung woman gives birth without expert assistance.

14. Her older sister helps her through labor.

15. Her mother welcomes the baby, a boy, by gently "molding" his head with her hands — a ritualized way of touching.

15.

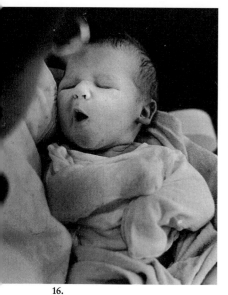

16.

17.

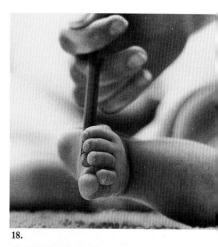

18.

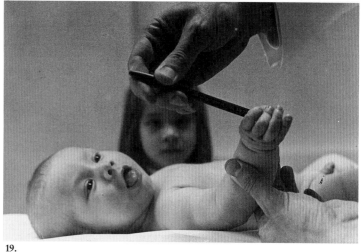

19.

Babies are born adapted — equipped to survive.

16. In "rooting," a newborn reflexively turns toward an object that touches its cheek — here, a maternity nurse.

17. Some reflexes simply show the undeveloped state of the newborn brain. The Babinsky reflex, for instance, wanes in the next few months but reappears in an adult with spinal cord damage.

18. Others appear functionless, but supply evidence of our monkey and ape ancestry.

19. A newborn's grasp is strong enough to support its whole weight.

20. Dr. Arnold Meltzoff, now a distinguished professor, doing the controversial study that made him famous. Not true imitation but a crude, reflexive mimicry, these responses to adult faces nevertheless show how strongly inclined newborns are to be social.

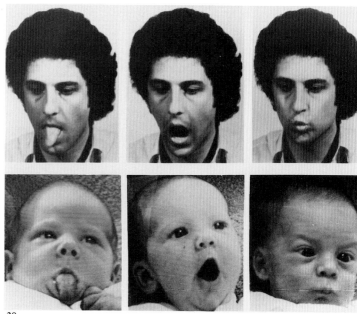

20.

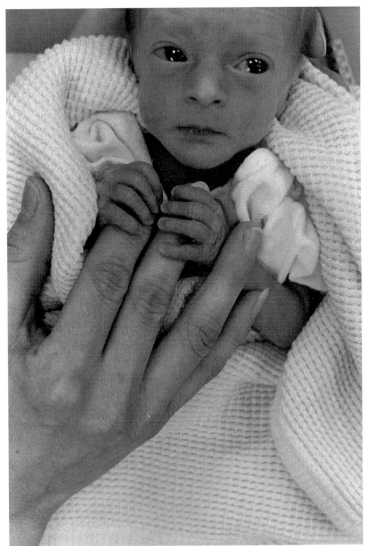

21. Even premature babies show adaptive reflexes...

22. ...but for many, including some cocaine-damaged babies, adaptation is inadequate for survival.

21.

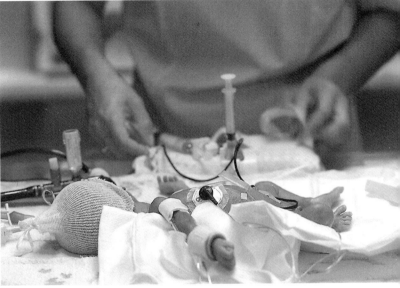

22.

Two

❧

Love's Labors

My mother groaned! my father wept.
Into the dangerous world I leapt:
Helpless, naked, piping loud:
Like a fiend hid in a cloud.

Struggling in my father's hands,
Striving against my swaddling bands.
Bound and weary I thought best
To sulk upon my mother's breast.

— WILLIAM BLAKE, *Songs of Experience*

―――――――

A WOMAN TAKES a man into her embrace. For our purposes there need not be love, but despite this indisputable fact let us say that there is love. Say too that although her monthly round is ripening to a purpose, the two have decided that there will be no separation between their biological selves, no artificial barrier to the purpose.

In due course — remember, there is love — the man edges into a basic animal reflex, and billions of tiny gene-bearing cells he has made in the past few days are mixed in a creamy fluid and squeezed out of his body into hers, by rhythmic contractions of the muscles of his pelvic floor. This fluid blends with the woman's resident fluids, and the tiny reproductive cells swim in all directions, including upward and inward toward the place where the future lies, waiting to be set in forward motion.

Earlier, the woman has shed a gene-bearing cell of her own — much larger and more impressive looking, but probably only one of them. It burst out of a bloody capsule on the surface of the ovary, leaving behind a miniscule scar, and began to be urged, by the beating of microscopic living threads called cilia, down the tiny ridges and valleys of the fallopian tube — the cavernous passageway from the ovary to the uterus. There, before moving very far, this cell will encounter the energetic mass movement of the much tinier germ cells fielded in the fluid from the man.

Although the egg will be crowded by sperm, only one will successfully cross its external barrier, after combining with a protein on the surface. As the head of the sperm penetrates, a set of biochemical changes is triggered around the surface of the tiny sphere, preventing any other sperm from entering. Only the gene-bearing head of the sperm enters, while the tail is shed, and the woman's genes soon combine with the man's.

Rapid reorganization produces the first cell of the new human being; it has forty-six chromosomes, in pairs — one of each pair from each parent. The roughly one hundred thousand genes strung along these chromosomes heavily influence a human being's destiny. Though subject to many influences themselves, they will not fundamentally change throughout the life and growth of the individual, and some of them can determine events that will not occur for eighty or ninety years.

Now the cell is ready to divide and transform itself. It divides every few hours and, under the direction of the genes, the daughter cells become different from one another. How this happens is poorly understood, but has something to do with polarity — asymmetry — within the very first cell itself.

All the cells carry the same genes, yet they don't get the same results. Chemical substances around the genes in the different cells can turn the genes on or off; if not for this possibility, cells would not become different, organs would not form, and there would be no real organism, just a blob of identical cells. But at the same time, this turning on and off of genes provides the first evidence that genes do not control everything themselves — that the context they are in exerts a profound influence over them. Here we encounter a fact that repeats itself endlessly throughout human life: a gene alone does nothing; context is always important.

After some more doublings, on around the eighth day, a still relatively formless embryo has been urged down the fallopian tube from the ovary to the womb, and it begins the process of implantation. At this time it looks nothing like a baby, yet it is already influenced by its environment as well as its genes. Implantation, for instance, requires receptivity. If the wall of the womb is not ready for the embryo, or if there is a mismatch between the embryo's genes and the mother's, the embryo may be discharged before or soon after implantation. In fact, many late menstrual periods are really failed early pregnancies. Not only that, but many pregnancies fail even earlier, so that there is not even late menses to alert the mother that one of her eggs has been fertilized. More important, a mother may be unaware that she is *successfully* pregnant, and thus may be consuming substances dangerous to the embryo. Thus the child-to-be, still small enough to be just this side of invisible, is already strongly affected by the mother's interactions with her environment.

Meanwhile, back in the womb, the normal embryo implants and continues to grow according to plan. As far as sex goes, the egg has combined with a sperm that carries either an X or a Y chromosome; this will determine whether a male or female will grow in the womb. The Y holds one or more genes that will set the growth of male sex organs in motion — particularly the internal testes that will make the male hormone testosterone. If this gene's product is not present — or if, as in a few rare cases, it is resisted — the body plan will inexorably develop as female, even if there is only one X chromosome. So the human body plan is female in essence, and maleness is a sort of biochemical afterthought. Interestingly, we will see that throughout childhood boys are more vulnerable to more sorts of damage than girls are.

In any case, the forming of the internal, then external sex organs mostly occurs during the first eight to twelve weeks of pregnancy — although all organ systems continue to grow throughout development. The heart, arms, legs, ears, teeth, and palate undergo their major formation during this period. While the brain and eyes continue to change and grow fundamentally, they also have formative periods during the first months of pregnancy. The significance of these patterns of timing is that damage caused by things the mother takes in depends on the stage of pregnancy, and of organ development. Here nurture makes a massive incursion into a process so far controlled by nature.

But for fetuses that grow and mature normally, there is a remarkable train of transforming events that continually surprises those who observe and chart them. Recall that the brain is developing throughout the course of prenatal life, and as it develops it governs fetal activity. Although the brain is certainly subject to outside influence in the womb — calories, drugs, hormones — it is also growing and changing under a remarkably thorough genetic plan. Consider just the convolutions that corrugate the surface of the cortex — the highest part — of the brain. Human beings have far more of these convolutions than even our near primate relatives, and the reason is that the cortex has become much larger while preserving the six-layer cellular depth necessary for function; the result is that it can fit into a skull-sized space only by folding.

The folding is very far from haphazard. It takes a species-specific pattern, and an experienced neurologist or brain surgeon can name the convolutions in any newborn baby's brain. The only way for such a complex pattern to be so constant from person to person is for it to result from a species-wide, genetically guided plan. This is only one aspect of how the genes shape the brain, and we understand very little about the overall process as yet. Brain cells are born in very excessive numbers, and many billions of them — possibly the majority — must die a preprogrammed death; likewise the trillions of connections forming networks among the brain cells that survive.

The cells don't just have to be born, of course; they have to migrate to their destined places in the fantastically intricate and precise plan of the brain. Then they must put out the snaky extensions of themselves that will form the "wiring" of the circuits. The cells and the extensions alike find their way to the right places following a combination of physical and chemical signals that tell them continually whether they are getting "warmer" or "colder" until they are in place.

But the genes do not control everything. As Jean-Pierre Changeux, a leading French brain scientist, and many others have shown, the "dying back" of countless brain cells and connections is not random. The fetus is active, and this activity shapes the brain's cell composition and circuitry. Even at twelve weeks of prenatal age, the fetus responds to stroking on the palm of the hand or the sole of the foot by clenching the fingers or toes. Yet at this stage it is only an inch or two long and hardly looks human. Spontaneous activity is also present — a kind of slow rhythmic squirming of the body and limbs, combined with occasional jerks and kicks that cannot even be felt by the mother because the fetus is so small. A month later other reflexes appear, including the sucking and swallowing of the amniotic fluid in which the fetus is bathed.

At around the same time or soon after, the fetus can be observed sucking its thumb. This is an extraordinary accomplishment; it not only requires the coordination of two completely separate organ systems, but it also has a less reflexive, almost voluntary quality — not like the reactive curling of toes, which can be coordinated purely through the lower part of the spinal cord. Reflexes do continue to develop, and some are very complex. By the seventh month, the nervous system is mature enough to generate modest breathing movements, as if the fetus is preparing for the day when she will have to breathe air.

In fact, she *is* preparing. Each of these reflex or spontaneous movements in the womb exercises a function in the developing fetus that will serve in one way or another to aid in the baby's survival after birth. Immediately upon birth she will begin to breathe air; perhaps she could do so without having practiced "breathing" movements, but this is doubtful. Soon after birth the baby will be put to the breast or the bottle; months of sucking and swallowing fluids in the womb have exercised the needed organs and brain circuits over and over again.

At some time during the first few days of life the baby, while crying, will find that she can bring her thumb to her mouth and suck, changing her own state from an extremely unpleasant one to one that is quite comforting. Best of all, it is a comfort achieved by the baby's own action. It may not be voluntary, it may be merely a discovery in the midst of many spontaneous squirming movements; but there it is: self-comfort.

Yet there is more to these prenatal preparations than practice. Since so many brain cells, and even more brain circuitry, must disappear by dying back throughout fetal life, the very shape of the brain's circuitry can be influenced by these calisthenics-in-the-womb. The cells and circuits that are exercised are more likely to survive the selection process than those that are not; the fetus's steady activities shape the emerging circuits of its own developing brain. This is the paradox that governs all of development: Genes guide a process as specific and intricate as the folding of the surface of the brain; yet the final honing and shape of the circuitry inside it depends on activities — transactions between the developing organism and the world outside.

• • •

Kicking is one of those activities, and although it begins much earlier, it becomes detectable by the mother, often as a mild tickling at first, shortly before the middle of pregnancy. Quickening is what this sensation has been called, to denote the mother's sense that something is coming to life in her. If it has not already started, this can also be the beginning of bonding between the mother and her tiny, emergent baby. Since this is a time when the movements cannot be felt through the abdomen, fathers cannot participate in this form of bonding until later, except through imagination and proxy.

But here technology can be a real help. When my wife was carrying our first baby, we went to the midwife for a scheduled visit and after much searching she found the fetal heartbeat with an ultrasound echo device. *Whsshh! Whsshh! Whsshh!* came the loud rapid whispering beat, distinct from the slower rhythmic slushing of the mother's own heartbeat, reflected down in the pulse of the uterine artery. My wife had already felt the changes in her body, and had begun the process of transformation and bonding. But for me the coming birth was more dreamlike and unbelievable, until that moment when — five months before our daughter would push her way out into the world — through the electronically amplified pumping of her tiny heart, I was in effect born as a father.

So much for the nature-lover's notion that technology always and everywhere interferes with natural processes like love. Today it is easily possible, and very safe, to get a visual image of the beating fetal heart as well as the sound — not to mention seeing the arms, legs, spinal column, face — even the telltale visual evidence that the baby will be a boy. Gradual bonding before birth is good for fathers as well as mothers, and psychological preparation for the advent of the baby will soften the shock of adjustment for all three.

But how about what the fetus senses and knows about the outside world? From studies of prematurely born infants, we know that all five senses — vision, hearing, touch, taste, and smell — are functioning to some degree by the seventh month of pregnancy. It is possible, though not certain, that the baby in the womb can detect bright light or darkness through the mother's abdomen, the amniotic fluid, and its own closed but translucent lids. Much more certain is that the fetus responds to sound. Fetal heart rate and body movement have been shown in many studies to respond to tones systematically delivered, even when the mother could not hear or respond to the tones herself. These studies confirm the impression of many mothers that when they go to concerts or even movies their babies are responding directly to the music. More recently, as we will see a little later, a few studies have suggested that it is not foolish to talk or even read to a baby through the mother's abdomen, because at least minimal traces of such experience may be detectable after birth. In any case, if it makes an impression on the parent talking or reading — if it helps to shape the parent's side of the bond — then it is not a wasted effort.

But by far the most advanced sense in the womb is none of the classic five but a sixth sense known as proprioception — the ability to sense movement of one's body, and to detect the position of the body's parts in space. Studies of brain development confirm that the circuits involved in this mature long before those that manage the other senses. This means that the main business of life in the womb is motion, both passive and active, and that exercise both in the circuits that control movement and those that detect it makes this the most advanced system after birth. Studies by Annelise Korner, a psychologist at Stanford University, and others have shown that premature infants do better by several measures when they are kept in an incubator that features a gently rocking water bed. Most newborn infants, premature or not, are very responsive to being held and rocked, as all parents know. This is partly because of the maturity of the system, but also probably because of the endless chain of experiences with movement in the womb; because of knowledge laid down that makes the new experience, even right after birth, familiar; because of learning.

• • •

But learning is not the only kind of nurture. We pause at this point in the story, and back up to early pregnancy, to consider how drugs and other substances taken in by the mother — or not taken in — can act as powerfully determining environmental forces. In effect they make up the first strong winds of nurture blowing over the natural landscape of development.

For example, the drug thalidomide, used in the late 1950s to help with nausea and anxiety during pregnancy, turned out to be one of the most devastating poisons on record — not for the mother, who was unaffected, but for the fetus growing inside her. Some eight thousand children were born with severe birth defects, including the absence of arms or legs or major defects of vision or hearing. Yet thalidomide had little effect when taken later in pregnancy, when the major organs it could distort or destroy were already basically formed.

This is a fairly exotic example, but it is very instructive. First, some things in the environment that seem benign or even helpful can turn out to have colossally damaging hidden effects. Second, the developing organism may be resilient, rolling with most environmental punches, but the resilience has limits, and transgressing them entails great risk. Third, timing can be important; some environmental influences can be benign for most of development, yet there may be a sensitive phase during which strong effects can occur — a demonstration that to understand the effects of nurture we must very often first understand the plan of nature.

Fortunately thalidomide is long since off the market, and although too many drugs are still prescribed during pregnancy, physicians are much more cautious and regulation is much tighter. Of greater consequence today is the most commonly abused nonprescription drug, alcohol. An estimated 2 percent of all potential mothers are alcoholics, and many more drink moderately. In the past decade research has established fetal alcohol syndrome, the disastrous consequences of heavy drinking by a pregnant woman. Among them are underdeveloped heads and brains, malformed eyes, heart defects, and a distorted face — eyes that are exceptionally far apart and a broad, flat nose. Severe mental retardation is common in these children, who have usually been heavily exposed to alcohol, especially in the first third of pregnancy.

But exposure later in pregnancy and exposure at lower levels can also produce some of this damage, especially in the brain. This is in keeping with the very long course of brain formation as compared with that of other organ systems. Research has demonstrated that this subtler type of damage, known as fetal alcohol effects, can be found in some at birth and for a long time afterward. As a result of such studies, health authorities recommend that the consumption of alcoholic beverages be reduced to zero in pregnant women throughout the course of pregnancy.

But it also must be considered what the beginning of that course is. If a woman who misses her period waits a few days or a week before going for a pregnancy test, then two to three critical weeks of development will have gone by before she determines that she is pregnant. If she waits until then to stop drinking — or any other behavior that may be damaging to her baby — she will perhaps have already done the baby irreparable damage. While any baby has a potential to be realized, and deserves every opportunity to achieve that potential, one thing is clear from all we have learned about childhood: You usually cannot make a high-quality child out of a badly damaged baby. The responsibilities — as well as the burdens — of parenthood begin for both parents with the decision to conceive.

The risks are many. Unfortunately, almost everything that enters the mother's bloodstream can cross through the placenta to make an impact on the fetus, and in addition there are indirect effects. Smoking a cigarette reduces the flow of blood to the fetus, and the birth weight of the newborn babies of pregnant smokers is at least 5 percent lower, on average, than that of nonsmokers. Pregnant addicts using heroin, methadone, or cocaine give birth to babies who are themselves addicted, and who must go through classic withdrawal as soon as they are born. In the case of cocaine at least, as with alcohol, there is often permanent damage to the brain, including hyperactivity and reduced intelligence throughout childhood. Although fewer babies are exposed to cocaine than to alcohol, crack-damaged children are making an enormous new impact on our services for children, from neonatal intensive care to special education. Finally, pollutants ingested inadvertently by the pregnant mother — things that are no fault of hers — as well as certain infections and several kinds of radiation, can cause irreversible damage during sensitive stages of fetal development.

Not surprisingly, the adequacy of the mother's diet can and does affect the fetus, and this — not drugs or even infection — has throughout history been the main distorting influence that the environment has on babies before they are born. Low birth weight — 5½ pounds or less — has generally been considered a reflection of undernourishment during pregnancy. On average, according to United Nations data, at least 18 percent of babies in developing countries suffer from low birth weight, and this is likely to be an underestimate because so many babies go unmeasured in some countries. On the Indian subcontinent, the figure is between 25 and 30 percent. In the United States and Britain the rate is 7 percent, but some developed countries, including Japan, France, and Spain, do significantly better than this. Still, in developed countries substance abuse by pregnant mothers contributes much to low birth weight — probably more than malnutrition itself.

"Childhood" series observer Marian Wright Edelman, an attorney who as head of the Children's Defense Fund is a tireless advocate for children, visited the Neonatal Intensive Care Unit of the D.C. General Hospital in Washington with a film crew. She talked with two doctors and a nurse about the tragedy of crack babies in the unit. These tiny creatures, prematurely expelled from the womb, must go through the two sicknesses of drug withdrawal and respiratory distress both at the same time. They must also suffer procedures such as blood-drawing and injections at least every six hours. We now know that, contrary to what we thought, premature infants *do* experience pain. Doctors hope and believe that they forget the pain — but pain later forgotten still hurts when it happens.

Because of the timing of brain cell formation, these babies often have permanent brain damage. They are sometimes abandoned by their parents. Their care can cost a hundred thousand dollars or more, and the outcome in terms of their quality of life can be quite unsatisfactory. They tremble unnervingly at times, and unlike full-term babies, some have to be taught to suck.

Yet, as Dr. Mikal Young points out, many of these outcomes could have been prevented with an aggressive outreach program for prenatal care of girls and women in urban ghettos. And, as Marian Wright Edelman says, "The fact that they are abandoning their children here says to me that there is a disconnectedness, a loss of family, a loss of a sense of future and hope that is unprecedented. . . . We had the capacity to give their mothers a sense of hope in their lives, and we did not."

Inadequate intake of calories is only one form of malnutrition. Deficiencies of vitamins and of minerals such as iodine and iron can affect the fetus profoundly, and are extremely common in the developing world. Anemia alone — overwhelmingly iron-deficiency anemia — affects about 60 percent of pregnant women in the developing world as opposed to around 15 percent in the developed world. Many such deficiencies have well-established effects on the child in the pregnant woman's womb.

The impact of disease and malnutrition on the developing fetus is great, but there is another stunning tragedy that deserves separate emphasis. Worldwide, an estimated half-million women die each year as a result of pregnancy and childbirth — most with inadequate nutrition and negligible prenatal care. The pregnant state is a profound biological transformation that changes every major organ system in some way, and it can bring out diseases that the mother may have a predisposition toward, such as diabetes or high blood pressure. Pregnancy may be normal, but it can be very risky, and the woman without prenatal care may be taking not just her baby's but her own life in her hands.

But many of those half-million deaths are due to childbirth itself — one of the great killers of young women throughout history, and still a great killer in the developing world today. What war has been for men, childbirth has been for women: an inherently dangerous act calling forth great courage. It seems an evolutionary anomaly: Obviously none of us would be here if not for an endless chain of successful births; yet birth is extremely painful and difficult in our species, and the women who were our ancestors ran grave risks and paid a heavy price to produce their cherished children. Why didn't evolution work out a better way?

Evolution isn't perfect, of course, but human evolution seems to have made a real botch of birthing. The fact is, it was our brains that made the trouble. Our closest animal cousins, the great apes, have an easy time at birthing, as do most monkeys. This means our own apelike ancestors must have had to endure at most two or three hours of discomfort during labor. So the curse of Eve is the product of our human evolution. Not only did an enormously expanded brain, already gestating mightily in the womb, confront the real Eve and her sisters with a newly challenging passage; but over the same few million years they became adapted for upright walking. This meant a strong, tough, inflexible pelvis, all the more difficult for those budding brains to squeeze their way through. Little wonder that humans throughout history have looked on the births of other animals with envy; little wonder that we have turned, relieved, to medical technology, to manage and reduce the risk and pain.

• • •

But for seventeenth-century women like Anne Bradstreet and Elizabeth Joceline, there were no such choices. This is how Bradstreet, the first distinguished American poet, addressed her husband in the mid-1600s as she approached the then terrifying experience of childbirth:

> *How soon, my dear, death may my steps attend,*
> *How soon't may be thy Lot to lose thy friend,*
> *We both are ignorant, yet love bids me*
> *These farewell lines to recommend to thee.*

Thus Anne, a young mother, marked the beginning of another child's life by preparing herself and her husband for her death. She went on,

> *And if I see not half my dayes that's due,*
> *What nature would, God grant to yours and you . . .*
> *And when thou feel'st no grief, as I no harms,*
> *Yet love thy dead, who long lay in thine arms:*
> *And when thy loss shall be repaid with gains*
> *Look to my little babes my dear remains.*
> *And if thou love thy self, or loved'st me*
> *These O protect from step Dames injury . . .*

Appealing to her husband's love for her, Anne reached as it were from her own imagined grave to appeal to him to love their children well — not to let them come to harm at the hands of a thoughtless or cruel stepmother. And she ended the poem by asking him to "kiss this paper for thy love's dear sake, / Who with salt tears this last Farewel did take."

Her fears were well founded. Although she did not die in connection with childbirth, countless women of her era did. Elizabeth Joceline of Cambridgeshire, England, approaching first motherhood in 1622, wrote an entire book of advice and instruction to her unborn baby, to guide the child in case of her own death. In the preface, addressed to her husband, she wrote,

> Mine own dear love, — I no sooner conceived an hope that I should
> be made a mother by thee, but with it entered the consideration of a
> mother's duty, and shortly after followed the apprehension of danger.
> . . . And in truth death appearing in this shape, was doubly terrible
> unto me. First, in respect of the painfulness of that kind of death, and
> next of the loss my little one should have in wanting me.

She gave birth to a daughter, Theodora, but died of childbed fever nine days later. The book served not only as a guide for Theodora but as an aid and comfort to many in the England Joceline left behind; it went through three editions by 1625.

Through their writings these women speak to us of what "natural childbirth" really meant for most of history. Although today in the United States one woman at most will die for every ten thousand births, at the turn of the century the rate was perhaps a hundred times higher, and back in Bradstreet's and Joceline's century the numbers were much higher still. Widowers and stepmothers were common figures of life and lore — both Cinderella and Snow White were orphans — and the most likely cause of loss of life in young women was death during or shortly after childbirth. Another Anne, the queen in an English folk song, says after a long labor, "Please pierce my side open, and save my baby" — knowing that this act will end her life.

The great Russian novelist Leo Tolstoy described the same fears from the viewpoint of a father. Levin, the character in *Anna Karenina* who stands in — sometimes comically, always poignantly — for the author, loves his wife Kitty to desperation. As she goes through labor, *his* anguish is sheer torture:

> He sighed, and flung his head up, and began to feel afraid he could not bear it, that he would burst into tears or run away. Such agony it was to him. And only one hour had passed.
>
> But after that there passed another hour, two hours, three, the full five hours he had fixed as the furthest limit of his sufferings, and the position was still unchanged . . . every instant feeling that he had reached the utmost limits of his endurance, and that his heart would break with sympathy and pain.

Many hours later — Kitty is having a somewhat longer-than-typical first labor, though most are sluggish, frustrating, and very painful — Levin and Kitty begin having the same dark thoughts that Anne Bradstreet and Elizabeth Joceline had had two centuries earlier and thousands of miles away:

> Kitty's swollen and agonized face, a tress of hair clinging to her moist brow, was turned to him and sought his eyes. Her lifted hands asked

for his hands. Clutching his chill hands in her moist ones, she began squeezing them to her face. . . . But suddenly her face was drawn, she pushed him away.

"Oh, this is awful! I'm dying, I'm dying! Go away!" she shrieked, and again he heard that unearthly scream.

Levin clutched at his head and ran out of the room. . . . He had long ago ceased to wish for the child. By now he loathed this child. He did not even wish for her life now, all he longed for was the end of this awful anguish.

"Doctor! what is it? What is it? By God!" he said, snatching at the doctor's hand as he came up.

"It's the end," said the doctor. And the doctor's face was so grave as he said it that he took *the end* as meaning her death.

What it was, of course, was the delivery, as Levin soon found out by reentering the labor room, falling on his knees by the bed, and hearing in Kitty's own voice the words, "It's over." Twenty-two hours had passed.

> If Levin had been told that Kitty was dead, and that he had died with her, and that their children were angels, and that God was now standing before him, he would have been surprised at nothing. But now, coming back to the world of reality, he had to make great mental efforts to take in that she was alive and well, and that the creature squalling so desperately was his son.

• • •

But in the United States and England by this time, rising expectations about life and health produced the first revolution in childbirth — the beginnings of the transfer of control from home to hospital, from midwife to physician, from women to men. Early disasters in the mid-nineteenth century — maternity hospital physicians were actually transferring deadly infections from mother to mother by way of their hands — gave rise to caution. But nevertheless childbirth became increasingly medicalized, and by the 1930s most American births took place in hospitals with physicians in attendance. Still, death rates for mothers and infants were unacceptably high.

Medicalization intensified. By the 1950s, almost anyone watching a delivery would think that doctors had invented motherhood — not the primitive mammals who first got the hang of it some two hundred million years ago. "Twilight sleep" — a type of general anesthesia — took the mother out of the picture, as a conscious presence at least; yet she still had to be strapped down in some rough deliveries to be able to bear the pain without dangerous thrashing. Delivery rooms were all tile, chrome, and steel, difficult to distinguish from surgical operating rooms. Fathers were nowhere near the place — they were out chewing their fingernails in the waiting room — nor was anyone else allowed in to provide support and companionship to the mother.

Then, in the 1960s, mothers and fathers, acting from impulses fundamental to human nature, began to insist on taking the process back. So a continually advancing birth technology has had to work around some fundamental spiritual requirements: full consciousness on the mother's part, for instance; an atmosphere in which the surgical and medical apparatus that ensures ultimate safety is very much in the background, so that the room provides a sense of familiarity and calm; a father or a friend at her side for emotional support from start to finish (such support, we now know, shortens labor); and that amazing trio that leaps into existence as the crying starts and stops again, and the baby is laid down on the mother's breast, and the father leans over to kiss her sweaty forehead, grinning one of those face-cracking grins.

Ironically, even this natural childbirth revolution has not stemmed the tide of technology. During the same thirty or forty years, the rate of cesarean section — a safe modern version of Queen Anne's proposed piercing — has in the United States gone from fewer than 10 to more than 25 percent of births. Electronic monitoring during labor, using a device attached to the baby's scalp, has become commonplace. Newer forms of anesthesia, such as the epidural injection through the spine, which deadens the lower half of the body, have replaced twilight sleep, but they also may slow down labor. Artificial speeding of labor, using hormonal substitute for oxytocin, has become more common. All these technological interventions, and others besides, have spread in some sectors of the American population, even while natural childbirth has become the rule in others. Meanwhile the Soviet Union, the descendant of Tolstoy's Russia, has just about caught up to the U.S. style of birth circa 1960 — doubly ironic, since childbirth preparation was invented there.

The apparent paradox is easily resolved with an old doctor's saying:

"Childbirth may be physiological for the species, but it's damn near pathological for the individual." *Physiological* is a medical word for a normal variation in biology — difficult or painful perhaps, but not in the realm of illness. So what the saying means is: This childbirth thing may be natural, but it's still very dangerous. By 1975 or so, physicians and parents found themselves to some extent in confrontation. On the medical side, most practitioners believed that their technology was preventing injury and death, and could do so even more if it were applied more often. Yet parents felt a strong pull toward conscious, family-oriented childbirth, prepared for with physical and psychological exercises, and protected from any unnecessary medical intervention. Some laboring mothers went so far as to stay at home for their births, with or without the aid of a midwife, just to avoid giving up control to an impersonal hospital environment.

This risky strategy made doctors sit up and take notice. Since they couldn't force such couples into the hospital, they had to lure them in, or take a chance on losing infants and mothers. No matter how good the prenatal evaluation, at least 10 to 20 percent of perfectly normal pregnancies — previously classified as low risk — will end with a serious problem in delivery. So the doctors began to let the mothers and fathers shape the experience.

Fathers came into the delivery rooms increasingly as a matter of course. Prepared childbirth, according to the Lamaze method and others, became more common. Laboring mothers were allowed to refuse pain medications, scalp monitors, even intravenous lines, as long as the process was going normally. Surgical suites were still used when necessary, but in many hospitals a woman could labor and deliver in a room that looked like a bedroom at home — a "birthing room."

Even midwives made a comeback. These are now usually highly trained, certified nurse-midwives working in hospitals under the supervision of obstetricians, but they are midwives nevertheless. Most are women, and together with the increasing number of female obstetricians, they have made many childbirths once again the province of women. (I remember well the delivery of our second child, a boy, in 1981. The obstetrician supervising our midwife came into the room at one point. Since nothing untoward was happening, we didn't want him around. We had made an agreement, and we glared at him until he left. As it turned out, the poor man only wanted a look — he loved to watch babies being born.)

The remarkable thing about all this new naturalness was that childbirth remained quite safe. None of the dire predictions that had been made about these changes came to pass. In fact, technology itself began to be called into question by the very scientists who were introducing and studying it. Questionable cesarean sections numbering in the scores of thousands became a source of embarrassment to American obstetricians. They pointed to declining infant mortality, but some European nations — Ireland, for instance — achieved the same declines with cesarean section rates less than a third of the U.S. rate. Research began to seek ways of reducing the section rate, which seemed to be rising relentlessly for no very good reason — even, some speculated, because of the rise in malpractice litigation.

Electronic monitoring became almost universal in better American hospitals, except when mothers steadfastly refused it. Yet a respected study in Dublin, in Ireland's leading obstetrical hospital, proved that a midwife checking the baby's heartbeat the old-fashioned way — with a stethoscope, through the mother's belly — was just as effective as the electronic method in preventing injury or illness in the baby. In 1990, a similar study was published in the *New England Journal of Medicine,* showing that in the United States and Canada, as in Ireland, there was no long-term benefit to infants from electronic monitoring as opposed to regular listening with a stethoscope. A leading physician labeled it "a disappointing story."

Perhaps most surprising, a 1989 study reported the outcome of births in almost twelve thousand women who attempted to give birth outside of hospitals, in eighty-four free-standing birth centers throughout the United States. Almost four out of five of the births were supervised by midwives. One in six of the women had to be transferred to a hospital, but the cesarean section rate was less than 5 percent. Complications and infant mortality were no higher than for low-risk births taking place entirely in hospitals. None of the mothers died. Physicians were compelled to recognize that free-standing birth centers provide a safe alternative to hospital birth, although most still prefer that such alternatives be located within or adjacent to hospitals.

In other words, mothers and fathers have restored the concept of childbirth as a rite of passage. They have reinstated some of the naturalness it had had since the beginning of our species. Once again it could be a conscious family ritual, a chance for the expression of love and loyalty in a time of stress. Pushing through the pain is itself a part of the ritual, complete with specialized breathing rhythms, hand-holding, even swearing like a sailor. And after the pain subsides, and the baby is out and doing well, doctors and even midwives stand back while the trio emerges. At this moment the grins can be colossal. *We are bringing new life into the world,* parents seem to say. *We need to be fully there, to take this very seriously. We are creating not just a new life, but a new or a changed family.*

• • •

Barbara and David Kaufman, the Manhattan couple filmed by the "Childhood" series, reached what was for them a happy compromise. They decided early on that Barbara would have an epidural injection that would deaden sensation below the waist. An unanticipated delay of about a week and a half beyond the expected due date led them, together with their obstetrician, to decide to induce labor with an artificial form of the hormone oxytocin. This option would not have been open to her under the original natural-childbirth conditions, and she and her baby, called Michelle, would probably have had to face the grave risks of carrying and delivering a significantly post-term baby. The epidural protected her from "natural" levels of pain, yet she was awake and active throughout the labor, talking with her husband and being comforted by him, and after the baby's head crowned she was able to bear down and push despite the epidural — and she pushed hard, making her own will one of the forces that caused Michelle's birth.

During part of the pushing, she played Wagner's triumphant "Ride of the Valkyries" on a cassette player — a personal touch that gave her one more dose of psychological support, but that would have been unthinkable in a 1960 delivery. And that was not all that was possible. Not only did her husband accompany her into the delivery room, but her mother and father were also there, not to mention a camera crew and a "Childhood" series observer, me — allowed in through Barbara and David's remarkable generosity in sharing their experience with others. Michelle emerged perfect into the hands of Dr. Louis Lissak, the obstetrician, and was immediately given to Barbara and David to hold, and they lost no time in warmly welcoming her. Thirty minutes later, after being properly ministered to by the nurses — vitamins, antibiotics, blood sample, footprint — Michelle was handed to me (more Kaufman generosity) for an examination of her normal reflexes.

This was a very safe birth. But today, looking around the world, we can still find cultures in which great fears about birth are justified. A third of the world's nations have death rates in infancy greater than 10 percent, and about half of these deaths occur in the newborn period. In São Paulo, in 1990, Maria Oliveira gave birth in a hospital, under the eyes and hands of a physician — and thanks to her and her husband Manoel's kindness, a camera crew as well. She had taken a saint's image with her to the hospital. In the delivery room she was horizontal, with her feet raised and tied into the stirrups. Her belly and vulva were unceremoniously doused with iodine. The result was Sydney, a perfect baby boy, but the risk of injury or infection, possibly deadly, was much greater for her than for her counterpart in the United States or Europe. And in Moscow, in 1990, Vitaly Popov was born in a way that was clean and safe, but quite reminiscent of maternity hospitals in the United States in the 1950s.

Even the U.S. woman has, on average, a higher risk for herself and her baby than do women in at least fifteen or twenty other nations — the rank varies a little from year to year, but does not show steady improvement. However, this often-repeated fact is very deceptive. None of those nations has a population anywhere near as ethnically varied as ours, and experts agree that further reductions in infant mortality will come mainly from improvements in prenatal care and other public health measures. In a way, and paradoxically, the natural childbirth movement can spread only so far in the United States; a higher degree of safety must precede it — and what that means now is not more technology, but fewer high-risk births. And this can be achieved only by understanding, as we have seen, that the relationship with the baby begins long before birth.

In fact, it begins, in a sense, before pregnancy. Some of the most dramatic events in the development of a human embryo have already occurred by the time the prospective mother has noticed that her period is late. Ideally, the care of her baby should begin before she attempts to become pregnant, with abstinence from alcohol, cigarettes, and all other drugs of abuse, and the sort of attention to nutrition that reflects concern for a child. Within a few weeks, the first contact with a physician should occur, followed by appropriate examinations. These may involve a certain amount of technology, which some parents view as obstacles to their experience.

But technology is also a window. We can look, now, with ultrasound, at a fetus's growth and movements. We can monitor how she is doing during the birth, alert for signs of distress or danger. Research in the 1980s has begun to suggest that this information can do more than identify major abnormalities; it can also tell us subtle things about the little person-to-be. That it is healthy and whether it is a boy or a girl are among the easier insights. Possibly, infant activity level or irritability will soon be to some extent predictable from observations made in the womb. Even more interesting is the likelihood that learning begins in the womb. The fetus not only squirms and kicks; her heart rate jumps in response to sudden loud noises on the outside, and these and other external events may make an impression on her.

We certainly know from studies of mice and other animals that psychological stresses on the mother during pregnancy can change the behavior of the baby after birth; something similar may occur in human infants. Most recently, a few studies have suggested that newborn infants prefer the sounds of their mothers' voices, on the basis of having heard them in the womb. Far-fetched as this sounds — and it is not yet proven — it would only be a human version of what we know happens routinely in chicks: They learn the sound of their mothers' calls — or an artificial sound played to them — through the shell and fluid of the eggs in which they are brooding, and they waddle toward those same sounds after hatching. If chicks can do it, why can't we?

But more important, unquestionably, than any effect such experience may have on the fetus, is the effect we know it has on the parents. Through the ultrasound heart monitor, my wife and I established contact with our baby, even though she was still very far from being born. And what happened to Barbara and David Kaufman in their Lamaze classes and prenatal checkups was far more than medical care and preparation for childbirth. It was the establishment of a relationship — one-sided, to be sure; much more subjectively powerful for the parents than objectively real for the fetus. Yet in relationships, the subjective *is* real.

Conscious childbirth itself may be of the same order. In natural childbirth today — as in the much less safe Baka and !Kung childbirths over the centuries — mother, baby, and sometimes father greet each other immediately after the birth. As this custom became prevalent during the 1970s, a tempting hypothesis called "bonding" grew in popularity. Many studies attempted to show that mother-infant pairs allowed to be together during the hours right after birth were different a year or more later. It always seemed somewhat implausible that these few hours of contact made a critical impact on the baby — nothing we knew about how newborn babies work made this kind of instant learning seem likely.

Yet the impact on the mother or the father was something else again. It was difficult to prove, but pediatricians John Kennell and Marshall Klaus suggest that some mothers, especially poor or unwed ones, were vulnerable to forming inadequate relationships with their babies. Such mothers, it was thought, got an extra boost from these few hours of early contact, and were more attached, or "bonded," to their babies as a result. Many were skeptical of even this effect; some wags called it derisively the "epoxy theory" of mother love. Whether or not such bonding occurs — the research jury is still out — there is no doubt that mothers and fathers experience something powerful when their baby is handed to them, as Michelle was to Barbara and David Kaufman. I know, because I experienced it three times myself. Some experiences are so powerful that they don't need to be justified by any sort of lasting effect. They simply justify themselves — by their emotion, their beauty, and the memories they leave behind.

• • •

In some ways every human infant — Michelle, Sydney, or Vitaly, for instance — summarizes the whole evolutionary history of our species. We look at the newborn and we say: Future Human. But the baby is not just an unformed creature developing *toward* something else; we flatter ourselves with this notion, seeing *us* as the ultimate endpoint. In reality the infant is also a survival machine. At every stage of her growth she must be adapted to the conditions she faces *then*. The newborn must start breathing just-like-that; and it usually does, the old wives' tales about bottom-slapping notwithstanding. In one of nature's most astounding physiological transformations, the circulation to the placenta shuts down as birth withdraws the mother's contribution, and the infant's heart suddenly changes its priorities, drawing oxygen from tiny lungs newly filled with air.

The behavioral transformations seem almost as dramatic, although these have more to do with new opportunities than with physiological rearrangements. Some newborns have an exceptionally alert period right after emerging, surveying the passing scene with wide open eyes. My first child, a girl, opened her eyes when she was halfway out, uttering a faint "waaaah." My brother said this was baby language for "Where's my legs?" but I suspect it meant something more like "What's this all about?" Of course, we don't really know what babies are thinking. But after years of research, we know quite a lot about what they are looking at, listening to, and doing.

Take, for instance, the Moro reflex, named for a German pediatrician who himself called it the *Umklammerungsreflex* — the clinging reflex. Newborn babies, experiencing a loss of support under their heads, will throw out their arms and legs and then, in a second phase, clasp them to their bodies. The second phase looks a lot like what monkey babies do when their mothers get up and walk away — they end up clinging to the mother's fur by their hands and feet instead of falling. Modern infancy researchers, with their panoply of technology — notably Heinz Prechtl of the University Hospital in Groningen, the Netherlands — showed that if a human baby's hand is loosely clasped around something, then when the reflex occurs it skips the throwing-out part; instead, it looks and works just like monkey clinging. So it really is Moro's clinging reflex — or at least a behavioral vestige of it, like the vestige of an ancient tail we have at the base of our spine. In fact, a newborn infant grasping on to some grown-up fingers can support its own weight for a time, hanging just as calmly as you please.

These abilities don't mean that we begin just like monkey infants; but they do tell an evolutionary story that ends in an adapted, capable infant. More relevant to our modern situation is the set of reflexes known as rooting, sucking, and swallowing. Stroke a newborn baby's cheek, and pretty soon she will turn toward your finger, open her mouth, and lock on with surprisingly powerful toothless gums. If she is luckier, the stimulus will not be your finger but a nipple brimming with that remarkable fluid that our early mammalian ancestors began to invent a couple of hundred million years ago.

In a concatenation of movements that cannot in any meaningful sense be learned, she then makes expert use of her tongue, lips, and gums to extract same fluid, not omitting to swallow and to breathe. If you think this is easy, try writing a computer program to do it; you have to make many millions of nerve cells fire in a precisely coordinated rhythmic fashion, responding to the unique shape and character of the breast, and to the degree of fullness of the belly. It's impressive.

And yet it's only a tiny part of what a newborn baby can do: get her fingers into her mouth, and stop herself from crying; protect herself and withdraw various body parts from a spectrum of pains and irritations; lift her face out of the sheets to breathe; study the cracks on the ceiling with amazing concentration; burp, spit up, and defecate, sometimes even without losing her composure; coo; stop crying at the sound of a human voice; sleep twenty hours a day without developing bedsores; probably, dream. Michelle Kaufman may have been thirty minutes old when I examined her, but she had thirty thousand generations of human evolution behind her, readying her to survive and thrive in the world as it exists.

But the most startling discoveries about infants' abilities have been in the realm of the senses. For instance, twenty-five years ago scientists got the hang of watching infants' eyes. Just by measuring the length of time infants spent looking at different things, you could begin to surmise their preferences. With fancier techniques, you could actually trace the flickering point of focus where she trained her eyes, moving restlessly over a pattern she was studying. It became clear, through studies by Robert Fantz and others, that sharp boundaries between light and dark were especially interesting. Checkerboards and bull's-eyes compelled her attention, provided that these patterns were not so fine that the boundaries blurred.

A 1973 book, *The Competent Infant,* became a bible of the period. In it some two hundred studies were collected, each somehow confirming the premise of the title. Marshall Haith, of the University of Colorado, then as now a leading investigator of infant perception, suggested "a few tentative conclusions" about infant vision: "The newborn may come into the world with a few programmed statements to get him on his visual way . . . (1) if alert, and light is not too bright, open [eyes]; (2) if eyes open, but see no light, search; (3) if see light but no edges, keep searching; (4) if see edges, hold and cross." Alfred Steinschneider and his colleagues showed a clear increase in the heart rate of newborns while a white noise was played to them — proportional to the loudness of the noise. A group led by Peter Eimas showed that one-month-old infants reliably increase their rate of sucking — another indicator of attention — when the sound they are listening to is changed from "pa" to "ba." In effect this was a sound boundary, and its recognition suggested a very early, perhaps innate, ability to discriminate sounds basic to speech.

Whether the preferences were indicators of pleasure or mere reflexive curiosity, they were consistent enough, and they clearly said something about what was going on in the infant's mind. Equally interesting was the discovery that newborn infants modify their behavior with experience. In the simplest approach, a stimulus — say, a light flash — is repeated, and the response — an eye blink — gets smaller with each equal flash of light. This change is called habituation, and is fairly ho-hum. But other changes are more striking. For instance, Lewis Lipsitt and Herbert Kaye trained newborn infants to suck when they heard a tone that had previously been paired with their getting a nipple to suck on. In the end they sucked with just the tone — no nipple. Classical conditioning, it's called — or in plain words, a simple form of learning.

Yet these proofs of infant competence were only the beginning. Consider: At an average age of nine minutes, newborns will turn their eyes and their heads to follow a sketch of a face more than they will a similar sketch with upside-down or scrambled features, and still more than a face shape with no features at all. A few hours later they prefer their mothers' voices to those of strangers, probably because of prior learning in the womb. Simple stories with striking language, such as *The Cat in the Hat* by Dr. Seuss — if read to babies during the last weeks of pregnancy — influence their attentiveness to those stories after birth.

By age forty-five hours, newborns already look longer and differently at their mothers' faces than at the faces of unknown women presented to them in the same way — *post*natal learning. In less than two days, they have become a bit acquainted with the most important person in their lives. And by two or three weeks, according to some scientists, they will crudely mimic two facial gestures — tongue protrusion and mouth opening. This is not true imitation, and it is certainly not imitative learning. It is more like contagious yawning, perhaps — a primitive sort of facilitation rather than imitation. But it does highlight the newborn baby's predisposition to be social.

All these facts about babies have come to light in the last twenty years. Some people call this the "Gee whiz!" approach to infant study, because scientists keep feeling surprised by what infants can really do. I may be easily impressed, but I have to say that my considered, expert, professional opinion is still more or less *Gee whiz!*

And yet with a knowledge of anthropology and evolution, we should have anticipated quite a good chunk of this new research. After all, getting a sense of the world — and one biased toward stimuli from people — is precisely what newborn babies are designed for. In communities like the Baka and the !Kung, full of dangers and devoid of protective technologies, the only thing newborn infants have going for them — other than their five senses and two- or three-dozen reflexes — is an inborn orientation toward people.

The human touch, the human voice, the human face; these produce an interest on the newborn infant's part that bias her growing thoughts and feelings toward relationships. The richness of social life surrounding a Baka or !Kung infant speaks volumes about why all human infants are the way they are. Because these are among the environments of human evolutionary adaptedness — the social and physical worlds into which human infants were born for thousands of generations. What can babies be, in evolutionary terms, except creatures designed to enter relationships?

· · ·

In one sense it matters little whether the infant is born among Baka or !Kung hunter-gatherers, in New Guinea among the Eipo, in a poor hospital in São Paulo, under sedation in Moscow, or to an alert mother in Manhattan. The design of the creature has long since been clinched by evolution, which has left her with a certain kind of nervous system at birth. On average, the state of development of the brain at the time of birth is the same in any collection of newborns in the world. My own studies of !Kung newborns in the Kalahari Desert of Botswana, Africa, showed them to have basically similar capacities to ours despite being formed in a different climate, with different nutrition, health conditions, and style of life. Though subtle differences unquestionably exist — much more so between individuals than between populations — the basic behavioral repertoire is the same in newborn babies throughout the world.

The reason for this relentless similarity is that there is a universal maturational plan for the human brain. Coded by the genes, it is set in motion during the first week of embryonic life, when the neural tube that is destined to grow into the brain and spinal cord first folds itself into the back of the embryo. We have seen how, under the guidance of the genes, brain cells are born by the millions, move along physical or chemical paths to predestined places, produce fingerlike extensions in all directions, make planned, brilliantly intricate connections with each other — and finally begin to die back, in a process of streamlining that will continue throughout life. In the nine months allotted to humans for the supposedly blissful, irretrievable circumstance of gestation, this brain growth and shaping can go only so far. Hence a basic universal functional state at the time of birth.

Now no one is saying that the process is independent of the environment — genetic guidance notwithstanding. On the contrary, the environment can do things that derange the process tragically, as with thalidomide, alcohol, and crack cocaine. On the positive side, good nutrition helps build better brains, and psychological influences must shape and strengthen connections among brain cells — otherwise how would a baby just out of the womb respond as if she knew that she had been hearing *The Cat in the Hat?*

Yet the most basic features of the system are predestined; they just grow. In this respect the shape of the brain resembles the shape of the face. And the transformation does not end at birth. The streamlining of brain connections, the appearance of new ones, a dozen different changes in the physics and chemistry of brain cells — all these continue the process of growth surprisingly smoothly across the immense divide of birth. The power of experience becomes much greater after birth, but the power of growth does not become much less.

Think of metamorphosis — the process by which a caterpillar is changed into a moth or a butterfly. It so happens that in some species the kinds of leaves the caterpillar is raised on will influence the kinds of leaves the butterfly seeks out. Even so simple a nervous system can be engrained with the biasing force of experience. Yet the transformation itself — the amazing set of predictable changes that molds the butterfly out of the crawling fuzzy worm-shaped bug — owes little or nothing to experience. It emerges from the chemical magic of the genes.

Similarly, the growth of the human brain after birth responds in a thousand ways to the impact of each day's perceptions. Yet the fundamental growth events, at least for the first few months of life, make up a kind of human metamorphosis. In the first year alone the brain doubles in volume, reaching 60 percent of its adult size. The size change goes along with an increased number of non-nerve brain cells called glia — Greek for glue; with the dying back of some connections and the formation of others; with profound change in the chemical environment of the brain; and with the laying down of a fatty substance called myelin, which sheathes the connections between brain cells, making them much better conductors of neural electricity — the stuff of brain function.

The brain will keep changing in these ways for years to come. Robbie Case, a psychologist at the Ontario Institute for Studies in Education, has built an impressive theory of mental development on some related concepts, such as the changing speed of information-processing in the brain, and the increase with age in short-term storage space, which is needed for many mental functions. Such theory promises to link psychological studies of the infant's developing mind with biological studies of the brain.

But here is a key additional fact: Whichever aspect of brain growth is studied, the changes are not uniform throughout the brain. Different parts of the brain have different rates of development. To some extent it can be said that the "lower" parts — both physically lower in the head and lower in the evolutionary sense of being found also in simpler animals — develop before the "higher" centers, which house the great attainments of human language and thought. Motor coordination and voluntary action grow in a head-to-tail direction: first eyes, then arms and hands, then legs and feet. But there are more specific disjunctions. For instance, the part of the cerebral cortex that handles visual-pattern learning develops much earlier than the part responsible for the learning of patterns of sound. Without knowledge of these relationships it is difficult, if not impossible, to understand the psychology of infancy.

• • •

The point is that this developmental process, with its somewhat evolutionary progression and impressive regional brain differences, determines much about the development of behavior, emotions, and mind. This is especially true in infancy and early childhood, when brain development is most dramatic.

Consider a crude analogy: the newborn's brain as a computer — not like an advanced computer waiting to be programmed by experience, although it shares some features of such a learning machine — but like a simple computer slowly but surely *becoming* an advanced one. More memory is added to the central processor, increasing the amount of information stored short-term; an extra floppy-disk drive comes on board, improving the way information is managed; speed is added to some of the machine's functions, making them faster while other functions lag behind; another memory card comes on line, making room for more programs; a slow modem is replaced by a fast one, enhancing communication; one of the floppy drives is replaced by a small-capacity hard disk, increasing the volume of long-term storage; and so on.

But in the brain, unlike in a personal computer, these changes do not occur as the result of rational decisions. The new functions and power emerge gradually and seemingly haphazardly, a developmental course designed by an unknown evolutionary history. Meanwhile, the system is being programmed in more and different ways, always straining at its emerging capabilities. Are this year's new functions more the result of newly added software — programs — or more due to new hardware that made the software usable? The difficulty we experience in answering this question resembles the frustration some experts feel when confronted with questions about the relative roles of maturation and learning in infancy.

Yet the question remains fair. If we were assigned to examine the changing computer system described above, say on a monthly basis, to try to figure out how its powers were being augmented, we would want to know at least three things. What can the system do at any given point in time? How, if at all, has the hardware been modified behind our backs since the last examination? And what new software has been loaded on?

These are analogous to three of the great questions of child study. Probably we would not be surprised to find that the relative contributions of software and hardware are sometimes very tricky to tease apart. Also, in some months there would be more change in capacity than in others, and the relative importance of software and hardware would vary too. Finally, from time to time we might see very big changes that seemed to result from an unpredictably large effect of combined hardware and software changes — a whole that is functionally more than the sum of its parts. These would correspond to what are known in child development research as interaction effects; they are some of the most difficult changes to interpret, yet are quite common.

Infancy is the time in human life when the role of "hardware" changes — in reality, brain development — is greater than it will ever be again. As impressive as we now know the newborn is, its brain will be transformed in a few months' time into a far more powerful one. As often as we have said "Gee whiz" about the social graces of the newborn, they cannot hold a candle to the manners the same child will show a few months later.

Consider smiling. Newborns smile sometimes in sleep, especially during the rapid-eye-movement (REM) kind of sleep that in adults is often linked with dreaming. Occasionally, they smile while awake, and, rarely, they even smile in the context of social interaction. But three months later they will smile so frequently in response to an active human face that the gesture begins to seem automatic. In the 1970s I measured the change in infants among the !Kung San, where it is just as dramatic as in the United States, despite enormous differences in how the two sets of infants are treated.

Jacob Gewirtz, of the National Institute of Mental Health, studied the same phenomenon in four different baby-care environments in Israel. In a foundling home where the level of social reward for smiling (or anything else) was fairly low, smiling to the experimenter's face did lag behind that in typical middle-class homes. But the lag was a mere two weeks; "statistically significant" but practically unimportant compared to the rapid parallel rise in the rate of smiling in both groups. Elsewhere in the anthropological universe — the Baganda of Uganda, the Navajo, the Baka, and the families filmed for the "Childhood" series in places as different as São Paulo, Hino, Japan, Moscow, and White Plains, New York — the same growth pattern occurs. While we don't understand just which brain changes account for the pattern, we know it is universal. Regardless of what culture the infant is born into, the social metamorphosis occurs in the same time frame. There is no reason to think that it results primarily from learning.

• • •

And smiling is far from the only transformation in the first few months. While the newborn's gaze could be engaged only with difficulty, the eyes of the three-month-old will lock on to the gaze of the father or mother, resulting in long, soupy looks that recall those the same father and mother may once have directed at each other. Visually, the infant has matured greatly. Myelin develops rapidly after birth in the visual part of the brain, so that the vision of the three-month-old is probably almost as good as that of the adult. No slave to a mere sketch of a face, the baby can now study the real human version for fun and profit.

And the eyes have it, in more ways than one. They attract the gaze because of their bull's-eye shape and because parents find ways to reward babies for meeting eyes — if only with a squeeze, a kiss, or a coo. But it's not just the vision thing. The brain is blossoming in many other ways, subtle and complex, obvious and baffling.

These make it possible for the baby both to give and to receive social signals with an increasing amount of finesse. Ronald Barr, of the Montreal Children's Hospital, and others have shown that the simple act of crying in infancy has complexities that are regular and universal across cultures, in spite of profound variations in the caregivers' responses. For example, in Western countries, infants are allowed to cry for from five to thirty minutes, and spend a good deal of the day doing it. Among the !Kung, the average time to a response to crying is six seconds; crying is rarely allowed to continue if there is anything the mother can do to stop it. Yet in both these cultures, and others as well, crying increases after birth, reaches a peak at two to three months of age, and declines steadily thereafter. Clearly some characteristic of the developing brain accounts for these regularities — a fact that should be comforting to parents.

Also apparently built in is some sense of the meaning of *others'* expressions, indicated by contagious crying among infants, but also by many subtler responses to caregivers. As Charles Darwin, who among his other accomplishments published a diary of his own infant's development, put it, "An infant understands to a certain extent, and as I believe at a very early period, the meaning or feelings of those who tend him, by the expression of their features." Edward Tronick, Heidelise Als, Lauren Adamson, and T. Berry Brazelton, then at the Harvard Medical School, showed that over the first few months coordination of face-to-face interaction between mother and infant, as studied meticulously through analysis of videotapes, is both impressive and improving. And if the mother stops being expressive and shows a blank face, even a two-month-old baby shows signs of distress.

Carrying the analysis one step farther, Lynne Murray and Colwyn Trevarthen of the University of Edinburgh did an experiment in which mother and baby first had a positive interaction through reciprocal television pictures. Immediately afterward, the mother's side of the communication was replayed for the baby on videotape. It was the same mother, the same medium, the same pleasant and cheerful facial expressions, and on the mother's side the same timing, except in the replay the mother was not responding to the baby. As in the case of the blank mother's face, the baby showed grimaces, frowning, fidgeting, looking away — in short, withdrawal and distress.

• • •

These developments in the special realm of the social are paralleled by changes that would seem to be purely mental. For instance, over the first few months of life the baby tends to study her own hand in relation to an object dangled in front of it. This will lead by age five months to swiping at the object while looking at it, and by six months to reaching out deliberately to grasp it. Such coordination of reaching with looking is a prerequisite for effective action in the world.

Memory is also changing. Between three and four months of age a baby will store the image of an arbitrary set of shapes hung over her crib. We know that she can do this because she loses interest in those shapes by the end of the month, and is not very attentive to completely unrelated shapes either. But she looks much longer at shapes that depart *somewhat* from the pattern she has been looking at. Cooing, and the strange phenomenon of decreased heart rate — both, like looking, signs of a baby's interest — are also evoked by the intermediate shapes. This classic study by Charles Super, Jerome Kagan, and their colleagues at Harvard University is one among many that demonstrate the attraction for infants of a pattern moderately different from the one stored in memory.

Consider what a wonderful tendency this is: You've got this image in your mind, and you lock on to the next image over, the one that is just different enough to attract your attention. You study that one for a while, and then it too is stored in your mind. So you move on to the next somewhat different image, and the next. Gradually, eventually, you will have put all the world's variety in storage — and have had a lot of fun doing it.

Renée Baillargeon, in an ingenious 1987 study at the University of Illinois, surprised other researchers by discovering yet another four-month-old capacity — object permanence, or the tendency to act as if you think an object exists, even though it is no longer in view. Previous scientists, including famed Swiss psychologist Jean Piaget, had placed this ability later in infancy. But they had biased themselves against young infants' minds by relying too heavily on their hands.

Like other good students of the first months of life, Baillargeon looked at looking. The infants watched a screen slowly tilt away from them until it lay flat. A box was ostentatiously placed behind the screen and then, in half the trials, was surreptitiously removed. At this point the screen tilted away again, either stopping where the box was, or doing the "impossible" — continuing to tilt backwards *through* the place where the box should have been. The infants looked longer in the "impossible" instance, suggesting that they were surprised or puzzled by it. To be puzzled, they had to have had some sort of concept that the box they couldn't see still existed behind the screen.

Carolyn Rovee-Collier and her colleagues at Rutgers University have worked on an even more interesting infant ability. Their work paralleled that of John S. Watson (not the early behaviorist Watson) on how three-month-olds learn to control their environments. Watson noticed that young infants love to gain control of the mobiles hanging over their cribs — to make them move and stop at will. He gave them control by wiring the cribs so that by simply moving their heads from side to side, they activated a switch in the pillow that made the mobile move. Rovee-Collier uses a ribbon tied to the baby's foot, which serves the same purpose, and three-month-olds learn remarkably quickly to run the mobile "by foot," rewarded only by the visual display they themselves generate. In a study published in 1990, Michael Lewis, of the Rutgers University School of Medicine, found that changing the rules so that the baby's movements no longer had the desired effect produced facial expressions reliably identified as sadness or anger; but the reinstatement of control produced expressions of joy.

Watson called it "the game," because the babies so obviously enjoyed it, smiling and cooing while they worked. "Why," he wondered, "should the offspring of our species be so vigorously expressive of their pleasure in recognizing their control of the environment?" His answer was that "the game" is meant to be played with a person, not a mobile. The three-month-old infant is built to love that sense of control because it is just what someone who loves her has to offer. In this view, the mother and father resemble gigantic controllable mobiles that thrill and delight the infant precisely because she *is* able to control them — not with her feet maybe, but with her eyes, smiles, coos, and cries. Watson was offered an opportunity to market his head-control mobile, but he wisely resisted this temptation; he feared that if "the game" were the key to the infant's interest in people, this mechanical device might actually take their place.

Watson's analysis brings us to where we want to be: Somehow the emerging properties of the baby's growing brain must be such as to make it really ready for relationships. We know from the studies of newborns that at birth we all have a readiness — use whatever adjective you like: inborn, innate, inherent, basic, built-in, fundamental — a readiness for social life. But we also know that in a mere few months that wired-in capacity becomes far more impressive, and changes from a predisposition to a true desire for relationships.

We have seen the rise of the social smile and the decline of early crying, and traced the emergence of prolonged gaze contact, all in the first three to four months of life. We also have studies showing that something deeply social in the young infant's brain is distressed by a lack of reciprocity. But we have as well these cognitive transformations: the ability to store patterns in memory; to prefer new things that are just somewhat different from the ones that have been stored; to keep in mind an object that can no longer be seen; and to get pretty excited about learning to make interesting things happen — to exercise control.

Clearly each of these emerging abilities helps make a first relationship possible. You need to store the image of at least one key person in your mind. You need to learn that person's varied appearances and moods, expressed in patterns seen, heard, smelled, felt, and tasted. You need somehow to know that she exists though she has come and gone. And above all you need to know that you have some control over that person — or to put it less one-sidedly, that she responds to your very own actions out of all the events in the crowded hubbub of life. That, after all, is what a relationship means.

Daniel Stern, a psychoanalyst and premier investigator of mother-infant relations in early infancy, has conceptualized the problem more aptly than anyone. The ideal primary caregiver — it's usually the mother, but it needn't be — takes advantage almost instinctively of the infant's emerging mental bents. She doesn't need to have read a psychology textbook, she just somehow *knows* that her vocal and facial expressions, even her chants and lullabies, can be fine-tuned to attract the baby's attention, to give the baby a growing sense of mastery, and perhaps above all to give the baby excitement and pleasure. Somewhere inside she even knows, again without a textbook, that the baby's capabilities are changing from week to week, and so she adjusts her patterns of stimulation accordingly, always aiming for that excitement and pleasure that give her so much of both back in turn.

"Affective attunement" is Stern's apt term for it; but "good vibrations" would not be too far off base. Stern's game is a more complex one than Watson's — more of a two-way street. And though they are not quite there yet — not at three, not at four, probably not at five months — the pair, for that is what they are, are rapidly progressing from the excitement and pleasure of a relationship to the depth and passion of love.

• • •

This is also, of course, the time when children in different cultures begin to have drastically different experiences. Until now, folded up more or less comfortably in the confines of the womb, it might not have mat-

tered to them whether they were in Timbuktu or Oshkosh. But now they
are out and in the world. If that world is the middle class of Ann Arbor,
Michigan, they will be talked at almost incessantly; if a farm community
on the Russian steppes, they will be tightly wrapped in swaddling clothes.
If it is the most traditional corner of the Navajo reservation, near Lake
Powell, Utah, a baby will not merely be swaddled, but strapped to a
cradleboard — and, believe it or not, will find this comforting; if Japan,
taught to lie quietly and get in touch with her own sense of calm. And
after nightfall, if it is suburban Atlanta, the baby may have to cry herself
to sleep in a crib, while in virtually every non-Western culture in the
world she will sleep at the mother's side. Nevertheless, there are some
points of reference to go back to, not proofs, just points of reference;
biological guidelines that emerge from the study of baby and child care
in the environment of human evolutionary adaptedness.

For instance, in hunting and gathering societies like the Baka and the
!Kung, infants are carried by the mother most of the time, and are nursed
several times an hour. At night, the two sleep together, and nursing continues, though less frequently. All these seemingly strange things are also
true of our closest monkey and ape relatives. During our evolution, the
constant closeness served several functions: mothers stood between babies and creatures that might eat them; they kept the babies warm with
the warmth of their own bodies; they breast-fed often enough to ensure
water balance, nutrition, and protection from infection in the form of
antibodies in breast milk. As Dvora Ben Shaul, Nicholas Blurton Jones,
and "Childhood" series observer Robert Hinde have shown, there is even
evidence in the composition of milk that we humans were meant to be
frequent breast-feeders. Animals, such as rabbits and tree shrews, that
stow their young in nests and return to feed them once a day or less often,
have thick milk rich in fat and protein. Monkeys and apes, which carry
their young around and feed them very often, have thin milk with much
higher water content. Human milk belongs on the frequent-feeding end
of the continuum.

Do these evolutionary facts mean we must keep mothers and babies in
constant contact, breast-feeding several times an hour and sleeping together at night? Certainly not. Studies to date have not shown any quan-
tifiable advantage to such a strategy, in terms of the infant's health and

development. That means such choices can remain open to mothers and fathers, and factors such as work schedules and marital intimacy should count for a lot in these decisions. Nevertheless it is not surprising that some mothers and infants in our society find themselves drifting back toward an ancient evolutionary pattern. As in the case of childbirth, the relaxation of our Western cultural — and medical — pressures to *depart* from the natural have enabled some families to "drift back."

So, in the 1970s, Benjamin Spock's *Baby and Child Care* — by far the most widely influential book of its kind — began to describe infant-carrying devices, just as these were replacing baby carriages in much of the industrialized world. Between 1950 and 1980, official pediatric recommendations about baby feeding in the United States turned around about a hundred eighty degrees, from a universal recommendation of bottle-feeding to a universal recommendation of breast-feeding. During the same time period, organizations of mothers such as La Leche League expanded enormously, paralleling the growth of childbirth education networks and preparation classes. La Leche League recommended frequent nursing, late weaning, and minimal mother-infant separation. Books called *The Family Bed* and *Nighttime Parenting* appeared, advocating that parents and infants sleep together. Interestingly, Japan underwent its own industrial revolution without ever abandoning this practice of co-sleeping, and studies during the eighties have shown that American parents admit children into their beds at night much more than they have been told they should. James McKenna, an anthropologist at the Claremont Graduate School who has been a leader in tracing evolutionary perspectives on childhood, is studying the implications of different sleeping arrangements for certain aspects of infant health.

Yet at the same time that this "drift back" was occurring, American women were entering the work force in record numbers — numerically the most impressive social change of this era. Households headed by single mothers, many of whom had to support their children themselves, became common. Universal breast-feeding was not easily compatible with these changes. (Barbara Kaufman, an architect, exemplifies this fact in her decision not to breast-feed Michelle — a decision that also helped protect and equalize David's role in Michelle's care.) The concept of infant day-care took hold, and mothers by the millions began to rely on it.

As some parents began to revert to primitive patterns of infant care, others chose to or had to use the full power of the modern industrial state to organize a completely different kind of care for their babies. Both strategies worked.

The cross-cultural study of traditional societies might have suggested to us that they would. Navajo infants get so attached to the cradleboard that they cry to be tied into it. Kikuyu infants in Kenya get handed around among several "mothers," all wives to one man, a situation known as multiple caretaking. Mothers in rural Guatemala keep their infants quiet, in dark huts. Middle-class American mothers talk a blue streak at them. Israeli kibbutz mothers give them over to a communal caretaker for all but a few hours a day. Japanese mothers sleep with them. Russian mothers bundle them up in a soft version of the cradleboard.

We have yet to figure out how, if at all, these widely differing cultural practices shape infants' minds so that they turn out distinctively, whether in terms of emotional or intellectual predispositions. This shaping may prove to be much less impressive than we thought. Certainly no one child-care practice can shape a child's destiny. Probably, as Urie Bronfenbrenner says, the effects will prove to be cumulative — little drops of water and little grains of sand incrementally build mighty rivers and dunes. But one thing we can say with some confidence: All these tactics are compatible with normal health — physical and mental — and development in infancy. So one lesson for parents so far seems to be: Let a hundred flowers bloom.

• • •

But that doesn't mean there are no limits to resilience in infancy. Consider the following question: What is the leading cause of death from injury during the first year of life in the United States? Drowning? No. House fires? Guess again. Suffocation? Aspiration of food or objects? Motor vehicle accidents? None of these lead the list, although they contribute to infant injury deaths in ascending order.

Homicide.

The leading cause of injury deaths — 17 percent of such deaths — for children under a year of age in the United States in the first half of the 1980s, as analyzed in a paper published in 1989, was homicide. This, of course, is only the tip of the iceberg of infant abuse. I remember well the day in medical school when I followed a suspicious expert on children's burns down to the X-ray room, where she had ordered pictures of all the bones of a baby in her burn unit. There were fractures of different vintage — they'd healed to different degrees — all over the tiny body. The baby was nine months old.

This seems young, but in fact the peak time for abuse in childhood is the first six months of life. The timing may be related to the developmental events we have considered. Although some babies are more frustrating to parents than others, all newborns are emotionally and socially unrewarding compared to their six-month-old counterparts. This is simply a biological fact of our lives in the human species. At three months the emergence of smiling, the possibility of steady face-to-face gazing, the ability to conjure up the mother's image when she has turned away, and the keen interest in "contingent stimuli" all slowly converge to make a delightfully social creature out of a lately whining and relentlessly dependent one. Now the baby is really rewarding for parents, and their pent-up frustration starts to wane. The same parents who a couple of months ago gritted their teeth in fatigue and frustration are now chanting tickle-rhymes, making faces, and playing peekaboo, giggling unabashedly all the while. Soon most babies will have locked their parents into relationships that steadily reduce the chance of abuse and neglect. That is, they will have staked their destinies on the different risks, and the sublime and practical benefits, of love.

Except the unlucky ones. Just as homicide is the tip of the iceberg of abuse, so direct violence is only one dimension of the overall maltreatment of infants and children. To this we must add the passive violence of neglect, and the exposure of children to inappropriate parental sexuality — even newborns have been reported, albeit rarely, as the victims of sexual abuse. Such distortions of the experience of infants effectively set a limit on our tolerance for variety in patterns of baby care.

Even certain "approved" cultural practices, such as traditional Chinese foot-binding or surgical removal of the clitoris in parts of Africa are universally condemned by educated people, including those trained to sympathize with alternative cultural choices. But what of the fact that !Kung hunter-gatherer mothers consider Dr. Spock's advice about how to "unspoil" babies — five-month-olds, he believes, should be allowed to cry if they want to be held too often — to be a clear case of neglect? Or the fact that mother-infant co-sleeping, widespread in non-Western traditional societies, is considered by some American social workers to pose a clear risk of sexual abuse? Or that infant day-care, accepted by millions, is viewed as neglectful by others, while spanking, seen by some parents as crucial to raising decent kids, is in other homes labeled child abuse? After we have drawn the lines where all agree, we must begin to consider the subtler cultural variations. No one, whether scientist, doctor, pastor, or anthropologist, is going to impose some dismal futuristic uniformity on baby and child care. Even if they could, the kids would grow up differently, because they *are* different — temperamentally, biologically. But without abdicating our parental role to experts of any stripe, we still may want to know what they are learning about how human infants grow into different sorts of people; especially, how our different ways of caring for them contribute to their ultimate human distinctness. Notice that this is different from the question of what we want them to be. We can be as idiosyncratic as we like about that, and ultimately as smug as we like.

But what we can't be smug about is the question of *how* we get them to be that way — the way our baby and child care practices shape them in any given direction. We can't, because those questions are scientific, not ethical, and science has as yet discovered only a few answers. But it is posing the questions vigorously, and some hints are appearing on the horizon. And it is these glimmers of understanding to which we now turn.

1.

1. Born knowing how to coordinate sucking, swallowing, and breathing, a newborn can get her entire sustenance from breast milk for several months. While recommended, breast-feeding is not essential, and not every mother is able to work it into her life.

2. For centuries in European art, Madonnas have breast-fed the Christ Child openly, making the act seem sacred. Rogier van der Weyden, fifteenth century.

3. With our century came an option that would help transform the roles of men and women. Early-twentieth-century male "Madonna."

2.

3.

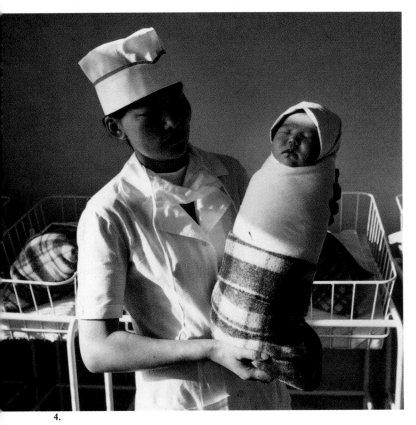

Some customs for handling infants seem to comfort them, but interpose a barrier to contact; nevertheless contact occurs, through rocking, humming, looking, kissing…

4. Swaddling in a newborn nursery in Mongolia.

5. A baby in James Chisholm's study of Navajo infancy; he showed that infants are comforted by the cradleboard and even become attached to it.

6. Nineteenth-century Native American (Chippewa) mother with infant tied in cradleboard.

7. Welcoming ritual: an Armenian christening in Marseilles, France.

4.

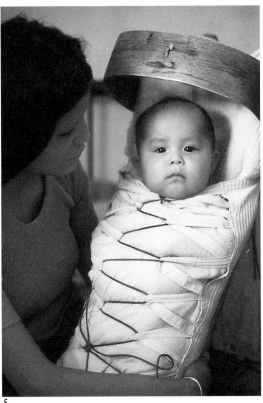

5.

6.

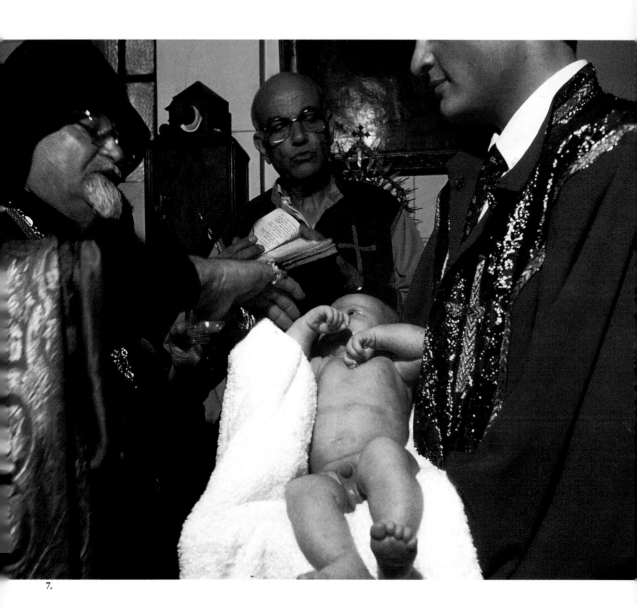

7.

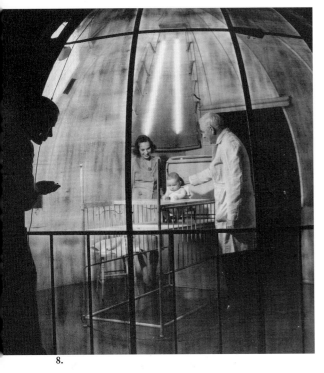

8.

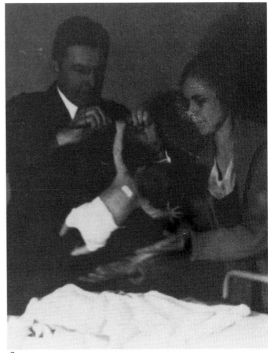

9.

10.

11.

8. Arnold Gesell and his colleagues — here being observed by students on the near side of the glass — did a comprehensive study of the normal growth of motor coordination in infancy, a basis for pediatric care.

9. John B. Watson, the behaviorist, demonstrates the power of the newborn grasp. His experiments on fear, and his child-care manual, which cautioned against hugging, were consistent with this image.

10, 11. Partway through the first year, babies develop object permanence. Until then, their rule seems to be "out of sight, out of mind."

12. This seventeenth-century Dutch painting by Nicolaes Maes shows an infant tossing objects onto the floor. He appears to forget them, consistent with a lack of object permanence.

13. Mary Cassatt, before modern psychology, shows visually directed reaching, joint attention between mother and infant, and just the right amount of helping, which according to recent theory places the act in the baby's "zone of proximal development."

14. "Childhood" series mother Natasha Kalugin guides her daughter Vera in picking daisies, Moscow, 1991.

13.

12.

14.

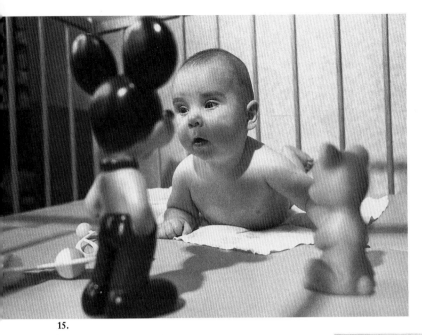

15.

15. Vitaly Popov, born in Moscow during filming for the series, gets acquainted with an American icon; *perestroika* in the cradle?

16. Carolyn Rovee-Collier studies the thrill infants get from being allowed to control an object — in this case a mobile tied by a ribbon to the baby's foot.

17. The sixteenth-century German artist Albrecht Dürer made proportional drawings of men, women, and children for thirty years. Unlike many earlier artists, the children he drew looked like children, not small adults.

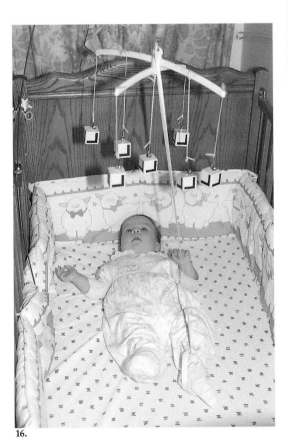

16.

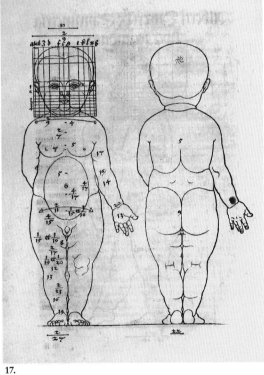

17.

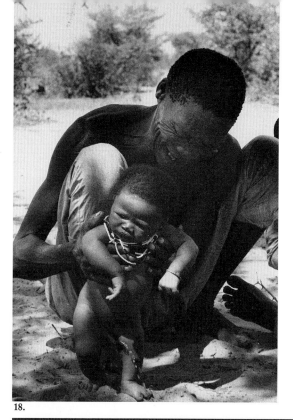

18. The !Kung encourage walking from early infancy. While walking will mature without practice of any kind, there is evidence — from research by Phillip Zelazo — that exercise of the newborn's "automatic march" reflex can accelerate *independent* walking by several weeks.

19. The first sequential photographs of a young child walking. Heel-toe progression is a hallmark of our species — and toddlers like it, too.

18.

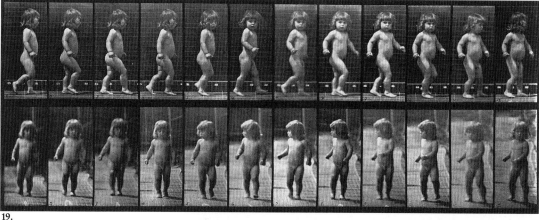

19.

20. The child who can walk, the !Kung feel, can dance. Here a one-and-a-half-year-old boy becomes the focus of all eyes as five women clap and sing to encourage him. He keeps the rhythm, and his arms are in the typical posture of adult men in the trance-dance.

20.

Love, Separation, and the Sense of Self

Summoned from a dream of your summoning
by your cry, I steal out of bed and leave
my doting husband deaf to the world.
We meet, couple, and cling in the dim light —
your soft mouth tugs and fills and empties me.
We stay that way a long time it seems, till
on your brimming face, where milky drops glide,
I see my body's pleasure flood and yawn.
We turn each other loose to sleep. Smiling
your smile of innocence, I return
to the bed of your begetting, and a man's warm side.

— JILL HOFFMAN, "Rendezvous"

WHEN MY DAUGHTER SARAH was four months old, her mother wrote this entry in her baby diary:

> Sometimes on the bed, when being changed, she looks intently at me, then breaks into energetic body gyrations — arms up and down, legs up and down, all parts moving separately and yet together. The expression on her face is priceless: intense, concentrated, working so hard, thrilled with her movement. I laugh and scoop her up with my hands. And we start all over again.

A four-month-old baby is already a far cry from the mewling, squirming, emotionally detached yet relentlessly demanding newborn. Brain growth changes and the transforming impact of loving stimulation and care have combined to make a new creature — one that is unmistakably human. Comfortable, even poised in the outside world for a couple of months now, she has found the resources to begin a project that will occupy her for at least the next two years: the formation and development of her main human relationships.

Sometimes, while nursing, she stops and stares quietly at my face. The other day she stared and stared, so intently, so curiously, so connectedly, so gently, so acceptingly. I looked back at her, receiving her glance, calling her name, talking quietly, finally laughing. She continued to look and look. When she was ready, a smile broke on her face, full of radiance.

This gaze contact, these smiles, so rewarding to parents, are beyond the ken of the newborn, and it is even possible that we are born before we "should" be. When Mikiko Nouhata breast-feeds Kenzaburo, her newborn, we see touching maternal solicitude, but it is still rather one-sided. But when Vera Kalugin, half a year older than Kenzaburo, interacts with her mother, Natasha, throwing playful glances, smiling, gurgling happily, even laughing, then we see a substantial proportion of the full, two-way power of human interaction.

Because our species experienced a disproportion between the infant's head and the birth canal, we may have evolved toward relatively earlier births, pushing the baby out a few months before she is quite ready for relationships. These relationships will require most of the machinery of her increasingly powerful brain — which improves in every respect from plain sight to foresight. Yet they rely most strongly on a still mysterious but universal human capacity built into the core of that brain: the ability to form emotional bonds.

As we follow the infant's transition into childhood, we can watch those bonds mature and change from inarticulate longings to complicated verbal exchanges complete with insults, compliments, protestations of love, cajoling, metaphor, even deliberate fabrication. But at their base will still, and indeed will always, be the strong emotions of infancy: love, fear, grief, comfort, joy, rage, and a frequent, if not continual, dissatisfaction with the way things are — a real as well as metaphorical hunger. This mild to moderate ache is nature's way of creating an imbalance that ultimately can make things better; but it also is a source of emotional irritations that generate existential anguish. Existential anguish in toddlers? Surprisingly so. But first we have to trace the growth of love.

• • •

We know that the four- to five-month-old is making her great leap forward into relationships because she is ceasing to be indiscriminate in her friendliness, her apprehensiveness, her disappointment. At three months she would have grinned at anyone giving the right cues — a smiling, open face moving up and down, say, combined with a melodic, spirited "Hi, baby," or the equivalent in any other language. More important, perhaps, she would, in disappointment or pain, have taken comfort from almost anyone's properly executed cuddling. By five months, these kinds of reactions have begun to be more privileged communications.

We know, of course, that glimmers of personal recognition are present two days after birth. But subtle statistical differences do not add up to a relationship. Five-month-olds show a much clearer preference for the mother or primary caregiver in social responses ranging from smiling, waving, and reaching to cuddling and the cessation of crying. Although they cannot walk or crawl they give every impression of trying to get to the mother or primary caregiver when they are in distress or simply when she has been away; to the mother or primary caregiver *particularly*. Others in the baby's life — fathers, siblings, friends of the family, nannies, day-care workers, grandparents, uncles, or aunts — can certainly still give comfort. But they appear to participate in a hierarchy of preference, a slope on which the baby edges or slides toward the most comfortable resting place.

Parts of this concept remain controversial. Some psychologists — "Childhood" series observers Jerome Kagan and Sandra Scarr, for example — feel that the infant's love or attachment can be distributed equally among several caregivers, but I am not persuaded. Studies of attachment in day-care or communally reared babies show that they usually prefer the mother to the substitute caregiver in situations where they need comforting. This is true even where the secondary caregiver has spent as much time with the baby as the mother has. But we know this for certain: The primary caregiver does not have to be the biological mother. It can be an adoptive mother, a single father, a married father who has a true primary-caregiver role, a grandmother, an older sister or brother, or a nanny in a situation where the parents are physically or emotionally quite removed.

But in most situations, not merely in our culture, but throughout the world — for example, in all the families filmed for the "Childhood" series — the primary caregiver happens to be the mother. A ten-year-old may roundly declare that she loves her father and mother the same, but a baby is not so solicitous of paternal sensibilities. When my son was just under five months old, I noted in his baby diary that he had begun to show "clear (to me) differential responsiveness to me and his mother, being less positive in his interactions with me, less responsive to my entertaining him . . . than he had been. This was consistent and fairly evident. On several occasions he was visibly comforted on seeing his mother after watching me warily for a while." I was a very involved father, yet I now had cause to be jealous.

By the middle of the first year, most babies seem to choose. When distressed, they move, under the force of emotional gravity, toward ever more powerful, more comforting relationships, and usually one of these is the most comforting. They can and frequently do prefer another caregiver, often the father, as an exciting, entertaining social partner. They may prefer grandparents as indulgers of their every whim, siblings as playmates, and nannies or uncles as teachers. But these relationships usually do not have the weight of the one with the primary caregiver. This emotional force is what psychologists call attachment, and it is a major part of what most of us call love. Out of reach for the two-month-old, at five months it has started to take its place in the infant's repertoire. And by seven or eight or nine months, it has taken an impressive, darker turn.

Consider the classic experiment. A baby plays beside her mother, occupying herself with toys on the floor, for three minutes in an ordinary room strange to the baby. A stranger, a woman, comes in, sits for a minute, talks with the mother a minute, tries to engage the baby a minute. Then the mother leaves. What will the baby do?

The answer turns out to hinge on the baby's age. The five-month-old we have been getting to know will most likely continue playing, interact a bit with the stranger, and, if distressed, even allow the stranger to comfort her. The eight- or nine-month-old — we can't specify these transformations precisely — will often show no such equanimity. The exclusivity of the baby's love has apparently intensified so that something between wariness and outright fear begins to raise a protective wall around it. Fear of strangers and the more consistent fear of separation — these can be and have been tested separately — tend to emerge during the second half of the first year. Together they might be called the social fears.

A separation experiment, the Strange Situation, was developed by psychologist Jean Arsenian, and later used by Mary Ainsworth and her colleagues to test John Bowlby's theory of attachment. Bowlby, a leading English psychoanalyst, viewed the mother-infant bond as an evolutionary adaptation, designed to prevent infants from straying away from their mothers and into the jaws of predators. For the infant, in this theory, fear was the other side of the coin of love. It seems a cynical view of love, but such strong emotion must have some practical purpose — or it must at least have *had* one in what Bowlby called the environment of evolutionary adaptedness: that of hunters and gatherers. This way of life, as studied by anthropologists, resembles in some important respects the life lived by our early human ancestors.

As one of those anthropologists, watching infants in one such group of people — the !Kung San, or Bushmen, of Botswana — I had a couple of years to think about what the evolutionary purposes of infant attachment might be. There are at least four others besides not getting eaten: maintaining energy and water balance through frequent nursing; stabilizing body temperature through physical contact; reducing the baby's risk of infection by reducing exposure to others, as well as through the immunological properties of breast milk; and providing an emotional foundation for cultural learning. But the fourth of these is paradoxical in a way: How can an attachment to one or two caregivers provide a basis for cultural learning, which ultimately must come from many?

The answer lies in widening the circle of relationships after infancy. In the human species this outcome is attained in a uniquely powerful way, through language — the vehicle for complex relationships that do not have to be based on, or even include, touching. Thus the coherence of this phase of life: it begins in the middle of the first year with the growth of the capacity for intense emotional bonds; and it ends around two years later with the emergence of language, which has two dramatic effects. First, it helps the toddler to conceive of herself as separate — not just to feel separate, but to think and talk about her separateness. Second, after this sense of self has developed, the further growth of language delivers the little person into a wider cultural world. Or, to put it another way, it delivers the infant — Latin for "not a speaker" — into childhood. Most of this chapter will dwell on and between these great events, and set forth the known details of both growth and experience that slowly but surely bring them about.

• • •

The baby game of peekaboo — peep-bo in England — would seem to have little to do with love or fear, but at second glance those emotions are just what it is about. It has been called the baby's first joke, and it certainly can provoke smiles and laughter. But good jokes, we know, delve into serious emotions, and peekaboo is no exception. In the last chapter we saw evidence even in the three-month-old of a joy obtained from controlling the environment, as with a mobile controlled by a ribbon tied to a foot. Peekaboo gives the baby an illusion of control over something in the external world that provokes very strong emotions. The face of the other player seems to disappear and reappear in response to the baby's own emotions of wariness or delight.

In effect, if the grown-up playing the game is good — attuned to the baby — that is exactly what is happening. As with "the game" the three-month-old plays with her grown-up partner in face-to-face "conversation," the adult tunes in to the baby's most fleeting mood, and acts so as to ride it, or stretch it, or, just to the right extent, disrupt it.

But in peekaboo with the older infant, more is at stake. As Sigmund Freud pointed out in his study of anxiety, the pair are in effect toying with the baby's most profound fears — that of loss of the loved one, or that of the threat posed by a stranger. Kenzaburo Nouhata at ten months demonstrated the connection: he played peekaboo with his mother, showing great delight; but when she actually left the room, he cried. The cycle of disappearance and reappearance in the game gives the baby the illusion of control over the scariest possibilities of his tiny social world. And the laughter perhaps, like the younger infant's smile during the interactive game, releases the tension raised by toying with the fear.

The separation experiment is not quite so funny. It's not cruel either — many infants never cry, and for those who do the mother is sent in very quickly. But in most studies throughout the world the *likelihood* of the baby's fretful or wailed protest rises steadily from the middle to the end of the first year. Even when crying doesn't occur, wariness is often present, and cessation of play or smiling — a good sign of mild discomfort — is very common. Searching for the mother, at least with the eyes, is usual. All in all, most babies don't experience it as a game, but as something more like a mild to moderate stress.

One of the first things surmised from this experiment was that babies' increased protest or wariness as they mature seems, on the surface at least, to track the growth of love, as subjectively experienced by caregivers. It seemed sensible to take the experiment to other cultures around the world — and to subcultures of infant care within our own society — where variations in the care given babies, the number of caregivers, the time spent with the mother, the role of the father, and so on, would make it possible to relate behavior in the strange situation to the baby's past experience.

One thing was very consistent: the rise in the proportion of protesting or wary babies during the second half-year of life. Among !Kung hunter-gatherers, where I did the experiment, infants are in physical contact with their mothers the great majority of the time during the first year. In Israel, kibbutz infants and their mothers spend the majority of their time, including sleep, in separate houses. And in rural Guatemala, infants are kept as quiet as possible, near their mothers in darkened huts, but with little of the constant babble and patter that links mother-infant pairs in middle-class America. Yet in all these settings the rise in the proportion of infants who cry is evident between six and twelve months of age.

Still, there are some clear differences. For example, all !Kung infants between one and two years of age cry when the mother leaves, while many American infants show little or no fear. Protest also persists much longer in !Kung infants, extending way beyond the first year. But it soon became clear to investigators that separation and stranger protest were too crude as measures of something as subtle and complex as attachment. So after the first wave of studies with the Strange Situation, researchers began to turn their attention to very detailed descriptions of what the baby does when the mother comes back. Videotapes of the reunion are played over and over again and trained observers code the behavior and categorize the infants. It seems an approach that would be subject to many biases, but in fact trained independent observers classify babies the same way.

There are basically three types, arbitrarily labeled A, B, and C. B babies are the most numerous (though not always the majority) in almost all samples. They are the ones who freely greet their mothers on reunion, either by voice and eye contact, or by approach and physical contact. Group A babies are called avoidant, because they avoid or ignore their mothers predominantly, although some may also show proximity-seeking. C babies, who mix anger and rejection with some attempts to contact the mother, are called resistant or ambivalent. These *classifications* of Strange Situation behavior, especially on reunion, are no longer controversial. They can be reliably identified.

What *is* controversial is whether the Strange Situation experiment really measures attachment, or any basic aspect of the primary relationship, as it is lived and felt by both partners. That this is the bottom line is shown by the label for B babies: securely attached. Both A and C babies are said to be insecurely attached. These labels not only imply something about the present relationship, they intimate something about the long-term mental health of the child.

In this they hark back before Bowlby and Ainsworth to an idea introduced by psychoanalyst Erik Erikson: basic trust. According to Erikson, the main task of psychological development in the first two years of life is to form a trusting attitude toward the world and toward life itself. This attitude, Erikson believed, was most likely to come from an indulgent, loving mother (although it could be the father or any primary caregiver). If you developed basic trust, you could rely on it for the rest of your life to help you pull through psychological challenges. If you didn't, you might be permanently plagued by insecurity, anxiety, and sadness.

It's an appealing theory, and one that runs counter to conventional wisdom about "spoiling," which holds that indulgence of early dependency results in a child who is insufferably demanding and tied to the mother's apron strings. According to Erikson's view, in contrast, dependent demands of infants are *not* bad behavior to be systematically snuffed out but normal needs that cannot be ignored without placing the growing mind in peril. So from the beginning investigators have tried to relate the attachment categories A, B, and C to independently measured aspects of the primary relationship.

In Ainsworth's original study, the sensitivity of the mother to the baby, as assessed in the home at six months of age, predicted secure attachment at twelve months. When sensitivity, defined as responsiveness to the baby's special needs, moods, and signals, whatever these might be — today we would call it attunement — was rated as high, the infant was more likely to land in the B category later on. Many psychologists were skeptical of this discovery, but it has been found to be true in at least five other studies, all independently done. They have not convinced everyone, but they add up at a minimum to a very viable hypothesis: *Good attunement now, good attachment later.*

A study of mothers and infants living in poverty seemed at first to support the idea. Of a group of two hundred poor mothers in Minneapolis, thirty-one were identified as inadequate — consistently failing to change diapers, leaving the infant alone without care, neglecting wounds and illnesses — while thirty-three at the other extreme were labeled excellent. These classifications were checked every three months throughout the first year. At twelve months the Strange Situation test was given. The proportion of securely attached (B) babies in the excellent-care group was 75 percent, slightly higher than the usual proportion in educated middle-class families. But B babies made up only 38 percent of the inadequate-care sample, a highly significant difference from their luckier counterparts. This was seen as strongly confirming the attunement-attachment connection.

The trouble was that at eighteen months, when the test of attachment was redone, the difference was no longer significant. This was because many of the inadequate-care babies had changed groups, especially by entering group B, and some of the excellent-care group had also changed. These facts suggested that inadequate care compromised attachment at twelve months, but that changes in the quality of care — due perhaps to improvements in the family's economic and social stability — could reverse the ill effects. Tellingly, perhaps, some of the resistant babies in the inadequate-care group switched to being avoidant at eighteen months; this could mean that after months of protest, they had become resigned, and had basically given up on their mothers.

Another approach psychologists have taken to test these effects has been cross-cultural comparison of reunion behavior. They have set up the same experiment in Germany, Sweden, the Netherlands, Britain, Japan,

China, and the Israeli kibbutz, among other national and cultural settings, as well as in many different settings within the United States. Alan Sroufe, of the University of Minnesota, has been a leader in this line of research, but excellent work has been done by Mary Main, Klaus Grossman, Eleanor Maccoby, and many others. A recent compilation combined the results from almost two thousand runs of the experiment in eight different countries. A-B-C classifications of babies in this combined analysis are of exceptional interest.

First, the standard distribution in the United States was 20 percent avoidant, 70 percent securely attached, and 10 percent resistant. This was quite close to the average distribution for the world as a whole and, incidentally, very close to the pattern for Mary Ainsworth's original sample — for years a standard of comparison. In one German sample — the first in that country, studied in Bielefeld — there was a majority of avoidant babies. This was a marked departure from the world range; securely attached babies predominate in every other sample. At first it seemed related to a pattern of mothering that included more strictness and less nurturance. But two other samples in different parts of Germany proved to have more usual distributions. One Japanese sample and one Israeli kibbutz sample were atypical in a different way — they had a larger minority of resistant babies. Yet in each case a second study in the same cultural setting came up with a more typical pattern.

On the whole it is possible to say that samples within countries vary more than do averages for different countries. In other words, there is so far no support for broad generalizations about how different patterns of child care in different countries may lead to different numbers of avoidant, securely attached, and resistant babies. Perhaps further study may turn up some systematic differences, but for now the cross-national comparisons seem to say more about the resilience of babies and the universal importance of attachment than they do about cultural or national differences.

Other differences in care, such as day-care versus home care, have also been studied, and we will return to them. For the moment we can just say that there is *some* evidence that the A-B-C groupings really do reflect the quality of the relationship; but such effects seem to require major differences in the quality of care, and even then are not necessarily lasting.

Skeptics have mounted another challenge: What if the differences in the test situation really reflect temperamental differences — mostly innate — among the babies? For example, difficult babies might exasperate mothers, producing both inadequate care and insecure attachment. But this hypothesis has not been proved. In most studies, measures of temperament from birth through the first year do not show strong relationships to the A-B-C groups. Securely attached babies have a range of temperaments — active and inactive, "easy" and "difficult," irritable and calm — resembling the range for insecurely attached babies. However, temperaments *do* relate to the *kind* of secure or insecure attachment. Remember that B babies can show their positive reunion behavior toward the mother in different ways. Some of them reunite but keep their distance, greeting the mother with words and glances from a distance. Others actively approach the mother and stay close to her for some time after her return.

It turns out that temperament classifications make the most sense if you split the B babies according to how actively they try to stay close. Babies in group A — avoidant — sort *temperamentally* with those B babies who keep their distance while talking with the mother. B babies who maintain physical contact, in contrast, sort with the C group in temperament — resistant to contact, and difficult to comfort. Thus the temperament measure split both the securely attached and the insecurely attached types of babies. We gain little or no knowledge of the security of attachment by measuring temperament, or vice versa. So the attachment psychologists understandably conclude that the Strange Situation measures something about relationships, not just something about the baby's inborn personality. Although this is still not certain, it now seems very likely that the test does give some insight into the growth of love.

• • •

Of course, the affections are not the only things that grow and change toward the end of the first year. Between birth and the first birthday the brain doubles in volume, reaching more than half of its adult size. The nuts and bolts of behavior, from muscle coordination to mental processing, are being tightened into place by brain changes promoted only in part by experience. I shy away from labeling growth changes with ages, because ages are given only as averages, and individual babies are not averages. Nor are they medians — the age at which half of all babies have grown into the particular behavior or capability. Such statistics are of use only if they are properly understood. Only a minority of babies will actually attain a "milestone" during the month in which it is said to develop on average. As for the median, by definition half the babies will be "early," half "late." Great damage can be done through rigid parental expectations.

More important, correlations between the age milestones are attained and the child's ultimate status in a given realm of behavior — and such attempts at prediction have been made many times — are usually negligible or low. Superstitions about the advantages of precocity are counterbalanced by sayings like "Slow and steady wins the race," and by tales of slow developers who turn out to be geniuses. Either myth can seem true in individual cases, but neither passes the acid test of prediction for children in general. As Jerome Kagan has said, infancy is a time of transformation. Underlying continuities between the infant and the older child or adult — if they exist — will be subtle, individualized, and difficult to discern. The main purpose of infant study is not predicting the future but charting the transformation.

Nevertheless, it is useful to have a structure in time against which infant development can be viewed — a metaphoric skeleton for the growth of the mind. With these cautions firmly in hand, we can make some reasonable estimates.

Babies tend to sit independently at around seven months of age, to crawl around nine, to walk independently around thirteen. Although experience can affect these "motor milestones" — they vary somewhat in different cultures, as much as two or three months for walking, and training can modify them a bit — every serious student of infancy believes that such milestones are basically "locked in" to the sequence of physical development by preprogrammed changes in the nervous system. We know from studies of the brain in infancy that marked changes in the cerebellum, which helps to coordinate movement, and the spinal cord, which carries messages between the brain and the muscles, are occurring at this time. It is likely that these and other brain changes explain the growth of the infant's abilities.

There is also a "cephalocaudal," or head-to-tail sequence of development of motor control, as well as a near-to-distant sequence, beginning at the trunk and moving outward, for the arms and legs. Head control is one of the first signs that a baby is leaving the newborn stage, and control of the arms and hands, in a gross sense, precedes the control of the trunk that makes sitting possible. We traced, in the last chapter, some consequences of arm and hand control for the growth of reaching and grasping between three and six months of age. But the six-month-old still has a clumsy whole-hand sort of grasp, which must gradually mature into the precise "pincer" grasp, with which the one-year-old picks up a pea between forefinger and thumb. Yet the same one-year-old is just starting to get the hang of walking (in a stumbling sort of way), and her leg and foot control will not permit the smooth heel-toe progression of fully developed walking until months later.

None of these changes takes us into much controversy about what is controlling development. Most theorists agree that they involve the unfolding of a growth plan in the brain, controlled by the genes. Cross-cultural studies confirm this view. Among the Hopi and Navajo Indians, for example, babies traditionally spent most of the first year of life tied into a cradleboard, with very limited movement of limbs. Yet they began to walk at roughly the same age as their conventionally reared counterparts. Throughout the world, samples of babies in many different cultures start to walk at an average age of a little over a year.

All these simple changes mean a great deal to parents, and make a major impact on attachment. "Childhood" series cameras captured some important motor milestones in several infants. For instance, Vitaly Popov, only a few weeks old, is lying on a couch on his back. His father, nearby, turns his own back for a second or two, and finds Vitaly lying on his belly. His surprise is delightful: "You turned over all on your own? By yourself? Wow! — good for you!"

At around age seven months, Vitaly's hands are held by his father as he bounces, and by his mother as he walks. This exercise may not make him stand or walk much sooner, but it certainly looks like fun. Not long afterward, Vitaly crawls — able, for the first time in his life, to mobilize and explore the world on his own.

There is little controversy about what causes these events. The verbal battles begin when psychologists start to look at mental and emotional development. But as we have already seen in the case of the social fears, some key components of cognitive and emotional development are also products of brain maturation. Changes in the cerebral cortex, especially the regions that serve higher mental life, and in the limbic system, or "emotional brain," are occurring at this time under the same kind of genetic guidance present in the cerebellum and spinal cord. This means that some pretty fundamental features of mental life develop in infants according to the same laws of brain growth that govern the emergence of walking and grasping.

• • •

Consider for example the emergence of "object permanence," first extensively studied by the Swiss psychologist Jean Piaget. The five-month-old will lose interest in an object, even a toy she has really been excited about, when it disappears under a cloth or behind a screen. Or, more strangely, she will act as if she has no idea where the object is. Try the same trick a few months later, and she won't be fooled. She will readily search under the cloth and find the toy.

But at this stage she is still easily misled by a simple maneuver, like changing which of two cloths the toy is hidden under. If it is hidden beneath cloth A repeatedly, the baby will find it every time. But if it is then — in full view of the baby — hidden beneath cloth B, the baby, astonishingly, will search again under A, seemingly denying the evidence of her senses. This is known as the A-not-B error.

Piaget thought the error was due to the tendency of physical action to dominate the baby's mental life. But research in the last few years has shown that by changing the tasks involved in testing object permanence, younger babies can be shown to be capable of the concept, and older ones can be led into error. Renée Baillargeon, as we saw in the last chapter, showed that even four-month-olds have some object permanence — at the most elementary level — if the measure used is visual attention rather than manual reaching.

Adele Diamond, a psychologist now at the University of Pennsylvania, focused her work on the A-not-B error in older infants. She discovered that the baby's tendency to search under A when the toy has been hidden under B depends on the delay between hiding and the chance to search. A seven-and-a-half-month-old will slip into error when the delay is only two seconds; a twelve-month-old will get it right until the delay is more than ten seconds. But many younger babies who make the error can get the problem right if the delay is shortened. And most any baby who has mastered the task during the latter part of the first year can be made to fail it again by lengthening the delay. Jerome Kagan did this on camera with eleven-month-old Aia, showing that imposing a trivial barrier, and increasing the delay, abolished the baby's ability to find the object. She seemed simply to lose interest in it. (Incidentally, girls can tolerate longer delays than boys at almost every age. But this is most likely because girls mature faster, not because girls are inherently smarter.)

The importance of these deconstructions of Piaget's object-permanence task is neither to deny his observations — made initially on his own children — nor to claim that the baby's mind is infinitely flexible. The point is to define more precisely the mental skills involved in meeting the challenge or making the error. In Diamond's case, her novel view of the task led her to study how brain development underlies changing abilities.

She had read about many experiments on the effects of delayed response on performance, and she surmised that the frontal lobes of the brain are crucial in enabling babies to wait through the delay without losing the thread of thought about the object's whereabouts. There was evidence that the frontal lobes mature during the period in which babies' performance was improving. Diamond decided to study monkeys in parallel with human infants; she was able to study both normal infant monkeys and adult monkeys that had suffered frontal lobe damage. The results showed that monkeys between one and four months of age go through changes similar to those in human infants between six and twelve months. Remarkably, adult monkeys with frontal lobe damage failed the object-permanence task at the same delays (between two and five seconds) as did two-month-old normal infant monkeys and eight-month-old normal humans. All three of these groups have similarly "impaired" frontal lobes.

In my view Diamond's is one of the most important infant studies of recent years. Its approach illustrates perfectly how brain function and behavior, human and animal, and normal and abnormal functioning can be measured in parallel, and integrated to produce a powerful discovery. Diamond was also able to show that these age changes cannot be explained by learning, and indeed that opportunity to learn within her experiments made little difference. Improved performance awaited not learning but brain growth, largely controlled by the genes. Infants, in this view, are a bit like brain-damaged adults — except, of course, that the infants are recovering.

Piaget used to call his field of study by the grand name of "genetic epistemology," a reference to one of the great questions of philosophy. Epistemology, or the study of how we know things, has always been a battle between those who claim that some of our knowledge of the world is inborn, and those who insist that all we know must be learned through encounters with things in the real world. The adjective *genetic* did not have its current meaning for Piaget; rather, it meant developmental. Piaget was trying to solve the great question of how we know by asking children, even babies, and tracing how their knowledge appears and grows.

Yet on the question of inborn knowledge, Piaget always equivocated. He understood that the mind (and its brain) were developing, and that gaining knowledge from the world requires readiness. But he gave at least equal importance to experience, which had to engage the mind at every stage before the next step could be taken. The mind was a bit like a wobbly toddler climbing a staircase: the impetus for taking the next step has to come from within, but without a pull on the banister — in this metaphor, experience — you could be stuck in one place for a long time, perhaps indefinitely.

This ratcheting, or lockstep, idea of maturation and experience allowed Piaget to dodge the question of inborn knowledge. Since neither he nor, to be fair, anyone else at the time knew much about brain development, his reluctance to take a stand was probably wise. But in the future we will certainly be bolder.

· · ·

At this point we might ask whether responses to the disappearance of objects may somehow be linked to separation protest; whether in order to miss your mother you have to have gotten the idea that she remains real and whole despite the fact that she isn't there. Infant psychologists have wondered the same thing, but several studies have shown that no such linkages exist. With hindsight, this is not surprising, since it suggests that emotions and intellect can develop in ways that are partly independent of each other. Object permanence is related to brain hardware that processes fairly cool perceptions and thoughts. Fear of separation, on the other hand, engages some of the most powerful and primitive of all human emotions. It should be based on partially separate, emotional parts of the brain.

In fact, there are dramatic changes in the limbic system, also known as the "emotional brain," during the same period of development. For example, the nerves linking various emotional-brain centers acquire, during these months, the fatty sheath called myelin that greatly improves speed and precision of messages. The evidence linking these growth changes to the social fears is not yet in. Still, it is likely that such marked changes in the limbic system would have to produce emotional growth in the infant.

But the best evidence so far about the brain basis of infant social fears concerns the relationship between the frontal lobes and the emotional brain. Psychologists Nathan Fox and Richard Davidson are using the latest techniques of electroencephalography, or EEG, to trace brain function during separation and stranger challenges. Their approach, which places harmless recording electrodes on the baby's head, has supported well-known ideas about the differences between the right and left sides of the brain. In most people the right side appears to be more important in processing emotion, while the left is more important in analytical and language functions.

What Fox and Davidson found, for ten-month-old girls, was that the right and left frontal lobes play different roles in infant emotion during the separation experiment. Infants who cried during mother separation showed high activity on the right side, while infants who babbled pleasantly during the mother's approach showed mainly left-brain activation. We know that the frontal lobes are maturing at that age, and that the connections between the frontal lobes and the limbic system — the core of the emotional brain — are also rapidly growing. Fox and Davidson's experiment suggests that the connections are functioning well enough for left-right differences to help determine behavior. It is not yet clear whether these brain-wave patterns reflect the effect of mother-infant relations, or are a more basic, perhaps temperamental, characteristic of the infant. Still, it's a very exciting beginning. The great mysteries of mental and emotional development are starting to yield some of their secrets to careful study of the brain.

· · ·

Now we have grown the baby to a point at which both objects and people are perfectly real and whole to her — whether or not they are in her view at the moment. We are poised for a most extraordinary development. Until now, objects and people have occupied quite distinct realities. At around nine months of age, she begins to put them together. That is, she begins to care about whether a given object is of interest to someone else.

The evidence for this transition comes in part from observations by Colwyn Trevarthen and Penelope Hubley at the University of Edinburgh. They study videotapes of mothers and babies together, beginning in the first weeks of life. Their work confirms the view that we are innately sociable; we are biased toward human interactions from the beginning, and by three months we have got the hang of nonverbal communication. The first stage of this ability, called "intersubjectivity," requires only that the baby take delight in face-to-face interactions. She shares herself, so to speak, with others — especially those closest to her. And she seems to know something about what the other person is thinking or feeling.

Even at four months of age the baby can be comforted by tracking the mother's reaction to new events. If, for example, we loudly play a few bars of Mozart's lilting, melodic chamber piece, "A Little Night Music," the baby may quickly drop her pleasant, playful interaction with the mother and become suddenly wary. But then she will often search the mother's face for clues about how to react. If the mother is smiling and talking warmly and excitedly about the music, the baby will convert the arousal of her wariness into a new burst of pleasure. She may even laugh. But in any case she has found out once again that her mother is a good guide to how to react to her constantly changing world.

But this primary intersubjectivity, with its rudimentary form of "consultation" with the mother, gives way, at around nine months of age, to what appears to be an intentional sharing of experiences. The evidence for this new, or secondary, intersubjectivity comes from studies of babies and their mothers not just with each other, but with objects too. Among the new capabilities of this last quarter of the first year are: looking readily where the mother is looking; pointing to an object and waiting for the mother to notice it; passing a toy back and forth as if playing with it together; staring at what the mother does with an object and imitating her actions; and checking the mother's face to find out how she is reacting to the appearance of a new or strange object.

These tendencies, also called "joint attention" or "social referencing," are of considerable importance to the baby. They give an inherently social and emotional dimension to the whole process of knowing. And for infants in our species, who face the weighty task of lifelong cultural learning, this social dimension is the crux of epistemology. The baby has entered a realm in which her searchings and experiments are guided by a loving eye. We have already established her as so tied to her primary caregiver that departure can put an end to joy, to mental activity, even to composure. These same strong emotions — and of course, their joyful counterparts when the caregiver is there — now prevent the baby from testing the world alone, from developing a completely idiosyncratic — and in a social species, potentially disastrous — world view. Her love for the most important adult figures in her life becomes the vehicle for transmission of knowledge from their generation to hers. She is now, as it were, for good or ill, caught up in her culture.

· · ·

Which brings us to the question of how that culture handles her — the other side of the first relationships. Our species belongs to the group of animals known as higher primates, including the monkeys, apes, and us, as well as the ancestral forms that gave rise to them and us. All monkeys and apes carry their infants and nurse them for the first phase of development, and the emotional bond that grows between mother and infant is two-sided and very strong. Mothers generally do not insist upon independence until months or years later, when the infant has grown to readiness. Deprived of this relationship in infancy, the young primate may grow up with severe, even grotesque behavioral abnormalities, such as stereotyped rocking or self-biting, hyperaggressiveness, sexual incompetence, and even abusive parenting. Monkey and ape species vary in the extent to which adults other than the mother normally participate in caregiving, but leaving the baby alone is simply unknown, except in grossly abnormal circumstances.

Mothers and infants thus have months, or, in more slowly developing species, years to get to know each other. "Childhood" series observer Robert Hinde, of Cambridge University in England, spent twenty years studying this process in monkeys, and then went on to study human relationships. In monkeys he showed decisively that subtleties of mother-infant relations were correlated with the development of independence. But more important, he showed that quite brief separations of the mother from the infant — as little as six days — had lasting effects on the infant, making it more fearful in strange situations at two years of age.

This experiment is important because it shows something that can't be shown in human infants for ethical reasons. Deliberate intervention in the mother-infant relationship, randomly assigned — what scientists call the one independent variable — has lasting effects. Because of random assignment, preexisting temperamental peculiarities of the infant cannot be the explanation of the long-term effect. The experiments of Harlow and Hinde, respectively showing effects of major and minor intervention in this relationship in monkeys, enhance the meaning of many human studies that are purely correlational. Together they make it unlikely that differences in the human primary caregiver–infant relationship would be without some measurable effect.

It is in the nature of this bond that it grows on you. Ten or fifteen years ago there was an intense flurry of interest in what is called maternal bonding. This, as we have seen, was supposed to rely heavily on contact between mother and infant in the first day, even the first hours after birth. In part this was derived from an analogy with herd animals such as goats, in which many mothers have kids at about the same time. Each mother has to imprint on the smell of her own infant to be sure to be able to identify it, and not respond to some other kid in the herd as her own.

In some maternity wards in the 1980s the application of this concept to mothers and babies reached an extreme. Some nurses believed that there was a critical period for contact in the first few hours, and that failing to give the baby to the mother right after birth could permanently compromise their relationship. The evidence for such a powerful early bonding effect is very weak. Although it is possible to imagine adverse circumstances in which early contact might make the difference, the truth of the matter is that for most human mothers the attachment to the infant develops gradually, beginning during the pregnancy and continuing to grow as the infant grows.

Hinde's research on both monkey and human relationships underscores the gradualness of this process. Contact right after birth can only be one step in a long creative process. As the mother experiences a three-month-old who starts to gaze at her face and smile, a six-month-old who responds especially to her, and a nine-month-old who cries for her when she leaves, the baby becomes more and more the object of her reciprocal love. Still most mothers — and fathers, too — are way ahead of the baby.

But being human, we don't settle for simple, natural burdens and pleasures, even in a biologically critical realm like parenting. Each culture has its own biases, and in a rapidly changing culture like ours, each era does as well. Among the Efe, hunter-gatherers like the Baka, but in Central Africa, parents hold their infants close and nurse them for years, but they also pass babies around to caregivers other than the mother in the close-knit extended-family band. East African mothers use their older daughters as nannies, leaving babies in their charge while the mothers go out to work in the fields. Brazilian mothers living in extreme poverty care tenderly for their infants, but seem to withhold the strongest form of love because of the high risk of infant death. Japanese mothers sleep with their infants, apart from their husbands, and keep stimulation and excitement of the infant to a minimum, valuing calm and quiet in all realms of life. In traditional families Russian infants are swaddled in blankets and Navajo infants are bound into cradleboards, where they come to feel warm, calm, and protected.

As we reread the frayed pages of our advice-to-parents manuals, consult our pediatricians and even our neighbors with trepidation, and generally agonize over the consequences of changes in the care of our babies — breast-feeding or not, mother at home or not, toddler allowed in the parents' bed or not, day-care or not, siblings present or not — it is relieving to know that throughout the world people have been experimenting for centuries with drastically different patterns of infant and child care, with results that are surprisingly normal. Anthropology gives parents a lot of room to maneuver; and yet there are limits to flexibility.

It would seem, for example, that no greater contrast could be offered than that between the !Kung San pattern of infant care and that of the Israeli collective farm, or kibbutz. The !Kung are a traditional society whose pattern of infant and child care have been handed down for centuries, even millennia. The kibbutz is a society that invented itself two generations ago, when committed pioneers made up their minds to create a new, truly cooperative form of social life. The !Kung are in constant close contact with their infants, sleeping beside them and breast-feeding until four years of age. The kibbutz baby sleeps in an infant house with other babies, and grows up with them as they pass through childhood and adolescence. !Kung children are given almost no responsibility for chores, and are allowed to explore their environment playfully, at will. Kibbutz children have a markedly more programmed life in which work and schooling take up most of the time. !Kung children play in naturally formed, multi-age groups in which older children watch and teach younger ones. Kibbutz children play in deliberately formed same-age peer groups, in which all members have roughly equal abilities, by design.

The first remarkable thing about this contrast is that children in both settings grow up to be basically normal psychologically. Each group has its own share of problem children and poor outcomes. But as far as we can tell, the number and kinds of problems are roughly similar in both, and not so different from those of our own children, whose treatment would seem to be somewhere between these extremes. The !Kung and Baka child-care pattern seems overly indulgent to us; and as for the kibbutz, well, it seems a sink-or-swim method that deprives children of the tender mercies of parenting and family life.

But neither turns out to be quite what it seems. !Kung infants and young children are in fact just that indulged in their dependent needs, but even toddlers have this dependency offset by their inclusion in a play group with older children. The play group combines nurturance with adventuresome exploration, and draws the child away from her mother even before she is weaned. A study I was involved in, together with Nicholas Blurton Jones, an ethologist now at the University of California at Los Angeles, showed that by age four or five !Kung children are wandering greater distances from their mothers than children do in comparable settings in England.

As for the kibbutz, it may strike us from the descriptions as little better than an orphanage, but the reality is quite different. The kibbutz is a closed community that resembles in some ways a large extended family. The quality of the care in the children's houses is extraordinarily high, partly because the personnel are parents in the community — their own children are at stake too. More important, no attempt is made to keep mothers and fathers out. On the contrary, mothers and, to a lesser extent, fathers visit infants several times a day after age four to six months — and before that age, the mothers have maternity leave and the infants are at home. Mothers do most of the feedings throughout infancy. At four o'clock both mothers and fathers are finished with work; they pick up their baby and retire to their apartment home.

They remain with the baby until bedtime, around nine o'clock, having what Americans call Q.T. — "quality time." There is no shopping to do, no dinner to prepare — all kibbutz members eat in a communal dining room — little cleaning to be done, and no work taken home. In fact there is little to do except be together as a family, playing, talking, feeling, creating. There are books around, drawing materials, board games. All are well used. At bedtime the mother or father takes the baby or toddler back to the infant house, and tenderly puts her to bed, in much the way a parent would in our culture, complete with bedtime story or lullaby. (I observed a charming reading to a group of four-year-olds of a Hebrew version of the classic story of Ferdinand, the bull who refuses to fight — after which the parents tucked the children in and kissed them good-night.)

Given these facts, it is little wonder that kibbutz children and adolescents identify their parents as the targets of their strongest feelings — positive and negative — just as kids do in nuclear family cultures like our own. This ranking was established in research by Israeli psychologist Eli Regev, who hosted the "Childhood" camera crew and me at Kibbutz Bar Am. After that, he found, the next strongest feelings are toward biological siblings; and only after that, toward the other children in the peer group of the children's house. Their method of rearing does give them a tendency to identify with and form friendships with a larger number of friends, and also a strong loyalty to the community. But their tendency to show group and community loyalty does not seem to interfere with their even stronger feelings toward their families.

Regev simply does not see a conflict here: "The child has to be raised within his close intimate group of people, which you call a family and we call kibbutz. If you see the kibbutz as a family, a big extended family, you don't have a problem explaining how they grow up outside of the family because they are *not* outside the family."

Nevertheless, today there are many parents in this kibbutz and others who are trying to chip away at the kibbutz child-care method: lengthening the time during which the young infant remains at home before going to the infant house; increasing the number and length of parental visits; and in some cases reverting to a pattern of having all children sleep in their parents' apartments. At the same time, many young mothers, themselves products of children's houses, defend the classic system. "It makes me a better mother," one said to me as she dandled her baby boy on her lap in the infant house. "And it lets me be more than a mother. It lets me be myself." Yet others insist on more conventional patterns of child care. Parents long for their children. Even a society that invents itself has to come to terms with human nature.

As for !Kung children, despite their intense early dependency, they grow up to give birth alone or bravely drive lions away from a kill. They are as tough and independent as young adults in the kibbutz, who in their turn will farm a recalcitrant land and defend their country from its numerous and very determined enemies. And they have a commitment to their extended family bands that rivals the loyalty of kibbutz children to their collective. There are some apparent lasting effects of early treatment: !Kung adults are very casual about physical (not necessarily sexual) contact, which may reflect the impact of their early skin-to-skin carrying; kibbutz adults perform extraordinarily well in the army, where self-sacrifice and group loyalty are crucial. But on the whole it is rather amazing that quite normal adults can arise from such very different childhoods.

• • •

With this cross-cultural background we can begin to tease out the implications of our own baby-and-child-care choices. To do this properly requires a bit of history. Advice books about child-rearing go back at least to the ancient Greeks, but in the United States official advice, beginning in the early twentieth century, came from a federal government agency, The Children's Bureau. This agency got up to 125,000 letters a year from parents, mostly mothers. The following one from Blainey, South Carolina, written in a large, round, childlike hand, is typical:

> I would like to have the baby feed. I am the mother of 12 head of children. I would like for you all to help me if it is your desire. I would like the medicine. The whooping cough is now down here in this country . . . please help me, with your help, I'm in need of it.

Another, from 1920, was addressed personally to Julia Lathrop, the director of the bureau:

> Dear Mrs. Lathrop: I am a busy mother with three dear babies, aged 3 years, 20 months, and 3 months. I have wanted babies for years and now I am so tired and with the unfinished work everyday and everywhere I turn, I could scream at their constant prattle. . . . Is there some way I can do all of the scientific and hygienic duties for my babies, keep my house up in a proper fashion, and still have time to rock and play with my babies?

This letter fairly brims with a poignant blend of responsibility and mother love; and yet, *I could scream at their constant prattle.* Everyone who has had children has felt that way from time to time, and will sympathize with the intense longing, expressed in these letters, for some kind, any kind of helpful and authoritative advice.

Lathrop wrote back, "If you've not tried putting your children away at 6:00, you have no idea what a relief it will be for you." In popular pamphlets and films, The Children's Bureau advised parents to keep absolutely rigid schedules and precise routines. Daily timetables assigned tasks, minute by minute from dawn until late at night. A "good mother" would train herself and her baby and follow the schedule religiously; a "bad mother" would run behind schedule, irritating her child. In many homes the schedule became an end in itself, and the dire predictions about the results of departure from the schedule became a self-fulfilling prophecy, as the tension level rose for parent and infant alike.

In the atmosphere of this period, it is perhaps not surprising that John B. Watson, a reigning figure of American psychology (not the Watson of the mobile-control studies), gave such advice as the following:

There is a sensible way of treating children. Treat them as though they were young adults. Dress them, bathe them with care and circumspection. Let your behavior always be objective and kindly firm. Never hug and kiss them, never let them sit in your lap. If you must, kiss them once on the forehead when they say good night. Shake hands with them in the morning. . . . Try it out. In a week's time . . . you will be utterly ashamed of the mawkish, sentimental way you have been handling it. . . .

In conclusion won't you then remember when you are tempted to pet your child that mother love is a dangerous instrument? An instrument which may inflict a never healing wound, a wound which may make infancy unhappy, adolescence a nightmare, an instrument which may wreck your adult son or daughter's vocational future and their chances for marital happiness.

This advice appeared in his 1928 manual for parents, which was dedicated to "The first mother to raise a happy child." Plainly he did not know what a happy child was, and his recommendations, if put into practice, would be viewed by many today as psychological abuse. Yet they emanated from a leading American psychologist, not only in this popular book but in regular columns in *Harper's* magazine and other forums throughout the 1930s. Among his other accomplishments, he trained a baby named Albert to be frightened of furry animals, although the child had started out liking them; he went on to lend his skills in the manipulation of behavior to advertising agencies on Madison Avenue.

Meanwhile, Margaret Mead, a brash young anthropologist at the American Museum of Natural History, was formulating her own sort of advice. But in contrast to Watson, her approach was not to try to control behavior, but to observe it in its immense variety — and in all modesty try to learn something from it. In 1928, the same year Watson's manual appeared, Mead published *Coming of Age in Samoa*, an account of the first of seven cultures in the South Seas where she would study childhood during the course of her career. Far from training children to be frightened, she mainly watched them, and she herself displayed remarkable bravery in her research. The only similarity between her and Watson was that she too wanted to share her findings with the general public.

[108]

But the lessons she drew were liberating, not confining. In her second book, *Growing Up in New Guinea,* she wrote of traditional societies,

> Although most of these fragile cultures . . . are lost to us, a few remain. Isolated on small Pacific islands, in dense African jungles or Asiatic wastes, it is still possible to find untouched societies which have chosen solutions of life's problems different from our own, which can give us precious evidence on the malleability of human nature.
>
> Such an untouched people are the brown sea-dwelling Manus of the Admiralty Island, north of New Guinea. In their vaulted, thatched houses set on stilts in the olive green waters of the wide lagoon, their lives are lived very much as they have been lived for unknown centuries. . . .
>
> The manner in which human babies born into these water-dwelling communities, gradually absorb the traditions, the prohibitions, the values of their elders and become in turn the active perpetuators of Manus culture is a record rich in its implications for education. . . .
>
> I made this study of Manus education to prove no thesis, to support no preconceived theories. Many of the results came as a surprise to me. . . .

Her career in field research was indeed one surprise after another, and she always approached the process of drawing implications for our own patterns of child care with great respect for its complexity. By studying seven different societies in addition to her own, she protected herself from simpleminded inferences about the need to imitate this or that cultural practice. In an appendix directed at psychologists she wrote,

> Such investigations as these involve a fairly drastic rearrangement of thought and daily habit. The willingness to make them, and the knowledge of the special techniques necessary to ethnological research, are the equipment which the ethnologist brings to the solution of psychological problems. He says to the psychologist . . . , "Let me take your results and submit them to a new test. You have made such and such generalizations about the thought content of young

children, the relationship between mental and physical development, the connection between a certain type of family life and the possibility of happy marital adjustment, the factors which go to the formation of personality, etc. These results I find significant and important. Let me therefore submit them to the test of a different social environment. . . .

Over the ensuing decades psychologists have shown relatively little enthusiasm for such tests, while opportunities for making them have steadily disappeared. But Mead and other anthropologists went on with them, and established a cross-cultural framework in which to examine psychological generalizations. Among those demolished by these tests were the notion of rigid and unvarying sex roles, the idea that strict schedules were necessary to make a child happy, the claim that every child must have and resolve an Oedipus complex, the belief that adolescence is necessarily full of turmoil, and Watson's ludicrous advice about shaking hands once a day instead of kissing.

Mead also had reservations about the claims of pediatricians. Based on her observations in traditional societies, she recommended breast-feeding, straight through the era of the fifties, when scheduled bottle-feeding was advised for all babies. In 1978, two years after her death, the American Pediatrics Association officially recommended breast-feeding for all babies. By that time, too, the Oedipus complex was viewed by most psychologists as a quaint relic of theory past, and sex roles in the United States and Europe were drastically changing in a direction Mead had recommended fifty years before.

• • •

This was the background against which Benjamin Spock, a pediatrician influenced by Freud's theory, introduced his own approach to baby and child care in the 1940s. To get an idea of how influential Spock has been, consider that his book *Baby and Child Care,* before the 1968 edition, had been through 179 printings, and according to the publisher was "the best-selling new title issued in the United States since 1895, when best-seller lists began." Before the 1985 edition it had sold eight million more copies for a total of thirty million. Just as Robert Hinde was a Truby King baby — Dr. King, a sort of English Spock, was one of the strongest proponents of strict schedules — I in a subsequent generation was a Spock child. I still have the frayed, crumbling copy of the 1946 edition — "A Pocket Book Special: 35 Cents" — that my mother consulted while trying to come to terms with my brother and me. The reason this book was so extremely successful was that it gave parents in simple terms the practical advice they needed every day. It also very wisely made parents feel confident: "You know more than you think you know" is the very first sentence.

Spock was considered by many to be indulgent and permissive, since he allowed physical affection and was not very impressed with the over-riding importance of schedules. But against the background of people like the !Kung, Spock does not seem so indulgent. It is not just that !Kung babies are picked up whenever they cry. In addition, they are not expected to do chores until adolescence, have no rules or regimentation in their lives, and are rarely disciplined except for wasting food. Even then, no one would think of striking a child, and toddlers can be seen throwing tantrums in which they hit their mothers repeatedly, sometimes with a stick.

As a Western observer, my gorge always rose watching this, but the mothers would smile, warding off the blows as if they were part of the natural flow of events. *We* believe in a spoiling theory of development. "Spare the rod and spoil the child" is not taken literally anymore by most American parents, but less brutal echos of this idea can be found in every family, and explicitly in baby and child-care guides like that of Dr. Spock. I once translated a passage ("How do you unspoil?") from Spock for a !Kung mother. In the 1985 edition, it goes in part like this:

> [I]t takes a lot of will power and a little hardening of the heart. To get yourself in the right mood you have to remember that . . . you are reforming them for their own good.
>
> Make out a schedule for yourself, on paper if necessary, that requires you to be busy with housework or anything else for most of the time the baby is awake. Go at it with a great bustle — to impress the baby and to impress yourself. . . . When he frets and raises his arms, explain to him in a friendly but very firm tone that this job and that job must get done this afternoon. Though he doesn't understand

the words, he does understand the tone of voice. Stick to your busy work.

The !Kung mother looked bemused and disapproving. "Doesn't he understand he's only a baby, and that's why he cries?" she said. "You pick him up and comfort him. Later, when he grows older, he will have sense, and he won't cry anymore."

Note that there is a theory of development here, and it is the opposite of our own theory of development, which says that if you pick the baby up you will train him to cry more and more. The !Kung bet on maturation — and they have never yet had a child who didn't outgrow crying.

Spock (with co-author Michael Rothenberg, who joined him in 1985 but did not change these passages) goes on to discuss chronic resistance to sleep in infancy — "going-to-bed" type and "waking-in-the-night" type — which "can be thought of as a kind of spoiling."

> The cure is simple: Put the baby to bed at a reasonable hour, say good night affectionately but firmly, walk out of the room, and don't go back. Most babies who have developed this pattern cry furiously for 20 or 30 minutes the first night, and then when they see that nothing happens, they suddenly fall asleep! The second night the crying is apt to last only 10 minutes. The third night there usually isn't any at all. . . .
>
> If the several nights of crying will wake other children or anger the neighbors, you can muffle the sound by putting a rug or blanket on the floor and a blanket over the window. . . .

The recommended treatment for night-waking is the same. If the baby vomits from excessive crying, parents are told, this is a sign of anger, another product of spoiling. "I think it essential that parents harden their hearts to the vomiting if the baby is using it to bully them. . . . They can clean up later after the baby has gone to sleep."

These recommendations, reminiscent of advice from The Children's Bureau sixty or seventy years earlier, would be placed squarely in the category of child abuse by parents in most traditional cultures. Among the "Childhood" series families, the Kalugin children sleep in the same room as their parents because of lack of space in their Moscow apartment, but the Nouhatas keep Koichiro and Yojiro beside their mother through the night as a matter of Japanese cultural choice — a choice also often made in modern Italy. (The Japanese co-sleeping pattern was extensively studied by psychologist William Caudill.) And among the Baka, as among the !Kung, the infant or young child is always kept beside the parents at night, and other children may be adjacent to them as well. In a cross-cultural study by Herbert Barry and L. M. Paxson, of the University of Pittsburgh, 173 societies in the anthropological record were found to have ethnographic information about their sleeping arrangements. Forty-four percent of them — 76 societies — typically had mother and infant sharing a bed; in 42 societies they shared a room but not a bed; and in the remaining 55 societies they shared a room with the bed unspecified. There were *no* societies in which infants routinely slept in a separate room.

In our society infants may sleep in a separate room from birth. This is the middle-class cultural ideal, and some adoption agencies may even insist on it. Yet the reality is more variable. Steven Tulkin, a psychologist then at Harvard University, found that in his sample of ten-month-old girls, the babies were more likely to be in the same room with their parents in the working-class families. Interestingly, this was not just a function of space; working-class couples with extra rooms might keep the babies in their room, while professional-class couples with tiny apartments had the baby sleep in the kitchen. Clearly cultural values have a lot to do with this.

But even in middle-class families, the cultural ideal seems to buckle under pressure from sleepless babies. A study in the Cleveland area by Betsy Lozoff, a pediatrician at the Case Western Reserve School of Medicine, asked parents how often they take their babies into their beds. Eight percent replied "frequently, full night" and another 16 percent said "frequently, part of night"; only 55 percent claimed to have attained the cultural ideal of never bringing the baby into their beds.

And some middle-class American parents routinely and unabashedly sleep with their babies, notably members of La Leche League, a nursing mothers' organization with more than two thousand chapters around the nation. I was involved in a study led by Marjorie Elias, then at Harvard University, which found that many La Leche League parents practice full-night bed-sharing. There are even books of advice about how to do this, such as *Nighttime Parenting* by pediatrician William Sears, and *The Family Bed* by Tine Thevenin, a La Leche League counselor. Apparently being put away in a separate dark room is difficult for many babies, and even the mere loss of consciousness may have its frightening aspect. (My youngest, at twenty months, used to wail "No seeep! No seeep!" just before dropping off to the sound of lullabies in her father's arms.)

Spock was right about one thing: Elias found that babies who are nursed when they wake at night take months longer to learn to sleep through the night. But what law says that sleeping through the night is always better? Perhaps we just need to keep a more open mind about the options before us. As Dr. Spock himself has said,

> I think that parents ought to get some idea of how the so-called "experts" have changed their advice over the decades, so that they won't take them deadly seriously, and so that if the parent has the strong feeling, "I don't like this advice," that the parent won't feel compelled to follow it.

He goes on to say, again very wisely, "So don't worry about trying to do a perfect job. There is no perfect job. There is no one way of raising your children."

• • •

Of all the child-care choices confronting us today, none is more difficult than the choice between home care by the primary caregiver and daycare by relative strangers paid for their effort. And few have probed the implications of this choice more thoroughly than "Childhood" series observer Sandra Scarr, a psychologist at the University of Virginia. But before we find out what she advises, we need to face a few pertinent facts.

The first concerns the need for help with children. I sometimes tease my students with the question, "What is the most impressive sociological trend of our time?" Aging of the population? Decline of the birth rate? The rise in divorces? Religious fundamentalism? Without doubt, the most dramatic trend in the Western industrialized world is the entry of women into the labor force — although, given the real history of women's relationship to work, "reentry" would be more accurate. More than half of American mothers of infants and young children are presently employed, and for all children the proportion is higher. Eighty percent of today's women will combine work and parenting at some point in their reproductive lives. In effect this is a cultural transformation with potentially profound implications for infants and children.

One of these implications is that large numbers of infants and toddlers have been placed in day-care situations where they spend much time outside the home, along with other babies, cared for by relative strangers. This is not necessarily bad, and in fact may be good. But from the outset child psychologists have been concerned about the effects of day-care on the minds and emotions of babies. A series of studies during the 1970s consistently showed no negative impact of high-quality day-care. The Strange Situation was used repeatedly, and the percentage of infants who cried when the mother left was the same in the day-care and home-care groups. As with the kibbutz children, day-care babies know who their mothers are. In other areas of development, day-care babies become toddlers who are somewhat more aggressive and obstreperous, but they are also more socially skilled and more comfortable with peers. Finally, good day-care promotes more rapid intellectual development, though only temporarily.

Contrary to some claims, multiple caretaking is not new. Many cultures have had it in their traditions for generations. Among the Efe of northern Zaire, a hunting-and-gathering group resembling the Baka, Gilda Morelli, Edward Tronick, and their colleagues at the University of Massachusetts showed that mothers take care of their infants 40 percent of the time during the first few months of life. But the infant interacts regularly with several different individuals. Although males, including fathers, spend little time with infants, women and girls interact a great deal with them — even to the point of breast-feeding another woman's infant.

A different kind of multiple caretaking was found by Herbert and Gloria Leiderman of Stanford University, who studied the Kikuyu of Kenya's highlands. There the mother's main helper is a young girl between ages seven and twelve. Very often the girl is an older sister, but she may come from another family, usually related. Occasionally a boy may play this role, known as the "child nurse." These children take their jobs very seriously, and they genuinely care about the infants. As the Leidermans say, "In many agricultural societies the mother does not have the luxury of arranging her time to provide exclusive attention to an infant."

Their research showed that children in this society form multiple attachments, but with the mother as the main attachment figure. It also indicated that "caretakers contribute substantially to the infant's social and cognitive development during the first year."

The same is true of infants in our kind of society, and the point extends beyond the first year. Consider Avery Gholston, age nineteen months, who one day cries briefly when left by her mother at an excellent day-care center. Her mother, Anita, a college counselor, says that she feels guilt pangs sometimes, but that "it frees me up to do some of the things I need to do. And one of the things I need to do is work, to do my thing, whatever that is. And my thing right now is working with students, college students. And I would be really unhappy if I gave that up to be a full-time mommy." Her statement echoes that of the kibbutz mother who said of the infant house, "It makes me a better mother. And it lets me be more than a mother. It lets me be myself."

And what about Avery? Well, it turns out that in a short while she is not merely laughing, but fairly squealing with delight as she plays "Open, shut them" with her teacher and follows her two-year-old friend Daniel, trying fiercely to do everything he does, stretching to do things slightly beyond her. If day-care helps Anita to do her thing, it also helps Avery — despite her initial protest — to do hers. If it helps her mother to be *her self*, it also helps Avery to find and become *hers* — as it does for children throughout the world. Reggio Emilia, for example, is a small city in the north of Italy known for the beauty and antiquity of its architecture. Its mothers need and want to work, so a superb network of nurseries and preschools serves most neighborhoods. They weave a web of support for children and parents that affirms the responsibility of the community for the well-being of its children. Appropriately, the Italian for nursery school is *asilo nido:* "Safe Nest."

Still, three caveats about day-care are required. First, this good news applies to high-quality day-care programs — like Avery's Union Day Care Center, or Reggio Emilia. It is not likely that run-of-the-mill or poor day-care centers produce such good results. A few have even been found to be guilty of abuse and neglect. Still, careful parents can find places where children will be safe — provided that they can afford them, or that governments provide them, as in Reggio. Second, as present-day pediatricians know, you can tell which preschool children are in day-care by the thickness of their charts — the file folders where notes and records from each office visit are kept. Day-care means more colds and other minor infections, and that means more visits. It also means more germs brought home to siblings, Mom, and Dad. Still, everything in life is a trade-off, and minor infections are minor annoyances.

Finally, there is now a little bit of evidence that despite the absence of differences in the percentage of infants who cry during separation, day-care and home-care babies may act differently during reunion. Specifically, Jay Belsky and his colleagues, working with the Strange Situation, found that day-care babies are more likely to be insecurely attached. This research is still controversial. But Alison Clarke-Stewart tabulated data from the Belsky research and sixteen other studies done in the late 1980s, and found that overall 36 percent of babies with full-time working mothers were insecurely attached, while only 29 percent of babies with nonworking or part-time working mothers showed this insecurity.

This is a statistically significant difference, but that alone does not make it important. We have already seen that grossly inadequate home care produces more insecure attachment at a year of age than day-care does, yet even this effect seems reversible by eighteen months. That fact suggests that compensating for the difference between day-care and home-care babies in security of attachment might be fairly easy. We have an understandable bias in favor of good mothering. But as Sandra Scarr points out, the superiority of day-care babies in social and cognitive skills does not lead us to muse on the deprivations caused by home mothering. Yet home care can be inadequate just as day-care can, and in fact it would be easier to regulate the quality of day-care centers than to intervene in the home.

On the other side of the scale we must carefully weigh the importance of primary caregivers in infants' emotional lives. If we imagine the ideal day-care staff member, we will be led to think that substitution for the mother is easily possible. But day-care staff is often part-time, and rapid staff turnover is a recognized problem. What if John Bowlby was right, and our evolutionary heritage made the first attachment relationship to some extent an exclusive and unique one? This is certainly not a proven theory, but neither is it decisively disproven. Then, too, we are talking about day-care for millions of babies, year in and year out, in the United States alone. The difference between 29 percent and 36 percent insecurity — if it proved to be true — could translate into scores of thousands of babies every year. If there proved to be problems in only a vulnerable small percentage of these, that could still be very undesirable.

Perhaps an ideal compromise is day-care at the mother's or father's place of work, which has already been instituted at some companies — the Stride-Rite shoe company, for example. This in some ways resembles the kibbutz system of day-care, keeping parents involved with their babies and children. It allows a high degree of freedom for the parent while also enabling visits, surveillance of the day-care situation, and prompt parental response to medical emergencies or other crises. B.E.&K. Inc., a construction company in Birmingham, Alabama, has gone a step further. Since their "place of work" is a moving target — the latest building site — they have ingeniously set up a day-care center in five 14-by-40-foot trailers that move with them. This strategy has enabled them to recruit and keep excellent women workers, whom they happen to need badly in the current labor market.

In addition, authorities on childhood are recommending *both* more government support for day-care centers *and* much more forceful maternity/paternity leave policies. The apparent contradiction here is resolved by individual choice: The parent who wants to stay home should have a formal leave of absence and a job to come back to after the baby care; the parent who wants to work should have high-quality day-care. But whatever specific solutions we try, we can be sure that this problem will not go away. As Alison Clarke-Stewart aptly put it recently, "Maternal employment is a reality. The issue today, therefore, is not whether infants should be in day care, but how to make their experiences there and at home supportive of their development and their parents' peace of mind."

• • •

The superior social and intellectual skills of day-care toddlers, and even their obstreperousness, bring us to the question of self-reliance — the other side of the coin of attachment. One of my most poignant experiences in Africa was watching a two-year-old girl among the !Kung San in the Strange Situation experiment. She was left alone in a grass hut, according to the study plan, while I watched through a chink in the grass.

Now, all !Kung infants between a year and two years of age cried when the mother left. But the reason this child's behavior was so affecting was that she was struggling *not* to cry. Her troubled face revealed that she was trying to comfort herself, not completely successfully. She certainly stopped playing and looked around for her mother, but when her eyes filled with tears she obviously tried to stifle her sobs. She was trying, in effect, to be more grown-up.

The "apron strings" or "spoiling" theory raises the concern that indulgence of attachment demands will slow or even prevent the normal development of independence. Though there is little evidence that this is true (and a lot against it), the concern with independence is legitimate. Because the same child whose most important task during the first year of life has been the development of powerful relationships must during the second year devote a large share of her attention to the development of a separate and unique focus of consciousness. She must, in effect, become herself.

Of course in some ways she has always been separate. Although some early theories depicted the newborn baby as unaware of being separate from the mother, this notion is implausible. Any creature with a nervous system knows, as soon as it takes its first breath, the boundary beyond which it does not feel pain or stimulation or pleasure, and this is a primitive form of the separate self. What begins to happen toward the end of the first year and culminates around the end of the second is that the child can put herself in the place of another person. And as she learns to do this, she begins to be forced to see herself as if from the outside — she experiences the dawn of self-consciousness.

We have looked at social referencing, or secondary intersubjectivity, which the baby becomes capable of at around age nine months. That is, she becomes interested in what the caregiver is looking at; she checks the other's face for information about how she should react to what she is looking at; and she generally begins to share experiences. Does she have at this point a clear concept that her caregiver, like herself, has subjective experience and self-consciousness? We can't ask her, so we don't know. But we do know that she takes into account another person's parallel experience of the same events and things in the world.

It is unlikely to be an evolutionary accident that the behaviors of social referencing and separation protest come seriously into play just as crawl-ing begins to allow the child to get away. The risks entailed in this great step toward physical independence gave an adaptive advantage to those infants who maintained a pattern of checking in with the mother — either through social referencing or, in a more threatening situation, by crying to bring the mother to their side. Thus the dramatic emotions of attach-ment: natural selection favored attached mother-infant pairs. After the end of the first year, as crawling gives way to walking, and then about six months later to running, the physical distance between infant and caregiver, and also the baby's increasing control of that distance, ensure that the baby is more and more aware of her separateness.

But despite the fact that independent movement guarantees certain ex-periences that lead toward self-consciousness, motor development is not the driving force. The brain continues to mature in many other ways, and this growth is reflected in cognitive, or intellectual changes. We are far from a clear understanding of how this works, and we know that like Piaget we will have to answer the question of maturation versus experi-ence with an ambivalent "both," even when all the discoveries are in. But then we will be able to answer the question "how?" by specifying the way brain development interacts with experience. For now we must be patient; but we can at least appreciate that when we study and talk about and write about mental development, a good part of what we are talking about — especially in infancy — is simple, and not-so-simple, brain growth.

• • •

The changes in the second year are not quite as dramatic as those of the first, but neither are they small or subtle. Growth slows somewhat, and our hero becomes more streamlined as she drops some baby fat and adds muscle mass. But between the first and second birthdays she will gain an average of five pounds and five inches, and brain growth will continue impressively. Not surprisingly, cognitive and emotional devel-opment continue at a rapid pace.

At ten months babies are interested in relating two objects together — by banging, inserting, or just touching them to each other. By the end of the first year or shortly thereafter, they progress to relating two objects for a purpose — retrieving a toy with a stick, say, or building a tower with two blocks. They can pick up a raisin with a pincer grasp, and have usually mastered one or two words. Between eleven and fifteen months they improve greatly in language comprehension. They also become avid imitators and develop a capacity for symbolic (pretend) play. In a subsistence-level society such as the !Kung, these abilities are expressed as sometimes remarkable executions of activities they have seen their mothers doing, such as pounding roots, cracking nuts, or digging in the sand with a stick.

The desire for mastery, also known as competence motivation, can be intense at this age. When my son was fifteen months old, I noted in our baby diary "his love affair with the staircase" on a visit to my brother's home in Los Angeles:

> He absolutely screamed and fought for a chance to climb it — even Susanna [his older sister, then four] insisted that I follow closely behind him but *let him do it!* After getting to the top landing he sat there breathing hard, looking around, and with a smile of complete satisfaction on his face. Later he had a fall — fortunately only a step or two — but resumed his enthusiasm for climbing as soon as he stopped crying.

Between fifteen and eighteen months the child masters many new words and begins to use two-word "sentences." She also uses words to get what she wants, as in the imperious declarations "More!" "No!" and "Mommy!" Given a small bottle with a raisin at the bottom, she will soon up-end it and get the raisin by shaking it out. Only a few months earlier she would have poked hopelessly (and rather comically) at the raisin, trying to reach it with her finger. The great achievement of the new approach, which affects other behaviors as well, is that it is indirect, roundabout, not tied to the immediate data of the senses. It involves a *mental* solution to a problem.

But the great drama of this age period is the emergence of a new global capacity, sometimes referred to as "the self," or more accurately, self-consciousness. Consider the following elegant and justly famous experiment by Michael Lewis and Jeanne Brooks. A baby is encouraged to play in front of a mirror, looking at her own image. After a time the baby is picked up briefly, and during this encounter the experimenter surreptitiously puts a spot of rouge on the baby's nose. What will she do when set down in front of the mirror again?

The answer depends crucially on age. Babies nine to twelve months of age directed no behaviors toward the rouge spot, and their facial expressions were mainly just attentive, although some also showed positive and some negative faces, in equal numbers. In the fifteen- to eighteen-month-old group, in contrast, none of the babies showed predominantly positive faces and more showed negative ones as compared with the earlier trial. Most important, half of these older babies touched their rouged noses. Between twenty-one and twenty-four months, three-fourths showed this behavior, and again no babies showed predominantly positive faces.

• • •

The ability to recognize that the image in the mirror is yourself — which is the minimum inference one could reasonably make from the behavior of nose-touching — is a key step in the emerging consciousness of identity. The dropping out of positive facial expressions at the same time suggests that a sense of unease is associated with that recognition. It is reminiscent of what Adam and Eve experienced after eating the fruit of the Tree of Knowledge of Good and Evil: They lost their innocence and became self-conscious about their nakedness.

The baby in the middle of the second year also experiences a kind of loss of innocence. From a creature who experiences life directly, smiling at the rouge spot on the face in the mirror, she becomes a typical self-conscious human, imposing self-awareness between the senses and the flow of experience, hesitation between her desires and her actions on the world. Jerome Kagan has studied these changes extensively, and he sees the second half of the second year of life as the most important step in the development of the self.

Kagan calls it self-awareness, and his research on toddlers in Cambridge, Massachusetts, and in the Fiji Islands in the South Pacific (the Fiji part was carried out by his student Mary Maxwell Katz) supports the idea of a universal cognitive change at this age. The advance is made up of a series of impressive changes toddlers undergo — increases in certain categories of behavior. One is smiles of mastery — the kind that my infant son gave at the top of the staircase. Another is directives, orders or urgent requests to adults. Yet another is self-descriptions; the use of the words *I, me,* and *mine* become more frequent. (When my youngest child was twenty-one months old, "*My* mommy" became a constant refrain. Once, when her older brother, whom she called "Aba," got up from their mother's lap, she sat down in his place, saying "My mommy. Not Aba's mommy.") In keeping with the idea of a loss of innocence, they also develop a rudimentary sense of shame and guilt, as shown by a hesitancy to break rules and discomfort after breaking them. Kagan calls these feelings "moral emotions." But we might perhaps call them the fruit of the Tree of Knowledge of Good and Evil.

Still, the most surprising finding, both in Cambridge and in Fiji, was in a situation in which the experimenter modeled symbolic or fantasy play with the toys available. At younger ages this would be something like feeding a bottle to a zebra or washing a doll's face. Toward the end of the year it would be a more complex sequence, like making three animals walk, simulating rain with the hands, and then having the animals take shelter under a cloth. The surprise was that an increasing number of children showed distress after the modeling as they progressed through the second year. Some attempted to get their mothers to take over the task, and if she refused — as instructed — might begin to fuss or cry. Kagan's interpretation of this distress was that they increasingly appreciated the difference between what they had been asked to do and what they were actually capable of. In other words, they had developed standards, and were disappointed in their inability to meet them.

Reasonably enough, Kagan has interpreted all these changes as collectively showing an increased self-awareness — an ability to reflect objectively on themselves. He does not claim that they are inexorably yoked together, but he does argue that as they are achieved, in whatever order, in the second year, the child reaches a new level of consciousness. Daniel Stern, a physician, psychoanalyst, and infancy researcher, has considered the implications of these changes for the development of the emotions. In his masterful book, *The Interpersonal World of the Infant,* he refers to this new pattern as the sense of a verbal self.

It is the culmination of a series of major changes beginning in early infancy. According to Stern, at two or three months, the sense of a core or physical self emerges. This is the subjective impression of a physical entity with a boundary. At nine months the infant has added the sense of a subjective self — what we have been calling secondary intersubjectivity — with joint attention and social referencing. The hallmark of this sense is the ability to see the world, and even oneself, from another person's perspective. Finally, during the second year, there arises a new sense of self, based on words. This allows the child to go beyond mere guessing at what someone else is thinking; she can now enter into a primitive conversation in which subjective states are openly shared.

Unlike previous psychoanalysts — notably Sigmund Freud — Stern does not consider these selves to be separate stages, which have to be passed through on the way to maturity. Rather, he sees them as successively integrated together, so that normally functioning adults experience them in some sort of balance. To grasp the meaning of the three selves and how they work together in adults, consider his evocative analogy to making love:

> [It] involves first the sense of the self and other as discrete physical entities, as forms in motion. . . . At the same time it involves the experience of sensing the other's subjective state: shared desire, aligned intentions, and mutual states of simultaneously shifting arousal. . . . And if one of the lovers says for the first time, "I love you," the words . . . perhaps introduce an entirely new note about the couple's relationship that may change the meaning of the history that has led up to and will follow the moment of saying it.

For infants, the five-month-old we began this chapter with has a core or physical self that can act on and be acted on by others; the one-year-old has an ability to see her relationships from both sides; and the two-year-old has words, which, as Stern puts it, "permit the old and persistent issues of attachment, autonomy, separation, intimacy, and so on to be reencountered . . . through shared meaning of personal knowledge." Avery Gholston, at two and a half, picks up the phone and hears Grandma saying, "Avery, go get your mother." But Avery says, "No, I don't want to do that. I want you to talk to me." She has language now, and with it she can insist upon a new level of discourse, a new kind of bonding, a new variety and intensity of relationships.

At the same time, language drives a wedge between the self and experience. Words are inadequate conveyors of feeling; they inevitably alienate the speaker or hearer, to some extent, from physical and emotional reality. They are not as direct as gaze contact, or smiling, or hugging, or crying. Also, like the earlier loss of innocence in the rouge-spot experiment, the child, with the added self-reflective power of language, and the ability to understand spoken rules of behavior, becomes even more self-conscious, and correspondingly less self-satisfied. By the force of words she is banished from infancy's Garden of Eden. In later years, she may find herself in a psychotherapist's office, using the same self-reflective power of words to recover some of her lost emotional innocence. This is no dire prediction, but rather a very hopeful one; it presumes that she is healthy enough to know when she needs guidance, and insightful enough for self-examination. And oddly, it may be only through the use of language to talk and think about emotions that she will be able to find her way again.

1.

1. A !Kung boy meets his big sister about an hour after birth.

2. But there are other ways of feeling about the new sibling.

3. Koichiro Nouhata shows a wary ambivalence as his mother breast-feeds Kenzaburo.

2.

3.

4.

Reflections of the self...

4. ...at six months, in a mirror...

5. ...at nine months, in a friend.

5.

6.

7.

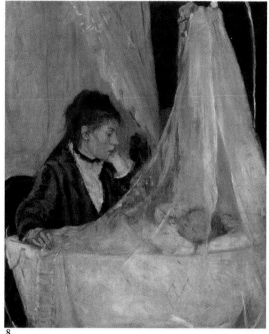

8.

9.

Since God couldn't be everywhere, He (or She) invented mothers... and fathers.

6. "Tandem" nursing of twins in Doti, Nepal.

7. Hmong father and child, Laos.

Child care choices — and chances.

8. A Parisian mother painted by Berthe Morisot in the late nineteenth century — a high point of what has been called "the cult of motherhood."

9. Nap time, circa 1890.

10. High-quality day-care promotes social and cognitive growth, and does not appear to weaken attachment to parents. Two five-year-olds at an outstanding day-care center in Reggio Emilia, Italy.

10.

11.

12.

Children have always had to learn, whether in school or not.

11. A Yanomamo boy takes aim.

12. A three-year-old !Kung girl has a go at a melon. Toddlers may handle knives almost as big as they are.

13. A small girl runs a taxi service in Hong Kong.

13.

14.

15.

14. And they learn by watching.

15. Beginning in the early 1980s, boys and girls ages eight to seventeen received military training on weekends at a Marine Corps center near Pasadena. This boy was eight.

16. Stas Popov, five, borrows an army cap from his father, who served in the Afghan war.

17. Mikiko Nouhata teaches her sons Koichiro, five, and Yojiro, three, a traditional Japanese sword ceremony.

16.

17.

18.

18. For millennia, throughout the world, the extended family has made life without siblings — or a reasonable substitute, cousins — almost impossible. *The Holy Kinship*, Lucas Cranach the Elder, sixteenth century.

19. A !Kung mother, daughter, and granddaughter prepare a meal together.

19.

20. This grandmother takes over the role of her daughter, who is a crack addict.

21. In Sicily, as in most of the world, grandparents indulge children more than parents do.

20.

21.

Language, Play, and Imagination

On Lammas-eve at night shall she be fourteen;
That shall she, marry; I remember it well.
'Tis since the earthquake now eleven years;
And she was wean'd. . . .
For then she could stand alone; nay, by the rood
She could have run and waddled all about;
For even the day before, she broke her brow:
And then my husband, — God be with his soul!
'A was a merry man, — took up the child:
Yea, *quoth he,* dost thou fall upon thy face?
Thou wilt fall backward when thou hast more wit;
Wilt thou not, Jule? *and, by my holidam,*
The pretty wretch left crying, and said Ay.

— WILLIAM SHAKESPEARE, *Romeo and Juliet*

"Hook or me this time."

— SIR JAMES BARRIE, *Peter Pan*

IT IS THE MOST ENTERTAINING PHASE of child life, more thoughtful than infancy yet still charged with emotion, full of frustrating enigmas and charming absurdities. Americans call it the pre-school period, but there is a culturally neutral phrase: early childhood. Well-nourished children in this phase of life grow about five pounds and two-and-a-half inches a year, which makes them gradually leaner — and less babyish in appearance. They also lose the fat-pads over their cheeks, which gives them a more grown-up-looking face. Children in hunting-and-gathering cultures only give up breast-feeding at around the same time — age three or four — and make way for the appearance of a sibling.

But the most crucial growth is going on in the brain, and that growth is the key to great changes in the mind. We have taken the toddler to the point at which the word *I* has real meaning, at which there is an uneasy truce between attachment and autonomy. If there are watchwords for the next phase, they are: *language, family, play, playmates, identity, fantasy, emotion.* Of these, the first four have more meaning in early childhood than they had in infancy, and the last three have a meaning they will rarely, if ever, have again.

If there is one process that frames this phase of life, it is the growth of language: by two it has begun in earnest; by six, except for vocabulary growth, it is essentially done. It has been well said that language doubles the child's world: till now she has had only things to manipulate and understand, where now she has both things and words, and also their relations with each other. But this formula simplifies one-third of the child's world almost out of existence. It exiles human beings into the category of objects, and human relations into the category of language — mere communication.

People — relationships — belong to a world of their own. It is a world of intense emotions, critical to the evolutionary struggle for survival and reproduction, processed by a very ancient and to some extent separate group of brain circuits. This part of the brain, the limbic system, evolved at about the time of the origin of mammals. Much later, the cerebral cortex — notably the frontal lobes, which neuroanatomist Walle Nauta has called the cortex of the limbic system — evolved to secure the profound connection between emotion and thought.

In the development of the child, the parietal cortex, which handles language, develops even more slowly than the frontal lobes, and much more slowly than the limbic system. So it is not surprising that the infant's emotional world is both very intense and comparatively thoughtless. But with the symbolic capacity of, say, the five-year-old — language again — elaborate fantasies can be thought up, even acted out, in such a way as to make this world more comprehensible and thus less fearful. It is the world grasped by Sigmund Freud and his followers, who assigned to early childhood some of the most crucial steps in the origins of character, normal or abnormal; grasped by them, but then largely ignored by developmental psychologists, who have often depicted early childhood in a way that could be better described as dry thoughts in a dry season than as an "I" in the center of a three-year-long emotional storm.

Still, it must be granted them that the growth of language drastically changes the rules of the game of childhood. Speech: words that can wound and heal, change the flow of experience, color it differently from moment to moment, stand in symbolically for the most important people and things, represent and express emotion, control the social world — all this and more. It is a power no other creature on this planet really has. What is the nature of this faculty of speech? Where does it come from? How is it mastered? And from the child's viewpoint, why is it needed? But before we can solve these puzzles, we need to consider some more primitive, less flexible but still very powerful forms of expression.

. . .

One of these, the early social smile, we have already traced in its emergence during the first three months of life, and in its remarkable cross-cultural universality. In fact this is only one of at least several facial expressions that can be reliably identified by objective observers. A recent study of eight-week-olds by Michael Lewis, based on Rovee-Collier's procedure, showed that when they are trained to move a mobile with a string attached to a foot, they exhibit three distinctive expressions: one of joy, when the mobile responds; and one of either sadness or anger when, according to the experimental plan, the string no longer works. By this age, too, it is easy to see and measure disgust and interest.

A few months later, certainly by seven months, fearful expressions appear distinct from the others. All these basic expressions — smiles and grins, angry frowns, expressions of surprise, disgust, and many others — have parallels in chimpanzees and other higher primate species, and there is every reason to believe that they are unlearned, genetically encoded, and passed down through evolution as part of the human phylogenetic heritage. Darwin recognized this in the 1870s, and it has been proven time and again since.

Irenäus Eibl-Eibesfeldt, a German ethologist, has devoted his prodigious energies for over twenty years to one main task: candid filming of nonverbal communication in traditional cultures throughout the world. He has documented the cross-cultural universality of responses ranging from facial expressions of disgust at a foul odor, through the combined smile and eyebrow flash — a quick, brief raising of the brows — to the complex and ambivalent sequence in flirting. In a life that would be the envy of many anthropologists, he has spent about a fourth of his time in primitive cultures, including the Yanomamo of Brazil, known as "the fierce people"; the !Kung of Botswana, known as "the harmless people"; the "gentle" Tasaday of the Philippine jungle; and others including the Eipo of New Guinea, the Himba of Namibia, and the Trobriand Islanders. He has also not neglected to study films of Russian leaders, French dancers, and courting couples on the street in his own Germany. The result is an unprecedented body of film taken in a uniform way and representing large and widely dispersed segments of the human species.

Eibl-Eibesfeldt's films not only demonstrate the universality of basic facial expressions; they also demonstrate universal occurrence of more complex sequences. Some of these, such as ambivalence — alternately looking at and away from a stranger, while also switching from smiling to sober expressions — are evident in the first year of life. Others, like hitting combined with an angry expression, are evident in the second year. Pointing — which we have already encountered as one of the signs of social referencing — occurs in all the cultures by around a year of age. And in all the traditional cultures where breast-feeding is carried on for years, toddlers were filmed playing with one nipple while nursing on the other.

Behavior *toward* infants and toddlers is just as consistent. Languages differ, of course, and the simplified speech used with infants — "motherese" — varies from culture to culture. Yet in all the settings the register of infant-directed speech is about an octave higher than for normal speech to other adults. (Not surprisingly, experiments in infancy laboratories in our culture have shown that young infants attend better to high-pitched voices — a fact that parents throughout the world had apparently already discovered.) The face a parent shows to an infant is also fairly standard: broad smile, wide-open eyes, raised eyebrows, with the head bobbing up and down and accompanied by a high-pitched, somewhat musical vocalization — some variant of "Hi, baby!" In many traditional cultures, "kiss-feeding" is found; this offering of prechewed food seems unsanitary to us, but these cultures have no baby food; the babies have the parents' germs in any case, and some antibodies are delivered with the food. The advantage of softened food, partly predigested by the mother or father's saliva, is probably considerable.

• • •

These universal, or at least very widespread features of infant-parent nonverbal communication speak to the unity of the human species and the centrality of our common evolutionary legacy. But verbal communication — speech — is something else again. Its most obvious aspect, as we look around the world, is the one biblical legend traces back to the Tower of Babel: the mutual incomprehensibility of languages. They number in the thousands — an estimated eight hundred in Africa and four hundred on the island of New Guinea alone. Not dialects; *languages*. Joseph, the biblical patriarch and viceroy of Egypt, was said to have spoken seventy. This prodigious and not-too-likely accomplishment would have given him mastery of perhaps 2 percent of the world's presently known languages.

If there were to be any argument for the flexibility of human behavior, for its domination by learning and the subtleties of culture, this vast diversity of natural languages would seem to be the clincher. As far as we know, you can take any two six-month-olds in any two cultures and switch them, like the prince and the pauper in the Mark Twain novel. Each will acquire the language of his new home as surely and flawlessly as if it were the language he was born to. What more evidence of human malleability would you need?

Such was the outlook of behavioral scientists until the 1960s, when Noam Chomsky, a linguist, and Eric Lenneberg, a psychologist — both were at the Massachusetts Institute of Technology — staked out a new theoretical position that has dominated research ever since. According to their theory, language is simply too complex to be learned, in any conventional sense, in the time in which it is learned. In the natural world of the young child, the schedules of reward and punishment for correct and incorrect speech are too inconsistent to form the answer. And in an environment in which deliberate instruction is rare and the sentences the child hears vary infinitely, direct imitation cannot be the answer either. In fact, imitation is an impossible source for some of the things the child says, which could never have been heard, and imitation is even resisted when the child has a strong idea of how he should say what he wants to say.

Consider the following exchange between my son Adam, then twenty-one months old, and me concerning the most important people in his life:

> "Adam, say 'Mommy.' "
> "Mommy."
> "Say 'Daddy.' "
> "Daddy."
> "Say 'Susanna.' "
> "Arara."

"Arara" had been his name for his sister, three years his senior, from the time he was fifteen months old — a time, perhaps, when "Susanna" was too difficult to pronounce. But by twenty-one months he could pronounce many more sounds, including those of his sister's real name:

> "Adam, say 'Su.' "
> "Su."
> " 'Zan.' "
> "Zan."
> " 'Na.' "
> "Na."
> " 'Susanna.' "
> "Arara."

Adam's stubbornness reveals an inclination to ignore or even resist correction and instruction. But persistence in error is still more interesting when the error is a grammatical one. By twenty-seven months Adam had learned a few letters, and we were playing with some plastic ones.

> "That's a *A*," he said, pointing correctly.
> "You mean 'That's an *A*.' "
> "That's a *A*."

I emphasized the word 'an,' and I finally initiated this exchange:

> "That's an *A*."
> "Hm?"

"That's an *A*."

"Hm?"

"That's an *A*."

"Hm?"

By being stubborn myself, I had finally gotten him to pay attention, and some such utterance as "Hm?" is a wonderful mechanism toddlers have for conning lazy adults into teaching them things. They notice a discrepancy between what they hear and what they know, and they emit that puzzled monosyllable that virtually compels repetition. In !Kung children the equivalent was a nasalized "Hih?" It had the same effect. Still, Adam never did say the word *an* that day, nor any day soon after.

Yet by that time he routinely said "Susanna," not to mention such utterances as "The cars . . . um . . . the cars gonin' up there and . . . um . . . gonin' to the store . . . and . . . um . . . buy some milk and . . . buy some milk and buy some chickens and mayonnaise and . . . ," at which point his mother burst out laughing and he laughed too.

In six months he had gone from tongue-tied toddlerhood to virtual speechmaking. At this time he and I also had another exchange, regarding a pair of feet in a jigsaw puzzle:

"What's that?"

"Two foots."

Here Adam made a classic overgeneralization error. He had learned the rule for making plurals in English, but was ignoring evidence that not all plurals followed the rule.

"You mean 'Two feet,' " I said.

"Two feets."

"Two *feet*," I emphasized.

"That's a two feets."

It was not that he paid no attention to me, just that he could not believe I really expected him to make a plural without an *s*. So strong, in fact, was his conviction that although he was willing to change the sound of the noun according to my whim, and even to add another grammatical error, the indefinite article, he was not willing to give up his pluralizing rule. In the course of the same conversation about the puzzle, Adam gave me an insight into the nature of such persistence. I pointed to a jigsaw dress.

"What's that?"
"That's a ress."
"Say 'dress.' "
"Ress."
"Say 'dress.' "
"Noooo! I wanna say 'ress.' "

This seemed a revelation. It not only showed that Adam heard the difference between his word and mine — a pronunciation problem was unlikely here — but also that his choice of "ress" was to some extent deliberate. In all these instances he had generated his own patterns, and he was not prepared to give them up just because I claimed primacy for a different one.

Persistent errors like this, particularly in the realm of grammar (as in the pluralizing error) were among the kinds of observations that led Chomsky and Lenneberg to find imitation implausible as a sole strategy for acquiring language. "Ress" could be initially a flawed imitation of the adult pronunciation, but "two foots," and more especially, the switch under pressure to "two feets" cannot be randomly imperfect imitations. These imperfections follow a pattern that can only be the product of an internal rule. A learning theorist might fairly say that the rule was learned, but that does not explain such fierce insistence on it, or even the toddler's ability to abstract the pluralizing rule from adult English — a tongue that contains many strange things, but no such thing as "foots" or "feets."

So the then-new theory was a biological one. It claimed that the young child's brain (and, therefore, mind) must have strong built-in biases. It enabled him to derive rules of grammar from a bewildering array of inputs, and then to apply them tenaciously to the ordering and transformation of new words — words being mastered at the astounding rate of about ten per day during much of early childhood.

Chomsky's contribution was to see the common features of function and thought underlying the great variety of the world's languages. He called these features *universal grammar,* and argued that each language transforms the universal grammar to generate its own special rules and forms. Along with the universal grammar came the concept of a Language Acquisition Device, or L.A.D., which all human beings were thought to share. This "organ" of the mind appeared in the growing brain during early childhood; thus the interchangeability of babies, and the incredible speed with which young children acquire their native languages, during the same two or three years, in all the cultures of the world.

Lenneberg's contribution was to point out the enormous variety of conditions that still allowed language to flourish and grow. These included barriers to communication such as deafness in the parents or the child, many forms of mental retardation, child abuse and neglect, and minimal stimulation of the child with adult speech. There was no claim that individual differences in language and its development were not important, nor that learning could not help explain these differences. It was just that attention needed to be called, at that time, to the remarkable similarities — especially in the realm of grammar — in the attainments of children growing up in vastly different conditions.

• • •

The fact that my own parents could not hear made me understandably friendly toward this theory. I knew that my linguistic environment during my own language learning had been very distorted. My parents were legally deaf, and hearing children of deaf parents who sign can do very well, sometimes acquiring sign as their first language. But my parents had themselves been raised without sign language, by hearing parents who believed in lip-reading as an adequate form of communication for the deaf — common then, but now a largely discredited notion. Lip-reading is very inefficient even between adults who are making an effort to enhance it by staying face-to-face and articulating distinctly.

When the speaker is a two-year-old torn by emotions and running on instinct, it is impossible for the nonhearing parent to grasp more than a small fraction of his communications. Although a firstborn, I certainly had the opportunity to speak to grandparents and other adults more than just occasionally; this must have helped. But still I felt a wave of recognition and assent as I studied the ideas of Chomsky and Lenneberg, which made it plausible for language to be acquired under unfavorable conditions, by assigning a large role to the child himself — or, more precisely, to the child's maturing brain.

I soon went off to Botswana to study !Kung infants and children, and they made the biological theory seem more plausible than ever. Here was a remote population of hunters and gatherers whose language utilized clicks and, like Mandarin Chinese, tones. Neither the words nor the grammar bore the remotest resemblance to English. Yet infants and toddlers were charging through the process of language learning in a way that was uncannily similar to American children's parallel progress. Babbling, or meaningless positive vocalizations, reached a peak at eight months of age in both cultures, followed within three or four months by the beginning of a steep, long rise in the rate of meaningful vocalizations — words.

In both cultures the first phase was dominated by one-word utterances that seemed to stand in for whole ideas. Common first words among the !Kung included *Aiyo* (Mommy), *Mba* (Daddy), *na* (gimme), *ihn* (take it), and *ihn-ihn* (no). Adam's first words were to be *Mommy, Daddy, Arara, no* (meaning either yes or no), *uh-oh, ihn-ihn* (for refusal), *open,* and *woop* (for woops). For his younger sister, Sarah, the one-word utterances at twenty months of age would include *aiee* (hi), *Mama, Papa, Ali* (Susanna), *Aba* (Adam), *Lala* (Sarah), *oosh* (shoes), and *take-you,* an effective blend of "thank you" and "take it," used to mark exchanges of food or objects in either direction. The similarity of the timing and nature of such achievements in these widely different cultures was impressive.

Yet even while I was becoming convinced of the reality of the L.A.D., some psychologists were beginning to challenge the idea that language involves a lot of innate preparedness. Their main strategy for doing this was to show that parents routinely provide more supports for language learning than Chomsky and Lenneberg claimed. They made the valid point that language acquisition constantly demands and uses social contexts, and so the child was learning a new form of social behavior, not just a bunch of labels for things and dry grammatical rules. Researchers like Katherine Nelson, of the New School for Social Research, and Catherine Snow, of the Harvard School of Education, began to study this process with impressive techniques of analysis. One result was the demonstration that children growing up in rich social contexts with lots of conversations — around the dinner table with their parents, for instance — learned language better and sooner than children relatively deprived of these contexts.

Avery Gholston, at age twenty months, gave a good example of how this works, at breakfast with her father, Felton, and her three-year-old brother, Malcolm:

FELTON: Pancakes!

AVERY: Panpakes! Mal . . . Panpakes!

FELTON: It seems she refuses to eat my pancakes.

AVERY: Panpakes! Panpakes!

FELTON: Yes, pancakes. Are you eating your pancakes?

Here she must cram all the meaning she wants to express in one word or at most a two-word phrase. But they serve. Among other things, they elicit corrected pronunciation by her father, a type of adult shaping of child language. Margaret Mead wrote that among the Manus of New Guinea she observed up to sixty repetitions by a parent of the same child utterance, the repetitions alternating with the child's mispronunciation of the word. I observed at least twenty repetitions in the same kinds of exchanges among the !Kung.

Also characteristic of this phase of language acquisition is Avery's conversation with her two older brothers, at a backyard dinner on her second birthday:

BENJAMIN: It's almost time for you guys to eat dinner.

AVERY: Eat dinner.

MALCOLM: Yeah, it's almost time for you to go to bed.

AVERY: Go to bed!

BENJAMIN: And tomorrow you'll come back.

AVERY: Come back!

BENJAMIN: Tomorrow.

AVERY: 'morrow.

Her abbreviated repetitions, sometimes with added emphasis, are a perfect adaptation for learning new words. But in addition she is learning the social skills of conversation, including gracious turn-taking and replying specifically to the other person's last remark. Only four months later, not yet two and a half, she would open a conversation at breakfast by saying, "Where's my muffin, Daddy?" and go on to joke about her father eating something inedible. She had moved from simplistic repetition to complex invented sentences in a remarkably short time.

• • •

These kinds of observations fit well with the ideas of a Soviet psychologist, Lev Vygotsky. Piaget had claimed that mental development, interacting with objects, changed the child's way of thinking about the world. Vygotsky, influenced by Marxist-Leninist philosophy, made a more radical claim: that all thinking derives ultimately from relations between people. In this view, the child's mind is inexorably imbedded in — and molded by — society, and the link between the mind and the world is none other than speech.

One prominent American psychologist who began to think this way in the 1970s was Jerome Bruner. In Oxford, England, he studied interactions between mothers and their infants or toddlers prior to language-learning. He noticed that certain preverbal patterns, such as pointing at or playing with an object together, seemed to precede the first words. Could such interactions be preparing the child's mind for language learning? Bruner believed that nonverbal interactions, such as joint attention to objects, provided a "scaffolding" to assist the child in developing language. As the painter uses a physical scaffold to climb the side of a building, so the toddler's mind climbs the social scaffold, supporting itself while it attains ever more impressive heights. Bruner even proposed, half-seriously, an L.A.S., or language acquisition scaffold, to compliment Chomsky's brain-based L.A.D.

There is now considerable evidence to support the idea of social scaffolding. But there are a few problems with this evidence. First of all, almost all of it has been gathered in observational studies of middle-class, well-educated, English-speaking families like the Gholstons. Such families, anthropologists know, hold more conversations with children — provide more verbal "scaffolding" — than those in most other cultures. Don't the rest of the world's children learn to talk? To an anthropologist, the cultural narrowness of these studies makes the conclusions drawn from them seem dubious.

Second, almost all the studies are correlational; that is, they show that the more parental coaxing now, the better the child's language later. But that does not prove that the coaxing *causes* the improvement. The parent could be responding to a verbally precocious child. Or the verbal facility of both could be the result of social and economic status, or even of shared genes. Only experiments can prove cause-and-effect. In addition, most of the correlations in these studies are low. So even if they *are* causes, they may not be very *important* causes.

Finally, these interpretations lack almost any reference to the actual facts of brain development — even though what they are often supposedly disputing is how much of language learning can be explained by brain changes. In addition, just as psychologists have not faced up to the many questions about other cultures, they have given little attention to the classic cases of deviant language learning, such as occurs in blind children, deaf children, or hearing children of deaf parents.

· · ·

The few studies that have addressed these deficiencies do support a role for interactional learning; but others are more consistent with the Chomsky-Lenneberg maturational theory. It has been shown, for example, that in middle-class college-educated families, a substantial proportion of young children's errors are followed by adult corrections. Such corrections often stimulate "recasts" — attempts by the children to get it right. However, the only study that controlled for genes by including adopted children showed that toddlers' verbal performance can be predicted best from the general intelligence of their biological parents, not by any measure of the adoptive parents' responses to their children's linguistic efforts.

The most convincing proof of the role of parents has come from a few studies using the experimental method. Two were done in the child study laboratory of Michael Tomasello. The first, done with Michael Farrar, showed that in teaching seventeen-month-old toddlers the names of unfamiliar objects, such as gauge, clip, bow, and wrench, the parents could best ensure learning by "following-in" to the child's focus of attention. For example, they might be told to say a sentence emphasizing the word *gauge* only when the child was already playing with the gauge. As an experimental control, the word *wrench* might be used with equal emphasis, but only when the child was not playing with anything. Two weeks after training, the child would understand "gauge" better than "wrench."

In another study done by Tomasello with Ann Cale Kruger, an invented verb, "plunk," was highlighted to fifteen-month-olds in a sentence either before, during, or after pushing a button that made a doll slide down a ramp. Learning was facilitated most by using the verb for an impending action — "Look, Jason, I'm going to plunk it." For an action, the label apparently needed to come in advance, or the child would be less able to link it with the event. In terms of the child's attention and learning, this advance labeling was the equivalent of "following-in" to objects with nouns.

Both experiments proved the power of some form of joint attention by adult and toddler in promoting language-learning. They went beyond the concept, advanced by Chomsky, that the child learns by simply hearing adult speech. Each was inspired by an observational study that called attention to the mechanism of learning (or scaffolding), which was then tested experimentally. As a result we now know not only that middle-class American children's environments include such scaffolding, but also that these tactics promote language-learning. How *necessary* they are — the real question posed by Chomsky's theory — remains an unsolved puzzle.

One approach to solving it is to go outside the middle class of Western countries. Anthropologists like Bambi Schieffelin, who studied how children learn language among the Kaluli people of New Guinea, and Elinor Ochs, who did similar studies in Samoa, have failed to find adult responses that correspond to recasts and expansions of child speech. Ochs summarized a wide range of anthropological studies of language acquisition in 1986:

> It is important to note here that *all societies do not rely on the very same set of language-socializing procedures. Indeed although prompting a child what to say appears widespread, expanding children's utterances, using leading questions, announcing activities/events for a child, and using a simplified lexicon and grammar to do so are cross-culturally variable* [emphasis in original].

These and other tactics of social scaffolding are considered very important by some researchers; yet in many cultures children do without them. Not only do they acquire their respective languages, but oratory is admired and is a route to success in many of these same societies.

In addition, the child's own speech shows strong cross-cultural consistencies despite differences in input. Dan Slobin, who studied the acquisition of Russian, and Elizabeth Bates, who studied the acquisition of Italian, both concluded that some important aspects of children's language capacity are universal, and must be genetically encoded within the developing brain. Although both see fewer universals than Chomsky does, they accept a major role for innate mental abilities — partly because they have compared different cultures.

Special cases like deaf children or hearing children with deaf parents also invite much more study, but what we know so far does not suggest that scaffolding is crucial, though some is present. For example, signing parents of deaf children exaggerate the size of their signs when addressing young children, and may make signs in contact with the child's body. But no one has asked whether this information matches the adult input provided to upper-middle-class hearing children of hearing parents. Those who have studied deaf children's communication consider such a scenario very unlikely. Indeed, what deaf babies do in sign is amazingly similar to what hearing babies do in sound.

For instance, Kevin Berrigan, filmed for "Childhood" at age eleven months, has been "babbling" for several months now — repetitively making signs that may be components of words, but are still unformed or meaningless. His deaf parents sign in front of him all the time, but still the impetus to "babble" visually at the expected age for babbling is remarkable. At eleven months, he produces some individual words with his hands, just as a hearing baby would at that age. And within a few months, he will produce two-word sentences with his hands.

But his parents do supply scaffolding for his signs. Like hearing parents the world over, they have a signed form of "motherese" that they use with Kevin — large, broad, deliberate, exaggerated signs, slowly repeated, and accompanied by encouraging expressions. Sometimes they even shape the hands of a babbling baby into the nearest meaningful sign. And that is not all. During the filmed sequence, Kevin's mother, Sheryl, recognizes that he is trying to make the sign for Daddy. She shows him how to make the sign properly in ASL — American Sign Language — and she points at Terry, his father.

> SHERYL (*signing to Terry*): Look at Kevin.
> KEVIN (*signing*): Da . . . Da . . . Daddy . . .

Kevin also makes the sign "bye-bye" to a balloon that slips away from him while he is holding it. Terry signs to Sheryl, "He's tired. It's nap time. He'd better sleep." Then he signs to Kevin, "Wave bye-bye. Let's go to sleep."

Terry and Krystle, age five, talk about a basketball game they are going to for deaf players. They can't hear the whistle Terry blows as umpire, although it is very loud; but if they are standing in the right place, they can feel the vibrations. Di, the three-year-old, signs with the same charming hyperbole of any other preschool child: "We'll go to the store and get many, many batteries and many, many envelopes. Many, many batteries and many, many envelopes." It's the sort of speechmaking by hand that Kevin himself will be doing in just a year or two — a product of signed linguistic input combined with a human child's language-prone brain.

But what will happen if there is no signed input? Susan Goldin-Meadow and her colleagues at the University of Chicago have for over a decade studied children in an unfortunate but common situation: they are deaf, but their parents are not, and the parents do not "speak" sign language. The children are exposed neither to heard nor seen language. Yet, amazingly, they invent a language of their own — "home sign," which is quite distinct from standard ASL.

Years of research on this homemade language show that these children structure their invented signs in ways that resemble true natural languages — those transmitted from adult to child for generations — whether signed or spoken. The structure is evident both at the level of early one-word signs and at the level of phrases and sentences. "For example," Goldin-Meadow writes, "one child pointed at a tower, produced the HIT sign [fist swatting in air] and then the FALL sign [flat palm flops over in air] to comment on the fact that he had hit the tower and that the tower had fallen."

These made-up signs are conventionalized just as words are, and appear as two-word phrases — two-word "telegrams" — at the same age at which hearing children, exposed to the full power of adult speech, achieve the same milestone. That these deprived children do not achieve the full subtlety of natural languages is worth noting but is not surprising; what they do achieve without such input is truly remarkable. As Goldin-Meadow and Carolyn Mylander modestly phrase their conclusion, "some aspects of linguistic analysis may be strongly guided by internal factors."

If this is not the Language Acquisition Device in action, I don't know what would be. But we don't have to stop there; we can see it not just in action but in the flesh. We now know enough about the development of the brain to cast doubt on any notion of language-learning that fails to note the brain's growing power. This means not merely the nod given in textbooks of child development — something about the increasing power of the brain to learn. It means recognition of what we know about development in specific regions and pathways of the brain, which can be seen to correspond to specific aspects of mental development.

For instance, every child with a normal brain experiences maturational changes in what is called Broca's speech area, adjacent to the brain region that controls the mouth and throat. This maturation follows a largely predetermined plan, with a timetable roughly corresponding to the acquisition of early speech. It is not difficult to imagine that in the deaf child, the next closest brain region, which controls the hand, becomes responsive to Broca's speech area. This is significant adaptation, but it is still based on specific brain maturation. The brain is, of course, also responsive to input. It has been shown — for instance, by Helen Neville of the Salk Institute — that deaf people have wider bands of responsiveness in the visual regions of their brains than do hearing people — likely to be the result of lifelong differences in input. But such subtle changes do not change the basic maturational plan.

I am biased in favor of the biological view, not just because I had parents who couldn't hear, but because I believe in the independent creative power of the human mind, especially as expressed through language. Since the world's children acquire different languages, they must learn the ones they are exposed to in one way or another. Discoveries about the learning process surely will help us to understand the very large learned component. Yet it should be a matter of pride to us to assert the independent power of the individual human mind — even when the mind is that of a toddler.

I once heard a fine lecture by Jerome Bruner about his work on scaffolding in language-learning. My question was friendly: What do we make of language-learning in cultures like the !Kung, where scaffolding patterns seem to play a minor role? And what about people like me — children of deaf parents, who were unlikely to have reproduced the scaffolding patterns he thought were so important? His candid reply was that he had been almost blind for the first six months of his life, and so his own development must have been quite unlike that of the children he was observing. We stood there smiling across the lecture hall — two people who each had faced significant early deprivation, yet had grown to independence and skill, linguistically and otherwise. Perhaps he was marveling, as I was at that moment, at the wonderful complexity, and persistent mystery, of human development.

• • •

But how language is acquired is only one of the great questions of this phase of life. How language is used, how it evokes, alters, and manages the three things that are central to the life of the child from two to six — emotion, relationships, and fantasy — is another. Not long after age two we can say to a child who is throwing a tantrum, "Use words." It won't always work, of course, but it is no longer meaningless. A new kind of following-in soon becomes possible — not attention to objects while naming them, but attention to and naming of those evanescent phenomena of the mind and brain: feelings. Words can draw the child away from the emotional here-and-now to another, imagined time or place where the source of the grief or anger will be assuaged.

And when the child finally controls her sobs, and as they subside blurts through them, "I didn't want the blue cup! I wanted the yellow one!" then the words can produce a solution, even if it is only a promise: "The yellow cup broke, but I'll buy you another one." Consider the child who has for the first time become able to understand this reply. She can *visualize* the new cup to come. The sounds idly strung together after the "but" carry immense weight; they pluck visions out of the air, so that the child herself can make the visions dance. The sounds are symbols. They are powerful. "Buy me it right away," she says, wiping away her tears. And Mommy, dabbing the drippy nose with a soiled, crumpled napkin says, "*I promise.*"

Even in this exchange the words are doing wonders, teaching the child about loss, anger, patience, love, and truthfulness — not to mention cups, their colors, and where they come from. But now consider the quite different exchanges that might begin with the words, "I didn't want a baby brother!" or, "I didn't want Daddy to move to a different house!" or, "I didn't want Mommy to get dead!" In the response to such anguished phrases, hugs will help a lot; but carefully chosen words will be worth a king's ransom. If they are good, they will give meaning to experience, dwell on feelings, and yet get beyond them, to a future time or a past one, perhaps painting a fantasy that seems safe and beautiful. The four plain words *I, still, love, you* — each a symbol of something in the child's personal world that bears enormous force, outlasting change and sorrow and loss — mean little to a two-year-old, but to a three-year-old they can serve as a compass in a savage emotional storm.

Consider what poetry does for us grown-ups. "O that this too, too solid flesh would melt, thaw, and resolve itself into a dew" expresses Hamlet's anguish, certainly; but it also evokes the fear and the hope of dissolution, making the end of life — the end of pain — seem almost beautiful. It calls upon us to let our attention dwell on this man's tragic plight, so that our own feelings about loss, grief, injustice, courage, and mortality resonate with his. "It is the east," sighs Romeo, "and Juliet is the sun. Arise, fair sun, and kill the envious moon, who is already sick and pale with grief that thou, her maid, art far more fair than she." This speech expresses love, of course, but it also evokes love; and yet its delicious hyperbole leaves room for a hint of self-mocking humor. And it pulses with overtones of a hoped-for, tenderly yet recklessly imagined future.

To a three-year-old, in a sense, all sentences have the freshness of poetry. Questions, explanations, promises, protestations of love — all create a transiently vivid fantasy that the child's new mind, fresh from the workshop of development, can dwell on in a brand-new way. "I love you this much," she grins, stretching her arms like skinny wings; and the tiny poem, spoken and seen and thought and felt, crosses the gap between two spirits like an arc of light, and moistens her mother's eyes.

It also says something about the tiny "I" in the child's head: "I am the one who loves you." When the child approaching age two begins to use the word *I*, it seems to mean mainly "I am separate." It helps the gem of autonomy to crystallize from the dense solution of attachment. But a year later it is not just a separateness; it is also an identification of the center of that separateness. This process of identification is a main job the child must get done during this period. I am a girl, I am small, I am black, I am loved (and therefore lovable), I am a Christian, I am a big brother, I am handicapped, I am Kathy's friend. Obviously some self-labels can hurt, but that does not prevent the child from wearing them on her sleeve. It is up to those who care for the child to help her define how the label will feel.

• • •

Two of the nice things about young children are that, unlike babies, they can tell you what's on their minds, and, unlike older children, they do. A few of my daughter Sarah's sayings over the last few months have as much to say about her emotional concerns as they do about the growth of language complexity:

- "Don't forget me to bring that" (age two years, eleven months).
- "That little girl stuck her tongue out at me two times!" — said with brows strongly furrowed, three years.
- Chris, three and a half, and Sarah, three, have set up house. Sarah, in "bed," says, "Chrissy, I want you to come to bed now." "No," comes the reply, "I'm watching the news."
- After falling and briefly crying, Sarah controls her sobs and says, "I hurt my knee and I also fell my shoe off" (three years, one month).
- "Papa, are you listen-to-ing me . . . listening to me?" (three years, three months).
- At a live performance in English of the opera *Hansel and Gretel*, Sarah is very frightened, actually shaking as she sits on her mother's lap, watching the witch. At last she asks, "Is this a movie, or is this real?" (three years, seven months).

Aside from the three instances of bad, or perhaps I should say creative, grammar — including one Chomskyan error and self-correction — these remarks are a veritable catalog of the central concerns of early childhood. In the first, she shows an ability to enlist adult help to prevent future loss — and also a bit of self-knowledge: she is acting to shore up her own forgetfulness. In the second, she shows distress as a baby could, with her furrowed brow, but goes on to explain the emotion; like many young children, especially girls, aggressiveness distresses her.

In the third, she and Chris — whom she calls her boyfriend — enact a scene they have watched their parents go through more than once. Already, they have identified themselves as future husband, future wife, and play out a domestic scene of marital familiarity and tension. Another friend of Sarah's, also three, had an imaginary husband and six children, one of whom was named "Dirty." Yet another, age four but in lively step with the times, had picked, from among the boys she knew at preschool, both a husband *and* a boyfriend. This is play, of course, and displays the rich and growing power children have to create waking dreams. But its importance lies in the recognition they newly have of who they are, and to what strange human forces they owe their existence.

In the fourth remark, after the fall, she explains how it happened. She has cried already, babylike, adaptive, announcing the crisis and summoning help for the pain. But then, she feels, she must suppress the sobs and give the details to her father; this is no animal cry, but a shared human experience, hung in the air between two people in a vessel of simple words. She uses words and, as my mother used to say, she gets her troubles off her chest.

In the fifth remark she catches me in one of my lapses of attention — it's a hazard of having an egghead father — and properly calls me on it, with a question I couldn't have asked at her age. She identifies here another central fact of early childhood: There is no point in telling your woes (or your joys for that matter) to someone who isn't listening. And listening — "listen-to-ing" may be the better word — doesn't just mean sitting there; it's active. The words are a way of touching across a little expanse of space; if the child is lucky, they will always be that, with someone, for a lifetime.

Last but not least, Sarah shakes like a scared kitten, unable to suppress her fear as pretend Hansel and Gretel seem fated to fatten the witch. The play focuses all the terror a three-year-old can see in the grown-up world. She is on her mother's lap, and her brother and sister have tried to calm her, without success. Finally she asks the question, aiming to get an answer that will help her draw a firm line between imagination and reality — a line that her siblings, at eight and eleven, readily draw for themselves.

•   •   •

The daughter of a friend of mine, an historian, made a remark when she was three that gave her father pause. Coming home from preschool, she dropped her depth charge nonchalantly: "I want to have a penis." For her skeptical father this was a jolt, and he asked me if it didn't prove Freud's theory. Freud believed that little boys are anxious about the possible loss of their penises, partly because, having masturbated pleasurably, they are fond of them; and partly because they imagine that girls have lost theirs. Little girls, in their turn, were supposed to envy boys their penises, and to see the prospect of pregnancy as a substitute.

I was not impressed with the evidence Freud or anyone else had offered to support these notions. As an anthropologist, I found more evidence and logic in Margaret Mead's concept of womb envy. Being able to bear a child, Mead thought, was a lot more impressive than having a penis, and boys were more likely than girls to be envious. Not only that, but there was some evidence: Many Indian cultures in native South America had a custom called the *couvade*. In this ritual men set about pretending they were in labor whenever their pregnant wives began contractions. In some cultures, they even took herbs and food that made them constipated during the wife's ninth month, so that they could trundle off into the woods and simulate the strain and pain of childbirth with a colossal defecation. This sure sounded like womb envy to me.

So when my friend's daughter, mixing it up with boys for the first time, showed up with this Freudian-sounding wish, it gave him — and me, when he told me about it — pause. Fortunately her explanation of why was mundane and conventional: Having noticed that boys could do it, she wanted to be able to pee standing up. Nevertheless, it was well into the feminist revolution, and her liberal father was not going to sit still for his daughter envying boys. He decided to nip this thing in the bud. A search of toy stores turned up the world's biggest Wonder Woman coloring book. On the cover was the fierce-looking, shapely superhero, maybe not larger than life, but larger than his three-year-old.

Two or three weeks after the unwelcome penis-wish, he and I came back to his house after a jog to find his daughter decked out in red cape and tights. She was jumping off a two-foot-high ledge onto a mattress on the floor, stretching her arms out, yelling *"Wonder Woman!"* as she sailed through space. After the third or fourth launching, she looked up at her dad matter-of-factly and said, "I can be Wonder Woman 'cause I'm a girl, but you can't be Wonder Woman 'cause you're a boy but I can because I'm a girl and Wonder Woman is a woman." Then she went up on the ledge for her next takeoff. "So much for penis envy," I said to my friend under my breath.

But the Freudian theory has echoed down through the modern history of thought about how sex takes shape in the mind. It proposed not only penis envy and castration anxiety, but also a constellation of wishes in conflict that were said to be crucial in shaping identity. Boys of three or four were in love with their mothers, and desperately jealous of their fathers; the fear of castration was in part fear of the father's wrath. This Freud named the Oedipus complex, after Sophocles' tragic hero who un-luckily (and unwittingly) killed his father and married his mother. The normal little boy, though, would have to act quite differently, suppressing in the end the desire to do either. As for girls, in addition to penis envy they supposedly had an Electra complex, with the roles more or less re-versed.

None of this has been supported with good evidence, although there are certainly children that seem to have these thoughts and conflicts. Many children this age claim to want to marry the opposite-sexed parent, and some talk or fantasize about getting the "rival" out of the marital bed. But there is no evidence that all normal children must go through such a process, and cross-cultural studies since the 1920s have cast doubt on Freud's idea that the themes of this family drama are universal.

Nevertheless, some related concepts must be valid. First, boys and girls differ anatomically, and most notice the difference by age three. Boys, through self-exploration and play, find out that their genitals can produce both pleasure and pain, and some probably worry about injury and loss. Girls soon learn of their future procreative power, and some discover the pleasures of the clitoris. Cultures and families where nakedness and mas-turbation bring reprimands, or even punishments — like the Austria where Freud grew up and practiced medicine — can certainly heighten children's conflicts. Among the !Kung San, fathers occasionally joked with boys about taking their penises, in much the way that American fathers and uncles "steal" noses. In a lighthearted, loving context, such jokes might help boys handle their conflicts — especially in a culture where people are comfortable with such jokes; in a harsh or threatening context, the opposite could easily occur.

• • •

But when we think today about the development of gender identity, we frame our questions in very different terms. When do boys become aware that they are boys, and girls that they are girls? What process leads to this knowledge? How large are the *real* sex differences in behavior, and how do they relate to the child's *concept* of gender?

Decades of research enable us to give at least provisional answers to these questions. A few children develop a sense of their own gender identity — the ability to label themselves consistently as boy or girl — by age two, but almost all do by age three. Also by age three most children will be able to identify the toys, games, clothing, tools, and work that in our culture are stereotyped as masculine or feminine. In the first phase of such stereotyping, they are more rigid than they will be later. At around this time they also correctly classify others, including the same-sex parent, as sharing the label "male" or "female" label with them.

As they move from age three to seven, they gradually learn that gender category is something permanent, not influenced by personal choice. It is fascinating that this change, to gender constancy, is associated with a *decrease* in the rigidity with which most children hold their stereotypes about how the sexes play, work, and dress. It seems that three-year-olds, uncertain about gender constancy, shore up their sense of identity by exaggerating the differentness of the two sexes in play, work, and dress. They also prefer to identify with and imitate the same-sex parent or other same-sex adults. A parent may actively encourage children to identify with traditional models, as Mikiko Nouhata does when she teaches her sons a traditional Japanese sword ceremony — a strongly male-oriented behavior backed by centuries of tradition, with the added power of fantasy and ritual. Not surprisingly, exposure to models whose lifestyle runs counter to stereotype helps make the child less rigid about it, both conceptually and behaviorally.

However, it is now clear that behavioral differences between girls and boys precede the time when the first concepts of gender begin to fall into place. In our culture one of the most dramatic differences is in choice of toys to play with; these begin to be sex-stereotyped (trucks and soldiers versus dolls and baby bottles) by age one and a half. There is overlap in the early years, but the sex difference is statistically significant, and it widens for the next few years.

Another dramatic difference in Western cultures is that girls play with girls, boys with boys. By age three, children are more likely to approach and to play with a peer of the same sex than one of the opposite sex. By age four and a half, in preschool situations where choice is possible, children spend only a third as much time with the other sex as they do with the same sex. By age six and a half, this threefold difference is increased to elevenfold, and a wide gap is maintained for five more years. The gap is not much affected by the choice of toys and games; sex-segregation is quite pronounced even in gender-neutral play settings. Deliberate efforts to influence children toward less sex-segregation have shown that they resist such influence.

We don't yet know why even young children allowed to choose freely tend toward stereotyped toys and sex-segregation. Eleanor Maccoby, a Stanford University psychologist and a leading authority in this line of research, believes that part of the explanation lies in inherent differences in the tendencies and reactions of the sexes. However, sex-segregation by individuals is not related to how "masculine" or "feminine" their personal behavior is, compared to others of their own sex. So part of the explanation must also be rigidity of sex-stereotypes and uncertainty about identity.

As Maccoby also says, children are socialized by friends and playmates, not just (and perhaps not even mainly) by parents and teachers. Therefore the power of voluntary sex-segregation must be of concern to anyone who would like to see a reduction of sex-role stereotyping in our culture. Once exposed mainly to same-sex playmates, the child will be influenced by their distinctive behaviors; after that, modeling and behavior will effectively reinforce each other. This cycle could maintain undesired sex-specific behavior patterns even if adult models were neutral.

Last but not least among potent environmental influences, television delivers a frequently sex-stereotyped message to young children. Cartoons, commercials, and a large proportion of other programming shape children's choices from very early ages. Lonnie Sherrod, a child psychologist then at Yale University, wanted to study children's television-watching in New Haven, Connecticut, during the late 1970s. Aiming to capture the early phases of the habit, he began with three-year-olds. He was stunned to find that at that age children had been watching for months or years, and averaged twenty hours a week. Such a dose of entertainment-cum-modeling must certainly affect sex-role stereotypes. However, certain gender differences appear in so many different cultures — and in our culture before the television age — that they clearly are independent of electronic media.

One of these is sex-segregation — it appears whenever there are enough children to provide a real choice. Another is aggression, whether playful or real, in deeds or in dreams. In every corner of the world where children have been studied, boys are rougher and more violent than girls, and the difference begins by toddlerhood. Most investigators — including leading women in the field, such as psychologist Eleanor Maccoby and anthropologist Beatrice Whiting — have concluded that part of the explanation for this difference must be sought in biology.

Whiting, with her husband, John — both at Harvard University — led a famous study of children in six cultures around the world, using parallel, objective, observational research methods. The six cultures were a New England town ("Orchard Town"), and rural farming villages in Kenya, the Philippines, Japan, Mexico, and India. Statistical analysis, done in collaboration with Carolyn Pope Edwards of the University of Massachusetts at Amherst, showed that aggressive assaults and rough-and-tumble play (real and play fighting) were more likely in boys than girls in all the cultures, and the difference was apparent in three- to seven-year-olds.

Some years later Nicholas Blurton Jones, then at the Institute of Child Health in London, and I compared !Kung two- to five-year-old children with a similar sample of children playing outdoors in the summer in London parks. Sex-segregation was seen in London but not among the !Kung — perhaps because of the smaller number of children typically available. Also, boys exceeded girls in overall activity level in London children only. Yet in either real or playful aggression, boys exceeded girls in both cultures.

Given that kind of cross-cultural consistency — plus many parallels in monkeys, apes, and other mammals — it is not surprising that most authorities on gender development, including leading some women scientists, now accept that biology plays a small but irreducible part in determining the psychological differences between the sexes. Here is a sketch of how this may happen.

As we saw in chapter one, the basic body plan of the embryo in mammals is female; without special instructions that is how it will grow. But in males, the presence of the Y chromosome beside the X — as opposed to two X's in females — makes the difference. When the Y is present (even if there are also two X's), the body plan will diverge and become male. In 1990 scientists zeroed in on the gene for maleness, and soon we may know just how that gene works. But other genes are involved too; it is possible (though rare) for an XY individual to be resistant to the maleness gene, and to grow up with a woman's body.

This difference — genetic sex — is followed by hormonal sex. Late in fetal development, males have high levels of circulating testosterone, the male sex hormone. Animal experiments and a small amount of human clinical evidence, collected by Anke Ehrhardt of the Columbia University School of Medicine and June Reinisch of the Kinsey Institute, among others, point to the possibility that the brain is actually "masculinized" at this time. That is, it is given a greater tendency to spew out aggressive behavior later in life, among other differences. In any case, we know that male and female newborn infants differ a bit — males show greater muscular strength, females greater skin sensitivity.

But before such differences are even noticed, their sex is identified and influences caregivers. The same babies, dressed alternately in pink and blue, were treated differently by average adults in one study. So when, by a year of age, boys are more likely to attack a barrier to get a toy on the other side, while girls are more likely to cry — as shown by Susan Goldberg and Michael Lewis — we are already unable to say whether biology or experience has made the difference. The best answer now is "both." But by the age of three, patterns of self-typing, same-sex modeling, and sex-segregation — together with the influence of television — have created an environment that surely must exaggerate any biological predisposition toward boy-ness or girl-ness.

• • •

What we have now begun to realize is that biological predispositions toward sex differences are not the only, and probably not the most important, effects of biology. More powerful and more pervasive effects are being found for individual differences in behavior and personality — boys compared with other boys, girls with other girls. We now have about fifteen years of good research comparing identical with nonidentical twins, and comparing biological parents and children with adoptive parents and children. These studies have established that for many traits of personality a very large component of differences among children is caused by different genes. This includes such important general characteristics as sociability, emotionality, and activity level, as well as some very specific traits, such as fear of strangers, physical risk-taking, anger, persistence, and fidgeting. These traits have been repeatedly shown to be more similar in identical twins, who share the same genes, than in nonidentical twins, who are only as similar genetically as ordinary brothers and sisters. They are also traits in which adopted children resemble their biological parents more than they do the parents who adopted them.

Such biologically influenced personality traits are often called temperamental differences. Temperament is easily identified in babies — in fact, parents usually change their minds about its importance when their second child is born, since they know they are not responsible for differences at the outset. Here, for example, are observations made of two of my children, each at seven months of age:

> He's a pleasure to feed. He sees the spoon coming and he opens his mouth, waits gently while the spoon enters and smacks his tongue against his upper palate.

> Eating is an experience. She insists on holding the spoon as it goes into her mouth — spreading the contents everywhere. She enjoys herself.

It is only anecdotal evidence, but later in childhood I would say that she is still, among our children, the most insistent on managing her own world, while he is more easygoing and compliant while thoroughly enjoying life — a difference, incidentally, that runs counter to gender stereotype.

Still, it is harder to show that infant temperament lasts. By early childhood, though, many children have distinctive personality traits that are relatively stable. One of the most impressive new research findings about temperament comes from Jerome Kagan's laboratory, where he and his colleagues have spent most of the 1980s studying timidity. In children as young as fourteen months of age they are able to identify a subgroup that is unusually bold, and another subgroup that is the opposite — unusually timid. Those who at the earlier age were inhibited in a strange or novel situation grew up to be four- and five-year-olds who tended to be restrained and socially avoidant with unfamiliar children and adults, as well as more likely to show unusual fears — fear of television violence, for instance, or of being alone in their rooms at night.

This stability of timidity or shyness surprised many psychologists, including Kagan himself — during the 1970s he had emphasized the difficulty of proving the stability of *any* trait that could be measured in early childhood. Not only is the trait of timidity stable, but it is also associated with biological measures that may link genes to the behavior. In particular, there are signs of a higher tension or tone in the sympathetic nervous system — known in biology as the "fight or flight" system.

The signs? — a higher resting heart rate, with comparatively little variation from moment to moment; a greater increase in heart rate and higher blood pressure in the strange situations; greater dilation of the pupils of the eyes during questioning; greater tension in the vocal cords; higher levels of the stress hormone cortisol; and greater activity in the manufacture and processing of norepinephrine — the principal chemical produced by nerve cells in the same "fight or flight" system.

Animal experiments on the same physiological factors suggest that the limbic system, or emotional brain, may have a lower threshold for arousal — something more like a hair trigger — in inhibited children. Common parlance might say that such children are high-strung. Perhaps the genetic mechanism has something to do with the enzymes that process norepinephrine — a nerve chemical closely related to adrenaline, which the body pumps out during fight or flight. These speculations await further research on the relationships between the child's brain and behavior. But the identity of this special subgroup of young children — perfectly normal, yet distinctive in both their behavior and their biology — is now secure. They may be identifiable even at age four months. The pattern is one of the key childhood research findings of the decade. And it is probably only the tip of an iceberg of biologically related stable traits in children, most of which await discovery.

• • •

One of the ironies of recent research on children is that some of our keenest insights into the effects of the *environment* are coming from studies of the biological, often genetic, components of behavior. For example, Kagan points out that two-thirds of the uninhibited children in his studies are firstborn children, while two-thirds of the timid ones are later-born. Since there is no reason to expect a genetic difference between children of different birth orders, we must look for an environmental cause of the greater timidity of later-borns, bringing out some underlying genetic predisposition. Kagan speculates that later-born children may experience their older siblings as sources of stress that can bring out any timid tendencies they might have.

Robert Plomin, of Pennsylvania State University, a leading investigator of genes and personality in children, has emphasized a more general fact that emerges from such research: However the environment may have its effect on us, it works in such a way as to make children in the same family very different. The simplest way to look at it is to face this fact, one example of the concept: Identical twins — same genes, remember — are often more alike in personality, and certainly no less alike, if they are raised in different families than if they are raised in the same family.

This whole notion is a serious paradox and challenge for research. Given all the things that families try to provide equally to all their children — religion, schooling, television, bedtimes, diet, household rules, toys — it seems remarkable that environment cannot help much in accounting for differences between children in different families. At the same time, it does not seem that the environment for different children within the same family could be different enough to explain much of anything. Yet it does.

Birth order comes to mind as a possibility — certainly it is emphasized in the folklore parents pass around — "Beware the middle child," for example. But in fact careful analysis of all the research on birth order has shown that it just is not very important in explaining much of anything — Kagan's theory of timidity notwithstanding. The folklore about it has only a little more scientific basis than astrology.

Still, somehow siblings are getting very different environments in the same family. It might be that parents are playing favorites, not because of birth order, but on some other grounds — say, similarity to the parent in looks or temperament. Recall that one of the things we learned from the great wave of baby research in the 1970s was that children strongly influence their parents — not just the other way round. Every pairing of parent and child produces a unique relationship, and a unique environment for the child. In one case opposites might attract, in another similarities might produce sympathy, while in yet another similarities between the child and one parent might lead the other parent either to love or hate the child. Unfortunately, mere physical appearance, including simple attractiveness, plays a major role.

Clearly too, if we concede that children can influence their parents, then surely they must also affect each other. Take our identical twins. In the same family they may be constantly trying to assert their individual identities in the face of a sometimes unsettling similarity — thus becoming more different than identical twins adopted away and raised separately. *Those* twins, unaware of each other, are more free just to be themselves, and their shared genes may make them even more similar. A different process may operate between ordinary siblings. Through the luck of shuffled genes, they often present each other with marked personality differences. For instance, a plain, quiet girl with a flamboyant and pretty sister will have a very different childhood environment from the same girl with a devoted, gentle brother. Here the luck of the draw in personality and appearance could have much more of an impact than birth order.

One of the exciting research trends of the 1980s has been a focus on siblings with regard not to birth order, but to interaction. The question is: What do siblings do to and for each other, and how do parents shape relationships among their children? Judy Dunn, of Pennsylvania State University, has contributed much to answering it, with over a decade of systematic studies. She and her colleagues have identified the parents' treatment of two children as having an important influence on their relationship with each other. For instance, the mother who involves her older child — even a three- or four-year-old — in the care of the new baby promotes a better relationship between them. The mother who plays favorites promotes sibling rivalry. As expected, the random factor in the combination of temperaments also has an important effect on the sibling bond.

Consider Stas Popov, three and a half when his baby brother Vitaly was born. The four went to stay with a grandmother, and Stas watched the sleeping baby intently. "Who did you wish for, a brother or sister?" his father asks.

"A sister."

"But will you love your brother anyway?" Stas doesn't answer, and he and his dad begin some rough-and-tumble play. Then Stas continues it by throwing a big Mickey Mouse doll around. He jumps on it, wrestles it to the ground, and pounds its head against the wall.

A while later Vitaly is awake, sucking on his pacifier while Stas stares down at him again from the crib railing. "I'll kill you, you boob, I'll kill you, stupid. There. I'll kill you and that'll be all. You'll just lie there. Stupid."

A doctor comes in to examine Vitaly and talk with his mother Larissa. Stas keeps up his litany of death threats right through their conversation, and even directs some at the doctor and his mother, brandishing a toy gun. "You'll be left all alone," his mother says, but this consideration doesn't have much weight for Stas. Soon after the doctor leaves, Larissa muses while folding diapers:

> When they turn five or six they become more mild, more agreeable. I don't know though how he will turn out. But for the time being he's very difficult. And I try to be as tender as I can be, but sometimes I just don't have the patience, I get exasperated. Sometimes I just have to spank him. Of course, that's not a way out. I feel that physical punishment is — Yeah, there's some other way, but somehow you don't always have the patience.

Meanwhile Stas is clobbering his father's engineering books.

When they get to their new apartment, Stas is visibly upset. He has faced a physical and an emotional displacement both at the same time. He takes up a leather strap and begins whipping his father with all his might.

"It hurts, Stas. Stop it. Don't you ever feel pity?"

"Never. . . . I care for Mom, but not for you."

"Why don't you care for me?"

"Because you're bad. . . . You're gonna get it now. Take that!" More whipping, then hitting his father with other objects, and making faces.

A few weeks later, when Vitaly is able to roll over, Mikhail has apparently worked out a way to channel Stas's potentially destructive energy. They roughhouse together, and Stas does some flipping, hand-walking, and other gymnastics while suspended from his father's hands. His aggressiveness seems to have abated somewhat, but not so as to have made him mild-mannered.

Contrast Stas with the Nouhata brothers, Koichiro and Yojiro, respectively four and a half and two and a half at their baby brother Kenzaburo's birth. Despite being more closely spaced, they show no overt aggression with the new baby around, even when he is breast-fed. Yojiro seems to be too young to immediately conceptualize his displacement, and Koichiro clearly is wary and cautious about the new intruder. But neither shows overt anger resembling Stas's. The Nouhatas try to discourage favoritism and sibling rivalry, symbolically involving the boys in the baby's care. But the Popovs try to do the same with Stas, with much less effect — particularly on his expressions of jealous aggression. Temperament plays an important role in sibling relationships from the beginning.

So does age-spacing: More years between the siblings seem to mean less rivalry. This is interesting, because birth spacing among hunters and gatherers like the !Kung averages four years, due mainly to prolonged frequent nursing. This may be a "natural" birth spacing for our species, and it is longer than spacing in most modern families. Competition also seems to decrease as both siblings grow older.

The Gholston children demonstrate the folly of always thinking *rivalry* first and foremost when you hear the word *sibling*. Benjamin, Malcolm, and Avery benefit from each other constantly — as we saw clearly with Avery's language learning. Their interactions are tender and mutually helpful, and their parents set the standard and the tone for this tenderness. Urie Bronfenbrenner has said,

> The family is the place where we learn how to deal with other human beings. It is a kind of museum in which the outside world is brought in to play with, to work with, and to have fun with, before it gets to be real. It sort of tilts the future in this or that direction. It tells us how we relate to problems, and to solutions, and what obligations are, and what responsibilities are.

The Gholstons seem to have this ideal in their bones.

Consider Christmas 1990. The whole extended family seems to be assembled in the Gholstons' house, and the children are excited and happy. They open presents under their mother Anita's supervision. Despite how hectic things get, Avery (who is wearing her dinner) exchanges lovely coy glances with both parents across the crowded, heavily laden table. Felton, the father, calls Benjamin over for a delicious-looking hug. But he has spent most of the day cooking for all the relatives, and then has to drive some of them home. Meanwhile, Anita gets the kids into pajamas and up the stairs, where she reads them a traditional African story from a brand-new book with beautiful pictures. During the reading the boys mumble something about a train set, but Anita just says skeptically, "We'll see about that."

Soon Felton puts his head in the door. "C'mere, Daddy," Anita says. "Did you tell them that you were gonna set up the train set tonight?"

"Well, I did kind of stick myself into that position."

"Oh, well we're gonna have to undo that."

"Please! Please! Please!" start the boys.

"What time is it?" Anita asks.

Felton checks the clock. "Eleven-oh-seven."

"Uh-uh," says Mom. "No. I'll be the bad guy. Absolutely not. It's after eleven o'clock."

Sounds perfectly reasonable; but of course, here's where the crying starts. Benjamin and Malcolm in perfect unison, synchronized wails full of anguish, deepened by a desperate need for beddy-bye.

This is what you might call a united sibling front. After a minute or so of rhythmic moaning and crocodile tears, Benjamin, who is standing on the bed, vomits up some of his dinner. "Benji!" says his mom with an astounding degree of calm. Now Malcolm, seeing that his big brother has changed his approach, leans over his mother's arm and starts to throw up too. They're not exactly in synchrony with their retches, but even with close siblings nothing's perfect. Now, however, as a sort of last flourish, two-and-a-half-year-old Avery gets into the act. She stares at her two brothers' remarkable performance, toddles over to them, and starts to dry heave. She can't seem to bring anything up, but we have to give her credit for trying to keep the sibling front really united.

Felton not only whistles philosophically as he changes the sheets; he also gets it together to be a patient, loving father again when his kids troop back from the bedroom. He sits down with them on the edge of the bed, obviously sympathetic rather than angry. "All right, we got to talk about the train, guys. C'mere, c'mere, c'mere." His voice is gentle, patient, earnest, and almost formal.

"I know that Dad promised you all day that I would put the train together. Okay — I didn't. You're right. But I was cooking all day. I got to cooking, and I blew it. I know. I know. But I'll put the train together tonight." By this time Malcolm is sitting on his lap while Felton holds him close, Benjamin is in the crook of his other arm, and Avery is on his back with her arms around his neck. "Okay?" Felton asks. "Don't make yourself sick." Finally Felton releases a sigh of total exhaustion.

But he keeps his promise. The train set is ready, even though he has had to leave for work before they awaken. As I watched Felton Gholston handle this episode, what I was thinking was, Here is a man who respects his children. He also clearly loves them, of course, but respect is something additional. If Urie Bronfenbrenner is right about the family, then it's a good bet they will grow up respecting themselves and others.

•   •   •

Psychologists have also looked at how experience between siblings affects experience between peers outside the home — say, in a day-care center. Little has come out of this effort so far. Perhaps it will one day; but in most anthropological settings, especially in small-scale societies such as the !Kung or the Baka, *peers* in the child psychologist's sense simply don't exist. Given the wide average birth spacing and the small number of families that make up a band or village, the chances of finding other children *the same age* to play with are very low.

But there is no cause for concern about children's restricted experience in such societies. It's only in our kind of society that "peers" have come to be synonymous with "playmates." In most societies playmates are not agemates, but they play perfectly well together — better, in fact, than agemates do. Child psychologists have made the study of social play synonymous with the study of peers. Conventional wisdom used to have it that two-year-olds were capable only of parallel play — they looked as if they were playing together, but actually they were quite egocentric, playing separately next to each other. Later, went the C.W., they engaged in "joint monologues" — these looked like conversations but each interlocutor was in a world of her own, taking turns but not really communicating.

Later research challenged the C.W. No, said the new studies, young children aren't as egocentric as all that; if you look hard enough, you can find ways that they actually interact. Now there is a new C.W. that finds a series of stages in which interaction between peers slowly and subtly improves — but, like most things in child development, comes earlier than was previously thought.

All these ideas, old and new, about playmate interaction, may just be experimental artifacts, caused by relentless insistence on only studying playmates who are just the same age. This sort of stubbornness is true of society at large, at least in the United States — teachers, parents, Little League coaches, everybody thinks that playmates should be the same age. But outside our society, in most of the world's traditional cultures, such a prejudice would be unworkable. Play groups are made up of children of different ages; if two are the same age, it is only by accident. In many settings they also include different sexes, breaking one of the strongest habits observed in Western children's groups.

Consider the advantages of multi-age groups. Younger children get playmates who are partly caretakers and teachers. They go through no wrenching transition such as Western children do, from a social world full of loving adults who make few demands on them, meeting them much more than halfway in the interaction, to a world full of socially inept toddler-peers with whom they have to eke out a stuttering semblance of relationships. Instead, they graduate slowly from adult caregivers to ten- and twelve-year-olds, then to seven-year-olds, and so on down to infants younger than they are. Each of these categories makes increasingly challenging demands on the toddler's social skills, shaping her up bit by bit until she becomes a competent playmate. The play setting is safe for her, and she has the opportunity to learn language, survival skills, and games from children ahead of her in the process of development.

As for older children, they get practice for parenting, the cognitive stimulation of having to teach what they know, and a chance to feel important and responsible. For some kinds of play, the group may break up into smaller units with narrower age ranges, but these will still be multiage groups. The culture as a whole gets a substantial amount of childwatching from children — or more precisely, from the play group — as well as an efficient means of transmitting the culture itself, without relying so heavily on the transgenerational adult-child confrontation that constitutes Western education.

In addition, these groups throw together siblings, cousins, even little aunts and uncles in a way that makes it hard to distinguish playmates from family. In a traditional society, in fact, it would be very unlikely for researchers to invent sibling relations and peer relations as separate fields of study, because they would grade so smoothly into each other. As anthropologist Thomas Wiesner, of the University of California at Los Angeles, has pointed out, our particular preoccupation with sibling rivalry would not have emerged so strongly in one of these societies, where sibling cooperation throughout life is a matter of survival, and foundations for it must be laid in childhood.

As for our cultural and research preoccupation with same-age peers, it seems likely to be an artifact of our obsession with competition in general. If you don't play ball and do spelling bees with children the same age — not to mention competing with them in dressing — how will you ever know who's better than you? Come to think of it, perhaps it's a valid preoccupation for a culture in which the quintessential social act is comparing oneself to someone else.

• • •

One day when my son, Adam, was just past four, I came home from a visit to Fermilab — the Fermi National Accelerator Laboratory outside Chicago. As I put him to bed that night, I started to regale him with details of my tour around the atom-smasher. Fortunately, it was not long before I realized that he was having visions of boys named Adam accelerating at colossal speeds around a mile-long ring, smashing together to produce a blinding flash of energy. He didn't lose his sense of humor; still, I think he was relieved to find out that atoms were not Adams, but were only teensy flecks of dust that released quarks when shattered. (Spontaneously, he proposed that quarks must have colors.)

I wonder whether he thought of this talk years later, while consoling his trembling sister (then three and a half) in her keen need to know if the Hansel and Gretel opera was "a movie" or "real." The distinction between appearance and reality is not an easy one at this age, and imagination can cause great emotion just because of a misheard word. One way of looking at it is that the child's mind is powerful enough to generate fantasies — basically, very elaborate symbols — but not mature enough to test them in the apparatus of logic.

Young children's command of the appearance-reality distinction has been an important subject of study in the past few years, partly because their testimony has been crucial to certain kinds of court cases — particularly those involving allegations of sexual abuse. This research has indicated that young children are more suggestible than older children, distorting their memories more in response to misleading information. But when they provide *spontaneous* memories, they do not make more errors.

Between three and a half and four and a half years of age, children improve markedly in their ability correctly to label objects and their properties as apparent or real — a paper flower, for instance, or a small object under a magnifying glass. Nicki, a grandson of "Childhood" series observer Urie Bronfenbrenner, says, "He's getting bigger," while looking at an ant under a magnifying glass, and there seems to be a moment of confusion before he concludes that this is just an illusion of bigness. This improvement occurs at the same age and in the same way in China and the United States, so it is likely to be the result of universal features of the developing brain working on similar information. But we also know that three-year-olds are capable of deliberate deception — to cover up a transgression, for instance; this shows a different kind of command of the appearance-reality split.

The growth of pretending follows an equally dramatic course. Piaget described its emergence in his daughter Jacqueline (at one year, three months, twelve days of age) in his book *Play, Dreams, and Imitation in Childhood.* He views it as the beginning of "make-believe":

> She saw a cloth whose fringed edges vaguely recalled those of her pillow; she seized it, held a fold of it in her right hand, sucked the thumb of the same hand and lay down on her side, laughing hard. She kept her eyes open, but blinked from time to time as if she were alluding to closed eyes.

In Botswana I made the following note on a !Kung boy whose age I recorded as sixty-six weeks:

> While playing his customary cloth game (pulling it over his head, face, behind his back while walking around with it) at one point lays it out on the ground, kneels and then lays down on it perfectly motionless for a short while. This is the same as Jacqueline Piaget's first step into representation. . . .

This emergence of pretend-symbolizing coincides roughly with the earliest emergence of those other great symbols, words, but the two abilities may be processed differently in the child's brain. By age three, children are capable of remarkably advanced pretending that integrates language and symbol perfectly. Consider this exchange between two three-year-olds, a boy and a girl, in a study in the laboratory of Willard Hartup of the University of Minnesota:

> "Hello, Mr. Dinosaur."
> "Hello, Mr. Skeleton."

In two years from the first appearance of language, the child has become capable of elaborate pretense, metaphor, humor, and collaborative imagining — all packed into three words.

Children this age throughout the world use dolls or other small objects to represent people and animals, and this gives them the power to make the world theirs. One group of three-, four-, and five-year-olds I observed among the !Kung were using clumps of earth to represent hyenas. The "hyenas" surrounded a hapless goat, represented in turn by a root. "Pudi zaha !ki," they shouted gleefully over and over — "The goat's already dead." They thus acted out the drama of competition, hunting, killing, and survival around which they knew their lives turned. In a study of puppet shows put on by three-year-olds in Paris — a more structured pretend-situation — children invented surprisingly complex sequences. In one, "Big Dog" frightens "Little Girl," and Little Girl hides successfully. In another, Big Dog "does poo-poo" in his pants, and is punished, but only mildly, with scolding. It is not difficult to see in these scenarios the working through of children's hopes and fears.

It is a realm, one might say, where Freud offers a more helpful map than Piaget. Take one recent Piaget-inspired study: It showed that most middle-class two-year-olds can make a doll act as an agent — a doer — in symbolic play; that three-year-olds can make the doll perform several acts involved in a role, such as doctor; that four- or five-year-olds can make two dolls interact in separate roles (patient and doctor); and that six-year-olds can imagine the same doll in two intersecting roles — say, doctor and parent. This is good standard developmental psychology, and it does teach some dry pale facts about small children.

But one would scarcely guess from it that it was done three decades after Erik Erikson, one of the pioneers of child psychotherapy, published his observations. In his book *Childhood and Society* he recounted 450 play scenes constructed and acted out by 150 children over the course of a year and a half. He wrote in summary:

> The microsphere — i.e. the small world of manageable toys — is a harbor which the child establishes, to return to when he needs to overhaul his ego. . . . [It] seduces the child into an unguarded expression of dangerous themes and attitudes which arouse anxiety. . . . [T]he pleasure of mastering toy things becomes associated with the mastery of the traumas which were projected on them, and with the prestige gained through such mastery.

It may seem odd to speak of prestige in mastering toys, but Erikson had great respect for children. And of play therapy, he says something that might be said of all imaginative play — that "to 'play it out' is the most natural self-healing measure childhood affords." At the same time, children play out fantasies with themselves and their friends or relatives as symbolic stand-ins, in many ways more effective than dolls and toys. Children at this age are beset with strong emotions, and many of these children generate rich fantasies. It is a time of imaginary playmates, invented husbands, wives, and children, scary animals and people, miraculous rescues, and overwhelming triumphs in which children win out over powerful grown-ups again and again. And above all, perhaps, they act out different versions of themselves.

Children, incidentally, also differ in their tendency to fantasize, and studies show that such differences are only partly responsive to teaching efforts. I had a chance to interview one four- (*four-and-three-quarters!*) year-old of my acquaintance in the afternoon sunlight of her parlor, and I asked her what interesting things she did that I might put in my book. Without missing a beat, smoothing her pretty dress, and with her most demure feminine smile, she calmly said, "I bite the heads off of fish, and suck their guts out. Then I spit 'em in the trash." It so happens she dotes on her goldfish, and in her daily life is quite devoid of aggression. But in this sudden fantasy she delighted in some fairly violent images, imagining someone utterly changed from the delicate small girl. Also, of course, she was tweaking my nose, mocking my serious adult project with a burst of unpredictable, wacky, and thoroughly satisfying invention.

But these imagined selves can be more serious. My eldest was sitting and bouncing on my chest once when she was just past three. After a while, to save my ribs (not to mention my breath), I engaged her in a chat about her future life. What would you like to be when you grow up? — a writer? or a doctor? or a dancer?

"I will be a doctor," she said. Why a doctor? "I will be a doctor, because when I grow up I will be big and you will be small, and I will be a doctor, and I will take care of you." I could imagine a real version of this fantasy; but more important is the meaning it had for her. Many children this age imagine that growth is reversible, and that their parents will grow small as they grow big. But the point here is the role reversal. She was imagining her grown-up self in such a way as to mitigate her anxiety about some of her most frightening glimmers of knowledge: that growth could eventually separate her from her parents; that her father could become old and die; and that she and I could each in turn need tender loving care. Doctor or not, I suspect I will feel quite safe in her hands.

• • •

Some people, including a few misguided authorities, believe that young children should be protected from the most powerful fantasies. They even go to the length of preparing cleaned-up versions of classic fairy tales so that children will not be distressed by violence. Some people even bowdlerize Bible stories. The point they miss is that parents and children have loved these tales for centuries because they help us — even the littlest of us — to deal with thoughts and feelings we are going to have anyway. This was the theme argued by Bruno Bettelheim, another pioneer of child psychotherapy, in *The Uses of Enchantment*:

> There is a widespread refusal to let children know that the source of much that goes wrong in life is due to our very own natures — the propensity of all men for acting aggressively, asocially, selfishly, out of anger and anxiety. Instead, we want our children to believe that, inherently, all men are good. But children know that *they* are not always good; and often, even when they are, they would prefer not to be. This contradicts what they are told by their parents, and therefore makes the child a monster in his own eyes.

Fairy tales, in contrast, get the message across to the child "that a struggle against severe difficulties in life is unavoidable, is an intrinsic part of human existence — but that if one does not shy away . . . one masters all obstacles and at the end emerges victorious." Similar views have been expressed by Maurice Sendak, the children's author, in defense of his immensely popular *Where the Wild Things Are*. In that book little Max, on his nighttime travels, encounters a group of ugly, terrifying monsters. They try to threaten him, "till Max said, 'Be still!' and tamed them with the magic trick of staring into all their yellow eyes . . . and they were frightened and called him the most wild thing of all."

We needn't go along with all of Bettelheim's psychoanalytic interpretations; the basic meanings of many tales are easy to follow. Children need and love fairy tales that show them triumphing over powerful, threatening strangers ("Little Red Riding Hood," "Jack and the Beanstalk," "Hansel and Gretel"), escape from evil parents ("Cinderella," "Rapunzel," "Snow White"), and recovery from vengeful enchantment ("The Sleeping Beauty," "The Frog Prince"). The stories in the last two categories all achieve resolution through romantic love; consider what they might mean to the little boys and girls we saw earlier, already fantasizing about their imagined spouses and girl- or boyfriends. The tales in the first category simply reflect the reality of life for all children — that strangers may be dangerous. It is also the reality of their emotions: Fear of strangers, we know, is primal in infancy.

Perhaps it is evil parents that disturb us most about fairy tales, although they are transformed into stepparents — not quite the real thing — in most stories. Still, in the real world as it is, parents, step- or otherwise, can sometimes be very dangerous. In moments of parental anger, a child's life may hang in the balance. In some sad, frightening sense, this possibility is part of the evolutionary and historical legacy borne by every parent, every child. Love them as we may, they have to fear us. And they certainly have to fear many others.

Is this a fantasy or is this real? asks tiny Sarah at the *Hansel and Gretel* opera. Child, it is both; I wish it were otherwise, but I can't remake the world. Watch the witch try to kill the children. She won't succeed — they will kill her instead. Watch, and work through the fear and trembling. Think, and hope, and dream your way through it. You are stronger than you think. Like Hansel and Gretel in the fairy tale, you can survive; you can win.

1.

2.

4.

3.

5.

1. Baka baby-sitting: Kamala gets care from Djadja.

2. The Gholston brothers, Benjamin, five, and Malcolm, four, in action.

3. In most of the world farming and child care go hand in hand, and the mother's work load determines much about child care. Fulani mother and child, Upper Volta.

4. Simone, fourteen, Suelen, two and a half, and Sergio, four, three of the six Oliveira children.

5. A slum boy get a lift from his brother in a turn-of-the-century New York City playground.

6.

7.

6. They need other children: rough-and-tumble, or maybe gentle-and-tumble play in Hong Kong.

7. They need imaginative play: !Kung children playing "truck."

8. And sometimes they need solitude: Avery Gholston, two, tries out a Christmas present.

8.

9, 10. Fathers often provide a jazzier, less tender sort of care than mothers do.

11. The Emporar Shah Jahan, builder of the Taj Mahal, and his son Shuja, India, seventeenth century. Another son was to make war against his brothers and imprison their father.

9.

10.

11.

12. A young girl, who is deaf, signs the word *butterfly*.

13. Little Red Riding Hood, as seen in an 1863 pop-up book. In traditional versions of the story, she and her grandmother are eaten and sometimes surgically removed from the wolf's body, but modern versions are milder. Psychoanalyst Bruno Bettelheim and children's author Maurice Sendak both argue strongly that children need to hear violent and frightening tales through which they can master their own fear and rage.

12.

13.

14, 15. Children love stories that toy with growth. Alice becomes tall and small at will (sort of) by drinking a potion or eating cakes.

16. An anonymous nineteenth-century illustration for *Jack the Giant Killer.*

17. A cartoon from the popular series "The Far Side" by Gary Larson.

14.

15.

16.

THE FAR SIDE   By GARY LARSON

"Big Bob says he's getting tired of you saying he doesn't really exist."

17.

18.

19.

20.

18. Pieter Brueghel the Younger's *Massacre of the Innocents* depicts Herod's army killing children in a vain search for the child Jesus Christ.

19. The god Saturn (Cronos) devours his own children in a Goya painting.

20. Yet reality can be worse than myth. History's largest and most systematic action against children was the Nazi Holocaust, in which one and one-half million Jewish children were murdered. German soldiers documented this accomplishment, which many were proud of.

21. An American photograph from around 1860, following the custom of formal portraiture after a child's death.

22. Wake of eighteen-month-old Gerlie Azura, Philippines, 1986.

21.

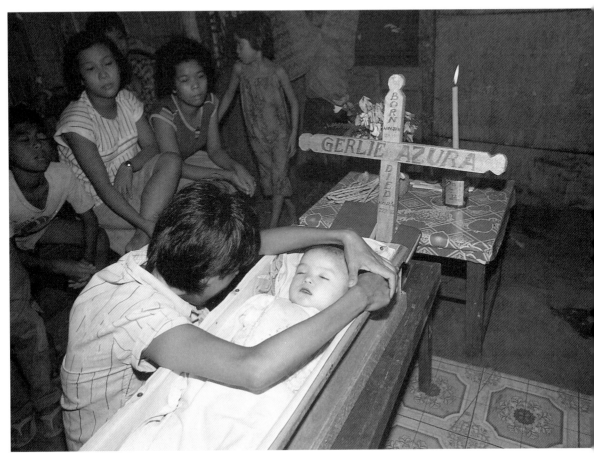

22.

FIVE

Vulnerability and Resilience

Now I was eight and very small,
    And he was no whit bigger.
And so I smiled, but he poked out
    His tongue, and called me, "Nigger."

I saw the whole of Baltimore
    From May until December;
Of all the things that happened there
    That's all that I remember.

— COUNTEE CULLEN, "Incident"

This world is so full of care and sorrow that it is a gracious debt we owe to one another to discover the bright crystals of delight. . . .

— HELEN KELLER

———

ONE-FOURTH OF U.S. BIRTHS Are to Unmarried Women"; "Addiction to Crack Can Kill Parental Instinct"; "Watching the Babies Die: Romanian AIDS Scandal"; "Shots Through a Bronx Door Kill a Baby in His Walker"; "CDC: Lead Levels Still Poisoning Kids"; "A Child's Nightmare in Italy Is Now the Nation's Shame"; "Child Labor and Sweatshops on the Rise"; "The Sex Abuse Puzzle"; "One-Fifth of the Nation's Children: Why Are They Poor?"; "Let's Stop Selling Cancer to Children"; "After an 18-Year Decline, Teen-Age Births Are Up"; "Growing Up Scared"; "Mom Goes to War"; "Why Is America Failing Its Children?" These are the headlines of some news articles in my lap at the moment, all from respectable, even distinguished publications.

Consider what is under just one of the headlines. On Saturday, July 14, 1990, on a stretch of highway not far from Florence, Italy, Vanessa

Moretti, six years old, was driving with her father, Marco, age thirty-three. They had just entered a tunnel when Mr. Moretti suffered a heart attack. Before his death minutes later, he managed to pull off to the side, near the tunnel wall. Dying, he told Vanessa to find her way home. She left the car and began to walk through the tunnel in heavy vacation-weekend traffic. Blasts of wind created by speeding cars knocked her down repeatedly, so that she stumbled along crying, scratched, and bleeding. She walked out of the tunnel onto the open highway, desperately searching for help among the rushing vehicles — for thirty minutes, covering more than a mile — a vulnerable, suffering six-year-old, ignored by thousands of drivers, almost any one of whom could easily have killed her.

Luckily, none of them did; Vanessa was not seriously injured. But the same could not be said of Italy's sense of its better self. Little Vanessa's lonely walk precipitated a period of national soul-searching, and the result was not favorable. One respected newspaper, *L'Unita,* put it this way: "A sheet of glass is interposed between us and the world that once and for all eliminates real, tangible and sensitive awareness of others." Even of children in desperate need of simple aid.

It is a comment that applies not just to Italy, but to all the nations of the earth. The saddest headlines deal with the developing world — for example, "25% of Girls in India Die by Age 15, Unicef Says," "Killing and Torturing of Children Charged in Brazil by Rights Panel," and "On Nairobi's Streets 50,000 Children Play Games of Despair." They and others that appear every day paint a picture of a nation and a wider world that has ceased to care about children. It is a world in which children are asked to fend for themselves, and in which — like the stranded, savage boys in *Lord of the Flies* — they do not fend very well.

The question on my mind as I lay this depressing news on the desk is "How much can children take?" Or maybe more precisely, "How much can children take and still . . ." What? Be happy? Learn? Contribute to society? Avoid mental illness? Master their impulses? Respect their elders? Carry on their culture and its values? Grow up at all? Survive?

• • •

One way to begin thinking about whether children's needs can be met in today's world is to look back. Two ideas about what childhood used to be like have gained such a wide hearing that it is necessary to mention them although they are now discredited. The first was promulgated by

Phillipe Ariès, a distinguished French social historian who is often credited with founding the history of childhood as a discipline. His idea was that people didn't use to recognize that children were really different from adults. One line of evidence for this view was the study of paintings of the pre-Renaissance period, in which children are depicted as having the same body proportions as adults but smaller in size.

Together with circumstantial evidence about child care (especially such things as children's chores) these studies of art led to the idea that, historically, people actually did not know that children are really different from adults — and so did not meet their psychological needs. Anthropologists found this notion implausible because although they could not directly study the people of medieval Europe, they were able to interview and observe living people in all kinds of societies throughout the world — including peasant societies quite reminiscent of the European past. They found many varieties of child care and training, and many strange and original notions about children, but lack of awareness of the profound differences between children's and adults' capabilities and needs was not among them. Every parent since the world began has had this awareness and alternately delighted in and bemoaned the differences.

Ariès, although he helped to found a whole subfield of social history — children had been quite neglected by historians — was more or less relegated to the domain of art history, where his theory is recognized as having more to do with painterly skill and representational tradition than with actual beliefs. Subsequently, in the 1960s and 1970s, a new theory came to dominate notions about childhood's past. This theory, spearheaded by Lloyd de Mause, then editor of *The History of Childhood Quarterly,* claimed that all past societies treated children brutally, and that all historical change in their treatment has been a fairly steady improvement toward the kind and gentle standards we now set and more or less meet. His 1974 book begins,

> The history of childhood is a nightmare from which we have only recently begun to awaken. The further back in history one goes, the lower the level of child care, and the more likely children are to be killed, abandoned, beaten, terrorized, and sexually abused.

Now anthropologists — and many historians as well — were slack-jawed and nearly speechless. Studies of parents, children, and the family in cultures on every inhabited continent had turned up not a single case — with one or two possible exceptions — of extant patterns of child care that corresponded to the brutal, neglectful approach that these historians were assigning to all the parents of the past.

On the contrary, serious students of the anthropology of childhood beginning with Margaret Mead have called attention to the pervasive love and care lavished on children in many traditional cultures. They even found much Westerners could admire and possibly emulate. And all known cultures made some major accommodations to the limited capabilities of children. Since many of the societies anthropologists observed roughly resembled those the historians studied through documents — especially peasant societies socially dominated by a hereditary nobility — it seemed dubious that the documents were being correctly interpreted. In any case, a generalization like "The further back in history one goes, the lower the level of child care" was very unlikely to be true.

The history of childhood is now in more capable hands. Scholars such as Ray Hiner, John Demos, Linda Pollock, and Shulamith Shahar are producing a more balanced and more believable account that weighs continuities with the past against important changes, and gives proper attention to enormous variations from place to place as well as from time to time — not to mention social class differences.

Hiner, a pioneer in this effort, has discovered and assembled a large body of new historical sources. He has called attention to the peripheralization of the father during the industrial revolution as compared with the agricultural past. Pollock has also assembled and published precious sources, and has played a major role in debunking de Mause. Demos has drawn attention to past echoes of modern problems, saying for example that "one can make the case that there was about as much dissolution of the family in the nineteenth century through desertion as there is today through divorce." Shahar, who meticulously disposes of both de Mause and Ariès in her new book, *Childhood in the Middle Ages*, challenges the view that people of that era were indifferent to children. She shows that putting a child out to a wet nurse was often as deliberate and careful a choice for families as day-care is today.

Without getting into subtleties that social historians still argue over, some things inspire almost complete agreement. I will forgo for now any mention of dates or places, in order to achieve generalizations that, surprisingly enough, will in each case apply to a centuries-long process affecting the whole world. This is not to say that the changes took place at the same time or the same rate in all these different instances. Rather, they are widely staggered in various parts of the world, having begun half a millennium ago in some regions and yesterday in others, having more or less run their course in some but going on at their peak rate in others. Nor does it imply that there are no exceptions or temporary reversals. What it does imply is that these broad trends can be counted on eventually to affect people in most of the world. Put simply, they can be summarized as the impact of modernization on childhood.

- Mortality — death rate — in children, infants, and mothers bearing those infants has declined steadily throughout the world. Contrary to popular belief, this change is not mainly the result of improved medical care, but of social and economic changes that prevent infectious disease.
- Several generations after these decreasing death rates, birth rates have declined in most societies. But they remain high enough worldwide to cause present and future disaster from crowding.
- These two processes, known as the demographic transition, have caused in turn an increase, and then a decrease, in family size.
- Rates of disease in childhood have decreased, while nutritional quality and quantity have improved.
- The size of children of a given age, their rate of growth, and the speed with which they reach puberty have all increased, mostly because of the factors just mentioned.
- Child labor and chore assignment have increased, then decreased, while schooling and literacy have increased.
- An increasing proportion of children have been growing up in cities — one of the strongest trends throughout the world.
- Mass electronic communication has reached an increasing proportion of children. This trend has its own momentum; in much of the developing world abject poverty somehow coexists with television aerials.

All these trends apply to the transformation of settled agricultural societies into societies based on industrial production. That is what is meant by modernization. But there is a deeper history to the human species, one that reaches down through many more millennia to the hunting-and-gathering past. Here the notion of harsh and neglectful parents can in most cases seem only surreal.

Recall, for instance, what we have seen among the !Kung. Infants are put to the breast within hours of birth, and are fed in this way an average of four times an hour for three years or longer. They sleep beside their parents so that their needs can be responded to without delay, and in the daytime, they are in physical contact with the mother or another caregiver 90 percent of the time. As for responsiveness to crying, Ronald Barr, Roger Bakeman, and Lauren Adamson recently calculated from my data on the !Kung that 92 percent of fussing or crying episodes are responded to by a caregiver within fifteen seconds.

Fathers take a definite backseat to mothers (as in every known culture) but spend more time with their infants and young children than do fathers in middle-class American families. Physical punishment is rare, verbal punishment infrequent. !Kung parents believe that children are mentally immature ("without sense") and must be allowed to be infants and children; the passage of time (growth) is seen as both necessary and sufficient gradually to eliminate their less-desirable behaviors.

Certainly not all small-scale traditional cultures, nor even all hunting-and-gathering cultures, maintain quite so indulgent an attitude toward infants and children. But throughout history, including prehistory, many cultures maintained patterns that make even ideal middle-class child-training seem harsh, even neglectful, by comparison.

In a pioneering 1953 study, John Whiting and Irvin Child examined the parenting practices of a broad cross-cultural sample — forty-seven traditional societies from around the world — and compared them to an American reference group of fifty middle-class families in Chicago. All the societies were rated on parents' indulgence of needs and severity of training in five different areas of children's behavior: nursing and weaning, toilet training, sex training (including modesty, and prohibition of masturbation and sexually explicit play), independence, and aggression. Overall, the Chicago middle-class families were at the extreme of low indulgence and high severity as compared to the traditional societies, although there were some primitive cultures at the same extreme. The exception was children's aggressive behavior, which was treated more indulgently in Chicago — making it more similar to the average for the other cultures.

With this background, it seems misguided to characterize American middle-class child care as the historical pinnacle of indulgent concern for children's needs. History, and what should be its sister field, ethnology, may be difficult to learn from, but we may as well start by getting the story straight. Cultures like the !Kung can teach us many lessons about generous and gentle ways of caring for infants and children. This doesn't mean we have to emulate them, just that we should stop feeling superior to them in every way.

• • •

Nevertheless, their children often did die — not just the children of hunters and gatherers, but those of all other societies from the dawn of the human species until about two hundred years ago, when death rates began a slow decline that, fortunately, continues. But before that, the picture was remarkably consistent for different countries of Europe and, in the more recent past, for societies on all other continents. In normal periods, free of decimating epidemics, about half of all children born alive died by their mid-teens, mainly from infectious diseases. Ten to 20 percent died in the first year — half of these in the first few weeks. Substantial, though in most times and places much smaller, numbers of newborn infants died at their parents' hands to prevent them from suffering needless, prolonged deaths — not to mention endangering the survival of their next-older siblings, toddlers in desperate need of care and in imminent danger of death from disease as soon as they were weaned.

The children's chanting game

> *Ring-around-the-rosy,*
> *Pocket full of posies,*
> *Ashes, ashes, we all fall down!*

is believed to have originated from the experience of the black plague. Posies were superstitiously pressed to the nose to ward off both the stench and the threat of death. "Ashes" may have been a sneezing sound victims made, and the ending means "fall down dead." And generations of parents have sung the lullaby

Rock-a-bye baby, on the treetop,
When the wind blows, the cradle will rock,
When the bough breaks, the cradle will fall,
And down will come baby, cradle and all.

Today, many parents are uncomfortable enough with its implications to falsify the ending by prettying it up, just as they do with fairy tales. But in reality, this was a good metaphor for the fate of many babies throughout the disease-ridden human past. Parents who sang this lullaby were simply facing reality and, perhaps, calming their own fears.

Were they also hardening their hearts to prepare for the inevitable? This is the viewpoint taken by anthropologist Nancy Scheper-Hughes, of the University of California at Berkeley, who has studied maternal reactions to infant mortality in poverty-stricken northeastern Brazil. "Death without weeping" is what she calls it in one eloquent essay. The idea is that because the rate of infant mortality is so high, mothers and fathers steel themselves against its inevitability, and even prepare for the infant's death by withdrawing love. This withdrawal is selective, so that the weakest will die more quickly, leaving more of the very scarce resources for those who have a better chance. One mother said,

> They are born already starving in the womb. They are born bruised and discolored, their tongues swollen in their mouths. If we were to nurse them constantly we would all die of tuberculosis. Weak people can't give much milk.

Another was less graphic but more explicit:

> They die because they have to die. If they were meant to live, it would happen that way as well. I think that if they were always weak, they wouldn't be able to defend themselves in life. So, it is really better to let them die.

Lack of loving care and inherent weakness in the baby reinforce each other in "a kind of macabre lock-step dance of death."

Scheper-Hughes's idea of withdrawal of love in anticipation of loss is a commonsense notion. The facts themselves have been challenged by other anthropologists who have worked in northeastern Brazil, and the Oliveira family of "Childhood" who originated there, love their children deeply and hold nothing back. But for the moment let's accept Scheper-Hughes's account. For twenty years I have been asked whether it isn't so of the !Kung whose infants I studied. There was certainly no evident withholding of love among !Kung parents, even though they faced a death rate for their infants that, if anything, was higher than in northeastern Brazil. And most of the parents I knew who lost infants showed full-blown grief reactions that were in no way discouraged by their culture.

When I look at the differences between the two cultures, the most evident are fertility and poverty. Women in northeastern Brazil have about twice as many babies as !Kung women do, and the babies come much closer together. Perhaps the time is not sufficient for equal attachment even to those babies who make it; and perhaps the inevitability of the next baby's birth has as much to do with the weakening of the mother-infant bond as does the likelihood of death.

But more important — and Scheper-Hughes is aware of it — is the fact that the Brazilian mothers are profoundly oppressed. They are at the bottom of a social hierarchy that forces them to do menial labor separated from their babies and children. They are under great external stress, and this stress wedges itself right into the mother-infant bond. Death without weeping, then, may not be an adaptation to anticipated loss but an adaptation to ever-present devastating poverty. It has been seen in war, in concentration camps, in starving populations, in epidemics, and in societies such as the central African Ik, where people have lost all capacity to care for their children or for anyone because their culture and their lives are being shattered by drastic social change. As for the Oliveiras, they may be more loving because their babies are more likely to survive.

But there is no doubt that profound parental attachment and profound grief are compatible with high infant mortality. "Childhood" series cameras filmed an interview with Maria Machi, a grief-stricken mother in Patulul, in highland Guatemala, where measles — a disease completely preventable with vaccination — has lately taken a great toll. She talked of her baby's death, controlling her feelings with increasing effort. "She would call Blanca, Blanca — this one," she said, pointing to her four-year-old daughter sitting beside her, to whom the baby was also attached.

> Mama, she would cry. I would give her my breast because she was still nursing, you see. She would call out my name, she would kiss

me, she would stroke my hair. When I saw her crying I cried also, to
see the sufferings that my daughter was going through.

Here Maria broke down and cried again, covering her face. When she
recovered her composure she went on, "We gave her so many medicines,
but the doctors just weren't able to cure her." They had sold their little
house to buy this medicine — not the action of people resigned to infant
death.

The point is underscored by historical data on families that lost children in relatively favorable circumstances.

Shulamith Shahar, writing of the Middle Ages, notes "the same spectrum of responses to bereavement which is known to us today: a weeping
and wailing mother, tearing her hair or beating her breast and head; a
mother fleeing to the forest after the death of her infant and refusing to
return home; a bereft mother refusing to hand over the corpse of her little
son for burial; a father totally paralyzed with grief."

Cotton Mather, the famed preacher and writer of colonial New England, lost fourteen of his sixteen children to infectious diseases, including
measles — which today continues to kill one and one-half million children worldwide each year. He once said in a sermon, "The dying of a
child is like the tearing of a limb from us." And in his terse but moving
diary, Mather mourned each and every loss. In 1694, during an illness of
his four-year-old daughter Katherine — then his only child — he wrote,

> My little and my only, Katherine, was taken so dangerously sick, that
> small hope of her life was left unto us. In my distress, when I saw the
> Lord thus quenching the coal that was left unto me, and rending him
> out of my bosom one that had lived so long with me, as to steal a
> room there, and a lamb that was indeed unto me as a daughter, I cast
> myself at the feet of his holy Sovereignty.

Katherine survived, but another daughter, taken ill in the year 1711, at
the age of two years, seven months, did not:

> I am again called unto the sacrifice of my dear, dear daughter Jerusha.
> I begged, that such a bitter cup, as the death of that lovely child, might
> pass from me. Nevertheless. . . .
> Just before she died, she asked me to pray with her; which I did, with

a distressed, but resigning soul; and I gave her up unto the Lord. The minute that she died, she said, *That she would go to Jesus Christ. . . . Lord, I am oppressed; undertake for me!*

It is difficult to know how historians who believed that all children of the past were cruelly neglected would construe these diary entries. Mather, incidentally, became a proponent of early forms of inoculation, for which he was heavily criticized.

Mother love in that era of high mortality was if anything even less resigned. William Byrd recounted his wife's reaction to the death in 1710 of their six-month-old son Parke:

> *On the day of the death:* . . . My wife was much afflicted but I submitted to His judgement better, notwithstanding I was very sensible of my loss. . . .
>
> *On the following day:* My wife had several fits of tears for our dear son but kept within the bounds of submission.
>
> *Three days later:* My wife continued to be exceedingly afflicted for the loss of her child, notwithstanding I comforted her as well as I could.

Clearly there is a standard here of submission to God's will — "God gives and God takes away, blessed be the name of God" — but no sense of inevitability, no lack of grieving, no withdrawal of love. In one witchcraft trial the defendant was accused of not having grieved over the death of his child; his proof that he did grieve played a key role in his self-defense. So in the death-ridden world of colonial New England, community standards expected grieving. And in the parallel culture of England itself, parental grief was rarely more simply or more poignantly expressed than by William Wordsworth, whose daughter died at age three:

> *She lived unknown, and few could know*
> *When Lucy ceased to be;*
> *But she is in her grave, and, oh,*
> *The difference to me!*

• • •

It might seem that the worst thing that can happen to a child is to die before having a chance to grow up. But, of course, that is not the worst.

Roughly one-and-one-half million Jewish children, and thousands of others of different ethnicity, were murdered by the Nazis — this was first-degree murder as defined by most criminal codes — between 1933 and 1945, but their lot was enviable compared with that of a number of children subjected to sadistic "experiments" before they were killed. These crimes, we must carefully note, were the product not of a primitive or historically backward culture, but of one of the most advanced civilizations that had appeared on this planet up to the middle of this century. They serve as a marker for the extremes people are capable of.

My own pragmatic initiation into crimes against children — already alluded to in an earlier chapter — occurred one afternoon at the Massachusetts General Hospital in Boston. I was lucky to be assigned that day to a pediatrician who was an authority on the treatment of severely burned children. I, the medical student, was to try to be her "shadow." The children she dealt with — whose lives she saved — on a daily basis were themselves a study in the stress that can be endured without loss of life or mind. There is probably no greater physical anguish in human experience than to be severely burned over a large proportion of the body. In a child who cannot stop being afraid of death and who, if old enough, may also fully appreciate the loss in function and physical appearance that will follow, the pain is compounded by grave psychological stress.

But on this particular afternoon we were pleasantly engaged in charting the growth of normal children in her walk-in clinic — the sorts of children whose biggest problems were things like whether they would feel more embarrassed or more proud about a change of voice or breast buds — until her beeper rang. Now, I had often seen doctors react to the beeper's insistent, methodical screech; the two dominant emotions were annoyance and urgency, depending on what was expected or what the telephone extension on the beeper's screen read. But her reaction was neither; rather, she was concerned and intensely curious. "Come with me," she said. "There may be something interesting." She wasn't smiling.

I followed her through the maze of hospital staircases and corridors — experienced doctors memorize these pathways with their bodies — and we ended in a darkened X-ray viewing room. Stuck to the light boxes in TV-doctor fashion were films of a tiny body, a nine-month-old baby. There were pictures of every section of the skeleton. The radiologist, a man with large hands, began drumming on the films with his forefinger. "Here. Here. Here, here, here," he said. There were partially healed fractures all over the body. None of them had been reported to the hospital emergency room. They were, in medical jargon, nonaccidental injuries. "How did you know?" I wondered aloud to the doctor. "Why did you order whole-body films?"

"I didn't like the pattern of the burn," she said simply. "Babies that fall into scalding water flail around. Their burns have ragged edges, random patterns. This one was too straight around the trunk and shoulders. The baby was immersed — held in the water deliberately." In addition to certain patterns and combinations of fractures and burns, some typical stigmata of child abuse include welts in a loop pattern made by folded lamp-cord wire and pattern burns like brands on buttocks, made by holding a baby with a wet diaper down on a radiator or gas burner.

C. Henry Kempe, a pediatrician who headed a major study of these kinds of injuries in 1961, coined the term *battered child syndrome.* Since that time, physicians have gradually learned to be suspicious of parental reports of falls and other accidents when these reports seem to be implausible explanations for the injuries — and particularly when wounds and fractures of evidently different vintage are attributed by parents to the same accident. A celebrated case in the late 1980s involved a Manhattan lawyer, Joel Steinberg, and his companion, Hedda Nussbaum, who had illegally adopted a child, Lisa. Lisa was found dead at age six, covered with bruises and other injuries after years of severe physical abuse and neglect. Nussbaum, who was complicit in Lisa's death, was terrorized by Steinberg's spousal violence. In this atmosphere of irrational brutality, compounded by drug dependency, Lisa was abused to death. Hers is one of many cases proving that such tragedies are not confined to the poor.

Some patterns of injury are more subtle; for example, the "shaken baby syndrome," identified by physicians only since 1972. An infant, usually younger than a year, is held by the arms and shoulders and shaken violently. There are no bruises, scars, cuts, or burns; there has been no impact injury. But inside the baby there is havoc. Relative to the small infant's physical fragility, enormous forces are set up that tear blood vessels in the neck, brain, and eyes. Blindness, mental retardation, and paralysis may result. In 1990 a Manhattan couple, Mary and Eugene Wong, were sentenced to eight to twenty-five years in prison for the shaking-caused death of a two-month-old they were baby-sitting.

To shake a child to death seems to entail anger, and that is probably also true for most other cases of child physical abuse. George Bernard Shaw once wrote, "If you strike a child take care that you do it in anger, even at the risk of maiming it for life. A blow in cold blood neither can nor should be forgiven." This runs counter to the This-hurts-me-more-than-it-does-you school of deliberate physical punishment. And however angry abusive parents may be, however bizarre the injury they have inflicted, they very often — once caught in their lie about accidental injury — say something like, "I had to teach him to mind."

Historian Philip Greven, of Rutgers University — in *Spare the Child: The Religious Roots of Punishment and the Psychological Impact of Physical Abuse* — argues that child abuse has its origins in a climate of opinion favoring physical punishment, and that this climate in turn derives from Western religious traditions. Proverbs 23:14 reads, "Thou shalt beat him with the rod, And shall deliver his soul from hell." Although this concept is absent from the teachings of Jesus, it is advanced in other words by the philosopher John Locke, by Susanna Wesley, whose sons John and Charles were the founders of Methodism, by present-day Christian fundamentalists, and by the saying "Spare the rod and spoil the child." Yet in Sweden it is outlawed — a 1979 law passed by the parliament there reads, "A child may not be subjected to physical punishment or other injurious or humiliating treatment" — so it must be possible to grow up without it. And there is some evidence that physical punishment increases the likelihood of aggressive and violent behavior in children. Finally, although it is not possible to prove causation, it is remarkable how many people who have mutilated or killed a child refer to the need for discipline as a justification.

Although most experts do not think the problem of abuse and neglect is increasing, the magnitude of the problem is great, and has come to greater attention in recent years. The National Incidence Study, conducted from 1980 to 1985 by the National Center on Child Abuse and Neglect, provides the best data. This study defined abuse and neglect very conservatively, requiring evidence of moderate or severe injury or impairment in the child, not just certain behavior in the parent — and definitely *not* including routine, culturally sanctioned parental punishment. Because many, perhaps even most, cases of maltreatment are not reported, the numbers almost certainly underestimate the problem. The hard core of maltreatment is probably physical assault, and that could be *proved* for at least 3.4 out of every 1,000 American children under eighteen in 1980. This number has remained fairly constant. Sexual maltreatment has affected at the very least 10 per 1,000 children in the mid-1980s, while the deprivation of necessities has affected 50 to 60 — over 5 percent. These, again, are the most conservative estimates; other estimates run much higher.

Breaking the numbers down by economic status and stress offers some insight into their basis. In 1980 the incidence of all types of maltreatment for families earning less than $7,000 a year was 27 per 1,000 children; but in families earning $25,000 a year or more, it was 2.7 per 1,000, or just one-tenth as many. However, the incidence was not related to the number of children in a family or to the rural-urban residential continuum. Many studies have tried to explore the reasons for child abuse and neglect, but few factors have emerged as clearly causal. Poverty is one of these, and this finding echoes the probable explanation of the "macabre dance of death" that develops in some mother-infant pairs in northeastern Brazil.

There are at least two other causes. First, abuse appears to be transmitted from generation to generation. Byron Egeland and his colleagues in Minneapolis have studied this in the city's public health clinics since 1975. They identified 267 new mothers who were considered more likely than average to become abusers, because of poverty, unpreparedness for the baby, and the general chaos of their lives. Eighty-eight percent of the mothers moved an average of four times in the child's first two and a half years. They lacked support from husbands, boyfriends, and family.

The mothers and infants were followed with home observations, laboratory tests, and questionnaires from the first few days of the infants' lives until they were nearly five years old. The focus was on identifying child maltreatment, but only 44 cases emerged — less than a fifth of the sample, including 24 cases of serious physical abuse.

Independently, the 267 women were asked to recall any abuse from their own childhoods. Forty-seven reported a striking sample of the spectrum of child maltreatment: "These women were burned with irons, scalded with hot water, thrown into walls and radiators, and hit repeatedly with belts, switches, and electrical cords." Thirteen of the women reported sexual abuse by an older male relative. None of the 47 had at the time received psychological treatment for their traumas. The result was a high proportion of transgenerational abuse — passing it on from grandparent to parent to child. Seventy percent of the 47 women who had been abused in childhood were currently abusing their own children. A vivid contrast was provided by 35 mothers who had been judged to have had emotionally supportive parents themselves: *only one* was currently abusive to her child.

The 30 percent of *abused* mothers who did *not* abuse their children were also of special interest to the researchers. These women currently had a stable home situation, an intact family, and a supportive husband who was the father of the child. Many also had themselves had a supportive parental figure who partially balanced the childhood abuse they had received.

The point about the supportive husband and father needs underscoring. Martin Daly and Margo Wilson, psychologists at McMaster University in Hamilton, Ontario, are interested in sociobiology. They have shown that the risk of maltreatment up to and including homicide is much higher for children — especially the youngest children — living with at least one stepparent than it is for those living with two natural parents. These are all two-parent families, and therefore the disadvantages associated with a single-parent family are not the explanation. The explanation has something directly to do with the presence of an unrelated adult — a stepparent. Thus research in the late 1980s, stimulated by Darwin's theory, confirmed to some extent the ancient fear of stepparents formalized in centuries of folklore.

Things the child brings into the world, such as irritability, sleep and feeding difficulties, and hyperactivity, can certainly also contribute, by provoking parents. Indeed, when I became the parent of a "colicky" child, I experienced sympathy for abusive parents' anger, and I even began to wonder why child abuse is not more common than it is. The answer, of course, is partly that we have built-in inhibitions, and partly that our circumstances usually buffer us against it. When I reached my wits' end, I could hand off the baby to a loving wife and mother who had been able to rest and gather her powers while I was doing the rocking and singing. Equally important, although we were not living in comfortable circumstances, we had ample reason to hope for a much better future. Many abusive parents lack such support and such hope.

• • •

One of the dramatic developments in child study in the last few years has been the recognition of much higher levels of sexual abuse than were previously accepted. Such abuse seems actually to be much more common than serious physical abuse, and its causes are more obscure. But all in all there seems to have been a long-standing, almost formalized conspiracy of silence regarding this form of child maltreatment.

This cover-up was inadvertently promoted by Sigmund Freud, the inventor of psychotherapy and the leading theorist of the unconscious mind. During the 1890s he dealt with women patients who experienced some physical symptoms. He tried to treat them with a "talking cure" he and a colleague, Joseph Breuer, were developing. He believed that in many cases the symptoms were psychologically caused, and that unearthing the childhood traumas that gave rise to each patient's neurosis would cure the psychological and physical symptoms alike. He was disturbed to hear some of the women describe childhood sexual encounters with adults. At first he believed their accounts, reasoning that they had repressed such horrible memories, and that the effort of keeping them out of consciousness gave rise to symptoms. In 1896 he wrote of their "grave sexual injuries; some of them were absolutely appalling." Among those implicated (overwhelmingly male) were domestic servants, teachers, fathers, older brothers, uncles, and occasionally a governess or nursemaid.

But neurosis was too widespread for this kind of explanation, which — if the theory were right — would have required equally widespread sexual abuse. Since Freud considered this implausible in most good families in nineteenth-century Vienna, he eventually hit upon an explanation that he viewed as revolutionary: The women remembered these kinds of incidents because they had, as children, *wished* for them. They had wanted to replace their mothers as the objects of their fathers' sexual love, and so they fantasized seduction scenes. Later they felt such guilt for their wishes and thoughts that they repressed all this far below the surface of normal memory, and the energy of repression caused their symptoms. Theoretically, they could be made healthy again by bringing these guilty thoughts to light.

Some of this new perspective may have been true — the switch in Freud's thinking was certainly crucial to the development of psychoanalysis as a theory — but the great mistake was totally to doubt the women's seduction stories. Neurotic they may have been, and perhaps the childhood memories contributed to the neurosis — but the things these women remembered were probably real. Freud himself continued to believe that two of his patients, whom he called Katharina and Fräulein Rosalia H., had in fact been sexually assaulted by their fathers. One patient had actually been raped by her father at age two. Indeed such events had been known to psychiatrists throughout the nineteenth century.

I remember the face of a twelve-year-old girl in Grady Hospital in Atlanta, undergoing the painful contractions of an induced abortion. She had been impregnated by her father, and her poised mother — twenty-eight years old — stood at her bedside sighing with resignation. My eldest daughter is twelve at this writing, and my basic reaction to such facts is rather like Freud's was: I simply don't want to believe them. But unlike Freud, I know that they are widely and tragically true. It is nearly impossible to estimate the extent of this problem — not just father-daughter incest but child sexual abuse in general. Still, it is clear that reflexively skeptical attitudes like Freud's — and mine — are obstacles to discovery, prevention, and treatment.

In retrospective surveys, from 20 to 35 percent of adult women recall having been forced by an adult male to have sexual contact (including exhibitionism without touching) when they were children. Only a small fraction of these events are reported either to health or to criminal authorities. The best current estimates are that more than 150,000 new cases of sexual abuse of children occur in the United States each year. Even those reported to health professionals often are not reported to the police. In a 1988 study of 156 sexually abused children in Boston, only 96 cases were reported to the police. The majority of victims were age seven or older, and 35 percent were between thirteen and eighteen. Underreporting was great, and was much greater among nonwhite than white victims.

The spectrum of reactions to such abuse recognized by psychiatrists today is even broader than that suspected by Freud in his first formulation; it includes depression, drug abuse, social withdrawal, delayed post-traumatic stress disorder, multiple personality, and Freud's old standby, hysteria, sometimes with physical symptoms. In cases of incest, it is often impossible to separate the effects of the sexual contact itself from that of the disruption of the family — temporary or permanent — that ensues, and in all cases it is difficult to rule out the effects of poverty, marital discord, and genetically inherited psychological problems. Nevertheless it is reasonable to conclude that at least some children must be psychologically damaged by such abuse.

Eliminating exhibitionist encounters from the statistics yields a consistent estimate from retrospective surveys: about 15 percent of adult women remember having a sexual encounter involving physical contact — as a child, with an adult. Their average age at the time of the remembered abuse was about ten years. Four to 10 percent of all women report having been abused by a family member, one percent by fathers or stepfathers. Between 94 and 100 percent of the remembered abusers were male — which, considering the fact that children spend most of their time with women, is an even stronger difference than it seems. Men's remembered sexual abuse has been less well studied, but the mean age is somewhat higher; family members, including fathers and stepfathers, are rarely involved; and women abusers account for only one-sixth of the cases. Almost all cases of parent-child incest are father-daughter, and even these are fortunately rare.

Some mental health professionals and many parents have become concerned about how increased vigilance regarding sexual abuse may impose abnormal limits on normal expressions of physical affection. I saw a frightened young father who had come to the Massachusetts General Hospital child neurology clinic with his ten-year-old daughter. The girl was being examined because of learning and behavior problems. But her father told a harrowing story of his investigation by social workers and then by the police because of suspected child sexual abuse.

According to his telling, a twenty-two-year-old school social worker had appeared at his door one day and told him that he was under investigation for sexually abusing his daughter. According to him, the only evidence was that his daughter had been drawing pointy objects and had said that she and her father had lain in bed together in bathrobes during vacation. The charge was not proved against him, and the child seemed happy enough with him. I don't know whether he was guilty or not. But I know that I have often thought of his story while lying beside my daughters. Somehow we have to find a way to encourage normal physical affection — probably, if cross-cultural experience is to teach us anything, *more* physical affection than is usual in most American families (*Have you hugged your child today?*) — without failing to pursue and correct the grave insult and injury of child sexual abuse.

• • •

These terrible facts about cruelty to children can only leave us with at least a transient sense of despair about the human condition. Such perversion of normal responses to infants and children — objects, one would hope, of an almost inevitable tender affection — make us wonder, and fear for, what we ourselves are made of.

But they also return us again and again to the question raised at the opening of the chapter. What happens in the development of such children? Assuming that they survive, what is it that they survive to be like? Other than the dreadful pain, fear, and grief that they suffer in the event, what is the nature of their lasting impairment and suffering? Freud, who at the turn of the century was very much a turn-of-the-century biologist, likened early psychic stress to the effect of a pinprick on an embryo during an experiment. Both were called *trauma* — a Greek word for wound. Just as the pinprick caused a divergence in the normal developmental path, leading to anatomical abnormality, psychological wounds would divert the child's mind from its normal course of growth, leaving emotional deformities — neuroses.

Corresponding concepts arose among educators and cognitive psychologists, who frequently asked themselves whether there were certain deprivations in the early growth of the mind that could not be made up for later. The now questionable notion of a "critical" period in childhood arose. This referred to the possibility that there were times in human development when certain experiences had to be lived, certain memories laid down, certain feelings felt, certain skills learned and mastered. Failing this timely intervention, the theory went, the functions of the psyche would be irretrievably impaired. A less extreme version of this concept, the "sensitive" period, is more widely accepted.

Unfortunately there were many examples of children whose life experience could help address this question. This included children raised in extreme poverty, those with handicaps such as blindness, deafness, or both, those raised in unsatisfactory orphanages and other institutional settings, and those raised in a severe form of social and cultural isolation. Children in this last category have always held a particular fascination, because they address questions about our most central needs for succor and knowledge from the world, and because they seem to tell us something about origins: for the religious, what God meant for us after all; for the scientifically inclined, what is given by evolution and biology.

Kings and emperors of legend have not been immune to this sort of curiosity. According to the Greek historian Herodotus, an Egyptian king in the seventh century B.C. arranged for two children to be raised by shepherds who never spoke to them; the king was supposedly curious as to what language they would end up speaking, but the result was not recorded. A similar experiment was attributed by a thirteenth-century chronicler to Frederick II, emperor of the Holy Roman Empire, who wanted to find out if the child would speak the Hebrew tongue — viewed by some in that religious, pre-anthropology era as the first human language. One can only hope that neither of these experiments — forerunners of Nazi experiments on children in the triumph of curiosity over decency — was actually carried to its conclusion.

But unfortunately such "experiments" have occurred inadvertently. Children have been raised with severe deprivation of normal social interaction and other benefits of the psychological and cultural world, by parents or caretakers whose attainments in the realm of neglect rival those of the curious kings. The most famous was the Wild Boy of Aveyron, whose case was described most completely in a book by that name by Harlan Lane. The boy was discovered in a forest in southern France in 1797. He seemed to be about twelve years old. He was naked and covered with scars. Apparently he had raised himself on the acorns and roots of the forest, and was able to swim, climb trees, run swiftly on all fours, find food and water, and burst forth with shouts and laughter.

He was not, however, able to speak or to understand speech. He thus seemed to offer an answer to the apocryphal question posed by the cruel kings of ancient Egypt and the Holy Roman Empire: the child who is not exposed to speech speaks no language at all. And in the words of an early observer, "His affections are as limited as his knowledge; he loves no one; he is attached to no one; and if he shows some preference for his caretaker, it is an expression of need and not the sentiment of gratitude. . . ." Still, the boy was fortunate enough to come under the care of Jean-Marc Itard, a young physician who was interested in the education of deaf-mutes. From 1801 to 1806 Itard devoted himself to the education of the boy, whom he named Victor.

His success was limited. In Itard's own summary:

> We find, among other real improvements, that he has both a knowledge of the conventional value of the symbols of thought and the power of applying this knowledge by naming objects, their qualities, and their actions. This has led to an extension of the pupil's relations with the people around him, to his ability to express his wants to them, to receive orders from them, and to effect a free and continual exchange of thoughts with them. . . . Victor is aware of the care taken of him, susceptible to fondling and affection, sensitive to the pleasure of doing things well, ashamed of his mistakes, and repentant of his outbursts.

Nevertheless, Itard also reported that Victor's intellectual achievements were "the slow and laborious result of an intense training in which the most powerful methods are used to obtain the smallest effects," and that his "emotional faculties, equally slow in emerging from their long torpor, are subordinated to a profound egoism." As he went through adolescence, Victor's sexuality emerged as compulsive masturbation.

Itard concluded with the philosophical inference that Victor had entered his condition of intellectual immaturity and emotional isolation through lack of "education," and that this lack could be only partly made up for later — a critical-period hypothesis. However, even at the time, debate about the wild boy showed an understanding of the problem with such cases: They have no history. The presumption of a normal infant somehow led to survive in the woods with no human contact is at the heart of Itard's interpretation. But perhaps Victor was retarded to begin with; or perhaps he was what we would now call autistic — of relatively normal intelligence but incapable of forming normal social bonds.

This has always been a problem of interpretation with such cases, but — fortunately for science though unfortunately for humanity — a number of modern cases have come to light in which the history is known. Ten of these children from six different families have been summarized carefully by David Skuse, of the Institute of Psychiatry in London, who himself intensively studied two of the children. Most of them spent some months after birth in normal environments, and were known to be normal before being subject to social isolation or other extreme psychological deprivation. Several, though not all, suffered nutritional as well as psychological deprivation. They were discovered at ages ranging from two to thirteen years, having spent their lives locked in tiny rooms or cellars, or tied to chairs or beds, with extremely minimal human stimulation. On discovery, they were withdrawn, fearful, and profoundly abnormal in their speech.

The recoveries of most of these children were simply remarkable. The oldest, Genie, who was thirteen when discovered, had made little progress toward normality by age eighteen; another died of liver disease at age ten. But all the other children were in school by their teenage years, six out of eight in normal schools. One pair of twin boys in Czechoslovakia, known as the Koluchova twins for the psychologist who studied them, had grown up in almost total isolation from age eighteen months to seven years. When discovered, their speech was very poor, they could barely walk, and they reacted with horror to normal objects. Placed with foster parents, they developed normal attachments, experienced astoundingly rapid language learning, displayed above-average I.Q.s, and at last contact (age twenty) were both working steadily at maintaining office machinery, had been dating, and had each fallen in love.

Such cases seem baffling. They fly in the face of everything we think we know about the normal development of children. I, like all the parents I know, have agonized over almost every choice in the care of our children. Breast- or bottle-feeding? Day-care or not? Preschool at two, or not until four? Strict bedtime or flexible time? Soccer or piano? Television on weekday nights, or only on weekends?

With these concerns dominating our thoughts, what can parents like us think about children who grow up locked in a cellar? Surely the Wild Boy of Aveyron must provide the standard model. Call him Victor or what you will, he will still be a wild boy after years of tender teaching.

Nothing, we think, could make him recover from such extreme deprivation.

In Victor's case, we will never know. But in these modern cases, where we do know most of the facts and can study the children with up-to-date psychological methods, the most dire predictions just do not come true. On the contrary, what is inescapable is the resilience of these children; and, in a scientific sense, a powerful channeling of development into normal paths even after very abnormal beginnings that last for years. "Canalization" is the technical term for it; the image is one of developmental canals into which children's maturation tends to flow — despite being turned aside again and again. *Canalization:* development's powerful tendency to return to, and stay, normal.

• • •

Harry Harlow, a psychologist who spent a lifetime studying laboratory rhesus monkeys, contributed as much to our understanding of this process as anyone studying children. He began serendipitously, simply raising monkeys for learning experiments. When he noticed that some of the monkeys behaved abnormally, he changed course and adopted the goal of discovering a method of emotional rehabilitation — psychotherapy, if you like — for monkeys with abnormal personalities. He started deliberately to raise monkeys in social isolation — taking good care of them physically, but withholding maternal care. The monkeys grew up unquestionably abnormal. They were socially withdrawn when introduced to companions, and would often hug themselves and rock, bite themselves, or bang their heads dangerously. They were fearful, and sometimes overreacted with inappropriate aggression.

Harlow and his students, including Leonard Rosenblum, were interested in discovering what techniques would allow monkeys to overcome the devastating effects caused by isolation rearing. Numerous efforts either failed or succeeded only partially. Introducing them to experienced monkey mothers, placing them with same-age playmates, giving them human affection, allowing years to pass — nothing worked. As in the case of the Wild Boy, the damage seemed permanent. When they grew up they were almost invariably inept in their social relationships. They continued to be fearful, with outbursts of aggression. Sexually, the males at least were so inept that Harlow joked about their pathetic attempts to copulate as "working at cross-purposes with reality." As mothers, the females showed a particularly tragic ineptitude with their babies — they were not merely neglectful, but abusive, clearly unable to adapt normally to the strains and stresses of new motherhood.

A few glimmers of hope for rehabilitation did, however, appear. First, it was found that if motherless monkeys were given play time with peers every day, they developed much more normally in their behavior — but this had to start very early in life, and could not be introduced after months of isolation. Second, it became apparent that motherless mothers improved in their maternal behavior when they had their second and third infants. William Mason, a psychologist at the University of California at Davis, did an ingenious experiment showing that isolation-reared monkeys would become attached — both literally and figuratively — to patient, long-haired dogs, clinging and riding under their bellies or on their backs. While this study showed that the potential for attachment persists in the monkey's brain through the experience of isolation, it did not address the question of long-term damage.

Then Harlow and his student Stephen Suomi, now at the National Institute of Child Health and Human Development, did an experiment that changed our ideas sharply. Taking a cue from what they already knew about peers and about the improved behavior of mothers with second and third babies, they took monkeys that had been isolated until six months of age and put them together with three-month-olds that had been normally reared. These younger infants acted on the isolates just as the successive babies acted on their own mothers. They were persistent, minimally threatening companions. And the result was an almost complete elimination of the isolates' abnormal behavior, which was replaced with normal social behavior toward the younger monkey. Later this same result was achieved with monkeys that had been isolated for a full year — the equivalent of about three years in terms of human age.

The book is not closed on the persistent problems of isolation-reared monkeys. They may continue to have subtle abnormalities that appear later under certain kinds of stress. But on the whole, the line of experiments started by Suomi and Harlow has changed the thinking of psychologists, who have become as fascinated by the resilience of the young organism — and by its ability to recover — as they were all along by the threat of damage through early deprivation. Together with the new evidence on isolation-reared children, these controlled experiments with monkeys show how the young of species related to ours can adapt to and survive deprivation.

• • •

Now that we have steeped ourselves in the worst things that can happen to children, and considered how well their minds and brains can recover from trauma, we are equipped to face with a certain equanimity some of the most pressing questions parents face in our time. These include the question addressed in an earlier chapter about parent-child separation and day care; the rise of divorce and of the single-parent family; the impact of economic depression and chronic poverty; the small but growing incidence of other kinds of unconventional families, such as those with two gay parents; and the impact of psychological stresses such as verbal abuse and bigotry.

It is worth remembering at the outset the great variety of situations in the anthropological record in which children have been able to thrive and grow. In most traditional societies subsistence activity was a daily struggle, and the possibility of shortages leading to starvation was always on the horizon. The loss of siblings and parents through death was very common — common enough so that the proportion of single-parent and stepparent families may have been as high as it is in Western culture today. And there has been a very great variety of "normal" marriage and family forms: Traditionally, Eskimos swapped spouses; Polynesians gave their children up freely for adoption; Nayar women of India married and sent their husbands off to war, remaining to take lovers as if the marriage almost hadn't happened. Some Nepalese women marry several men at a time; lots of men throughout the world, from native Australia to Utah, do the same with women — with the approval and encouragement of their cultures.

But we also need to know that the *extended* family was very strong in most of these cultures, and the embeddedness of a child and his or her caregivers in a wider circle of relatives was widespread. This provided a set of buffers and supports when stressful life events put pressure on the immediate family. Grandparents, aunts, uncles, and cousins were often involved with children's care on a daily basis. The kinship network also mitigated some of the more odd-sounding marriage practices. For instance, Eskimo spouse-swappers, Polynesian child-swappers, and jointly married Nepalese men all tend strongly to be relatives. A dense and supportive kinship network is not as available to children in our society as they go through a momentous change in the structure of the family.

The last generation has seen what might be called the single-parent-family revolution in the United States: of all children in the United States in 1960, 9 percent were living in single-parent families. This rose to 12 percent in 1970, 20 percent in 1980, and 24 percent in 1988 — and many more had spent some time in such families. These are national averages; the percentages are much higher for blacks than for whites; more than 85 percent of the single parents are women; and an additional few percent of children live with *no* parent. The rise in divorces only partly accounts for the recent change — millions of single-parent families have never involved marriage at all, and the divorce rate actually rose slowly and steadily from the 1860s until the mid-1980s.

Still, we have crossed a statistical threshold: Half of all marriages entered in the 1980s are projected to end in divorce. (It is also true that the number of divorces in a given year is about half of the number of marriages in that same year, but that is a different, less important statistic.) Since many divorces involve children, parents are justifiably concerned about how children will fare, and the subject serves as a suitable example of what might be called more "normal" stresses in childhood.

So far it has been very difficult to separate the effects of divorce from other elements of the situation children are in. The most well-known study of the problem, that of Judith Wallerstein and her colleagues, really does not deserve the attention it has gotten, because it fails to meet even minimal standards of scientific validity. Children were followed in the years after divorce, some up to adulthood. They were found to have adjustment problems in the immediate aftermath of the divorce, and to have bitter and sad memories of it, even into adulthood. But they were not studied before the divorce to determine whether their problems were new. They were not compared to children who remained in marriages full of conflict, or indeed to any other children.

Did they have adjustment problems before — problems that may have helped cause the divorce or that may have stemmed from marital conflict?

Would they have had more problems if their parents had stayed together? Would they have had bitter and sad memories of their parents' marriage even if there had been no divorce? Did the divorce itself produce their problems, or was it years of other stresses afterward — such as an absent father or a much lower standard of living? We will never know, because the study was not conducted in such a way as to answer or even raise these crucial questions. Yet the Wallerstein study has received widespread media attention as proof that divorce is very damaging to children.

The facts are more complex by far, as shown by better studies. For example, in a study by Mavis Hetherington and her colleagues at the University of Virginia, seventy-two children of divorce (thirty-six boys, thirty-six girls) were compared to a matched sample of children whose parents did *not* divorce. Certainly there were adjustment problems — such as disobedience, especially for boys — that were greater in the divorced families than in the controls. But these differences declined within two years, and by six years were present but even less prominent. The importance of factors other than the divorce, such as economic stress, was underscored by the study. As the authors concluded:

> In the families we studied we did not encounter . . . a divorce in which at least one family member did not report distress or exhibit disrupted behavior. However, if these effects were not compounded by continued severe stress and adversity, most parents and children adapted to their new family situation within 2 years and certainly within 6 years. It also should be remembered that many households headed by mothers are exposed to excessive stresses and that without adequate support systems such families may show more sustained deleterious sequelae of divorce. It is imperative to identify and develop effective support systems that assist the family members in adjusting to the stresses and changes associated with divorce.

Other studies have also emphasized these complexities, and especially the need for postdivorce intervention. One very recent, excellent study by Robert Fauber and his colleagues, then at the University of Georgia, compared fifty-one young adolescents from recently divorced families to forty-six from intact families. Conflict between parents was a strong predictor of children's problems (such as depression or acting out) in *both* groups, and the way marital conflict made its impact on children was by changing the parents' behavior — especially by making them withdraw from or reject their children. In a smaller study by Fauber's colleague Nicholas Long, young teenagers whose parents had a lot of conflict both before and after their divorces had more problems than children from intact families. But a third group of children, whose parents had high levels of conflict before the divorce but not after it, had no more problems than children from intact families. As in the Hetherington study, the message is clear: Intervention to reduce additional stresses in the postdivorce period could prevent many problems for children.

These studies still did not address the issue of whether the problem children had their problems before the divorce. However, another excellent study, conducted by Jeanne and Jack Block and their colleagues, at the University of California at Berkeley, began with families that were all intact, and then compared those that experienced divorce to those that did not. They followed children from age three to fifteen, and later looked at the predivorce problems of children who, although the researchers could not then have known it, would end up divorcing. They discovered that up to eleven years *before the divorce,* children (especially boys) in that group had more problems than children whose families were not destined for breakup. The child's problems were there before the divorce. Not only that, but they were very similar to the kinds of problems many studies have found in the wake of divorce itself.

The researchers believe that the children's predivorce problems stem from marital conflict, but that is only one possible explanation. The problems (disruptive behavior, for example) may begin with the children, and may actually help to bring about marital conflict. Or, problem-prone personalities may run in certain families — for either economic or genetic reasons. This could independently create both marital conflict and children's behavior problems. Either way, studies like this one show us how naïve we have been to look at families *after* divorce and think we could attribute all the children's problems to the divorce itself.

The Blocks' modest sample is only suggestive, but a large new two-nation study confirms their insight. Writing in the journal *Science* in June 1991, Alfred Cherlin, Frank Furstenberg, and five other investigators analyzed data from Britain and the United States. In Britain, 98 percent of all children born in one week in March 1958 — more than 17,000 — were studied at birth, and more than 14,000 were restudied at ages seven and eleven. Parents and teachers rated behavior problems in the children — temper tantrums, or being frequently worried, destructive, or tearful, among others — and reading and mathematics tests were given. Only children whose parents were together when they were seven were included, and the 239 who experienced divorce during the next four years were compared with those who did not.

Boys whose parents divorced had significantly more problems than those whose parents stayed together — a 19 percent excess. But after correcting for child and family problems already there at age seven — preceding all divorces — the difference dropped to 8 percent and was no longer statistically significant. For girls the pattern was similar, but some of the excess attributable to divorce remained significant after controlling for preexisting problems,

The American study involved over 2,000 children in intact families ages seven to eleven in 1976, restudied five years later. For boys the pattern was similar to the British one. Boys whose parents divorced in the interim had 12 percent more behavior problems — fighting, lying, restlessness, and withdrawal, for example — than those whose parents didn't; but after controlling for preexisting problems in the child and the family, the excess was halved to an insignificant level. For American *girls,* the pattern was more surprising: The excess of behavior problems was in the children whose parents did *not* divorce during the five-year-follow-up. The authors wisely caution against putting too much weight on this counterintuitive finding. Still, the study calls into question every single piece of research on divorce that did not begin with an assessment of children's problems when they were still in intact families.

Over a million American children each year now experience the divorce or separation of their parents. To continue sounding a hysterical alarm about the devastating psychological effects of this experience without better evidence is simply irresponsible. It preserves bad marriages that may harm children more than divorce does, and it creates an epidemic of hurtful guilt and shame in many millions of parents who failed at marriage after doing the best they could. Some of these parents may deserve the guilt and shame, but many do not.

In a meeting on this subject with Harvard psychiatrist Alvin Poussaint, a "Childhood" series adviser, I was struck when he said, "We need to start looking at the *positive* effects of divorce on children." I recognized from my own startled reaction that the thought had simply never occurred to me. I thought of the effects of divorce on children in one of two ways: very bad, and not all that bad. But of course, as Poussaint wisely says, the effects may sometimes be good. The chances of good — or at least less bad — outcomes are greatly increased by key interventions: guarantee of child support, continued nurturance by both parents, and reduction of conflict between separated parents after the divorce. These are easier said than done. But as a society we might as well realize that whether we support the process or not, it will go right on happening, and either way, we will take the consequences.

• • •

Of course they will be worse for some children than others, as is true for the consequences of all kinds of injury. Even given the same degree of injury, some children are resilient, others are not. Psychologist Jean MacFarlane expressed the common feeling of many who have done large longitudinal studies, following children's emotional growth from childhood to adulthood: "Many of the most outstanding mature adults in our entire group, many who are well integrated, highly competent and/or creative . . . are recruited from those who were confronted with very difficult situations and whose characteristic responses during childhood and adolescence seemed to us to compound their problems." Psychiatrist George Vaillant, now at the Dartmouth Medical School, completed another longitudinal study, comparing thirty men with "best outcomes" in later life to thirty with "worst outcomes." Almost half of those with the worst outcomes had emotionally inadequate childhood environments; but a sixth of the "best outcome" group did as well. Vaillant speculated that some of these men were compensating for their deprived childhoods by, for example, a close marriage or a dazzling business success. But he recognized too that this theory, even if true, does not detract from the quality of these men's later adaptations.

Charles Dickens is probably the paradigmatic case. When he was a boy his father struck financial disaster, and spent two years in debtor's prison while Charles and his family suffered in humiliating poverty. During that period he slept on a straw mat in a garret and worked in a blacking (shoe polish) factory. His father — Charles never wavered in his love for the man — was released when a relative left him some money, and life improved for a time for Charles. But in his mid-teens he had to drop out of school to go to work. Yet somehow he became the most celebrated author of his era, and one of the most financially successful of any era. Along the way he immortalized boys who triumphed over the poverty and mistreatment of their childhoods — Oliver Twist, David Copperfield, and others — and these invented stand-ins for their creator will serve as examples to other children for all time.

Who are these resilient kids and why do they make it? Norman Garmezy, a psychologist who pioneered the study of such children twenty years ago, has used the term *stress resistant* to refer to them. The assumption was not that *all* children could resist *any* stress, but that children in general could stand up to substantial stress, and some could actually thrive in spite of it. Garmezy summarized a number of studies of children of schizophrenic mothers by noting that some showed deficiencies of social competence and attention problems in school.

"But equally important," he went on, "were the large numbers of vulnerable children who provided little, if any, indication of current signs of pathology or incompetence." These children had been subject to abnormal mothering and separation from their mothers periodically for hospitalization — not to mention their genetic risk. Yet they were adapting well. Garmezy went on to study 600 children facing deprivation in an inner-city community. The results of this study are still preliminary, but there is already clear evidence of similar stress resistance.

Emmy Werner, another psychologist interested in resilience, followed a multiracial sample of 698 infants born in 1955 on the island of Kauai, Hawaii. So far she has followed them until age thirty-two. About one-third of these infants were considered to be at risk, because each had faced *four or more* of the following problems: biological stress during or shortly after birth, poverty, rearing by mothers with little education, and family environments marked by discord, desertion, divorce, alcoholism, or mental illness. Of this high-risk group, two-thirds — two-ninths of the original sample — developed serious problems with learning, behavior, delinquency, mental health, or pregnancy before age eighteen.

But the last ninth — 72 high-risk children, 30 boys and 42 girls — "developed instead into competent, confident, and caring young adults." The questions then were, who were they and why did they do so well? Some differences in these 72 were apparent in infancy. They were described as active, affectionate, good-natured, and easy to deal with, compared with the rest of the high-risk babies. At school, though not above average in ability, they used their skills more effectively and got along better with their peers than did the nonresilient children. They tended to come from families with four or fewer children, and with the births spaced farther apart. They all had at least one very nurturing caregiver in infancy — sometimes a grandparent, older sibling, or baby-sitter. And as they went through childhood, they sought out and "found emotional support outside their own families . . . an informal network of kin and neighbors, peers and elders, for counsel and support in time of crisis."

It is impossible to tease apart the complex web of factors that made these children resilient, but clearly both factors intrinsic to the child, and factors in the environment that provided support despite the stresses, were important. When studied at age thirty, even these resilient individuals had more problems — such as unstable marriages and stress-related medical complaints — than did their low-risk counterparts. But overall there were few long-term results of their early deprivations. This is in contrast to the other two-thirds of the high-risk group, who suffered more serious damage. Only a minority recover fully from the early insult.

But most interesting of all, perhaps, is this paradoxical fact: 44 percent of the *resilient* high-risk group, as opposed to only 10 percent of their low-risk peers, rated themselves as "happy" or "delighted" with their present lives. One of them, who had just gone through a divorce, was asked what he thought was the most important thing that had happened in his life so far. His reply:

> The realization of how harsh life really is — how relationships can leave deep, within, hurts that don't seem to go away. With understanding and care, much can be accomplished — with sincere motivation and determination. Believe in yourself, and accomplish the best you can do, and know it is your own achievement that brings you along. Enjoy life and respect it.

No wonder Werner titled her book *Vulnerable But Invincible*.

Again, two-thirds of the high-risk group were *not* invincible, but in-stead showed long-term damage. Still, our task is not just to repeat over and over again the fact that stressful experiences in childhood can leave lasting injury. Although we must never lose sight of that, the challenge is more complex. It is to figure out why some children do so well in spite of these experiences — and to attack the problem of stress on children in two ways at the same time: by reducing the part of the stress that *can* be reduced; and by supporting children through and after the part of the stress that is an inevitable aspect of life.

Some psychologists see every sort of childhood stress as leaving a per-manent scar on the human spirit. For example, the economic hardship of the Great Depression years is believed by Glen Elder and his colleagues at the University of North Carolina to have effects on the mood and behavior of children and adolescents, with interesting differences depend-ing on the father's behavior, the sex and age of the child, and (for ado-lescent girls) even the child's physical attractiveness, which surprisingly affected fathers' behavior toward their daughters.

But even Elder concedes that these mechanisms receive only "modest support" from his research, and that much past thinking has "resulted in an understatement of children as producers of their own socialization," and of the "complexity of interactions among social, psychological, and biological factors." Rarely if ever do such studies even consider such fac-tors as prenatal exposure to alcohol, nicotine, cocaine, and heroin, or pre- and postnatal malnutrition, or brain injury from accidents or abuse — let alone potentially problematic genes. Yet even biological dam-age need not be permanent. Depending in part on the age of the child at injury, the brain may be able to recover in remarkable ways from dam-age — whether biological or psychosocial.

"The American Century" was created by people who, as children, were torn from their homes and families to cross the Atlantic or the Pacific under horrendous conditions, and be cast into poverty while desperately trying to learn a new language and new customs; who experienced a worldwide economic depression of enormous proportions; who lived through one or two world wars; and who experienced racism, sexism, anti-Semitism, and other social ills to a degree much greater than is the case for American children today. As for the Japanese and German "economic miracles," they were created by people who, as children, belonged to societies that experienced devastating deprivation and humiliation in the course of utter military defeat.

Not every child is a Charles Dickens (or his stand-in, David Copperfield), able not only to withstand adversity but to thrive and grow in stature because of it. I would not like to back the theory that stress is good for children, for the simple reason that far too many are damaged.

Still, evidence is accumulating that many children handle stress well. The reason may perhaps be found in an old theory of Hans Selye's, a Canadian physician who specialized in the medical aspects of stress. In a book called *The Stress of Life* and in his many scientific papers, Selye distinguished between *dis*tress, which can be physically debilitating, and *eu*stress — normal or positive stress — which can produce adaptive responses in the body that strengthen its defenses and increase its effectiveness. As psychiatrist George Vaillant put it, "It is not stress that kills us; it is effective adaptation to stress that permits us to live." If this is true, then our responsibility is clear: It is not to eliminate stress from children's lives completely, since that is beyond our capacity; rather, it is to help shape responses to stress that will somehow permit them to live.

· · ·

We end our trek along the difficult path of vulnerability with accounts of two children who have trod the path before us. One continued climbing, and one fell by the wayside. They have left us two messages on behalf of all children: The first is, "You are big, make the path smoother"; the second is, "I will walk, but hold my hand." If we fail to rise to these two simple challenges, we had better cease to think of ourselves as anything we or our children could ever remotely, possibly admire.

Helen Keller's story is known throughout the world as one that inspires hope for the human condition and for the prospects of teaching the supposedly unteachable. In a play and film pointedly called *The Miracle Worker*, Helen's teacher Annie Sullivan was rightly credited with enormous dedication and creativity in reaching this six-year-old child locked away from the world by both blindness and deafness. She resembled Victor, the wild boy, in several ways. Yet Sullivan broke through all these formidable barriers to draw out a girl, and then a woman, whose thoughtful leadership, through writing and "speaking" in alphabetic sign language, was to change the way the world thinks about the handicapped.

But the rehabilitation was no miracle. Helen had lost her sight and hearing in a fever at age eighteen months, before she had learned to speak. She was cared for in a home that was nurturing (though ignorant of her needs) and safe. She seemed as autistic — cut off from people — as Victor, but in fact was not. She described in her autobiography many years later the astonished sense of discovering language through the letter-signs for water spelled out in her hand: W-A-T-E-R, which Sullivan signed for her while cool water from a pump flooded over her other hand. "Suddenly I felt a misty consciousness of something forgotten — the thrill of returning thought; and somehow the mystery of language was revealed to me."

It was revealed, of course, partly from within: "the thrill of *returning* thought." It could be the thought of the eighteen-month-old that she means; but more likely, the sense of return she got was really the sense of finding thought within her own mind — a mind that had been developing, not normally to be sure, but developing — for four and a half more years. If there was a miracle here, other than Sullivan's dedication (which in fairness was matched by Itard despite his failure with Victor), it is the miracle of the growth of a child's brain and mind. This growth somehow kept itself going despite what should have been devastating deprivation. The miracle is the mental life that is inside every child.

Finally, we return to a frequently quoted text from Anne Frank's *Diary of a Young Girl*. The words have been quoted often in the past because they express to us otherwise almost inexpressible hopes: that life is worth living, that growth and change are worth going through, even in unspeakably bad conditions — even in the valley of the shadow of death. They are becoming like the words of that Psalm, or of the Sermon on the Mount. It is no longer in spite of past repetitions that we repeat them again, but in part because of those past repetitions.

Here are the circumstances. A young girl begins a diary two days after her thirteenth birthday, in June 1942. Her family has moved to Holland from Germany upon Hitler's rise to power in 1933, so for all intents and purposes she is an ordinary Dutch child, except for being Jewish. She wants the diary to be her friend, so she names the friend: Kitty; and thereafter she writes in the form of letters. Nine entries occur in the first month, filled with the exuberance of a middle-class child's life — such things as, "We ping-pongers are very partial to an ice cream, especially in summer, when one gets warm at the game," and "Our whole class B1 is trembling, the reason is that the teachers' meeting is to be held soon." Then there is an entry beginning "Years seem to have passed between Sunday and now," in which the girl describes the cramped storerooms above her father's office where she and her family and several other Jews have gone into hiding, to avoid imminent Gestapo arrest — which would mean deportation to an extermination center.

This diary-in-hiding continues for almost exactly two years, and is filled with some of the most articulate self-description of the adolescent experience that we have in all of literature. But for now we are interested in the end of the entry dated Saturday, July 15, 1944 — the third from the last — in which she talks about her hopes. She has spent two years in cramped quarters in constant fear of arrest and death, desperately (and successfully) trying to keep growing up. In the next entry (July 21) she will have a specific label for her hopefulness: "Super news! An attempt has been made on Hitler's life. . . ."

But the end of the nightmare will not come in time for Anne. She will be arrested on August 4 and will die in Bergen-Belsen, one of the most notorious Nazi camps. And despite what she says about Hitler on July 21, we know that what she says on the fifteenth is not tied to the news. We know her too well by now; it is Anne. She writes:

> It's really a wonder that I haven't dropped all my ideals, because they seem so absurd and impossible to carry out. Yet I keep them, because in spite of everything I still believe that people are really good at heart. I simply can't build up my hopes on a foundation consisting of confusion, misery, and death. I see the world gradually being turned into a wilderness, I hear the ever approaching thunder, which will destroy us too, I can feel the sufferings of millions and yet, if I look up into the heavens, I think that it will all come right, that this cruelty too will end, and that peace and tranquillity will return again.
>
> In the meantime, I must uphold my ideals, for perhaps the time will come when I shall be able to carry them out.
>
> Yours, Anne

Si quebró el Cantaro.

1.

1. Child abuse is usually justified by the perpetrator as physical punishment, and some psychologists challenge the distinction between the two. "If the Pitcher Broke," etching by Goya.

2. The different brutality of famine. Mothers and children walk across what was once a lake, Mali, 1985.

2.

I was scared of the gun and The man. Donald Leggett age 8 - 2nd grade March 19, 1990

3.

3. Growing up scared. An eight-year-old depicts his neighborhood, in Maryland just outside Washington, D.C., 1990.

4. Drawing by an abused prepubertal girl, who said, "That's me" (the red eye) "and that's Jack's thing" (the red-tipped projection). Jack was her mother's boyfriend.

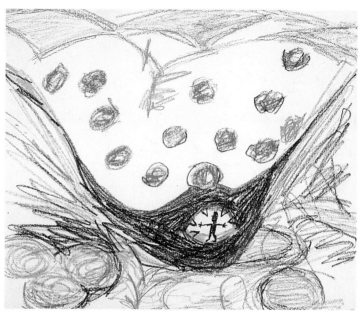

4.

5.

6.

7.

8.

5. When Harry Harlow found that baby monkeys got more comfort from a warm, fuzzy mother-substitute than from a wire one that gave milk, he thought he had found the secret of mother love.

6. But when grown, the same monkeys became inept, neglectful mothers to their own infants.

7. Yet giving them time to play with other monkeys their age prevented such abnormalities.

8. And, he and Stephen Suomi found, placing the abnormal monkeys with normal, younger infants — "therapists" — made them well again.

9.

10.

11.

12.

Children, too, are resilient — up to a point.

9. Mexico, 1985.

10. With the Sandinista army, Nicaragua, 1986.

11. A boy writes home from camp, Chatauqua, New York.

12. New York, 1979.

13.

13. Dagomba boys apprenticed at drum school, Ghana, 1990.

14. Russian children crowd their teacher with flowers on the first day of school each year — a national holiday.

15. Weaving in Zinacatán, Mexico, as studied by Patricia Marks Greenfield. It is taught by the mother in the daughter's "zone of proximal development" — with exactly the right degree of challenge, step by step.

14.

15.

16. The East European Jewish *cheder*, one of the oldest continuously functioning systems of elementary education, and one of the most successful. Here it is transplanted to the Williamsburg section of Brooklyn, New York.

17, 18. Muslim boys and girls are taught the Koran by traditional methods. The girls belong to the Al Argam sect in Malaysia.

16.

17.

18.

19.

19. A sixteenth-century open classroom? It illustrated a popular Persian love story of a boy and girl who meet at school. The teacher holds a rod, but the children's poses suggest that he must have spared it.

20. Breaker boys sifting coal in a scene all too representative of the nineteenth-century experience of childhood in the United States.

But mass education slowly but surely began to spread throughout the world.

21. A turn-of-the-century Chinese classroom.

22. A harmonica lesson in a Tokyo primary school.

20.

21.

22.

Six

Life's Lessons

When they have passed their fifth birthday they should for the next two years learn simply by observation whatever they may be required to learn. Education after that may be divided into two stages — from the seventh year to puberty and from puberty to the completion of twenty-one years. Thus those who divide life into periods of seven years are not far wrong, and we ought to keep to the divisions that nature makes.

— ARISTOTLE, *Politics*, circa 345 B.C.

———

O N A RECENT EVENING my almost-four-year-old, Sarah, stood rapt watching her twelve-year-old sister, Susanna, do her writing homework. Susanna, in a mood to be solicitous and kind, suggested that Sarah could go play instead. "No," came the answer, "I want to watch you." And then after a pause, "It's so amazing. You just make those squiggles, but it's really writing." Sarah can appreciate a level of mental mastery of the world that she cannot now attain, even though she does write some letters. What will happen to her in the next few years is first of all a physiological process and only secondarily — albeit crucially — a process of learning. She has set her foot on the bridge leaving early childhood, that wild land of imagination and amazement, and will slowly but surely pass over to middle childhood, a more developed country where travel is guided by cognitive maps.

The bulk of the changes occurs after age five and before age eight, and so has come to be called the five-to-seven or five-seven shift. Sheldon White of Harvard University is the psychologist who laid the foundation for our understanding of this change, and who first realized its biological nature. Among other things, there is a stabilization of brain-wave rhythms in a basically adult pattern. Children become capable of new kinds of learning, and mature grammar is attained in language development. These changes hint at fundamental growth in the brain at this age. Some experts point to the completion of myelination — the laying down of more rapidly conducting sheaths along the nerve paths. Others see changes in the granule cells — tiny, densely packed cells of the hippocampus, a brain region crucial to memory.

There are yet other theories, and we will not understand the neurology of these changes for many years. But even outside the brain there are physical changes — the loss and slow replacement of the "baby teeth," and especially the mid-growth spurt. This is a speeding up of the pace of physical growth — height or weight gained per year — which otherwise declines steadily from a peak while still in the womb to the growth spurt at puberty. This raw fact of purely physical growth seems to clinch the theory that the five-seven shift is in large part biological.

It also has led to a fascinating evolutionary speculation that points to the *human* meaning of middle childhood. Our closest animal relatives, the apes and monkeys, have a pubertal growth spurt like our own — which few other species do — but it comes much earlier, without a mid-growth spurt, and without the prolonged slow growth corresponding to our middle childhood. Evolution often works by changing the growth pattern of a species in order to produce a different adult form, and this has apparently happened as we evolved from our monkey and ape ancestors. Most phases of growth have been lengthened — for example, gorillas are developmentally ahead of us in infancy. But there may have been a specific change in which the growth spurt of adolescence was interrupted and most of it postponed from age seven, eight, or nine (when it occurs in gorillas) to the teenage years (the human timetable). The five-seven shift could be the evolutionary vestige of what was formerly the start of puberty, but with hormonal and sexual development — and the adolescent turmoil that often results — put off for years.

These years became what we call middle childhood. It is a time when the extreme dependency, emotional turmoil, and intellectual confusion of early childhood have been left behind, but the driven, sometimes chaotic, hormonally transformed mental and social life of adolescence has not yet begun. These are the years when the child is seen by societies throughout the world as a vessel into which knowledge, skill, and tradition — in short, culture — can be steadily and reliably poured. So a phase of human growth that has been more or less stuck by evolution into an otherwise uninterrupted race toward puberty — a sort of temporary braking process — has made possible the process that makes us most different from our ape ancestors: enculturation, or the imbuing of a child with a culture.

But before we get to the cross-cultural evidence, we must first understand the mental life of middle childhood, and that means defining the "extra card" added to the "computer" during the five-seven shift. The most widely known hallmark of this mental transition was discovered by Swiss psychologist Jean Piaget. It is called conservation — the idea that quantities of things often stay the same through transformations that change their appearance. We have already the germ of the idea in John Flavell's experiments on appearance-reality distinctions in four-year-olds in the United States and China: *before* the five-seven shift, children grow markedly in their ability to distinguish a real from a paper flower. But Piaget's classic experiments on the conservation of quantity are more demanding. I tried one with Sarah, age three years, eleven months — not long after the night when she stood amazed at her sister's writing.

Two straight rows of dimes, each with six pressed close together, lay beside each other on the table. I asked whether both had the same number or whether one had more. "They both have the same," she said. Then, as she watched, I spread out the six dimes of one line to make it longer. "Now, does one line have more, or do they still have both the same?" "This one has more," came the answer, as she pointed to the longer line. We tried it several different ways, including "Can you buy more candy with one of them, or would both buy the same amount of candy?" Her eight-year-old brother, Adam, was looking on impatiently; I had planned to test him, too, but I would only have insulted him. As soon as I turned him loose, he was giving his kid sister a gentle, spirited lesson on the conservation of number. None of this made any difference. Sarah stuck to her mistake.

Now, like most age-bound tasks for children, there are ways to set up the task differently, simplify it, or teach about it that will allow preschool children to show some degree of understanding. Such experiments have become a cottage industry among developmental psychologists, proving again and again that Piaget underestimated younger children in one way or another. But what they definitely do *not* do is abolish the difference between the younger kids and the older ones — who do the job promptly, easily, under a wide variety of conditions, and without being taught. No amount of teaching or manipulating the conservation task will give Sarah what the five-seven shift will give her: a better brain.

One of the convincing things about the shift is that all major theories of child psychology claim a major change at this time. For Freud, it was the time of resolution of the Oedipus complex; the child suppresses his or her infatuation with the opposite-sex parent and intense anger toward the rival in order to enter a less sexual, less emotional phase called latency. For Piaget, it was the time of transition to operational thought — not just conservation but a more general ability to stand back from the evidence of the senses, not through the imaginative exuberance of early childhood but through a new set of rational-thinking skills. For Vygotsky and other Russian psychologists, it is the time when "interior speech" begins to be used by the child to regulate action. In classical learning theory, it is a time when the simplest forms of learning — as in Pavlov's famous experiment in which dogs came to salivate at the sound of a bell — give way to learning in which mediating mental processes, especially words, help link the stimulus to the child's own response.

Cross-cultural studies confirm the importance of the shift. The latency concept is questionable in many cultures like the !Kung, where children play at sex games throughout middle childhood; when they play house, they simulate sexual intercourse, while our children mask their interest by "playing doctor." Still, attachment is less emotionally intense in !Kung children after age five, and the sex play of the next few years simply does not have the seriousness of sexual contact in puberty. In this sense even the !Kung have a distinct period of development corresponding to what Freud called latency.

As for serious activities such as school and work, !Kung children during middle childhood are about as free of responsibility as are younger children. But in many other cultures throughout the world, wherever responsible behavior is demanded of children, that responsibility is rarely assigned before middle childhood. Most cultures recognize what has in fact been proved in cross-cultural trials of Piaget's experiments: the mind of what we call the school-age child is qualitatively different from that of younger counterparts; they cannot really match it through training, only through growth.

• • •

Yet hunting-and-gathering cultures like the !Kung and the Baka have no formal training corresponding to schooling or apprenticeship. Consider, for example, how Baka children learn their tasks. Against the dense green of the rain forest, a four-year-old boy trails along behind a group of women cutting plantains in a banana grove. The boy hefts his own heavy machete with difficulty, trying to chop fungus off a fallen tree. Or, an eight-year-old boy goes along with his father in a group of men and boys of all ages to gather honey (steal is a better word; I gathered bee stings as well as honey during similar expeditions among the !Kung). The boy hacks at a big tree trunk with an ax, while grown men do the same nearby, and as they break out the honey, they and younger boys rush to eat it in the comb. Or, both a four- and an eight-year-old boy watch their father smoke termites out of their underground mounds. The boys watch, eat termites, and learn.

But in these situations the difference between age four and age eight is not a drastic one. The ability differences are there of course — they are biological. But the process of learning by watching, by playing, and by slowly doing is roughly similar at the two different ages. The difference is one of degree. Yet most cultures throughout the world recognize the five-seven shift. This was shown by Barbara Rogoff, then working with White, in a comparative study of cultures throughout the world as described by anthropologists. Rogoff and her colleagues found that whether cultures have serious task assignment or formal schooling for children, the earliest age at which they begin the process is sometime during the five-seven shift.

How can we reconcile these facts about task assignment in traditional cultures with the facts about the Baka and the !Kung? There — as in most other hunting-and-gathering societies, the type of culture from which we all evolved — there is neither formal instruction nor formal task assignment. Children spend almost all their time playing and socializing, and the learning they must do occurs in fairly casual interactions with adults and older children, where observation and imitation are embedded in the nature of things. Girls do spend some time caring for babies, and children of both sexes sometimes go on gathering expeditions where they make a contribution. But compared to the essential chores performed by children in agricultural societies — contributions without which their economies would founder — the work of hunter-gatherer children is very minimal.

This is not true of agricultural societies such as the Zinacantecans of Mexico's Yucatán region. There, children have major responsibilities beginning in middle childhood: hoeing for the boys, weaving for the girls. Carla Childs and Patricia Marks Greenfield, psychologists at UCLA, have studied the process by which girls learn to weave. Weaving is complex, systematic — six separate, difficult steps must be mastered — essential to the society, and a skill universally developed among Zinacantecan women, as well as in many other traditional societies throughout the world. Yet, like Baka honey-gathering, it appears to be transmitted completely informally — so much so that even some adults in the society say that girls learn to weave "by themselves."

In reality, they are taught in a one-to-one apprenticeship in which a skilled woman guides their learning. The process is interactive; "teacher verbalization is very much a part of [it]," but "teacher impels learner to *do* rather than *say*, through heavy use of imperatives in her own speech; and learner responds by weaving a lot and speaking little." Teaching "is adapted to the skill level of the learner" — in short, "scaffolding" is provided for cognitive growth. The result is "no-failure learning." The mastery of patterns involved in learning to weave does not generalize to settings where pattern recognition is formally tested. But it does allow universal performance of a crucial skill produced by patient, effective teaching in childhood.

• • •

True apprenticeship is generally more complex and intense than this, since the child is often as much a servant as a learner. It has been a common mode of teaching — and a common fate of children — in many parts of the world, and it is deeply woven into European and American history. In colonial Williamsburg, Virginia, for example, a young boy might be bonded to the masters of a foundry, and at the same time consigned to their care. He would be doing menial, sometimes dangerous work in the foundry, such as fetching water and tools and stoking fires, and in exchange he would be fed and clothed and have a roof over his head. But he would also, slowly but surely, learn the techniques of working with iron — "the art, craft, and mystery of foundering" as the contract said — that would ensure his adult livelihood and status in the community. The knowledge of these techniques — as with those of other crafts like cabinetmaking, stonemasonry, and printing — had an almost mystical quality. To give up a part of one's childhood in exchange for them was considered a fair trade. Of course, this concept was only for freemen's children. The child of a slave in colonial Williamsburg would serve, of course, but not be admitted to the mysteries of craft and guild; she would not trade her childhood for high-status knowledge, but for cooking and cleaning — or worse, would simply have her childhood taken away.

One of the most impressive *current* examples of apprenticeship is in the drummers' guild among the Dagomba, a traditional agricultural chiefdom in northern Ghana. It has a lot in common with apprenticeship in craft guilds and even professional guilds in medieval and Renaissance Europe. But its influence goes far beyond the craft of drumming. The rhythms themselves are extremely challenging to master, and the performances to mark rites of passage — weddings, naming of babies, funerals, installation of chiefs — are crucial and honored displays of ritual and skill. But drummers are also the historians in this society, and as such are the guardians of tradition. It is they who provide, from memory, the record of important past events, as well as the genealogies of all Dagomba citizens — essential, since all claim to be descended from chiefs.

Like the medieval guilds and the colonial crafts they gave rise to, this is a closed club, a fraternity that may be joined only through descent. The sons of drummers join, and the daughters each provide one son from the next generation. Apprenticeship begins at age five, and it takes at least four or five years of instruction and practice before public performance begins (some boys learn more quickly, but still have to wait). In parallel with drum lessons, boys memorize the genealogies, as well as other history, folklore, musicology, even drum-making and -maintenance. The teaching is oral, including informal and intimate sessions as well as group rehearsals and recitation. The boys live with their masters, and observation is crucial to learning. They also serve them as in other apprenticeships, doing chores, running errands, and carrying drums for their masters during performances.

Although this education is narrowing rather than broadening and is elitist in both theory and practice, it accords enormous status and power to the child grown up. (In these respects it reminds me of my medical school experience, an apprenticeship at a much later age.) The Dagomba drummers' guild school differs from our elementary and middle schools in that it tries to train a very specific set of skills in a very limited, hand-picked group of pupils. It combines some elements that we would consider traditional — rote repetition, authoritative teaching, chore assignment — with some that fit well with progressive trends in American education, such as observational and interactive learning embedded in daily life.

· · ·

But how much can we learn from it as we try, with increasingly intense effort, to improve that education? Apprenticeship in drumming, however complex and beautiful, or even in the memorization of tribal history, may not be similar enough to what we need to achieve in our schools. Yet the mastery of history and geography surely has something in common with drummers' knowledge of tribal lore. Also relevant to schooling is a kind of mathematical apprenticeship among the children of street peddlers in Brazil.

In Brazil's major cities, many poor families augment their income by selling in informal street markets — about a tenth of the working population. One or 2 percent of these entrepreneurs are children between eight and fourteen years old. They help their parents, or in some cases develop their own businesses, selling snack-foods such as popcorn, peanuts, and coconut milk. But don't confuse them with middle-class American children selling lemonade. This is not play, it is crucial family income.

Terezhina Carraher and her colleagues at the National Center for Scientific and Technological Development in Brasília studied how such children do their necessary roadside arithmetic. They chose Recife as their study site, and began by approaching children between nine and fifteen years old as if they were just customers. But they had specific problems in mind, and asked specific follow-up questions. One "customer" told a twelve-year-old, "I'm going to take four coconuts. How much is that?" The child answered, "Three will be 105, plus 30, that's 135 . . . one coconut is 35 . . . that is . . . 140!" Another asked an eleven-year-old, "What would I have to pay for six kilos?" (of watermelon, at 50 Brazilian cruzeiros per kilo).

CHILD: "[Without any appreciable pause] 300."

CUSTOMER: "Let me see. How did you get that so fast?"

CHILD: "Counting one by one. Two kilos, 100. 200. 300."

There is nothing astounding here, although some educators might be surprised at the speed and facility with which these barely schooled youngsters — they'd had about three years of very inadequate study — could calculate on the street. More surprising is what happened when they were later given problems of similar difficulty in a formal paper-and-pencil situation. The twelve-year-old who solved the four-coconut problem with ease was given the same problem (35 times 4) in abstract form, verbally, about a week later, and encouraged to write down the answer. The child explained out loud, "4 times 5 is 20, carry the 2; 2 plus 3 is 5, times 4 is 20," and then wrote down an answer: 200.

What seems to be happening here is that the child has learned very imperfectly some school-based strategies of paper-and-pencil calculation, and turns to them when formally tested. All street-calculation knowledge flees at that moment, and the child is helplessly trapped by the wrongly learned classroom strategies. The formal test, against the background of a little bit of schooling, makes the child temporarily stupid. This recalls the failure of Zinacantecan girls to pass formal pattern-recognition tests that are closely related to skills they have long since mastered in weaving.

Of course, school-based strategies are valuable. One twelve-year-old street vendor arrived at the price of ten coconuts by adding three groups of three and then adding one. An average well-schooled fourth-grader would have gotten the answer much faster by placing a zero after the 35. Also, the street vendor's strategy would break down under a challenge like "9 kilos at 187 cruzeiros," a problem readily handled by slogging through the method of paper-and-pencil carrying. So the issue is not whether school-based methods should be taught. Carraher and her colleagues

> do not dispute whether "school maths" routines can offer richer and more powerful alternatives to maths routines which emerge in non-school settings. The major question appears to centre on . . . where

to start. We suggest that educators should question the practice of treating mathematical systems as formal subjects from the outset and should instead seek ways of introducing these systems in contexts which allow them to be sustained by human daily sense.

•   •   •

But always, we must consider specific children, and what those children can really do. While still in high school, I was a summer day-camp counselor at the League School for Seriously Disturbed Children, and also volunteered to work with such children in the psychiatric wards of Kings County Hospital. These children — most were autistic, emotionally inaccessible, and unable to communicate meaningfully in any way — were a challenge to anyone's belief in universal educability, but my version of this belief remained temporarily impervious to the challenge.

An eight-year-old boy whom I got to know well — let's call him Timmy — spent almost his entire life walking stiffly on tiptoe with his head cocked as if listening for a message that might be hidden somewhere in the world. He moaned softly, continuously, and abstractly with neither positive nor negative emotion. But as vividly as I remember him I remember his mother's exhausted face, looking at me with a strange, profound, yet detached sadness as I applied my hopes on behalf of her hopeless son. He was moving toward the stage of puberty when he would almost surely face institutionalization. Looking back, I only hope that I did not add to her suffering any measure of new guilt, any further enticement of useless hope.

In Timmy we have an anchor point for our concept of educability. His unique and limited brain served to block almost all educational effort, yet he had to live and be cared for, and those around him had to find some teaching strategies, however minimal, that could connect him at least a little with his own special world. But even among the vast, highly educable majority, all children are individuals. Each has a slightly different mind and brain, a slightly different readiness for learning. And we can begin to learn about those differences by first looking at children whose minds are really different: those with learning disorders. These range from attention deficit and hyperactivity to specific reading and calculating disorders. Such children pose a special set of problems in our quest for universal education. If we are to take this goal seriously — and

I certainly do — we cannot avoid or skirt the general issue of children's internal readiness for learning. This is different from the question of overcoming social and economic disadvantage to achieve universal education, although both minority-group status and learning disorders are overrepresented in low-income people. We will come back to this connection, but for the moment let us look dispassionately at what we have learned about the prevalence of children with special problems.

Recent studies of children brought to doctors for all reasons and of children randomly sampled from American communities have arrived at this estimate: between 12 and 22 percent of American elementary-school children have diagnosable problems that could interfere in one way or another with schoolwork — one child in six. This is a conservative estimate arrived at after eliminating children whose problems were probably transient or otherwise basically normal problems of childhood. At least 2 or 3 percent of all children have a particular problem in paying attention — "attention deficit disorder," or ADD. Most of these, although not all, have hyperactivity — inability to sit still — adding to their classroom problems.

It is well established that these children can be helped by certain stimulant drugs. Such drugs — especially Ritalin, which is closely related to amphetamine — are now in wide use throughout the United States. The theory is that these drugs stimulate attention, thus paradoxically reducing restlessness. The drugs are relatively safe, often effective over a period of months or years, and praised by children and parents as well as teachers. School performance — not just conduct — improves. However, it is not yet clear whether the benefits extend into adulthood in the form of a more satisfactory educational outcome.

A larger proportion of all children, perhaps 10 percent, have what are known as oppositional or conduct disorders, which lead them into behavior problems at school, especially problems with authority. (As might be expected, separating these disorders from hyperactivity is a diagnostic challenge.) These, like attention and hyperactivity disorders, are much more common in boys than in girls. The remainder of the psychological difficulties in children are emotional disorders such as depression and anxiety, or behavior problems like bed-wetting, which may or may not influence school functioning. Significantly, this estimate of one-sixth of children does not include either general developmental disorders like mental retardation or specific ones like dyslexia. These are not classified by psychiatrists as mental disorders, but obviously they have an enormous impact on the children who suffer from them — as well as on their classmates and teachers.

Specific developmental disorders are an important category because most are treatable and do not imply a generalized lack of intelligence — a common mistaken inference. Even if untreatable, they can usually be gotten around in school because of the child's average or better skills in other areas. They may or may not be associated with a generalized attention problem. The best-studied specific disorder is dyslexia, or developmental reading disorder, which affects from 2 to 8 percent of children. Other less-common disorders include persistent problems with speech, writing, calculating, and motor coordination. The last is not something that schools emphasize; yet a deficit in motor coordination limits functioning in any activity involving use of the hands or the body — bike riding, sports, crafts, and mechanical tasks, among others.

No one really knows how these disorders come about. No doubt they often emerge from misunderstandings or emotional conflicts around a particular subject, even a particular teacher. Labeling the deficit can reinforce the failure in some children, so that the label becomes a self-fulfilling prophecy instead of a path to successful treatment. There is even some evidence that self-fulfilling prophecies can affect whole classrooms whose teachers have been told that their pupils are slow.

Yet we know that at least some cases of hyperactivity and dyslexia are *not* caused by a flawed educational process. In late 1990 the *New England Journal of Medicine* published a path-breaking study of the brains of hyperactive people, conducted by Alan Zametkin and his colleagues at the National Institute of Mental Health. For ethical reasons the study was done with adults, but it is likely that the results would be the same with children. The subjects were upper-middle-class people of average intelligence, free of alcohol, criminal, or major medical problems. But they had been formally diagnosed in childhood as having attention deficit disorder with hyperactivity, and were still dealing with it as adults. In addition, each had at least one child with the same symptoms.

These were matched with nonhyperactive adults for age, socioeconomic status, education, and I.Q. All performed a simple attention test using computer-generated tones. They had to choose the softest of three tones of the same pitch, presented in random order two seconds apart, a test known to be difficult for children with attention problems. While the subjects were attending to the tones, Zametkin and his colleagues were watching their brains. The method, known as PET scanning, follows the brain's use of glucose, a simple sugar that supplies the brain with energy, to determine how active the brain is, and where.

PET scanning showed clearly a lower level of brain activity in the hyperactive group than in the normal controls. Sixty different brain locations were measured, and the hyperactive people showed lower activity in thirty of them. The most significant differences were in areas, such as the frontal lobes, that help us inhibit action and balance thought and emotion. But the lower brain-activity level is general. The positive effect of stimulant drugs begins to seem less paradoxical; if lower brain activity is the basis of inattentiveness, then increasing brain activity could fight boredom and thus reduce restlessness.

These brain studies have not solved the puzzle of hyperactivity, but they open a very promising path of discovery. The same is true of brain studies of specific reading disability. Albert Galaburda and his colleagues at the Harvard Medical School have examined the brains of four individuals who had been diagnosed as dyslexic and who had died of a variety of causes unrelated to their brain function or behavior. The brains had in common a developmental defect — an abnormal arrangement of cells in parts of the left hemisphere that might well underlie a reading problem. In most people, the left hemisphere handles language and analytic thought, while the right processes spatial relations and emotion. But brain studies have been done on only a small fraction of dyslexics, and do not negate an educational or psychological cause for the disorder in many children. However, they do show that not all learning disabilities stem from cultural causes like bad teaching and emotional abuse.

•   •   •

This is even more true for generalized learning disability, or mental retardation. The I.Q. — "Intelligence Quotient" — is the quick and crude route to detecting this disorder. Like educators, psychologists, and physicians throughout the world, I rely on it here for convenience — not because I think it measures decisively what most people think of as general intelligence. In the 1970s Ulric Neisser, a founder of cognitive psychology, made a formal distinction between "academic" and "everyday" intelligence — not news to most of us, but something that needed to be said out loud by a leading authority. I.Q. tests measure best the kind of intelligence that schools value, but there are several other kinds.

Still, academic intelligence is important in our society, and schools are the place where it is discovered and nurtured. I.Q. can change to some extent at any age, but in practice it stabilizes during the five-seven shift, and from that time it predicts fairly well both later I.Q. and school performance. Contrary to popular opinion about testers, few who use this kind of test are unaware of its limitations. Many children score low because they are sick, moody, abused, or linguistically or culturally disadvantaged. Professionals, far from assuming that one number can express the whole of a child's mental ability, often use it precisely to show that the global score has been pulled down by a specific deficit in one or two areas, balanced by high-level functioning in other areas. Thus the test can help identify an attention deficit or a calculating deficit in a child of otherwise normal intelligence.

But what does "otherwise normal" or "normal" mean? For the purposes of I.Q., it means merely "average" — by definition. If you read a child's global I.Q. score, you are basically looking at a numerical summary of performance on a test in relation to all other children the same age at the time the test was standardized. Under ideal circumstances the I.Q. scores of a population of children at, say, age seven will follow a distribution resembling a bell or a Stetson hat with the crown rounded. The peak of the hat should be exactly in the middle, at a score of about 100, because that is where the largest number of children are. The truly exceptional small minority of children, for better or for worse, will be in the brims.

We want to believe, in the phrase that humorist Garrison Keilor made famous, that "all the children are above average" — at least in our town. (This has been called by some educators "the Lake Wobegone effect," after Keilor's imaginary town.) But by definition, half the children in a bell-shaped curve are below average. Most of those below-average children are perfectly normal. But if a child has an I.Q. lower than around

70 — this is not a strict cutoff point, just a guide to further, individualized assessment — the label "mentally retarded" is applied, because this level predicts that the child will need special services and care. Fewer than 5 percent of children fall below this line. The most severely affected will not appear in school, but most of the 5 percent can and do. Another 11 percent of all children have scores between 70 and 85; they are not mentally retarded, but they pose a formidable challenge to teachers who try to bring them along with the other children in typical classrooms.

Genes account for only about half the variation in I.Q. This is a lot, but it also means that education must affect I.Q., and many studies show that it does — it can add as much as fifteen points. But there are limits to these effects. More significantly, some of the environmental variation in I.Q. has nothing to do with education, except for the sad fact that it stands squarely blocking it. This is the damage sustained by children's brains under the influence of prenatal alcohol or cocaine, poor nutrition in pregnancy or infancy, poisoning by lead and other toxic substances, and head injury, whether accidental or not. These factors also limit the genes' effect on I.Q., but they are not part of the educational or cultural environment. They belong to what might be called the biological or biomedical environment.

The brain cannot always recover from these early insults, and they leave a biological legacy of learning problems that are not caused by genes, but are at least equally lasting. In the United States, elementary schools are facing an enormous influx of the first large cohort of "crack babies," and the effect will be both pathetic and burdensome. Possibly the most profound of the disadvantages sustained by children in poverty is that they are more likely to be exposed to any and all of these biological insults. No amount of goodwill or educational method will make things right for a child who has come to school with a damaged brain. It is necessary not just to help those children after they are damaged — often possible, but expensive and difficult. The goal is to stop the damage before it happens.

• • •

The studies showing that abnormal brain structures can cause dyslexia, a highly specific learning disability, underscore a fact that gets far too little attention in our educational system: Children have distinctive brains. Fortunately this does not always and simply mean worse brains. Physicians and educators have always known of individuals with general mental disability — either autism or mental retardation — who showed in one area of performance a skill that was far above average. I once met an autistic young man who was incapable of adapting to life outside a hospital but could multiply two three-digit numbers quickly in his head. He was not perfect, and once when he knew he was wrong the frustration led him to attack his neurologist. But his ability would have been re- markable in anyone, and against the background of his general disability, it was astounding.

Similarly impressive feats can occur in the arts. Nadia, an autistic child who began drawing well at age three and a half, went on to make mag- nificent pictures of roosters, pelicans, riders on horseback, composite an- imals, and other subjects that showed extraordinary maturity and skill. She was studied by Lorna Selfe, a psychologist in Birmingham, England. The drawings included perspective, anatomical knowledge, and sensitivity to movement at a level of competence achieved only by highly talented much older children and adults. Indeed, she never drew like a child. Un- like Robbie, the boy who grew tense and finally violent while trying to multiply three-digit numbers, "Nadia enjoyed drawing and this was when she was most animated and lively." At age nine and a half she had been in a school for disturbed children for two years, and she had improved somewhat in social relationships and acquired a small amount of speech. She no longer drew spontaneously, but on request could still produce drawings that were very good for her age — yet nowhere nearly as good as they had been when she was four or five.

Nadia had a somewhat abnormal electroencephalogram (EEG), and the abnormality showed itself differently in the two halves of her brain. She was left-handed. Selfe speculates that her left-brain/right-brain balance may have been abnormal — that right-brain areas governing drawing ability may have been pushed to develop more because of impairment in the left-brain language regions.

What is clear, though, is that children have different brains. It is easiest to show this in abnormal cases, but it is also true within the normal range. The differences are not completely the result of genetic or other prenatal causes. Head injury, lead poisoning, microbes, high fevers, and other problems of childhood may also contribute. And we cannot rule out the power of learning and culture to influence strongly the course of brain development. One of the few educational psychologists who take the brain seriously is Howard Gardner of the Harvard School of Education. He has done research on both the psychological effects of brain damage and the development of creativity in normal children, and his books — especially *Frames of Mind: The Theory of Multiple Intelligences* — make the connection between the two explicit and accessible.

Gardner confronts and undermines the idea of general intelligence, substituting an elegant conception of the differentness of children's brains. "We find," he writes, "from recent work in neurology, increasingly persuasive evidence for functional units in the nervous systems . . . a biological basis for specialized intelligences." In evolutionary terms, "human beings have evolved to exhibit several intelligences and not to draw variously on one flexible intelligence." But this serious academese doesn't show quite how radical Gardner's concept is.

> First of all, try to forget that you have ever heard of the concept of intelligence as a single property of the human mind; or of that instrument called the intelligence test, which purports to measure intelligence once and for all. Second of all, cast your mind widely about the world and think of all the roles or "end states" — vocational or avocational — that have been prized by cultures during various eras. Consider, for example, hunters, fishermen, farmers, shamans, religious leaders, psychiatrists, military leaders, civil leaders, athletes, artists, musicians, poets, parents, and scientists. . . . [Samuel Johnson] once defined "true genius" as "a mind of large general powers accidentally determined to some particular direction." . . . I strongly challenge the notion of large general powers.

In its place Gardner defines at least six kinds of intelligence: linguistic, musical, logical-mathematical, spatial, bodily-kinesthetic, and personal (he has since divided the last into two kinds that correspond roughly to outgoing and inward-looking personal intelligence). The sorts of people who might make use of them could be, for linguistic, a poet or interpreter; for musical, a rock star or violin teacher; for logical-mathematical, a theoretical physicist or accountant; for spatial, a painter or chess master; for bodily-kinesthetic, a pitcher or ballerina; and for personal, a community leader, psychotherapist, or parent.

Now, how can this outlook be reconciled with the I.Q. test, an alleged measure of general intelligence? Anthropology has always stressed the limits of Western-type, tested intelligence, and emphasized other kinds: !Kung hunters' knowledge of animal behavior, New Guinea adults' animistic intelligence, Zen masters' religious intelligence, and the interpersonal intelligence of nonliterate people throughout the world. Cross-cultural experience lays the groundwork for an acceptance of multiple intelligences. The evidence of neurology about the varied effects of damage to different parts of the brain proves that the brain has modules for different types of function, and that one of these can excel while others fail.

But the I.Q. test is useful nevertheless. First, it can bring out some of the multiple intelligences, when scores on different subtests differ markedly. Second, it does measure two of the intelligences in many children: linguistic and logical-mathematical. These, for better or for worse, are the ones we have expected our schools to foster. As long as our society needs these more than some of the others, this emphasis will be appropriate in general schooling. Gardner has helped start a school — the Key School in Indiana — where children can grow in any of the multiple intelligences he has defined. But critics think the children are being done a disservice if they are not told that some intelligences count more than others, or that a talent is not the same as an intelligence.

Also, many people considered outstanding in their fields excel in more than one intelligence, or combine excellence in one with better-than-average functioning in another. Becoming a surgeon, for instance, does not require genius; but it does require high levels of linguistic, logical-mathematical, spatial, bodily-kinesthetic, and (ideally) personal intelligences. Or consider George Balanchine, whose genius as a dancer and choreographer was matched by his leadership and teaching ability; or Mister Wizard, the great popularizer of science for children, who is as much an entertainer as a physics teacher. These are not people who, like poet/painter William Blake, had high levels of two separate intelligences. They are people who could not do what they do without *combining* several intelligences in one lifelong effort. Finally, there are few fields of endeavor in which high levels of linguistic and/or logical-mathematical intelligence will not be a boon to you. As long as this is true, there will be a role for the crude notion of general intelligence, and for standardized tests of something different but related, called I.Q.

Yet the lesson of multiple intelligences must not be lost on us. The question must be kept in mind: Are we looking at disabilities or simply at variation? Even the disabled learner shares in the universal human desire to learn, and in characteristics like curiosity, adaptability, and the joy of mastery. Educator John Holt once pointed out that although adults with Down's syndrome may show the intelligence of a child, they almost never show the happiness of a child — perhaps because they have been made to feel unhappy about themselves. Since every intelligence, at whatever level, has the spark of curiosity, the main determinant of how brightly the flame burns will be the amount and suitability of the educational fuel.

• • •

Anne Frank's ordinary fear of the teacher's meeting — "Our whole class B1 is trembling" — reminds us of one of the (ideally) positive forms of stress that all modern children experience. The replacement of work with school — it comes from a Greek word for leisure — has happened throughout the developed world at all social and economic levels. It is happening today — rapidly and sometimes dramatically — throughout the developing world. In many places school and work must coexist, as in northeastern Brazil, where cousins of São Paulo's Oliveira children work in the morning and go to school in the afternoon. Worldwide universal education is a laudable goal, with profound consequences ranging from democracy to industrialization to population control.

Yet it has by no means been a blessing for all children. Throughout history, for at least some children, school has been a place of punishment, humiliation, and failure. The complaints of an ancient Mesopotamian youth learning to be a scribe confirm that schooling has been stressful for thousands of years. Today in the United States school is a place where guns are often found in children's possession, hard drugs are bought and sold, and dropping out is expected and predictable — and these things are now true not just of high school but of elementary school. Even the best schools are often said to be doubly failing: in their educational mission on the one hand, and in preserving children's emotional balance and self-esteem on the other. For every child who does it, getting up to go to school for the day is the main job of life; and whether it goes well or badly determines much about not just the present but the future, stretching out to the end of life.

A few cultures depart from the historical generalization in a positive way — that is, they have instituted and maintained formal schooling not just for centuries but for millennia. This includes the elite classes of China and Greece, and more ordinary Jewish communities scattered throughout the world. The traditional Jewish method appears to have been successful in reaching its general goals — widespread literacy, at least for males; and the identification and nurturance of scholars. Whether its specific goals are close enough to ours is a separate question, but it is likely that we can learn something from it.

The tradition survived intact in the communities of eastern Europe before World War II, where the population was measurably more literate than in the surrounding cultures. For example, according to the 1897 census of the Russian Empire, there were almost twice as many Jews who could read Yiddish, their native language (39 percent, including 49 percent of males and 26 percent of females) as there were Russians who could read *their* native language (21 percent). This last figure was lower than the proportion of *Jews* who could read Russian — their second language, using a different alphabet. These literacy rates were also much higher than historians estimate for classical Greece. Paralleling this grassroots success was another at the level of the academy: These communities succeeded in finding and supporting the outstanding scholars in their midst.

These communities placed an extraordinary degree of cultural emphasis on learning — book learning. They were called "the people of the book" because of a religious relationship to the Torah (the first five books of the Bible), which tradition held was given to their ancestors on Mount Sinai after a mass exodus from Egypt. The central event of their weekly worship was the ceremonial withdrawal of this book, in the form of a parchment scroll, for the dramatic chanting of passages from it, completing the book over the course of a year. Other books, such as the books of the Prophets, the Psalms, and an encyclopedic legal and interpretive work, the Talmud, were given an important secondary place.

No one was more respected than the scholar who had mastered these books, and who could understand their messages on practical matters ranging from whether a chicken could be eaten to whether a couple should divorce. Even more important was the spiritual value of the scholar, whose studies kept him close to God. In these communities there was no route to respect through military glory. There was a definite awe of rich businessmen, who had local influence, but the highest regard was reserved for scholars. For parents, few joys could match that of finding out that their child was a good student. Parental concern was a crucial link that made school an extension of home. Regardless of how bright a child was, parents and teachers viewed the goal of learning with respect.

Cultures that place a high value on learning often have customs and rituals to mark the first day of school. In the Soviet Union the first day of school is a national holiday, the "Day of Knowledge." On that day in 1990 Seryozha Shlyapnikov, age seven, got advice from his father and mother, along with stickers for his notebook and "chocolate for the brain." At school the parents and children assembled in the schoolyard, many holding bouquets of flowers. Some of the children gave little recitations, and the principal, a young woman, made a warm, welcoming speech. A new first-grader was given the honor of ringing the school bell to start the year; inside, in Seryozha's class, the children crowded in on their teacher, raising and waving a dozen bouquets of flowers.

In Japan months earlier, Chizuka Nakayama sat with her mother and father eating a ceremonial breakfast of fish, beans, and rice — a special meal to mark a special occasion. After breakfast, as Chizuka talked to her bear, her mother was dressed by a neighbor in a floor-length, formal, ivory-colored kimono tied with a brilliant multicolored bow. After dressing, the two women knelt on the floor and bowed to each other, and then the mother walked a cheerful Chizuka to school. There she received a yellow hat — the sign of a first-grader — and joined in a formal assembly with all her schoolmates, with older children singing and playing musical instruments in celebration. It would be impossible for so much ceremony to be lost on a small child. It clearly reflects her parents' commitment to education. In fact, the kimono and all it represents may be more important than many aspects of school structure and curriculum.

The East European Jews had a school-starting ritual as well. As described by Diane Roskies, Mark Zborowski, and Elizabeth Herzog, on the first day of school the child of three or four would be carried ceremonially to the classroom, known as a *kheder,* and immediately introduced to some of the letters of the Hebrew alphabet. While the child was poring over the letters, candy and coins would mysteriously drop from above and behind him onto the slate. At the end of the lesson honey might be dripped onto the letters, to be licked off by the child, linking learning with sweetness. Later, when he was ready to graduate to Torah study — at the age of five or six — a ceremony at home would mark the event. Next to a table laden with nuts, cakes, and wine, the boy would discuss the Torah with his teacher, in the presence of his parents, relatives, and three older students who would bless him.

Just before the blessings, the teacher would ask him if he would perhaps like to say some Torah. The boy would reply as prepared, "Of course! That is what I was created for. Although I am not yet worthy to 'say Torah' before you, yet I will say a few words. My teachers and friends . . ." And he would go on with an interpretation of the first few passages of Genesis. The older boys' elegant blessings would follow, and then the women in the room would shower them with nuts and candy.

Good students would progress to more and more intensive and complex levels of study with better teachers. In the teenage years, some would drop out to become apprentice craftsmen, farmers, or laborers, others to become businessmen. But the ideal was lifelong study for everyone. Adults would set themselves the goal of mastering at some level a section of sacred writings, and then offer a celebration in the synagogue when they had reached the goal. For a laborer, such an accomplishment might seem trivial next to the knowledge of the advanced student, but that comparison was not made. The goal was suitable for the adult part-time student, and when it was reached it was celebrated with all joy and solemnity. The message was not lost on the children.

Nevertheless, this system had its dark side, especially at the elementary level, where teachers were paid a pittance and looked down upon by parents. They sometimes responded with punishment, humiliation, and cruelty to pupils. Many who attended these schools recall being struck with the rod or whip — and this was not just for misbehavior but also for poor performance. Thus the paradox: a centuries-old educational system that honors learning and produces both outstanding scholars and a high general level of literacy, yet mixes sweetness with pain, the reward of self-esteem with the humiliation of punishment. And it leaves some children with bitter memories.

• • •

My own memories are of an education in the public schools of New York City during the 1950s, along with intensive Hebrew school (four afternoons a week plus Saturday and Sunday mornings) modeled loosely on the system I just described. At P.S. 152 I sat in fixed desks deeply (though not, back then, obscenely) etched by generations of disgruntled pupils, and was taught largely by rigorous elderly women trained before World War I. In Hebrew school as in public school there was no rod, but I was there buried in books instead of outside in the sunshine playing ball, and a teacher did once throw a well-aimed blackboard eraser at my head when he thought I was dozing. From the early years of public school I was given about as much schoolwork as I could stand, and by junior high was engaged in a burdensome program of school, homework, and exam preparation that took up most of my time.

Today I look back on all this with some fondness. I attribute to it most of the status and stability I have gained in a harsh and competitive world. I started out in a basically working-class family with handicapped parents who were rightly confused and frightened by that world. But my parents said, "Listen to your teacher," and I did. To them, my accomplishments in school were a cause for celebration. They and I knew that school was my best way up and out of their limited sphere.

But I was not always so nostalgic or so thankful. Already at thirteen, that age at which ideals and plans dawn so dramatically on the human mind, I was awake in my bed at night dreaming of a giant educational complex I would design, to nurture children-as-learners from nursery school to college. (For some reason I placed my pedagogical empire in Canada, as if such a bold plan could be realized only outside our borders.) I did not exactly know how this system of mine would function, but it would be better — and kids would enjoy it, learning effectively at their leisure without humiliation, competition, or punishment. Of course, *I* would be fully in charge.

• • •

By the 1960s two extreme camps in educational philosophy had been well staked out. One was the traditional method in old-fashioned schools, less punitive perhaps but not far from the stressful and competitive approach that characterized Jewish education — and without the honey to sweeten the work of learning. The other was exemplified by A. S. Neill's *Summerhill,* which told of a school where children learned at their own pace in a joyful way without any kind of pressure or competition, and certainly without humiliation or punishment. One boy who could not be taught to read and who clearly enjoyed his resistance to it was left alone for a couple of years; one day, at age eleven, he was found secretly reading a book with a flashlight under the covers at night. Less extreme but in the same camp was Joseph Featherstone's *Schools Where Children Learn,* which offered an account of a "revolution" in primary school education in Great Britain — a whole country, and a pretty respectable one at that — where "open" classrooms and individually paced learning had replaced the fixed desks and rote, whole-class lessons and drills of my childhood.

The new trends in education seemed to echo at least faintly the transmission of knowledge and skill in cultures like the Baka and the !Kung where there wasn't *any* schooling. Although my field research among the !Kung would focus on infancy and early childhood, I wrote a paper called "Learning to Hunt: The Ultimate Education to Reality." It summarized anthropological writings on this subject, mainly descriptions of how the process worked in hunting-and-gathering societies. Mervyn Meggitt's account of the Walbiri of Australia was typical:

> After the boy is aged five or six, he roams the bush with other lads, and his father sees little of him by day. Men spend much time cutting up damaged boomerangs to make throwing-sticks for their sons to use on these jaunts; and the boys display remarkable accuracy in killing small birds and lizards with the weapons. They now learn which flora and smaller fauna provide the best foods, they develop their tracking skills and acquire an intimate knowledge of the bush for ten miles or so around the camp. During this period, men take little part in educating or disciplining their sons, whose behavior towards them often reflects this lack of control.

And of the !Kung, who were to capture my imagination for years, Lorna Marshall had written,

> In their parents' presence the children imitate adult activities in vital, active ways, very exciting to watch, and participate in actual work as they are able. The adults pause to show them how to hold a digging stick, or a toy bow or drill, so that play and learning merge.

During my two years with the !Kung, I confirmed the accuracy of her observations again and again. Boys began learning to hunt through the same playful process described for the Walbiri. Only as teenagers did they begin to accompany their fathers on hunting expeditions, where they could learn by direct imitation. Boys and girls went along with women on gathering expeditions, where they gradually gained knowledge of plant foods and how to get them, but they were not expected to work very hard. Skills were absorbed more than they were drilled or taught, and play and learning really did merge. Studies and films of the Baka show that the same traditions hold true for them. Children go out in groups to collect snails or honey, and they are obviously having fun — but they are also bringing home food. And, not incidentally, they are learning the facts and skills on which life itself depends in their culture — "the ultimate education to reality." It had to work, and it had worked, for the vast majority of the history of our species.

The contrast between this ancient hunter-gatherer learning and structured modern schooling takes to an extreme the most fundamental tension in American education: between excellence and standards on the one hand and self-esteem and mental health on the other. Some experts claim that no inevitable contradiction exists here, that self-esteem for all and a relaxed, robust emotional health are perfectly compatible with the highest standards of excellence. Yet this same rhetoric has led to much higher standards in Japan, Taiwan, and elsewhere than it has in the United States.

· · ·

The Japanese edge in education, paralleling their edge in industrial competition, has now received so much attention in the media that we have grown numb to hearing about it. But the facts have not changed, and will not go away. Japan is succeeding amazingly well in educating its children, while some other industrial nations are failing. This brings us to the best research comparing the mathematics performance of schoolchildren in Japan and the United States, and on the family and school background to this difference. That is the research program carried out in the 1980s by Harold Stevenson and his colleagues at the University of Michigan, which also incorporated a Chinese sample to achieve a three-way cross-cultural comparison. While preliminary results of this research have been discussed for years, the full presentation, appearing in 1990 and co-authored with Stevenson's student Shin-Ying Lee, has confirmed the earlier reports.

Briefly, here are the facts. Children in three roughly comparable cities — Minneapolis, Minnesota, Sendai, Japan, and Taipei, Taiwan — were selected and tested. Ten representative schools were chosen in each city; then two first-grade and two fifth-grade classrooms were randomly selected from each school; and finally six boys and six girls were randomly chosen from each classroom. The resulting total was 288 children from each city. Mathematics testing was done systematically and carefully, with an eye toward eliminating cultural bias from the tests. Minneapolis was chosen because of its "middle America" quality; compared to many other cities, it has a low proportion of minority-group disadvantaged children.

The basic results are simple. Children in Japan and Taiwan are much better than American children in mathematics. The difference is evident in the first grade and, for Japan, increases by the fifth grade because of Japanese children's improvement and American children's decline. The fifth-grade superiority of the Japanese and Chinese children is neither subtle nor slight. Look at it this way: The *highest*-scoring American classroom (i.e., the class's average for all its children) was below the *lowest*-scoring Japanese classroom and below all but one of the Chinese classrooms. Or this way: The worst-scoring American classroom in the *fifth* grade was only slightly higher than the best-scoring Chinese classroom in the *first* grade. Or, worst of all, this way: Among the top 100 children in first grade, there were only 15 Americans; among the top 100 fifth-graders, there was only one American; but among the lowest-scoring 100 first-graders, there were 58 Americans, and in fifth grade 67, or fully two-thirds, of the worst scorers were American.

In the title words of a recent *New York Times* editorial, "Johnny Can't Add, Hiroko Can." This gap widens as the school years pass, with the result that American high-school seniors simply cannot compete in mathematics and science with comparable students from Japan, Taiwan, or a substantial number of other industrial countries. But Stevenson and his colleagues were not satisfied with their initial accomplishment, which was to show that American inferiority in mathematics extends downward into the elementary years. They set out to understand why.

It is not because of a difference in native ability or general intelligence. American children are on a par with the other two national samples in reading and language arts. More important, on *aptitude* tests designed to assess general mental ability (for example, perceptual speed, coding, spatial ability, and general information), there was no deficit in American children.

It is not because of the cultural or racial homogeneity of Japanese and Taiwanese classrooms. Minneapolis was chosen because of its relative homogeneity. Moreover, there is no "tracking" in Japanese and Chinese schools and classrooms, so that children of widely differing ability are present in each class.

It is not a matter of years of teacher training; American teachers had by far the longest professional training of the three groups, with the Asian teachers getting roughly a community-college level of preparation. It is not a matter of class size, which was more than twice as large in Taiwan (48 at fifth grade, as compared with 23 in Minneapolis) and almost as large (39) in Japan.

And it is not because Asian children are being processed through a lockstep authoritarian program damaging to their mental health, independence, and enjoyment of life. This is one of the most common claims of Americans, but it is just not true. Japanese and Chinese classrooms, extensively observed by these researchers and others, are places of stimulation, concentration, and enjoyment of learning. Child interviews and attendance records show that children like school as much or more than their American counterparts. Children worry about school performance, but overall do not worry more than American children, whose anxieties are about nonacademic issues — social acceptance and sports performance, for example. *Parents* in Japan make enormous psychological sacrifices so that their children can learn, but children's mental health is not compromised — at least not at the elementary-school level.

What does account for the difference is revealed in extensive research by the same group and others on the practical organization of schools, the attitudes of parents, and the relationships between parents and schools. To begin with the simplest things, American children spend much less time in school over the course of their education than do the Japanese and Chinese. While the school day is longer for Americans in the first grade, the reverse was true by the fifth grade. Furthermore, the Asian children spent half a day in school on Saturday. But most important is that the school year is much shorter for Americans — not only compared with Japanese and Chinese, but compared with almost all other developed countries. On average, American children spend 180 days a year in school, behind twenty-four other countries; nine, including West Germany, Israel, South Korea, and Thailand, have 200 days a year or more; Japan has 243.

In the Stevenson study, the Japanese fifth-graders spent almost half again as many hours in school over the course of a year (1,466) as the Americans (1,044); the Chinese spent even more (1,655). At least equally important is the organization of time in school. The Asian children have intense forty-minute learning sessions followed by ten- to fifteen-minute breaks. They have five or more recesses per day compared with two or fewer for Americans. They tend to hang around the school for nonacademic activities at the end of the day, while Americans tend to rush off elsewhere. As for mathematics, American fifth-graders spent three hours a week on it, while the Japanese and Chinese children spent twice as long. These conclusions were based on more than a thousand forty-minute observation periods in each of the three cities. Within the schools, the level of order, organization, and planning is much higher in the Asian cities, and they follow national curriculums and lesson plans. This planning extends also to the numerous recesses, which systematically release children from the pressure of concentration — to breathe easy, have fun, and return to concentrate again.

To go beyond these timing factors to possible differences in teaching methods, James Stigler and Michelle Perry made observations of mathematics learning in Japanese, Chinese, and American classrooms. They worked with the Stevenson group, but explored classroom interaction in more detail. One of their most interesting findings is that Japanese and

Chinese classes spend much more time on individual problems. Of all five-minute segments in fifth-grade math lessons, 75 percent were devoted to single problems in China, 55 percent in Japan, and only 17 percent in the United States. American teachers were slogging through many more problems per unit time, getting to the heart of individual problems — and individual misunderstandings — less effectively.

Stigler and Perry, with their biased Western eyes, watched in horror as a Japanese boy was kept at the blackboard, trying to draw a cube:

> The class was typical by Japanese standards: thirty to forty students at their desks arranged in rows, facing the teacher who was standing at the front of the room. Each student was working in his or her notebook, but there also was a great deal of discussion from desk to desk, and the noise level was rather high. The discussions were not inappropriate, however; rather, they were directed almost completely to the mathematical topic at hand.

One boy could not do the task and was brought to the blackboard.

> After working for five or ten minutes, he asked the teacher to look at his product. The teacher turned to the class and asked: "Is this correct?" The child's classmates shook their heads and said, "No, not really." After some open discussion of where the problem might lie, the child was told to continue working at the blackboard and try again. This scene continued for the duration of the forty-minute class. As the lesson progressed, the group of American observers began to feel more and more uncomfortable and anxious on behalf of the child at the board. We thought that any minute he might burst into tears, and we wondered what he must be feeling. Yet he did not cry and, in fact, did not seem at all disturbed by his plight. At the end of the class he finally drew a passable cube, in response to which the class applauded.

One might ask whether the word *plight* is even appropriate here. This boy got a good deal of his teacher's personal attention, along with help from the class, and ended up mastering the task, to the sound of his peers' applause. As for the rest of the class, they got the benefit of focusing on the problem in a way that may have helped them to understand it better, even while getting on with their own work.

But some of the most important differences are not within the schools. They lie in what can be called a culture of educational achievement in Japan and Taiwan that does not exist to anything like the same extent in the United States today. It has to do with the ancient Confucian tradition of excellence through learning, including taking competitive examinations — a tradition that pervades not only China but also Japan and much of the rest of East Asia. Its modern result is an intensely education-centered family in which both parents (especially the mother; *kyoiku mama,* or education mother, is the Japanese term) fully support the goal of educational excellence, set high standards, provide a home environment that promotes learning, and maintain exquisitely close and positive relations with teachers and schools.

Studies like Stevenson's have produced no evidence to support the stereotype of Asian parents as driving taskmasters who steadily lower their children's self-esteem and cash in their children's mental health in exchange for high grades. They tend to be much less satisfied with their children's performance than American parents, even while their children are outperforming Americans. But they emphasize innate differences in ability *less* than American parents do. They reject heredity as explaining children's performance, stressing instead the value of hard work as the path to success. Merry White, a sociologist at Boston University, has called this "the path of pure endeavor." Of course, a child's self-esteem can suffer if expectations are inappropriate. But all evidence shows that, despite deemphasizing innate ability, Japanese and Chinese parents tailor their expectations to the needs and potential of the individual child. They set goals that are difficult but attainable; in a word, challenging.

"Japanese mothers have been likened to good coaches, individuals who guide the players but keep cool under stress," write Stevenson and Lee. In interviews with their children, they found that the children were *less* likely to worry about how their parents would react if they got a bad grade, as compared with Chinese and American children. And as for how well they felt about school:

> American children were the ones who regarded elementary school less
> positively. . . . American children's expressions of dislike for school

must reflect, in part, their belief that school is not an interesting place to be. . . . Large classes, crowded schools, long hours in school, and large amounts of homework do not necessarily result in a dislike for school when gaining an education is considered to be one of the paramount accomplishments of life.

But there is more: "There was no evidence that Chinese and Japanese elementary school children experienced more stress than their American counterparts. Instead, the Chinese children appeared to develop strong internal motivation toward learning and achievement." In fact, "The very high self-perceptions and high confidence of the American children may prevent them from acknowledging the need to work hard." An extension of this observation might be to conclude that American children are being deprived of the boost to self-esteem that can come from rising successfully to an appropriate but difficult challenge; from internal motivation to learn; from working hard, stretching oneself, and doing one's very best.

Bart Simpson, the television cartoon character who has recently been very popular in the United States, brings the leveling spirit of American anti-intellectualism to a new low. He is opposed to exerting the slightest effort to lift himself above his own mediocrity. "Underachiever and Proud of It!" proclaims one T-shirt bearing his image. "Don't have a cow!" is his answer to every conceivable criticism by an adult; he blames them for having expectations. But most amazingly, some American parents are proud of him for it. Calling him a "genius of self-esteem," a writer in the *Atlanta Journal-Constitution* applauded Bart's ability to accept himself in all his mediocrity, suggesting him as a good model for all American children. On this theory, self-esteem and the avoidance of neurosis are essential at all cost, even to the complete sacrifice of competence.

But unfortunately there is a contradiction in this theory; as any child can tell you, consistently losing does not promote self-esteem, no matter how impervious to reality you may be. So every educational system needs to make a choice. You can get short-term gains in self-esteem and continue to lose ground; or you can try this theory: that self-esteem can also come from making a great effort, from facing uncertainty and overcoming obstacles, from meeting a standard that we were not sure we could meet, from doing our level best. You may have to struggle with a child from time to time to get her to overcome her doubts about herself, to dig in and really try. We inevitably doubt ourselves and our methods at such times. It's a risk. But only by taking it do you get to see that smile — no, it's a grin, really, and the face is open in a hint of astonishment — that breaks over the child's face as she slams the pencil down on the page and says in a thrilled, surprised voice, "I did it!"

• • •

Just as we know that a schoolchild's unique brain can enhance or impede education, we know that education can change the brain. Many experiments in animals have established this as fact. Even rats raised in stimulating environments have thicker cerebral cortexes, with more complex branching of their brain cells for more elaborate circuitry, and with higher activity of chemicals in the brain that are known to be involved in memory. Similar effects of experience on the brain have been found in many species, including monkeys closely related to us. So the brain-learning relationship is a two-way street. In coming decades we may understand precisely what kinds of learning have the greatest impact on brain function for good as well as for ill.

But in the meantime we have increasing information about how educational methods affect performance. Particular techniques of teaching and learning make a difference in children's skills, whether they change the brain's structure or not. Educational experiments have finally gotten down to a level of detail where we can start really to understand how children respond to them. Excellent recent studies have shown that experience with rhyme and alliteration during the preschool period gives children an edge when they learn to read. This fact contradicts the modern notion that "sounding out" or phonics learning in reading should be completely replaced by word recognition (which is also useful). Ironically, it returns us to the insights of the New England primer and the East European Jewish *kheder*, by way of Dr. Seuss's *Hop on Pop*.

Other experiments have raised the hopes of educators for the future of older, seriously disadvantaged children. Learning to read occupies the first few school grades, but by the fourth or fifth grade reading must become a tool, a basis for learning almost everything else. Disadvantaged children at this age, *without* dyslexia, are severely impaired by difficulties in extracting information from what they read. Ann Brown, Annemarie Sullivan Palincsar, and Linda Purcell developed and tested an interactive technique to encourage children with poor reading comprehension to develop the skills of summarizing, questioning, clarifying, and predicting from what they read. It worked with one or two students and it worked with larger reading groups. It generalizes well to the classroom setting. Poor comprehenders start with a 20 percent level of correct answers, but "after the experience of the reciprocal teaching sessions, students reach accuracy levels of 80–90% correct. The improvement on the daily comprehension tests was large and reliable." The process takes about two weeks, and the improvement is still present eight weeks later with no further intervention.

Finally, the concept of "scaffolding" — providing learning challenges appropriate to the child's level — has become the center of a new line of research. Barbara Rogoff and James Wertsch are among its leading practitioners. This line of research was inspired in part by Lev Vygotsky, the Russian psychologist — although the same insights can be found in every introductory textbook of anthropology, where cross-cultural studies have long since required that they be taken into account. The idea is that thinking and learning are basically social activities in our species, and that social interaction between teacher and learner must be involved in most learning. At any level the child's abilities have a frontier of sorts — known as "the zone of proximal development" — where the child's present competence meets the social context of the culture. The good teacher "follows in" to that zone, teaching exactly there.

The !Kung, the Baka, and the Zinacantecan weavers come to mind, as do the theories and observations of anthropologists such as Margaret Mead, who studied cultural transmission in traditional societies in the South Seas. So do the studies of Jane Goodall and others on how nonhuman primates acquire the much simpler but equally crucial skills they need to survive and thrive. A little-known but valuable book by J. Gary Bernhard, *Primates in the Classroom: An Evolutionary Perspective on Children's Education*, provides a recent summary of this long history and its implications for schooling. Whatever we decide to do with schoolchildren, we need to remember that they are fancy social primates. They have fine brains compared with other primates, but they have very similar feelings; learning invariably has to do with feelings, and feelings have to do with people.

• • •

In *How Children Fail* John Holt gave precise and individualized accounts of children's misunderstandings of classroom problems and exercises. These accounts report one-to-one conversations — relationships — although they somehow sometimes occurred in the context of teaching an ordinary class. One ten-year-old girl gave 432 as the answer to 2×76. Holt then gave her problems such as 2×100, 2×80, and so on, but returning to 2×76 she stuck to her wrong answer. However, after slowly going through this process again, and giving the wrong answer again, she suddenly said, "Now *wait* a minute. This doesn't make sense. I'm going to figure this out." And with pencil and paper she did. Her insight was like the street sense of the Brazilian peddlers; his teaching, like the patient focus on the cube in the Japanese class. In these conversations, Holt was able to help children slowly sense their own errors.

A different kind of personal attention is in evidence in Tracy Kidder's *Among School Children,* an account of a year in the life of a fifth-grade class and in that of an excellent teacher, Chris Zajac. The setting is Holyoke, Massachusetts, a public school with a mixed student body — a lot of Hispanic-American children, a lot of Irish-American children, and mostly poor children in both groups. But for much of the school year Chris has to contend with Clarence, a boy with a conduct disorder — although she never uses that or any other label. Clarence comes in with a thick folder that she refuses to read, feeling it will bias her against him. She gives him every chance. His bad conduct, cutting up in class, refusal to do assignments, and general teacher-baiting occupy more of her attention by far than the needs of any other individual student. When, finally — not by her request — he is sent to a school for problem children, a colleague in the teachers' lounge asks her how different the class is. "Night and day," she answers.

Meanwhile, a Hispanic-American girl named Judith — "the brightest child she had ever tried to teach" — and eighteen others do not get nearly as much attention. Chris does well by Judith, who has a truly exceptional gift for both spoken and written language. But how much more might she have learned that year if Clarence had not been in the class? How much more within reach might her goals have been? It is argued that children like Judith need to experience children like Clarence. In fact, Judith — little Judith — teaches Sunday school at her father's church, and has her own much littler problem boy, whom she calls "my Clarence." So she is learning from Chris and Clarence. But she is paying a price. And so are the children in the middle, who might need even more of their teacher's time than a self-starter like Judith does.

• • •

There are 42 million public school children in the United States, and $150 billion a year is spent on them — a larger percentage of the gross national product than is the case for Japan, Germany, France, or England. Our schools are failing our children, and we have yet to really understand why, but first and foremost the failure is a simple failure of will.

John Goodlad, professor of education at UCLA, capped a distinguished career by conducting in the early 1980s a large, well-funded study of 38 representative schools around the nation. More than 8,000 parents, 1,350 teachers, and 1,000 classes with over 20,000 students were studied using classroom observations and interviews. In his book *A Place Called School,* Goodlad described American classrooms as overwhelmingly teacher-dominated. Seventy percent of class time was devoted to instruction, most of which was talk by the teacher to a room full of students. Five percent of the time an expectation of student response was created, and only 1 percent of the time was devoted to student responses to open questions that might provoke reasoning or opinion. In students, what stands out is "the extraordinary degree of passivity."

For teachers, what stands out is exhaustion, boredom, and lack of appreciation. The "flatness" of the profession is seen as a major problem — not only are starting salaries low, but the reward for years of experience is very small. Also, opportunities for specialization, innovative roles for teachers such as teacher training or curriculum development, and other paths of professional growth are blocked by intransigent bureaucracies. Since Goodlad's book was published, the further experience of teachers has confirmed these observations.

As for the reformers of the 1960s, several prominent ones have retreated from the front. John Holt, who died a few years ago, spent the last years of his career as a leader of the home schooling movement. It was an honest choice, and in a way the logical outcome of his technique of individual conversations with children. It is a good solution for some children, but not the vast majority. Others have retreated to writing and research. Few prominent authorities on teaching — critics or otherwise — actually stay in the classroom.

My own children are in a private school — part of the so-called white flight, a misnomer in this case, since they are well integrated with middle-class blacks who, like us, are fleeing the poor of both colors. The school, although relaxed in atmosphere, is thought of as one of the better ones in Atlanta. It is run by a talented well-educated schoolmaster who deftly balances the progressive trends of the 1960s against high academic content and standards.

American standards, that is. Fifth-graders there score better than 90 percent of their American peers in math, but will still not look very good by Japanese standards. They do like school. There are no rows of desks, fixed or otherwise, but rather tables around which kids sit and chat while working, getting frequent individual attention from the two teachers per class. They work at a flexible individualized pace, and the teachers can tailor work to children's particular needs. A sign on the wall in one classroom says "Make it messy to make it good." It turns out that this means revise and revise again to make a piece of writing good. That's excellent advice, and a far cry from the standards of neatness that prevailed when I went to school.

This is the model of the British open classroom, and it works very well here. The children are happier than I was, I think. They certainly get more in the way of arts, music, theater, and sports. In many ways the school is a perfect compromise between the two ideals that tug at my mind: the !Kung or Baka "primates-in-the-classroom" model, where informal, playful learning has a very large role; and the classical ideal in which a whole complex civilization must be mastered. The staff is well trained and dedicated, not especially well paid, but with superb working conditions and very good pupils. Still, I keep thinking about Japan, where with rows of desks, large classes, less-educated teachers, fewer resources, and little cost to self-esteem, the pupils do consistently better than ours.

And of course, the best compromise may be no guide for the 42 million, especially those with the least money, facing the greatest disadvantage. It is fitting that we end with some observations of what seems to be working for those children. A comparison of two elementary schools in one of the poorest neighborhoods of Brooklyn, New York — the borough I grew up in — has proved enlightening. The two schools are very similar. They are ten blocks apart in Bedford-Stuyvesant, a neighborhood filled with abandoned buildings and lots covered with uncollected trash. Drug trafficking and violence occur on every street corner. The student bodies have the same composition: 90 percent black, 10 percent Hispanic, 100 percent poor — every child is poor enough to get a free lunch. Both schools have dedicated teaching staffs.

But P.S. 28 has 80 percent of students scoring at or above grade level on standardized reading tests, while P.S. 309 has only 36 percent scoring that well. P.S. 28 is smaller, and has a smaller average class size (23 versus 26). Students prepare for the reading test all year long, which P.S. 309 pupils don't. But the key difference seems to be in expectations and discipline. Thelma Peeples, the principal at P.S. 28, says, "I honestly believe there's not much my children can't do. I believe it; the teachers believe it; the parents believe it." She tests children frequently to identify deficiencies. She insists on quiet throughout the school, strictly limiting bathroom excursions. Students walk in single file, and are not allowed to say "yeah" or "ain't." Most important, perhaps, 41 of the 315 students (13 percent) were suspended last year at P.S. 28, while only 8 of 833 (less than 1 percent) were suspended at P.S. 309. The principal at 309 is also responsible and competent, but Thelma Peeples is fierce, intent, insistent. Thelma Peeples is demanding.

So is Madeline Cartwright, principal of the Blaine School in North Philadelphia — a neighborhood possibly worse than Bedford-Stuyvesant. There, the issues were different; in a sense pre-educational. She made the school the center of the neighborhood, getting teenagers to feel like members who could borrow equipment instead of stealing it. She confronted abusive parents personally and *then* called the hot-line. She interposed herself between a fourteen-year-old prostitute and a customer. She forced parents to help her clean the toilets in their homes. She answered the phone herself in the morning so that teachers calling in "sick" had to speak to her. The first summer she shamed eighteen parents into helping her clean the school, encrusted with years of filth, scrubbing the whole place until it sparkled. "You must think you're in the suburbs," one mother said at the meeting.

Madeline Cartwright said, "The dirt in the suburbs is the same dirt that's in North Philadelphia — if you don't move it." She pulled every string in every bureaucracy, and gave some bureaucracies a pretty wide berth, to bring parents — the right parents — into the Blaine School. She twisted their arms, she bribed their children, she put them in some small way on the payroll, until the place was weighted with a responsible adult presence, ballast in the dreadful storm of inner-city life — until it began to look like a North Philadelphia version of the first day of school in Japan. And she said to them over and over again, "There's things you can do!" Madeline Cartwright is demanding. Madeline Cartwright has standards.

Many things are being tried. In Atlanta, "magnet schools" are being devoted to particular themes, like the clothing or printing trades, and are attracting superior teachers and students alike. In Rochester, New York, high teacher salaries *tied to performance ratings* are bringing teachers in from far and wide, and in a new home-based guidance program teachers are monitoring children's progress (twenty per teacher) through home visits and phone calls. In Milwaukee, two schools are devoted exclusively to black boys, who fail at epidemic rates in ordinary schools. Rising above traditional criticisms about segregation, Milwaukee officials are courageously pioneering an experiment that may staunch a gaping, hemmorhaging wound in their inner-city community. And throughout the nation, school systems are finally overcoming outmoded ideas about teacher certification to bring highly talented people, from retired executives to recent college graduates serving in a Teachers' Corps, into school situations where they are desperately needed.

But without standards none of these experiments will work. There are many kinds of standards. A reading score is a standard. A stunningly executed jazz dance is a standard. A clean toilet is a standard.

An ironic fact that has come out of recent educational research is that minority-group parents hold higher standards for their children than do either their white counterparts or the children's own teachers. This research was led by the same Harold Stevenson whose team compared Japan and China with the United States. Three thousand black, white, and

Hispanic elementary-school children in Chicago were compared on achievement, and their parents were interviewed about their beliefs. Stevenson and his colleagues Chuansheng Chen and David Uttal conclude:

> Black and Hispanic children and mothers evaluated the children and their academic abilities highly; they were positive about education and held high expectations about the children's future prospects for education. Mothers of minority children and teachers in minority schools believed more strongly than white mothers and teachers in the value of homework, competency testing, and a longer school day as means of improving children's education.

• • •

An old fable had the animals starting a school. The duck was excellent in swimming but not so good in flying and very poor at running. So he was made to drop swimming and take make-up lessons in running after school. These so ruined his web feet that his swimming suffered, but no one worried since his running was now average. The rabbit, who could run like the wind, had a breakdown because of too many swimming lessons. The squirrel could climb and run, but these abilities suffered because of his flying class. The eagle was reprimanded in climbing class because, although he was first to the top of the tree, he insisted on using his own method to get there.

Perhaps something like this was meant by the great philosopher of education, John Dewey, when he urged us to "think of the insolent coercions, the insinuating briberies, the pedagogic solemnities by which the freshness of youth can be faded and its vivid curiosities dulled." We need to ask, always, what an education is for. Is school a place where we make round pegs fit square holes or where natural curiosity, the impulse to explore and learn, is allowed to flourish? Is the goal indoctrination or liberation?

Education among the Baka, the !Kung, and other hunters and gatherers — quite possibly the model for learning among our remote ancestors — is informal, personal, imitative, and usually fun. It entails risks, and parents have to be willing to expose their children to risk. But adults or older children are there, "following in" to the place where the child's competence and confidence mark her frontiers. Children are helped and taught so that their confidence increases, with a view toward individually paced learning. Finally, their learning is emotionally meaningful, forming a part of the structure of the web of social bonds.

Consider a child learning to ride a bicycle, something almost always taught informally. In the United States, the Soviet Union, and Japan there are striking similarities. It is a difficult skill, rarely learned before middle childhood. A parent is usually present, walking along beside the wobbly rider, hands prepared to anticipate a fall. The child has substantial emotion staked on the process, and of course is made to feel secure by the parental bond. But despite all this, the child will fall and cry — and must be allowed to fall, if learning is to occur. Perhaps it is even necessary, to make the lessons sink in, but in any case, if the child does not fall, it is unlikely that he or she is taking enough chances; without taking chances there can be little increase in skill.

So we may need to do several things in education. First, contextualize it socially and culturally, with a basic recognition that children are primates — or, more exactly, hunter-gatherers — in the classroom. It should be playful enough so that it is its own reward; primate and hunter-gatherer learning is crucial, yet it's fun. And in the case of the Baka children gathering honey, the external reward is immediate as well: the honey goes from tree to hand to mouth. So perhaps we ought to find some immediate way to sweeten learning. But with this sweetness goes the risk of bee stings, and the very real pain when they occur. So children have to take some risks, and even feel some stress, or else their learning may not be adapted to life.

Second, we may need to do something specifically human and cultural: formally mark and support learning with rituals that dramatize, inspire awe, dazzle; invoke some signs that are weighty and old, conveying the wisdom of generations in support of every new child's natural thirst for knowledge. Hunter-gatherers do it in their rituals of puberty, which render certain kinds of lessons painful, large, and sacred. The Russians do it with flowers and poems, the Japanese with full-dress kimonos, bowing, and yellow hats, the East European Jews with a command performance, showers of candy, and honey on the slate. Such rituals punctuate and solemnize the long march of learning necessary in these cultures. They give mothers and fathers the chance to declare in no uncertain terms how much education means to them. After that, how can it help but seem valuable to the child?

Finally, we may need to think carefully about the ultimate rewards we promise children: Work hard in school and you will have a better life. Sometimes we are lying, and when we are, they know it. It is not irrational for a child to ignore school when he knows that what is promised there will never be fulfilled. But if we reward a child with fun, and sweetness, and ritual, and in addition keep our promises at the end of the line — really, truly a better life — we will have a system more in tune with human nature and with the wisdom of other cultures; and, maybe, even one that works.

1.

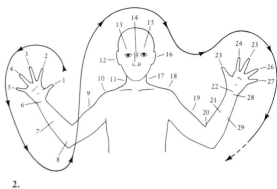

2.

3.

1. Reading, writing, arithmetic —
and much more. Howard Gardner
has defined a spectrum of different
kinds of intelligence.

2. The Oksapmin people of New
Guinea do their counting with
body parts as a mnemonic — a sort
of human abacus. Every culture
somehow challenges children's
ability to learn.

3. The famous New England
Primer, in a 1723 edition; but the
couplets date from much earlier.
Rhyme and rhythm have often been
used to facilitate learning to read.
Now we have proof that it works.

4. Parental involvement in learning
is the basis of school success. Here
Anita Gholston, a college counselor,
takes time from her busy life to
work with her son Malcolm.

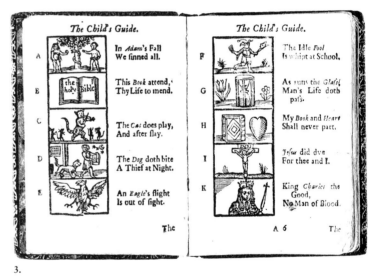

4.

24
This drawing is very detailed. Note the bridle, tunic, trumpet and hand, together with the inappropriate and disturbing face, and squirrel on the horse's side. Drawn at approximately 5 years 6 months.

5.

6.

Argentina   The Philippines   Japan   China   Syria

Iran   Hong Kong   Denmark

8.

5. Whether normal or abnormal, children have distinctive brains. Nadia, a severely autistic girl with a very low I.Q., drew this at age three.

6, 8. Two horse-and-rider drawings by slightly older normal children, almost a century apart. The "X-ray" technique is characteristic.

7. In early childhood, figure-drawing shows a certain constancy.

9. But thereafter cultures bring children into special ways of seeing, as in this drawing by a boy five years, nine months old, in Bali.

9.

10.

11.

10. Literacy may change the shape of family relations; Pietro learns to write, turn-of-the-century New York City.

11. The need for knowledge can be transcendent. Italo Renzotti, eleven, who lost his hands and eyes in World War II, reads Braille with his lips, Italy, 1948.

12.

Child labor:

12. U.S.A., farm labor.

13. Carolina cotton mill, 1908.

14. Bogotá, Colombia, 1979.

13.

14.

15.

15. *Children's Games*, Pieter
Brueghel the Elder, 1560.

16. *Children's Games*, detail.

16.

17. Hoop play in modern Egypt.

18. *One Hundred Children at Play,* China, twelfth or thirteenth century.

17.

18.

But some children's work imparts competence and pride.

19. A Parisian boy on an errand, 1958.

20. A boy waters his family's camels at the Niger River, Mali.

21, 22. Play or work — in this case, prawning — at the seaside? In the nineteenth century, it depended on social class.

19.

20.

21.

22.

SEVEN

Marbles and Morals

'Then come home, my children, the sun is gone down
'And the dews of night arise;
'Come, come, leave off play, and let us away
'Till the morning appears in the skies.'

'No, no, let us play, for it is yet day
'And we cannot go to sleep;
'Besides, in the sky the little birds fly
'And the hills are all covered with sheep.'

— WILLIAM BLAKE, "Nurse's Song"

———————

"PUNCH BUGGY RED! No punch back!" yells a twelve-year-old or eight-year-old or even three-year-old voice beside me in the car, while a small burst of pain spreads through my shoulder, the impact of a child's fist. One of them has been alert enough to be the first to spot a Volkswagen "bug" on the road. This, according to local child lore, allows you to punch the nearest unlucky person — *without being punched back.* All you have to do is see it first and come out with the formula, including the color. As Sarah has amply proved, even a three-year-old can do it. But a three-year-old could never invent it or formalize it. In that sense it belongs to the realm of middle childhood — a realm of aggressive feelings, to be sure, satisfied by an unpunished punch in the shoulder; but also a realm of rules, reciprocity, and fairness.

And of tradition. These kinds of games and spoken formulas are part of a substantial and entrenched child culture, a vast web of interconnected words and practices that link — and have always linked — children throughout the world. They change from time to time and place to place, responding to the opportunities of technology and history. But they stay remarkably constant in purpose and function, and their continuity even in form is sometimes astonishing. They make up an independent children's culture, one that only children control, and that dances continually in the spiritual nooks and crannies around such solid cultural edifices as families, schools, churches, and media. Even fairy tales and lullabies, those staples of natural culture, are semi-institutionalized now through an endless train of books and recordings. But "Punch buggy red, no punch back!" is a piece of culture that belongs to absolutely no one but children.

Much of what we know about this child culture is thanks to the tireless, lifelong work of Iona Opie and her late husband, Peter Opie. The Opies took child culture seriously when the great majority of anthropologists, folklorists, and child psychologists ignored its intrinsic richness and its many lessons about the nature of both culture and childhood. They found it a gold mine. Consider: not just games, but riddles, jeers, curses, ditties, oaths, pranks, tricks, songs, pacts — in the case of the English language, at least, even the words for all these things — have deep, ancient roots. And most of the forms found among children in any American city today have variations or parallels around the country and the world.

"Punch buggy red," for instance, is a trick that resembles one described by the Opies for the town of King's Lynn, Norfolk, in 1950s England:

> *I pinch you, you can't pinch back,*
> *For I see a man in a white straw hat.*

Straw hats have gone out of style, Volkswagens have been introduced in the United States, and pinching has changed to punching, but those alterations in content do not alter the striking sameness of form. The key elements of alertness, one-upmanship, aggression, and the rule abrogating vengeful reciprocity and escalation all apply in both cases, and the rhythmic formal utterance seals the ruling. Some Americans report a similar custom on passing a car with only one headlight, sometimes called a "pididl," on the road at night. The triggering event needs to be moderately uncommon, but not rare.

Some of these things have more extensive cross-cultural parallels. According to my children, if two kids happen to say the same thing at the same time, they must try to count to ten aloud fast and then say the word *jinx*. Whoever gets through the whole thing first has put a curse on the other one, who must remain silent until someone speaks his name — or else face seven long years of bad luck. He is allowed to write to get a friend to do that, and if he has managed to say "Stop" before the count is over, the curse is averted. Rituals on saying the same word together are found throughout the world, although wishing is a more common form than jinxing. In Italy, the counting element is also present; children link little fingers and shake their hands up and down three times, saying "Uno, due, tre"; they then break their grasp and say either "Flic" or "Floc." If this word, too, is the same, they each get a wish. In Egypt, children who have spoken the same word say "Your life is longer than mine," a way of wishing each other long life.

"Made you look! Made you look!" is the formula Atlanta children utter when they have tricked someone into looking at something that isn't there. I remember it from the Brooklyn of the 1950s, where I was at a disadvantage because of my trusting nature. We used to say, "Made you look, made you look, made you buy a penny book!" — which price indicates that the saying was already old by then. Since my children leave off the second line, their form might be thought of as degenerate, a custom losing its traditional shape. Similarly, Atlanta children say, "No backs!" after a swop, when they want to ensure that the other child will not renege on the deal — crucial in a world without contracts. Back in Brooklyn we used to have to touch something black and say, "Touch blacks, no backs," a form identical to one in Liverpool, England, at the same time. "Finders keepers, losers weepers" was a Brooklyn formula to seal one sort of good luck, again to prevent the former owner from taking it back — in this case contrary to adult rules and to a more mature sense of justice. This slogan was also widespread in England.

But there does not seem to be evidence of any general decline in these customs due to television, family mobility, or other aspects of modern life, because in other sayings my children's version is more elaborate. We used to say "Liar, liar, pants on fire!" to humiliate a child caught in a lie, but my children add, "Hanging on a telephone wire!" (in another Atlanta version I learned from a seven-year-old, the hapless miscreant is sitting instead of hanging). While walking on pavement or flagstones we said "Step on a crack, break your back" (or "break your mother's back"), while my children say

> *Step on a crack, break your mother's back,*
> *Step on a line, break your father's spine.*

Various versions of this are found throughout the United States and Britain — as are variants of the pledge "Cross my heart and hope to die." We used to say it just like that, but one of my young friends says you should follow it with "Stick a needle in my eye."

Children who cry too easily must be brought in line, it seems, almost as rigorously as liars. Cry-baby is a common term, and in Brooklyn we had a singsong chant, "Baby, baby, stick your head in gravy" — related to a version collected in Bishop Auckland, Britain, by the Opies around the same time: "Baby, baby, brown bread and gravy." This seems a cruel turn, and children the world over are amply capable of cruelty, but look at it from another point of view: Sometimes a child cries half-deliberately to get his or her way, especially if there are adults around. Such a child rends the fabric of rules that holds the world of play together, appealing too often to emotions and influences that don't belong there. Like lying, crying can be a violation of fairness.

But these kinds of traditions are also frequently the vehicles of cruelty. In Brooklyn, when you got something away from someone, or got the better of him fairly or not, you could reinforce his hurt feelings with the simple chant "Nya-nya, nya-nya-nya," to the following tune:

My children in Atlanta, like children in many parts of the world, use almost this same bar of music for different syllables: "Nanny nanny boo-boo." But even this nasty custom gives form to hateful feelings and sets some sort of limit on them. As we shall see, when not limited they can become very dangerous. And in any case, the formal nature of the custom once again belongs to middle childhood.

Some bits of child folklore are not oral but written, and that makes it possible to show some long-term continuity. I recently found my mother's junior high school autograph book, filled with entries dated 1923. In New Brunswick, New Jersey, in that year, her older sister wrote on the last page, "The one who writes in this book after me is a better friend than I." In mine, from the Brooklyn of 1958, my best friend wrote, "If anyone thinks more of you let them right [*sic*] on the next page." Another near-match appeared in her book upside down:

> *As you go from city to city,*
> *from town to town,*
> *Remember the girl*
> *who wrote upside down.*

That girl was Marie Bly; and thirty-five years later "Pat Mc" wrote in my book,

> *Remember the girl in the city,*
> *"   "   "   "   " town,*
> *"   "   " who ruined your book,*
> *By writing upside down.*

Wendy A. wrote in my book, "Dated till hell freezes and all the devils go ice skating," while the corresponding message in an earlier era was written, "Yours till H--- freezes and the little devils go ice skating." But some were in my book only, and would never have slipped into my mother's: "Your face is a treasure — go bury it," for instance, and

> *Roses are red,*
> *Violets are blue,*
> *I killed my dog*
> *Because he looked like you.*

In fact, this charming ditty appeared in my book *twice,* penned by two different companions.

But some of the most interesting traditions in the child culture are games — not formal, grown-up–organized games like baseball and soccer, but playground and schoolyard games that children play, regulate, and reinvent *by themselves* throughout the world in every generation. Hide-and-seek is one of the most perennially popular of these, and my children and their friends play it in Atlanta more or less as we played it thirty-five years ago in Brooklyn. According to one twelve-year-old slightly beyond the hide-and-seek stage ("We used to play it a lot more last year"), the game goes locally as follows:

A base is defined, as are boundaries beyond which hiding is not allowed. One child is "it." That child covers her eyes and counts out loud, the size of the count depending on the size of the already defined boundaries. At the end of the count, the "it" child starts searching for the others. If she succeeds, the one she finds first becomes "it" next. If she finds no one, she is "it" again, but local rules provide a two-round limit to that. As for the beginning of the game, "it" is chosen by the "one-potato-two-potato" method. The kids stand in a circle, each holds out a fist, and one pounds her fist down on each other fist in turn, chanting:

> *One potato,*
> *Two potato,*
> *Three potato,*
> *Four.*
> *Five potato,*
> *Six potato,*
> *Seven potato,*
> *More.*

The child touched on "More" is *not* "it," and the ritual is repeated until only one is left and *that* child is "it." Notice that if the first child were "it," it would probably be possible to calculate and unfairly determine the outcome on one trial; but the process of elimination is too complex for advance calculation, even for graduates of the five-seven shift. The chant can also be "Eeny meeny miny mo,/Catch a tiger by the toe,/If he hollers let him go,/My mother says to pick this one,/Out goes Y-O-U!" This has the advantage of matching words to the process (not to mention stimulating literacy) but seems to be less in use — perhaps because of unpleasant echoes of an old version in which a racist usage is substituted for the word *tiger*. After the five-seven shift, for better or worse, racism is firmly understood.

Some games are known to have spanned enormous distances in time and space. A Greek wine jug of the fifth century B.C. — 2400 years ago — depicts a small boy pulling a toy wagon, or possibly a chariot. From Central America before Columbus, archeologists have unearthed what appears to be a toy cart with wheels — and this in a culture that did not have real wheeled vehicles. Children of ancient Greece are also known to have played with balls, tops, and hoops. Almost a thousand years ago, during China's Sung Dynasty, a painter depicted "One Hundred Children At Play," and their play included riding hobbyhorses, juggling, and dressing up as grown-ups.

A similar work, "Children's Games," by the sixteenth-century Flemish painter Pieter Brueghel the Elder, shows many familiar kinds of play, including a tug-of-war, a pretend wedding, hoop rolling, and a game played by two girls that looks very much like jacks. Rolling hoops with sticks looks the same in Africa and the Middle East today as it did to Brueghel in the Europe of four hundred years ago; and in a poster by nineteenth-century French lithographer Theophile Steinlen, a little girl holds a hoop and stick as she walks with her mother or nanny in the street. Brueghel's blindman's buff appears quite similar to the same game in a woodblock print by Kitagawa Utamaro, a leading eighteenth-century Japanese artist.

We don't know, and probably we will never find out, which of these correspondences come from imitation and influence, and which from independent invention by children far apart in geography but close together in inclination and fantasy. Certainly informal games like these can cross barriers of language, race, and polity. But children anywhere with a bit of cloth and a day to while away might conceivably invent blindman's buff. Either way, these games belong to children, and it is a privilege for an adult just to be able to look and listen in on them.

• • •

We have already considered the five-seven shift as one of the evolutionary bases of cultural transmission — a defining feature of the human species. So it is not surprising that it should also form the basis of the complex rule-bound games and elegant verbal traditions of middle childhood. What was less expected perhaps is that the shift even lays the foundations of social relations in later childhood, and of that supreme regulator of relationships, the moral sense. Indeed, one of the most astounding findings to come out of the whole history of child-development research is that morality stems not primarily from parental discipline, nor from the lessons taught in Sunday school, but from social development in the natural course of play.

Fairness, rules, oral contracts, sanctions against wrongdoers or even just against oddball kids — these things are what many time-honored child traditions are about. They are not the concerns of early childhood, but require the mental facility granted by the five-seven shift. This was why Piaget was so fascinated by the game of marbles — and why his experiences playing marbles with children could lead to a book he titled *The Moral Judgement of the Child.* He understood that marbles was part of that vast, intricate netherworld of primitive culture controlled completely by children. And he knew — probably from his own childhood around the turn of the century — that it was a game replete with rules and resting upon a strong foundation of fairness that had to be at least as important as skill.

Who can resist a book that begins with this sentence? "Children's games are the most admirable social institutions." He mastered the game of marbles thoroughly himself, along with all its local variants among the poorer children of Geneva, where he was doing his research. All research should be this much fun. Piaget not only watched and interviewed children, he spent many hours playing marbles with them — and experiencing their reactions to his breaking of the rules.

He was able to trace three stages in the development of the child's idea of the rules. Before the five-seven shift, the child may seem to play by rules, but in fact there is little understanding of what they mean. There may be some degree of conformity, but the child's behavior is really an empty imitation of older children's rule-bound play, full of obvious errors that point to lack of deeper understanding. Between roughly ages seven to ten, the child plays with a greater understanding of the rules, and the rules are said to stem from higher authority — although in practice they are still frequently broken. An eight-and-a-half-year-old girl named Ros offered the opinion that the rules were invented by "a Gentleman" and that it is best to leave the game as it is.

> *But if people want to, can they change it?*
> Yes.
> *Can children?*
> Yes.
> *If they invent something will it be more fair or less fair?*
> Less fair.
> *Why?*
> Because it isn't the real game.

What is the real game?
The one the gentleman invented.
Why?
Because that is the one you always play.

By around age ten or eleven, children grasp the fact that the game is subject to change, and that children are in charge of the rules. A new rule may be invented by children, and it will be accepted and welcomed provided it is seen as fostering the two main features of the game: fun and fairness — two features that are exquisitely interdependent. Most interesting, this stage of flexibility with respect to invented rules is combined with a stricter-than-ever adherence to the rules. A twelve-year-old boy named Blas was asked to try to invent some new rules, and came up with the idea of playing in two squares, one inside the other, instead of just one.

Would everyone want to play that way?
Those who invented it would.
Later on, if your game is played just as much as the square, which will be the fairest?
Both the same.

Blas has graduated to the most profound understanding of rules, where they come from, and what they mean. He and his age-mates know that the rules come not from authority on high but from consensus on the ground (in marbles, quite literally). Yet they obey the rules now with a much more fierce determination. In effect, they have become moral, because they have absorbed the essence of morality, which is not rules but reciprocity or fairness. In Piaget's words, "moral autonomy appears when the mind regards as necessary an ideal that is independent of all external pressure. . . . Autonomy therefore appears only with reciprocity, when mutual respect is strong enough to make the individual feel from within the desire to treat others as he himself would wish to be treated."

Marbles and morals? The connection had proved intimate.

• • •

Among the more interesting research on moral development in recent years is work done by Ann Cale Kruger of Emory University on moral reasoning in children. Her experiments have tested and confirmed some of Piaget's most radical predictions in *The Moral Judgement of the Child*. While respecting Piaget's work, she wanted to be more systematic in her approach so that she could be more definitive in her conclusions. The subjects were forty-eight eight-year-old girls, and the materials were pictures with set stories relating to questions of fairness. For example, one of the picture-stories told of a class of children working together on a project that earned money. At the end they had to divide up the money — but on what basis? Equal shares for all? Each according to her work contributed? According to her talent? Need? There were four such stories, all ending in problems of a similar nature, known as "distributive justice" problems.

Now for the experiment. All the girls were brought to the child psychology lab by their mothers, but half of the girls (according to the luck of the draw) were asked to bring a friend as well. Kruger sat with each of the forty-eight girls and discussed one of the stories, randomly chosen from the four, asking the child to comment on a fair solution. She made it clear to the girls that *there was no right answer*. The goal was not to get an answer but to study the process of reasoning the children went through as they considered what would be a fair distribution. Then half the girls were paired with their friends, half with their mothers, for a similar discussion of two more problems, while the experimenter left the room. By prior agreement, a tape recorder was running throughout the experiment.

After the two kinds of pairs had each talked through their two problems, Kruger sat alone with the girl and talked about the fourth, remaining problem. The question was: How would the experimental intervention — discussion of two problems with either a friend or the mother — influence or improve the girl's processes of reasoning between the "before" and "after" talks with the experimenter?

From previous studies by psychologist William Damon of Clark University, Kruger devised a scoring system — an "index of moral reasoning" — for the child's contributions to the "before" and "after" discussions. A separate coding system was used to score the conversations the children had with their peers or mothers in between. This scoring highlighted the use of *transaction* — remarks or questions involving "reasoning about reasoning" — children commenting on their own or the other's ideas.

The results, published fifty-five years after Piaget's book, would have warmed the old master's heart. First, girls paired with friends showed more sophisticated moral reasoning after the discussions than did girls paired with their mothers. Second, the subjects paired with friends used active transaction — "reasoning about reasoning" — in their talks, much more than did the girls paired with mothers. Finally, among the girls paired with mothers, the ones who used the most active transaction had the greatest improvement in the index of moral reasoning. Put another way, the more "peer-like" the mother's role in the conversation, the greater the gains in moral reasoning for the child.

The really remarkable discovery here is that an eight-year-old girl profits more in her development of moral reasoning by actively puzzling through a problem with another eight-year-old than by working out the same problem under her mother's guidance. This confirms Piaget's intuition about the importance of children's games in fostering moral development, and runs counter to the widespread belief that morals are inculcated in more or less wild children by systematic exposure to adult guidance and teaching.

In Kruger's conclusion, "Piaget's contention that symmetry of power leads to greater moral reasoning . . . is supported, and . . . active reasoning is the essential element in the process." Subsequent analysis, somewhat paradoxically, showed that the reasoning must be not only active but spontaneous; mothers who used the Socratic method of directive questioning leading toward a certain answer did *not* improve their daughters' performance; perhaps the girls experienced this as patronizing, or as a kind of meddling with their own process of thought. But mothers who somehow more subtly encouraged the girls to reason and comment *spontaneously* apparently did foster moral reasoning.

• • •

One would think that it might give comfort to a religious person, especially to a religious leader or teacher, to recognize that moral judgment is something already existing within the child — something that will be brought out naturally and almost automatically through play and talk with other children. One might even expect such a finding to inspire faith, and thus to be readily recognized and embraced.

Instead, we find the practitioners of organized religion throughout history viewing children as intrinsically evil creatures who have to have the evil stamped out of them through corrective training. For fundamentalist Christians, it is Satan in the child, for orthodox Jews, "the evil inclination." How could such a concept have taken hold, and held for so long? Part of the answer is that there is what is fairly called an evil inclination in children — a tendency to be selfish, do harm, break rules — and to be fair to the religious view, that inclination is not the whole story: the Jewish theory holds that the evil inclination is struggling against an equally given good inclination, the Christian that Satan in the child's heart is balanced by Christ. But religiously motivated child-training methods have at some times in history — for example, in the colonial New England of the Puritans, in traditional Catholic Ireland, and in some ultraorthodox Jewish sects today — seemed based on the notion that the evil inclination in children is far stronger than the good. The resulting methods have sometimes included extremely narrow restrictions and harsh punishments designed to stamp out undesirable behaviors, from immodesty and fighting to talking back and idleness.

The psychological burdens that were imposed on children by some cultures were deliberate and systematic. Elizabeth Mascall, a Methodist homemaker in England, wrote in 1738:

> I have been endeavouring to my utmost to convince my children of their natural sinful state, and the necessity of a saviour, and to teach them what to believe and practice that they may be saved . . . while others are mourning over the sins and follies of their children, I have the pleasure to hear mine mourn in secret over their own sins. . . .

Here an ordinary eighteenth-century mother openly takes pleasure in her children's self-punishing guilt — diligently instilled by the mother herself. An earlier letter written in America in 1638 is even more telling, since it comes from an eloquent twelve-year-old boy who has fully internalized this guilt. Samuel Mather writes to his father,

> I feel also daily great unwillingness to good duties, and the great ruling of sin in my heart; and that God is angry with me and gives me no answer to my prayers; but many times he even throws them down as dust in my face; and he does not grant my continued request for

the *spiritual blessing of the softening of my hard heart* [emphasis in original].

The boy's metaphor of total rejection by God Himself is stunning. Most poignantly, he goes on to speculate, "I think that the reason of it is most like to be because I belong not unto *the election of grace.*" In the religious framework of the Puritans, this meant that he was already destined not for eternal salvation but for the other place, the horrors of which had colonized his young mind like an army of foreign troops deployed there day after day by his parents and teachers.

In both England and America whippings were as common as tales of hellfire and damnation, and even the doubts some parents expressed about them show how widely accepted they were. James Erskine, Lord Grange, an English judge, recorded in his diary for 1712 his disagreement with the methods of Cumming, tutor of Erskine's son Charles:

> As to the perverseness of the poor young child, it rarely is uncon-
> querable in a boy so very young, if proper methods be taken. I know
> the boy had a wantonness, as such of his age use to have, and is more
> pliable by persuasion than by rough treatment. But Cumming's
> crabbed peevish temper made him use the last method, and often to
> beat him severely for trifles, and sometimes when the boy was more
> in the right than he, till I put a stop to it, and now he says himself
> that the boy does well.

But there were also fathers like Samuel Sewall, who in 1688 in New England whipped his sons regularly and "pretty smartly," as when his ten-year-old was punished "for breach of the ninth commandment, saying he had been at the writing school, when he had not." The fact that this is not a breach of the ninth commandment — it prohibits false witness, not general falsehood — must have added confusion to the boy's experience of cruel punishment.

In contrast, what Margaret Woods, a middle-class fifty-one-year-old Englishwoman, wrote in her journal of 1799, showed a wisdom that is essentially modern:

> The love of liberty and independence is strongly implanted in the
> human mind. How far it should be indulged in the education and

conduct of youth, will by many people, be differently determined. . . . Either extreme, I believe, is prejudicial. Too tight a curb sometimes makes young people fret under it, and produces an impatience to be entirely free, when more gentle discipline might have produced submission. Little benefit can arise from mere compulsion. . . .

Sixteen years later she wrote to a friend,

> I have always wished that they should be afraid of doing wrong, but not afraid of me. I would encourage them to lay open their little hearts, and speak their thoughts freely; considering that by doing so, I have the best means of correcting their ideas, and rectifying whatever may be amiss. I am, from judgement, no great disciplinarian; if I err, I had rather it should be on the lenient side. Fear and force will, no doubt, govern children while little, but having a strong hold on their affections will have most influence over them in their progress through life. Obedience I do consider as an indispensable thing in education; but perhaps it would be imprudent to call it forth too frequently on trivial occasions.

Here Margaret Woods showed herself to be far superior to many of her contemporaries, and more than a few of *our* contemporaries, in the understanding of children and discipline. Compared to her older compatriot, Elizabeth Mascall, Woods appears a virtual genius of child psychology. Still, the route to our current understanding of the role of discipline and punishment in moral development was circuitous and full of stumbling. Many of the key issues are still subject to vigorous debate, with some blaming modern liberal parenting — the natural extension of the views of Margaret Woods — as responsible for unacceptably high rates of divorce, drug and alcohol abuse, and crimes against people and property.

• • •

To people like the !Kung, the Baka, most other hunter-gatherers, and many other traditional peoples, the disciplinary methods of eighteenth-century parents in England and America would simply seem abusive. Even the middle-class of Chicago in the 1940s — far more lenient in its child-training than these predecessors of the 1700s — scored as being harsher in parental discipline in every area except aggression. Recall that the !Kung have an essentially Piagetian folk theory of child development. They believe that the infant or child behaves in a way that is appropriate to a particular stage of life. Children therefore do not need to be beaten out of sinfulness and into submission, nor to be carefully taught every desirable behavior they must one day show, nor even to be consistently rewarded for doing the right thing. What they mainly need, according to this theory, is to grow — and to play. Play — behavior with no apparent immediate survival purpose, but which looks like fun — is very widespread among birds and mammals. It serves the functions of exercise, learning about the environment and about other group members, and sharpening of subsistence and social skills. In some mammals, we know, including monkeys and apes, deprivation of opportunities for play in early life has serious consequences for social and reproductive skills. Play is a form of learning; social play is a form of emotional learning.

It can't be a coincidence that the most intelligent mammals — especially primates, carnivores, dolphins and whales — are also the most playful. If an animal is short-lived, the young do not play very much, probably because there is too little time for them to gain much knowledge or skill from playing. In humans, with our long life span, slow growth, high intelligence, and learning ability, it is no surprise to find that play serves a critical function during development, even among hunters and gatherers.

Play is children's main activity throughout their waking hours in hunting-and-gathering societies, in contrast to the assignment of at least some chores and schooling after age six in other types of societies. So middle childhood in hunting-and-gathering societies is characterized by an increase in self-reliant behavior, but not in obedient or responsible behavior.

In herding and agricultural societies — as in our own society — obedient and responsible behavior in middle childhood tends to be more emphasized. A seven-year-old girl may spend hours each day tending and carrying her baby sister while her mother is working in the fields; a boy the same age may have full responsibility for guarding a herd of cattle that represents his family's entire (and very considerable) wealth. In a hunting-and-gathering society, neither of these tasks is necessary. In a quantitative study of middle childhood among the !Kung, Patricia Draper, an anthropologist at Pennsylvania State University, tested the hypothesis in a single changing society. She found that as some !Kung became more settled, kept more goats, and hunted and gathered less, they began to demand more obedience and responsibility from their children, while the laissez-faire outlook of traditional hunter-gatherers persisted in other groups of !Kung that did not settle down to a way of life based on gardening and goatherding.

In essence, there were *two* major transformations in the human past that changed the experience of childhood. The one we usually think of as the main historical transformation was and is associated with the Industrial Revolution or modernization. The other, which might be called the anthropological transformation — also known as the Neolithic revolution — occurred around ten thousand years earlier and followed the spread of agriculture. In the historical transformation school has slowly but surely replaced work; but in the anthropological transformation work replaced play.

• • •

Marjorie Shostak's now-classic book, *Nisa: The Life and Words of a !Kung Woman*, captures what it feels like to be a hunter-gatherer child at play, within the context of adult realities in an ever-changing, ever-challenging environment. Consider Nisa's reminiscences of the beginning of the rainy season in an environment where dryness and thirst are common almost the year round:

> The rainy season had finally come. The sun rose and set and the rain spilled itself. It fell and kept falling. It fell tirelessly, without ceasing. Soon the water pans were full. And my heart! My heart within me was happy. We lived and ate meat and mongongo nuts and more meat and it was all delicious.
>
> My heart was so happy I moved about like a little dog, wagging my tail and running around. Really! I was so happy, I shouted out what I saw: "The rainy season has come today! Yea! Yea!" . . . My heart was bursting and I ate lots of food and my tail kept wagging, wagging about like a little dog. And I'd laugh with my little tail, laugh

a little donkey's laugh . . . I'd wag my tail one way and the other, shouting, "today I'm going to eat caterpillars . . . cat — er — pillars!"

Another story of Nisa's illustrates the impossibility of separating play, learning, and subsistence in hunting-and-gathering cultures — even when the process crosses standard gender-lines:

> Another day, when I was already fairly big, I went with some of my friends and with my younger brother away from the village and into the bush. While we were walking I saw the tracks of a baby kudu in the sand. I called out, "Hey, Everyone! Come here! Come look at these kudu tracks." The others came over and we all looked at them.
>
> We started to follow the tracks and walked and walked and after a while, we saw the little kudu lying quietly in the grass, dead asleep. I jumped up and tried to grab it. It cried out, "Ehnnn . . . ehnnn . . ." I hadn't really caught it well and it freed itself and ran away. We all ran, chasing after it, and we ran and ran. But I ran so fast that they all dropped behind and then I was alone, chasing it, running as fast as I could. Then I picked it up by the legs and carried it back on my shoulders. I was breathing very hard, "Whew . . . whew . . . whew!"
>
> When I came to where the rest of them were, my older cousin said, "My cousin, my little cousin . . . she killed a kudu! What have the rest of us been doing? We men here . . . how come we didn't kill it but this young girl with so much 'run' in her killed it?"
>
> I gave the animal to my cousin and he carried it. On the way back, one of the other girls spotted a small steenbok and she and her older brother ran after it. They chased it and finally her brother killed it. That day we brought a lot of meat back to the village and everyone had plenty to eat.

The children were not expected to do that, but they did; and Nisa's sense of pride, in remembering these events more than forty years later, is palpable.

• • •

Beatrice and John Whiting, anthropologists at Harvard University, headed a group that studied childhood in five farming and herding societies around the world — corresponding to the middle stage of human history, between the origins of agriculture and the Industrial Revolution — as well as in a New England town, which they called Orchard Town. Their main approach was systematic, randomly distributed recording of children's behavior, following a prearranged code, and distributed throughout the day over a period of a year. Six teams of young anthropologists, all now distinguished in their own right, were trained in behavior observation and dispersed to the corners of the world.

The study has been known as the Six Cultures Project, and it provided the first really systematic, quantitative cross-cultural comparisons of children's behavior. The five agricultural societies were the Gusii people of Nyansongo, Kenya; the Mixtecans of Juxtlahuaca, Mexico; the Boco of Tarong, the Philippines; the Hokan and Japanese villagers of Taira, Okinawa; and the Rajput Hindus of Khalapur, India. Averaging all five, the percentage of observations that included work was 17, while play occupied 44 percent, and casual social interaction, 34 percent. In Orchard Town, the corresponding figures were 2 for work, 30 for play, and 52 for casual social interaction. But there, formal learning took up 16 percent of the observations, while the average for formal learning in the agricultural societies was only 5 percent. If the categories of play and social interaction are combined, their total changes little, while formal learning seems to replace formal chores.

Yet the average of 17 percent work is not consistent with an "all-work-and-no-play," oppressive notion of farm life. The highest percentage among the five agricultural societies was 41 percent. The Dickensian world of child factory labor during industrialization, or the turn-of-the-century child miners made famous in photographs by Lewis Hine, fit this description better than the farming past that preceded industrialization. The historical hump of early industrialization had to be gotten over, at least for the poorer children, before their work was returned by law to a level found in farming communities, and then eventually to a much lower level, to be replaced by a steadily increasing dose of compulsory schooling.

Nevertheless, the switch from 17 percent to 2 percent for work and from 5 to 16 percent for formal learning is not small. How oppressive was this work? By most accounts, no more so than school is. To the objection that school is for the child's benefit while work is exploitation by adults we must reply: Not so simple. Chores, too, entail learning and can be a main mechanism of cultural transmission — and also of expanding horizons. A study in Africa by Carol Ember, an anthropologist at the City University of New York, showed that boys who were assigned to take care of infants were more nurturing than other boys. Many chores are outdoors, interesting, and fun. Current studies of farm families support this at-least-partly-positive assessment of children's agricultural work.

Peggy Barlett, an Emory University anthropologist working in Dodge County, Georgia, finds that despite their hardships chores give children skills they are proud of all their lives, and can bring parents and children closer together. It is not just a matter of needing children's help, and letting them know it, but also of transmission of certain farm values. One mother, speculating that some might find the chores they assign cruel, said, "It's important to make them feel a *part* of the farm" — to make them feel "*I have a purpose here.*" They are buying an old tractor for their thirteen-year-old son, who likes rowcropping, and some female hogs for the eleven-year-old. When he sells the hogs he breeds, he will pay his parents back for that investment, but keep the profit. "You have to let them make money when they're eleven, so they'll have enthusiasm [for farming] when they get older," the mother said. She also said, "You have to start them at birth, practically, to raise 'em to be what you are."

Major farm-family investments also often involve children. They are asked to make sacrifices — of toys or movies, say — so the family can buy irrigation equipment, or even a new piece of land. Barlett notes, "A child who shares in the decision to buy such a piece of land develops a context in which to understand his role in that investment as well as an attachment to that piece of land."

As farming becomes more and more a minority occupation, this transmission of values becomes increasingly difficult — and for some families, no longer desirable. But for those families who try to maintain farm values, children reap benefits, not just burdens. Glen Elder, a sociologist at the University of North Carolina, has made similar observations in Iowa: "Though faced with an uncertain future, rural farm youth in the midwest have something akin to an apprenticeship for growing up with a sense of competence." So farm work at least is not synonymous with exploitation. As for school, it is a form of child-tending for a society that demands two working parents, and it attempts to turn children into a work force with skills that the society needs. In these senses it exploits children just as much as work does.

• • •

Beatrice Whiting, along with Carolyn Pope Edwards, an anthropologist at the University of Massachusetts at Amherst, went on to do an even broader cross-cultural comparison, adding four more Kenya studies, representing the Kikuyu, Kipsigis, and Abaluyia peoples, as well as studies of the Kpelle of Liberia and the Oriya of Bubaneswar, India. These were studied by a new group of young anthropologists, who systematically observed children's interactions with the method developed for the original six cultures. This brought the total to more than five hundred children, observed for thousands of hours, by seventeen anthropologists of both sexes and different theoretical orientations. In addition, still another six were studied using "spot observations" developed by Ruth and Robert Munroe of the Claremont Graduate School — randomly ordered verbal "snapshots" showing where a child is, whom she or he is with, and what doing. These cultures extended the range to Guatemala and Peru, and to Claremont, California.

Given the cross-cultural variety of these studies, it would seem unlikely that any generalizations could be drawn that would apply in some form to all of them. Surely such a wide range of cultures would shape children's social behavior in dramatically different ways? However, Whiting and Edwards's 1988 book, *Children of Different Worlds: The Formation of Social Behavior,* turned up an impressive set of consistent findings. These children the world over were certainly being shaped toward different occupational futures and being socialized into different religions. Their worlds varied in population density, family size, illness, and mortality. But in their basic social behavior during childhood, they were similar.

Some of these cultures had child nurses, some didn't. Some had mothers who encouraged a great deal of physical contact, some didn't. The cultures also differed in whether they promoted segregation of boys and girls, whether they ignored or reprimanded children who dominated other children, and how much schooling children were getting, if any. Yet it was still possible to make firm generalizations applicable to all of them.

To begin with, infants and toddlers behave dependently in all the cultures, and successfully obtain attention and care from older children. Girls are more likely to be in the presence of infants and toddlers than boys are, and are more likely to behave in a caring way toward them. Girls are also more likely to be playing close to home than boys, and more likely to be in the presence of adults, mainly women. Both sexes become increasingly likely to segregate in play as they get older, and to announce their sex clearly to the community by means of dress. They also differ in their behavior.

> Of the five major categories of interpersonal behavior explored in this book — nurturance, dependency, prosocial dominance, egoistic dominance, and sociability — two emerge as associated with sex differences. Across the three older age groups [that is, between infancy and puberty], girls on average are more nurturant than boys in all dyad [interacting pair] types, while boys are more egoistically dominant than girls.

Egoistic dominance means ordering someone around for purely selfish reasons, while prosocial dominance means telling them to do something useful to the family or to another child, or giving an order in the course of training or teaching. In addition, "Boys engage in more of both informal, rough-and-tumble play and competitive games with rules than do girls. The competitive behavior of girls is more difficult to observe; it is more often expressed in insulting behavior."

Clearly, task assignment plays a major role in shaping the behavior of boys and girls. Girls are more likely to serve as child nurses, especially between ages six and ten. But girls who do more of it than other girls, *and* boys who do more of it than other boys, both show more prosocial and nurturing behavior *toward their same-sex peers*. This may mean that being assigned to care for little ones changes an older child's general behavior — not just the behavior toward babies. But as Whiting and Edwards recognize, it may only mean that more-nurturing boys or girls are the ones who get assigned to be child nurses or baby-sitters.

They use the interesting term *generic behavior* to refer to the cross-cultural uniformities they have discovered. This does not carry the implications of words like *genetic* or *biological*, and they reserve judgment about how important inborn tendencies are. Still, they conclude,

> The exploration of possible biologically determined sex differences remains an important research task. In particular, research should focus on the possibility that there are biologically determined differences in the strength of motives for physical activity, goal-oriented egoistic dominance, and responsiveness to human beings.

But they also say, "Through experience, we develop propensities for certain generic behaviors." This resembles the theory of social development proposed over a decade ago by anthropologist and psychoanalyst Robert LeVine, of the Harvard School of Education. He suggested that there is a wide variety of inborn responses, and that each culture shapes children by *selecting* some responses to emphasize while letting other responses drop out from disuse — a kind of cultural selection of behavior during childhood. But the new cross-cultural research summarized by Whiting and Edwards indicates that the variety of inborn responses is limited, may differ between the sexes, and may be less amenable to being selected or dropped out by cultural fiat than we previously thought.

· · ·

Jean-Jacques Rousseau, the Swiss-French philosopher, wrote that the work of children is play. He meant that they are not idle when they are playing; play *is* their work — real work that promotes learning and development. But today it could be interpreted as a way of turning play itself *into* work — a disaster for children and for childhood.

Play into work? Consider Little League baseball games. Ideally, such organized team sports promote the ideals of practice, discipline, skill, teamwork, fair play, and sportsmanship. But they may also take something inherently joyous and playful and turn it into a source of pain and humiliation. Parents at these games can be observed screaming at the top of their lungs from the sidelines, and very publicly showing their disappointment at their children's failure. Perhaps they have exaggerated expectations, or perhaps they have even transferred their own failed ambitions onto their kids. It is very ironic that some of the parents who, unlike the Japanese and Chinese, refuse to put any pressure at all on their children for school performance, willingly stuff those same children into a veritable pressure cooker of expectations for sports performance. Parental responses to failure at this supposed "play" can sometimes verge on psychological abuse.

Compare such games with sandlot baseball — that spontaneous, child-dominated, semidisorderly *pastime,* truly deserving of the name, that has always coexisted with organized baseball. As an urban child in a neighborhood with no sandlots, I played two street versions: stickball, played with a broomstick and a pink rubber ball, and punchball, played with a fist. Sewer covers and the tires of parked cars were bases, and even on the dead-end streets where we played we often had to call "time out" for passing cars. Sides were "chosen up" spontaneously at a moment's notice after two older or more-skilled boys were made captains by consensus. I was clumsy, and was never among the first picked, but I played — and with minimal pressure, far from the eyes of adults. I know that Little League baseball can be fun in spite of the pressure, but our impromptu games were much more like play.

In his book *Homo ludens* — the title uses "playful" as opposed to "wise" as the adjective in our species name — the Dutch historian Johann Huizinga explored the relationship between the related ideas of play and contest in the history of various languages. In many civilizations of both East and West, this linguistic connection is a close one. And unfortunately it even extends to the notion of killing contests — war as play. Without understanding this historical connection, it is impossible to grasp the role of war in what we call civilization, or the meaning of group games in complex societies. This understanding is key, too, for the traditions of such games in childhood, and how we "civilized" adults supervise them.

As we have seen, while true peer groups are common in more advanced societies, only the multi-age play group occurs with any frequency in hunter-gatherer bands, and it is ubiquitous. It is made up mostly of siblings and cousins, is mixed with respect to sex, and may consist, in a band, of six or eight children ranging in age from late infancy to adolescence, or may divide into two or three smaller groups with smaller age ranges. Infants begin to join in from the time they can walk, and the sight of a toddler edging away from his mother to more or less throw himself on a pile of wrestling two- to five-year-olds is not uncommon. Two-year-olds who are better walkers will follow the group around and, if it has wandered from the village-camp, will be carried by older children when they tire.

The main activity of the group is play, though this may and often does include watching adult work. It also includes play at subsistence — which, however playful, produces food, as in the case of Baka children collecting snails, or honey; "pretend" subsistence play, which does not produce food but assumes some semblance of adult work; rough-and-tumble play; and sex-play. It also includes protection, care, and teaching of infants and children by older children. There is no "child nurse" comparable to that found in middle-level farming societies — that is, children are not *assigned* the task of taking care of infants; and mothers are always within shouting (or crying) distance, receptive to infant needs. But there is care, protection, and teaching nonetheless, and, of course, older children are learning infant and child care.

What happened after hunting-and-gathering life passed from existence? This question has been approached through analysis of a large number of traditional cultures living widely differing ways of life. The sample used consisted of 182 of the 186 societies in the World Ethnographic Sample taken from the Human Relations Area Files, based at Yale University.

The variety of farming and herding societies is great, but two patterns are more common in them than at the hunting-and-gathering level. First, there is more care in early childhood by anyone other than the mother. Second, there is more assignment of children as infant caregivers. This type of child nurse, common in many farming communities where women's work load is heavy, is quite different from the care given infants by children among hunters and gatherers: the mother is farther away, working in the fields, and the child has more responsibility, for more time at a stretch.

The question of the ages of children in play groups is more difficult to answer from this kind of ethnographic data. It is clear that same-age peer groups become possible in some farming and herding societies, although they do not always occur wherever they are possible. Good information is available only for adolescence, and it shows that societies that hunt and gather, societies without social classes, and societies made up of communities with fewer than 1500 people are less likely to have competitive peer groups among teenagers than more complex societies.

. . .

In our culture, same-age peer groups are everywhere, both in and out of school, and at all ages including infancy. We seem to hold the belief that it is best for children to be with other children their own age. It is likely that same-age peer groups promote the learning of competitive strategies, and they may even be indispensable in a competitive society. Once a child has come through the five-seven shift, the cognitive task of seriation — rearranging a bunch of sticks in order of size, say — becomes second nature. But the child who can do "big, bigger, biggest" can also do "smart, smarter, smartest" and "pretty, prettier, prettiest." True, one of the major tacit purposes of school is to rank-order children on various dimensions. Still, we should consider what this intensely competitive peer system may cost us.

One famous study known as the Robbers Cave Experiment is relevant, although it addresses the general questions of group identity and competition. Muzafer Sherif, a psychologist at the University of Oklahoma, led a group that conducted two similar studies, one in Connecticut and one in Oklahoma. In the second and major study, a group of twenty-two average, normal eleven-year-old boys was chosen — all middle-class Protestants with similar educational backgrounds. During the summer between the fifth and sixth grades, the boys were taken to a two-hundred-acre camp in the Robbers Cave State Park, a densely wooded section of the San Bois Mountains of southeastern Oklahoma.

The study was divided into three stages. In Stage 1, which lasted one week, the boys were divided into two exactly matched groups — they differed in no obvious or measurable way. In this stage competition was discouraged, and there were joint activities, but the groups nevertheless began to show signs of feeling competitive — they named themselves Eagles and Rattlers, spoke disparagingly of each other, and began to react territorially to each other's "incursions."

In Stage 2 of the study, a tournament of planned contests was set up between the two groups — baseball, tug-of-war, tent-pitching, skits, treasure hunts, even cabin inspections. Trophies, medals, and four-bladed knives were offered as tempting prizes. Sherif and his colleagues write,

After the second day of the tournament, the "good sportsmanship" stated in specific words during the initial period and exhibited after the first contests . . . gave way, as event followed event, to increased name-calling, hurling invectives, and derogation of the out-group to the point that the groups became more and more reluctant to have anything to do with one another.

In time, they conclude, "derogatory stereotypes and negative attitudes toward the out-group were crystallized."

Again, there were no real differences whatsoever between these groups. Bigotry was easily created by arbitrarily labeling exactly matched boys. There would seem to be a sad message here, confirming the picture of boys in their natural state offered by William Golding in his novel *Lord of the Flies*. In this depiction schoolboys stranded on a desert island after a plane crash, without adult supervision, degenerate quickly into violent behavior toward the weakest members of the group. They begin by killing a pig, which they need to do to survive; but they perform an emotionally intense blood ritual afterward. Soon the group splits into factions led by Ralph, a basically good boy, and Jack, a prototypical bully. Most of the younger boys gravitate to Jack, whose strong destructive bent leads to savage acts that culminate in murder — first of the eccentric, "different" Simon, and then of Piggy, the fat boy with glasses.

But unlike Sherif's earlier study in a camp in Connecticut, the Robbers Cave study added a third stage, in which the two groups were reblended and given important goals to reach together — such as fixing the water tank that had supposedly been damaged by vandals, so that all the boys would have water to drink. This third stage greatly reduced prejudice and conflict in just a few days; and while at the end of Stage 2 there was practically no crossover between the two groups in the question of whom the boys considered their friends, there was considerable healing of this split by the end of Stage 3.

This kind of finding is consistent with what we know about bands of orphaned street-children, such as *los abandonados* — the abandoned ones — of the cities of Colombia, Kenya, and elsewhere. Some of these children are probably runaways, but others are "throwaways" — children for whom no adult had any care or use. Yet in contrast to Golding's prediction, such groups, within themselves, leaven conflict and prejudice with cooperation and nurturance. "Childhood" filmed a group of *abandonados* — boys ranging in age from eight to twelve — in the streets of Guatemala City, and documented a remarkable cohesiveness. The younger, livelier boys are best at begging, while the older boys at the top of the hierarchy take responsibility for group protection and defense. Several of the boys were interviewed on camera: "How old are you?" one is asked.

"Eleven."

"You live in the street — why is that?"

"I live in the street because my father drinks a lot and hits me. And I don't have a mother."

Another boy, back from successful begging on a busy street, is asked why he stays with his friends. "They help me when I have nothing, and when they have nothing I help them." Sitting on the steps of a big building, smiling and talking, they share the money collected in a morning's begging and stealing.

"Why do you share?" the second boy is asked.

"Some of us make more money than others."

"You share it? You split it down the middle?"

"Yes. We can share it. We split it up."

"Why?"

"Because we're together and we have to stand by each other because some other boys will come and take our money."

They sniff glue many times a day; yet they say they know it ruins the lungs and the mind — "It makes you crazy." During the day they wander, hang out, beg, steal mirrors and other auto parts, and sell what they steal. They even go for a swim — obviously great fun — in a municipal pool. When together, they fall in step with each other, smile, laugh, and talk cheerfully about the camera trained on them. A big boy puts his arm around a small boy's shoulders. Two other boys wrestle gently. These boys are in some ways like a hunter-gatherer play group. In other important ways they are like a family.

They don't mix with the street girls, though. These girls keep aloof from them because they don't want to be touched by anyone who can't pay. One, about thirteen or fourteen, said:

> In the street they teach you a lot — they teach you how to sniff glue
> and things like that. My first time, they took me by force — some
> men. I was passing in the street, and they were grabbing me. After
> that I lived in the street. Because I was in disgrace . . . I was ashamed
> to tell [my parents]. My friends taught me — they taught me how to
> sell my body. But I don't sell it all the time. Just once in a while.

But the girls, like the boys, show solidarity. Three of them stroll across
a bridge in brightly colored clothes, laughing, touching, teasing, pulling
at each other's shirts. Clearly and simply, they are together.

At night, the boys return to their *gallada,* or "roost" — nothing but
the sidewalk under the slight overhang of a storefront. They sit around,
some breathing glue out of paper bags, others laughing and talking softly.
Then a boy approaches with a bag of food. *"La comi-da! La comi-da!
La comi-da!"* they chant cheerfully. They share the sandwiches without
competition, dominance, or resentment. In fact there is much laughter,
some funny remarks, a little gentle roughhousing. "I'm hungry!" say a
couple good-naturedly — in no way a distress call. "I need some water,
it's dry," says one, wolfing a sandwich down, and another boy gives him
some water to drink. "Whoever is really hungry should have this big
one," says another, holding a sandwich out. There is no struggle over it,
just matter-of-fact sharing. I would like to see my own children share
food with the same degree of order, aplomb, and mutual respect as is
evident in these abandoned street boys.

This tenderness is impressive, as is the internal loyalty of the group.
But the face the *abandonados* turn to outsiders is not a friendly one. They
steal and prostitute themselves when begging and menial work do not
suffice. And they behave territorially with respect to other groups of
street-children; when they come into situations of conflict, they often exhibit the kind of bigotry that the Robbers Cave boys showed in Stage 2.
In our culture, the cliques that seem to form so naturally among school-
age children of both sexes — to the great pain of boys and girls left out
of them — further attest to the power of these tendencies.

• • •

During the 1960s, at the height of the Cold War, "Childhood" series
observer Urie Bronfenbrenner did an influential study called *Two Worlds*

of Childhood, comparing children's experience in the Soviet Union and the United States. He had spent part of his own childhood in Russia, was fluent in Russian, and was considered an authority on child care generally. In terms of out-group animosity in those years, child training in the two countries was something like a gigantic Robbers Cave experiment — before the reconciliation. But Bronfenbrenner was more interested in the unique features of the two systems than he was in their mirror-image antipathy.

In the Soviet Union there was near-universal membership in two youth organizations — the Octobrists for ages seven to nine, and the Pioneers for ages ten to fifteen. Each classroom in school comprised a unit of one of these groups, and from the Pioneers were chosen the 50 percent of adolescents who would enter the Young Communist League, or Komsomol — a stepping-stone to Communist Party membership and bureaucratic posts. In some ways — as in the mottoes "Always prepared" and "A Pioneer is a friend to children all over the world" — Octobrists and Young Pioneers resembled Brownies and Girl Scouts, or Cub and Boy Scouts.

But scouting is an elective activity, and the Pioneers differ greatly in their extreme emphasis on collective solidarity. Public self-criticism sessions, resembling those in Communist Party cells, were frequent and obligatory. A poster of the period showed an angry-looking, handsome Pioneer pointing a stiff finger at a frightened, contrite companion, with the caption, "A Pioneer tells the truth and treasures the honor of his unit." On the wall behind the Young Pioneers is a poster-within-the-poster, showing Pavlik Morozov, a Pioneer who was killed by the people of his village after he denounced his own father to the authorities and then testified against him in court. He has remained a hero to Pioneers, "a martyr in the cause of communism. A statue of him in Moscow is constantly visited by children, who keep it bedecked with fresh flowers, and many collective farms, Pioneer palaces, and libraries bear his name."

Little could illustrate more strongly the different valuation placed on family as opposed to collective loyalty in the Soviet Union and the West. Yet in the Soviet Union of today, after years of confusion and changing values caused by *glasnost* and *perestroika,* the traditional role played by the Pioneers is now open to question, and the culture is attempting to adapt its socialization methods to a new future. Still, we see Seryozha Shlyapnikov, seven, inducted into the Octobrists, and Anya Krilov at fourteen wears her Young Pioneers scarf to school, but argues with her grandmother, who thinks Anya has a future in the Komsomol. These children are struggling to assess their roles and futures in a society that is changing its terms of existence day by day.

Twenty years ago no one could anticipate this change, and Bronfenbrenner talked about the two worlds of childhood as leading initially similar children in very different cultural directions. He was not enamored of the Soviet system of child training, yet he also had reservations about the egoistic, almost anarchic childhood experiences in the United States. Probably he would still say that the American culture has drifted too far from a sense of community, that it emphasizes individualism and self-reliance too much. The results of this philosophic excess may well be visible in the high rates of crime and drug abuse the United States experiences today.

Yet the recent events in the Soviet Union seem to teach the converse lesson. Seventy years of Octobrist and Young Pioneer indoctrination did not suffice to motivate people to set the collective above themselves. It did not turn children into adults who could be selfless members in a socialist utopia. Decade after decade of laying flowers on Pavlik's statue left the family still strong and the collective, in its Soviet form, too weak to survive. People who spent their childhoods being indoctrinated into communism became cynical black-marketeers as adults, "making a connection" to circumvent the collective and satisfy their personal needs. And a mere few years of partial freedom has left Communist culture almost everywhere in ruins. The lesson resembles that of the less extreme, much more successful kibbutz culture: a society can construct any childhood it wants, but it will still have to come to terms with human nature — and specifically, with the nature of the child.

• • •

In spite of the relative anarchy of American culture, or perhaps partly because of it, a great deal of play in our kind of society, and most of casual social interaction — together totaling up to four-fifths of children's waking time — can in principle come closer to Rousseau's ideal. Consider the following excerpt from novelist Robert Paul Smith's memoir, *Where Did You Go? Out. What Did You Do? Nothing*:

> But about this doing nothing: we swung on the swings. We went for walks. We lay on our backs in backyards and chewed grass. . . . [H]e walked me home to my house, and when we got there I walked him back to his house. . . .
>
> We watched things: we watched people build houses, we watched men fix cars, we watched each other patch bicycle tires with rubber bands. . . . For at least a month I watched my own sisters making beads. . . .
>
> We sat in boxes; we sat under porches; we sat on roofs; we sat on limbs of trees.
>
> We stood on boards over excavations; we stood on tops of piles of leaves; we stood under rain dripping from the eaves; we stood up to our ears in snow.
>
> We looked at things like knives and immies and pig nuts and grasshoppers and clouds and dogs and people.
>
> We skipped and hopped and jumped. Not going anywhere — just skipping and hopping and jumping and galloping. We sang and whittled and hummed and screamed.
>
> What I mean, Jack, we did a lot of nothing.

Thus, a boy's life in an American town between the world wars. But what would the "nothing" consist of today?

A study done in Oakland, California, in 1976, by Elliott Medrich and his colleagues at the University of California at Berkeley, traced how 764 sixth-grade children used their time out of school — the great majority of their waking hours. The sample was representative of boys and girls, black, white, Asian, and "other," in twenty different neighborhoods, with family income ranging from below $5,000 to more than $20,000, in 1970 dollars. Children and their parents were interviewed systematically about the children's lives.

In answer to the question "What do you like to do when you are with your friends?" children responded with over thirty different activities. Baseball was an answer given by 40 percent of children (51 percent of boys, 30 of girls), and the next three most common activities with friends were "general" play (32 percent), bicycling (29 percent), and basketball (26 percent — 44 percent of boys, 8 of girls). "Socializing" was a reply for 16 percent of boys and 25 percent of girls.

As might be expected, the question "What do you like to do when you are alone?" produced a very different pattern. "Reading and writing" was cited by 43 percent, television viewing by 34 percent, and listening to the radio or music by 16 percent. But in contrast to the children's claims, television occupied "more of a child's out-of-school time than any other single activity." Thirty-five percent of the families in the study were "total television homes," where the TV was on continuously throughout the afternoon and evening, regardless of whether anybody was watching it. Forty percent of the sample watched for three or more hours a day, and only 28 percent watched for an hour and a half or less.

Interestingly, in this study 81 percent of the children said they would like to spend more time doing things with their parents, and 67 percent said they wished they had more close friends. Forty-five percent said that they would be different from themselves if they could, and 41 percent said that they often felt bored and didn't know what to do after school. Yet parents claimed they wanted their kids to watch less television, suggesting that excess television-watching results from a pull by the kids, not from parents' need for an electronic baby-sitter.

Another approach is to study the time-breakdown of kids' activities. The Berkeley group calculated that by the time they are out of high school, children have spent only about 11,000 hours in school, but 65,000 hours out of school, including 15,000 hours watching television. In another study, based at the University of Michigan, mothers and children kept diaries of the kids' activities. On an average weekday, nine- to eleven-year-old children spent five and a quarter hours in school and half an hour studying. They spent two and a half hours watching television, an hour and a quarter eating (today some families blend the two, and even converse with the set on), a little over an hour "playing," and a total of about one more hour involved in sports, visiting, church, outdoors activities, art activities, hobbies, and other leisure activities (in declining order) *combined*. They spent an average of only nine minutes a day reading.

It would seem that today the experience of children when not in school is less exciting, more passive, and much less spontaneous than the childhood lives of Robert Paul Smith and his friends. Urie Bronfenbrenner has wisely said, "The primary danger of the TV screen lies not so much in the behavior it produces as in the behavior it prevents — the talk, the games, the family activities and the arguments through which much of the child's learning takes place and his or her character is formed."

But unfortunately for simplicity, research has shown that the impact of television can sometimes be good. In the Berkeley-Oakland study, children whose parents were worried about neighborhood safety were much more likely to be heavy viewers. In the urban United States of today, the safety issue is much more serious, especially for poor and minority parents, than it was in 1976 when the study was done. Television may be protecting these children from grave danger, not preventing them from having wholesome adventures. In addition, preschool children who watch "Sesame Street" show gains in academic skills in proportion to the number of times a week they watch. For disadvantaged children, these gains may outweigh the losses involved in watching too much television and even the aggressive behavior that many believe it causes.

I once asked Beatrix Hamburg, a leading child and adolescent psychiatrist now at the Mount Sinai School of Medicine, what she recommended about television. She answered without hesitating: "Watch television *with* your children." Although this is not always practical, it seems likely that joint parent-child viewing combined with some degree of restricted or managed viewing would serve in most families to enhance the medium's positive effect. If the sound of commercials is clicked off with the remote control, then conversation about the programs can stimulate children to think about them, and to draw lessons about the parents' values. And if the programs are "soft" situation comedies that suggest a moral, rather than "hard" ones full of sex and violence, so much the better.

• • •

In our culture, siblings within the family provide a basis for social interaction that is separate and distinct from peer relations, and they often but not always provide a softening of competitiveness. They certainly do give parents the opportunity to intervene and influence their children's learning about social relationships. In the Kirkpatrick family of White Plains, New York, "Childhood" cameras caught an argument over Nintendo — a truly international game of industrial societies, which in a few years has spread from Japan throughout the world. The argument involved Michael, ten, and his sisters Shannon, twelve, and Kelly Ann, eight. It evolves quickly: One moment Michael is bright-eyed and alert, watching the TV monitor and punching buttons on the Nintendo controls, saying "Cool, man. Cool." Shannon makes a remark, and the next moment Michael throws down the control panel and stands up, saying, "I don't want to play anymore."

He goes to the kitchen and complains to his mother. "Honey, it's a game," she says expressively. "It's just a game. You get yourself excited." Michael says, "They laughed at me when I died" — a reference to a bad Nintendo outcome.

"Well, you laugh at them all the time. It's just because you're doing it that you're getting yourself upset over it." Nancy, his mother, is at the sink, which is in an island-type counter between them. As the exchange goes on, she increasingly stretches and leans toward him across the counter. Her tone of voice is a bit impatient but somehow also very loving. "You're getting yourself all teary." Then she asks, "Are you upset because Anthony can't come skating?"

Michael shakes his head no. "Look at me," she goes on. "When they're finished, then you can play it all by yourself like Kelly did."

Nancy goes into the living room where the girls are still playing. "When you're finished, Mike's gonna play Duck Hunt. We really haven't played Duck Hunt in a long time. Okay? Girls!" They ignore her and she begins to sound angry. "Girls! — Shannon and Kelly Ann, look at Mommy!"

Shannon finally turns and says Mike is a sore loser. Nancy is not impressed. "So last year you were a sore loser. All right, so this year he's a sore loser."

"He's a more sore loser than I am!" Shannon replies sullenly.

"Give it a break," Nancy says, turning back to the kitchen. "He's disappointed Anthony's not gonna come skating."

It's a beautiful piece of parenting, and a very informative one. Nancy's tone with Michael is just impatient enough to let him know that getting teary over Nintendo is changeworthy behavior. But she also lets herself feel his mood, and sympathizes with his plight. She guesses at an underlying disappointment that might explain his low threshold for tears. He denies it, but she sticks to her theory anyway; it helps her to sympathize — to do more than just call Michael a crybaby.

It also helps her to justify her position to the girls: She's going to turn the game over to Michael alone for a while. Shannon calls Michael a sore loser — the child culture's time-honored jeer at a bad sport. But Nancy not only knows her children, she knows their history, and that of their relationships. Shannon is reminded that she herself was a sore loser not so long ago. And when Nancy cuts off the interchange with "Give it a break," and repeats her theory of Michael's tearfulness, she is letting all the children know that the specific current details of their falling out are not of great concern to her. She is interested in meting out justice, but she is more interested in taking good care of them.

• • •

Since so many cultures, and so many parents in our culture, have seen children as having natural tendencies that could be considered evil, it is not surprising to find that there is a piece of the truth in their claim. Their judgment of them, of course, is a separate matter. But the tendencies they identified certainly exist, and neither the developmental process itself, nor any amount of interaction with other children, nor any known process of adult-directed child guidance has been found to control them completely. Nor, in my opinion, should they. The tendencies — idleness, fantasy, risk-taking, sexuality, selfishness, and violence — are all part of the adaptive equipment left us by eons of organic evolution. If we didn't know that before the past twenty years of research in sociobiology — the science that applies evolutionary theory to social relations — we certainly do know it now.

Yet any of these inclinations can get out of hand and interfere with adaptation in some situations. Individual children differ greatly in the strength with which they exhibit them. That is part of the solution to the paradox. We cherish the belief that we can find a method of child-rearing that will work for all children, but that is an illusion. Since children have different tendencies, we should by right have different goals for them, and we will be wise to adopt different methods that are responsive to the needs of different children.

The religious rigor with which the Puritans tried to instill a fear of God in their children now strikes us as cruel, but we should at least acknowledge the threat of mortality that was ever-present for those parents. Heaven and hell might be only a breath away, and they had continually to help their children adjust to deaths in the family and in the community, including deaths of children. Of course, death was equally frequent in hundreds of primitive cultures that did not impose a like burden of guilt and fear on their children. But given the Puritans' beliefs about hellfire, parents among them can perhaps be forgiven for trying to ensure their children's salvation, even through harsh means if necessary.

But children must deal with death in some way, even in a society where it affects mainly the old. And this process of dealing with death occupies a place in the inner mental life of a child as the transition to middle childhood takes place. Recently my mother died after two months of illness, and I had to spend a good deal of time away from my children both before and after her death. We had a memorial ceremony when I returned, and I explained things as well as I could without unpleasant detail. Sarah, the almost-four-year-old, brooded the least about this event, although all three of the children loved their grandmother. One day about ten days after the funeral, Sarah was in my office "writing" — that is, making line after line of squiggles, her version of her big sister's real writing. After some puttering at my desk, I asked her what she had written.

She came over, saying, "This is a note that I wrote to Grandma." Then, running her fingers over the squiggles, she "read" the note:

> I love you, Grandma. I hope you feel better. And I know Papa buried you in the sand. I love you and nobody else thinks you're dead. I hope you feel better. I know you are dead. And I know Papa loves you very much.

Her mood was self-possessed, even a bit light. She went back to write a second note, which she "read" as follows:

> I love you, Grandma. I hope you feel better. I know you are dead. And I'm sorry you're dead. I love you so much, that I hope you feel better. And I know you are happy. And I'm glad you're buried. Except I know you have fun. I know Papa buried you. And I love you so much. 'Cept I hope you feel better. Sights at the end of the days.

I couldn't find out what the last line meant; as far as I know she had had no exposure to apocalyptic notions, although she may have without my knowledge. But otherwise the meaning seemed clear. Sarah was trying to deal with her grandmother's death using concepts typical of young children, who see death as a reversible condition.

I later discussed Sarah's notes with a seven-year-old boy who had recently lost an uncle. Having completed the five-seven shift, he smiled at her misconception, saying (with a descriptive hand gesture) that she must have thought God would send her grandma down again. But actually his speculation about her thinking was still ahead of where she was — stuck in a much simpler misconception about the death of the body. She was keeping death at arm's length, but at the same time trying to control it — reverse it — with the magical force of her love. *I know you are dead and buried,* she says repeatedly; she doesn't want Grandma to think she doesn't know, because then what good would her wishful magic be? But also, "I love you so much," and "I know you have fun." She has not yet had any religious education, but she has perhaps absorbed the notion that people feel better when they are dead. Or, equally plausibly, she invented it.

There have been some studies of children's developing notions about death, and they confirm the difference between Sarah and Patrick, the boy I discussed her letters with. As summarized by Edward Cassem, a Harvard psychiatrist who is an authority on dying and grieving — and who was a Jesuit priest before he became a doctor — most studies have concluded that before age five children see death as reversible, similar to sleep, illness, or a journey — something that will not touch them or those closest to them. Sometime after age seven, they begin to see it as an inevitable and irreversible fact of life — and in an abstract way, something that will someday come to even Mommy and Daddy. But it remains a very remote prospect for several more years, and only after age ten or eleven do they grasp the central fact of death's universality: *This means me too.*

•   •   •

There are many individual variations, though, and no studies have addressed the obvious questions about cross-cultural differences — especially the question: How does a frequent experience of death, as in a developing country or in the human past, determine a child's views at different ages? Although it cannot take the place of systematic research, we are fortunate to have the work of Robert Coles, also a Harvard psychiatrist, whose sensitive interviews with children — especially children facing racism, poverty, and other stresses — have produced a series of books that have enriched our view of childhood almost incomparably. His 1990 book, *The Spiritual Life of Children*, departs from Freudian orthodoxy by rejecting the assumption that religion is merely a neurosis.

Instead, it takes an open-minded approach to find out how children — most between the ages of eight and twelve, and of various religions and cultures — use what they have learned about God, heaven, the devil, spirits, life after death, and other concepts of organized faith to explore and deal with their problems; although sometimes, as for the Puritans of colonial New England, religion does not seem much of a help. But consider the testimony of an eight-year-old Christian girl in North Carolina.

It was 1962, and she had been among the first black children to enter a newly desegregated elementary school. She described her then-recent walk through a mob of savagely bigoted whites — adults and children: "I was all alone, and those people were screaming, and suddenly I saw God smiling, and I smiled." As she approached the school door, "A woman was standing there and she shouted at me, 'Hey, you little nigger, what you smiling at?' I looked right at her face, and I said, 'At God.' Then she looked up at the sky, and then she looked at me, and she didn't call me any more names."

Many children feel that Jesus is with them — regardless of race or color. Yet religious differences enter into many ethnic conflicts, including violent ones, in ways that seem as arbitrary as the peer-group prejudices of Robbers Cave. Religious emotions can inflame ethnic ones in a potent blend of incendiary, negative spiritual power.

Some differences in the beliefs themselves are consequential, though, and interesting in their own right. Coles interviewed Hopi children, Native Americans of the southwestern United States. Natalie was a ten-year-old whom he had known for two years. She had been described by her teachers as neither especially bright nor especially good for him to interview. Coles noticed her looking at a cloud — a penetrating long gaze directed at a thundercloud that would barely enter the consciousness of an "Anglo" like himself. "The home of the noise," she finally said, pointing. About the differences between her beliefs and Anglo ones, she said this:

> The sky watches us and listens to us. It talks to us, and it hopes we are ready to talk back. The sky is where the God of the Anglos lives, a teacher told us. She asked where our God lives. I said, "I don't know." I was telling the truth! Our God is the sky, and lives wherever the sky is. Our God is the sun and the moon, too; and our God is our people, if we remember to stay here [on the consecrated land]. This is where we're supposed to be, and if we leave, we lose God.

If this seems a "primitive" concept of God, consider the possibility that the rise of a new kind of spirituality throughout the world, centered on nature and the earth's preservation, may make this ancient Native American kind of faith the ultimate religion of the future.

But even this faith lends itself to bigotry. Reciprocal animosity between the Hopi and the Navajo — I saw it during a month on the Navajo reservation — is as virulent as between any two peoples, and is fueled with this spiritual attachment to the land. Natalie said she prayed for the Anglos, but had this to say about the Hopi-Navajo land dispute: "They want the land, and we believe it has been here for us, and it would miss us . . . the land can feel the difference." Still, she felt sorry for the Navajo and the Anglos, who

> don't feel at home near their mesa, so they want all the mesas in the world! Then they have so many, they'll never be able to choose which one to call their home! Their ancestors must go from one mesa to the next, and they must cry, because they don't know where they can stay and be together, and they don't know if they'll ever be seen by the people. . . .

She loved to watch hawks in flight, and believed they were watching her — the transformed souls of the ancestors of her people, hovering over a most particular place on earth, vigilant, welcome, and benign.

But there is a side of Hopi religion Coles does not mention. Esther Goldfrank, writing in the *American Anthropologist* in 1945, described the traditional Kachina Society initiation rituals of the Hopi and other Pueblo groups. Children, especially boys between ages six and ten, were brought together in a sanctuary called a *kiva* and systematically terrorized by half-naked adults wielding yucca whips, costumed as exotic and threatening supernatural spirits; for example, "a We'e'e Kachina in a blue mask and carrying a long black and white ringed pole . . . [and] two Natackas with fierce bulging eyes and huge black bills fashioned from large gourds, each with a bow in the left hand and a saw or a large knife in the right hand." The express purpose of these rituals was to frighten children into good behavior.

> The children tremble and some begin to cry and to scream. The Ho Kachinas keep up their grunting, howling, rattling, trampling and brandishing of their yucca whips. All at once someone places a candidate on the sand mosaic, holds his (or her) hands upward and one of the Ho Kachinas whips the little victim quite severely. . . . Some of the children go through the process with set teeth and without flinching, others squirm, try to jump away and scream. . . . It was also noticed on several occasions that some of the boys, probably as a result of fear and pain, involuntarily micturated [urinated] and in one or two cases even defecated.

This is not the spirituality of Coles's friend Natalie, but it is very much a part of Hopi children's religious experience. Of course, as in all religions, this is for the children's own good — "to save their lives" — as well as to make them compliant. Some time later the children learn of the impersonations, and are angry and disappointed, but as one woman put it in adulthood, "I now know it was best and the only way to teach the children."

The Judaic religiosity of my own childhood was no exception to this rule about balanced pluses and minuses of spiritual life. On the one hand, Jews have a sometimes egregious ethnic pride in their status as "chosen" people. They celebrate biblical military victories over idolators, and look down their noses at other, "Johnny-come-lately" monotheistic faiths. They don't usually mortify children with beatings, but they don't shrink from imposing very heavy burdens of guilt, especially regarding sexuality and playfulness. And adults' expectations for a rule-bound religiosity, built on a foundation of relentless demand for study, can certainly create some pretty impressive neuroses.

But on the other hand, there are the pluses. An eleven-year-old named Leah became ill with leukemia after Coles had gotten to know her, and as she lay dying she impressed all who knew her with her faith. Her family was with her, but so were her favorite Psalms, which she read to herself and, when she had become too sick, her family read for her. Through the agony of severe disease and fruitless but painful and destructive chemotherapy, she took comfort from the Psalms and from the Jewish people's history of suffering. "Leah is part of Israel," was how her father summed it up. There was nothing fanatical about her; she also loved to hear her mother sing the old popular dance song "Three O'Clock in the Morning," which Leah had once learned from her grandmother. But just before she entered her final coma, her eyes and mind still very alert, she told her father she would like to go to "that 'high rock,' " an allusion to Psalm 61. Later, while she was unconscious and losing her hold on life, her father read it again and again:

Hear my cry, O God;
Attend unto my prayer.
From the end of the earth will I call unto Thee, when my heart faints;
Lead me to a rock that is too high for me.

It is an idea of great poignancy and subtlety: It is too high for me, but with help I will get there anyway. Leah, age eleven, facing death with all her mind and heart.

1.

1. Children must take risks to learn: Michael Kirkpatrick, eleven, New Rochelle, New York.

2. But some risks are just too great: a boy who lives in an abandoned building, South Bronx.

2a. Queens, New York, 1979.

2.

2a.

3.

4.

5.

6.

3. How direct is the link between television and violence? The question remains controversial. Chicago, 1985.

4. Peer behavior among boys can be violent...

5. ...or joyful. Philadelphia and Brazil, 1980s.

Some aggression in childhood is sanctioned by adults.

6. Father and daughter put 'em up, running against stereotype.

7. Dodge-ball, Boston, 1970s.

8. Boys Club in Spanish Harlem, 1988.

7.

8.

9.

9. They learn more from what they see than from what we say.

10. Amish girls in a mud puddle, Pennsylvania.

11. The past two decades have seen a complete transformation of athletic training for girls. Shannon Kirkpatrick, twelve, and friends.

12. "Old Roger Is Dead," a game we know was played by children in colonial Williamsburg — here staged for a "Childhood" episode.

13. Girls playing blind man's buff, turn-of-the-century China.

10.

11.

12.

13.

14.

15.

16.

17.

14. Apache girls' puberty ceremony, San Carlos, Arizona, 1970s.

15. Bar mitzvah, the traditional Jewish puberty ceremony, Wailing Wall, Jerusalem, Israel, 1991.

16. Young Xavante bachelors initiate boys, Brazil, 1950s. For days boys were run to exhaustion, taken hunting, and wakened in the night to sing. At the end they were deemed worthy of having sex.

17. In northern Kenya, Turkana girls' leather skirts get longer as they approach marriageable age.

Metamorphosis

*In the meantime, Martha, in an agony of adolescent
misery, was lying among the long grass under a tree,
repeating to herself that her mother was hateful, all
these old women hateful, every one of these
relationships, with their lies, evasions, compromises,
wholly disgusting. For she was suffering that misery
peculiar to the young, that they are going to be cheated
by circumstances out of the full life every nerve and
instinct is clamoring for.*

— DORIS LESSING, *Martha Quest*

A CERTAIN TWELVE-YEAR-OLD of my acquaintance was sitting at a very informal dinner with two friends, both also just twelve, and three adults. I asked the girls about songs they liked, and all chose as their favorite the song "Do Me," sung by a group called Bell Biv DeVoe. They played it, and I happened to catch a few phrases from the song, which is explicitly about sex. I asked them if they liked it for the music or the words, and with some giggling they insisted that they didn't know the words. So I tried a few lines on them.

" 'I love it when you touch my body all over baby,' " I offered first. Exchange of dreadfully embarrassed looks. Uncontrollable giggles.

" 'This girl's gonna do me,' " I volunteered. More giggles. Painful squirming. Incipient bolting and running.

" 'I just wanna lay your body down by the fire baby,' " I ventured. Blushing. One-hundred-decibel squeals. Amazed, shocked grins. "I think I have to go to the bathroom," said one. "Me too," chimed the others, one of whom had just accidentally sprayed a mouthful of water onto the table.

" 'Rub your body all over . . . Just watch your body shine,' " I tried next.

They were gone. Out of there. History. They were halfway up the staircase before I got to *shine*.

Now, please note that I did not quote any of the *really* explicit lines, like "kiss you from head to toe," say, or "take off your clothes, leave on your shoes," or the truly remarkable "smack it up, flip it, rub it down." Nor did I endeavor to capture any of the moans and groans deftly harmonized into the arrangement. I still cherished the fond hope that some of it might have been over their heads — plus I didn't want to do anything that would make *me* blush. But whenever they returned I could scatter them, screaming for cover, by offering any phrase at all from the lyric. Finally I had mercy on them and let them eat their dessert in peace, but the giggles never quite stopped.

The adults at the table differed on whether they were deliberately concealing their knowledge of the words, or truly blocking their meaning out of consciousness while bobbing and swaying to the music. Either way, at some level they knew what the words were — they weren't that difficult to hear. Not many months later at least one of the girls was innocently flirting with a boy at poolside, stretching herself to her full height, and making the best of her now-developing breasts. Although it was still not fully conscious, feelings that were once the cause of giggles had become the cause of longing.

It is much the same all over the world. In São Paulo, fourteen-year-old Simone Oliveira giggles uncomfortably in a sex-education class, as she identifies parts of the human anatomy. Yet a few months later the giggles are gone, replaced by a remarkable calm lightened with mature anticipatory excitement. In February, on one of her several visits to the dressmaker's, an older woman helps her on with an ornamented rope skirt, while women nursing babies sit in a row by the wall, watch, and comment. Then a hairdresser comes in to fix her carnival style. The transformation is deliberate and big; her face is now surrounded by appealing black curls.

She goes home to show her family, and the rite of passage continues. "You really look different," her smiling mother says. "Your face really looks different. You look pretty. You really look so cute." Maria's repetitive comments show just how stunned she is by her daughter's reappearance as a woman. She laughs in surprise and joy. "Simone, you look so different, but you look cute. I like it. I *like* it!" She calls Simone's sister

Sandra, a year older, to see it too. "When I saw Simone," their mother says, "I didn't recognize her right away." What statement could a mother make that would be more symbolic of transformation? The younger children are riveted. Even cousin Francisco gets into the act: "Oh, this is really shocking! This hair is really shocking!"

Yet of course the transformation doesn't erase Simone's persona. On the same night she is still a wonderful big sister — supervising toddler Suellen, horsing around with Francisco, entertaining, cajoling. She even lets five-year-old Sergio toy with her precious brand-new hair while she chats with her close friend Valeria.

Valeria says she won't go to carnival. "I don't like it . . . sometimes people throw stones, my grandmother told me." They are about the same age, but make different choices. Simone is deeply involved in carnival, turning it into her own coming-of-age ritual. During dress rehearsal for carnival at the samba school, the same Simone who giggled over anatomy in class views with serenity a sensuous, bare-breasted dancer wearing an enormous feather headdress, leading a whole community in evocative, sensual movement. Sandra, fully dressed and on the sidelines at this rehearsal, mugs for the camera, putting on an immense, terrific grin as she faithfully imitates the movements of the almost nude dancer.

Soon it is carnival for real. Simone, in full costume, smiling eyes framed by her new hair, proudly takes her place in the parade. She dances all night, right through the dawn that breaks over the city. You would never guess that she was from a poor and struggling family. Carnival is an equalizer. Among exotically clad men, and bare-breasted, bare-buttocked women, to the thudding of hypnotic drums, Simone dances her heart out in the pale morning light — grinning, confident, a future woman.

In Moscow, Anya Krilov, thirteen, does her own preparations for life by training in swimming and gymnastics — activities that will help produce both fitness and, eventually, sex appeal. But now she is a mild-mannered, gentle, intelligent girl who takes tea smiling and talking with her friends and goes on a picnic with her family. Anya, a Young Pioneer, is a girl coming to womanhood in a culture undergoing rapid, sweeping change. In conversation with her grandma on the picnic — while the two skewer meat chunks for shishkebab — she tests the limits of *glasnost* within her own family by saying that she has no interest in joining the

Komsomol. Grandma cautions her that this is the route to success — and especially, to the Communist Party. "You won't get a decent job — you'll end up as a milkmaid."

"You're behind the times, Grandma. Nobody is interested in Komsomol today." But the grandmother says, "It's still important, some things never change." For all the world it could have been a conversation between an American girl and her grandma about grades in school, or about the value of joining the local church's youth group. Yet Anya is not growing up in a stable tradition but in the midst of an historical convulsion. At such times adolescents do not merely imbibe the culture of tradition; they also create the culture of the future.

As for Igor Shlyapnikov, also thirteen, he is preoccupied with more personal things. He talks on the phone with his girlfriend — or is it his girl friend? — who tells him that she can't go out because her little sister is sick. So they visit at the girl's house and chat uneasily on the couch with the not-very-sick-looking little sister between them. When she goes off, they speak awkwardly to the camera, answering questions as Igor has done in an earlier interview. That they are drawn to each other is evident; what is touching is that they cannot explain why — they seem bemused. What does not seem evident now but will a year or two later is the pull of the undercurrent that draws them together. Igor's soft, handsome, almost peaches-and-cream face is awake with anticipation and embarrassment, and with feelings he cannot now name.

A nineteen-year-old friend who has been like a daughter to me seemed to take it all fairly calmly, but she has little good to say about the years she has just been through. "You have to do absolutely everything for the first time, and everyone around you is keeping score on who's ahead. There is competition in *everything* — who's first to wear a bra, to drive, to have sex. And the *changes*. One night I went to sleep a size five and woke up a size six — I couldn't get into my clothes. And the second or third time I menstruated I was sitting in a movie theater wearing white shorts and I didn't have a sanitary napkin. It was horrible."

Another friend tells this story, to illustrate "the angst and anguish of teenage dances and parties":

> I remember going to one party in my hometown at age thirteen for
> what was known as the "cool" crowd and being so shy and embar-

rassed (no one would talk to me) that I went upstairs to call my mother to pick me up early. When the mother of the boy who was throwing the party caught on to what was happening, she called her young son (not a great friend of mine) upstairs and insisted that he "entertain" me. Talk about a bad match and profound embarrassment. As he walked downstairs with me (the leper), my most angst-ridden teenage nightmare was realized. Soon after, since the situation had gone from bad to worse, I went upstairs (I got to the phone this time) and called my mother. Of course, the boy's mother insisted that I join the adult party in the living room until my mom arrived. Making conversation with teens was hard enough — adults, at age thirteen, were a different *species*.

Anne Frank had no parties to go to, yet she experienced the same combination of pride, embarrassment, fear, and longing in interactions with the eight people in hiding with her, and even in her solitude. And she confided all these feelings to her diary.

> *Wednesday, 5 January 1944*
>
> I think what is happening to me is so wonderful, and not only what can be seen on my body, but what is taking place inside. I never discussed myself or any of these things with anybody; that is why I have to talk to myself about them. Each time I have a period, (and that has been only three times) I have the feeling that in spite of all the pain, unpleasantness and nastiness I have a sweet secret, and that is why although it is nothing but a nuisance to me in one sense of the word, I always long for the time that I shall feel that secret within me again. . . .
>
> . . . After I came here, when I was scarcely 13, I began to think about myself rather early on and to know that I am a person. Sometimes, when I lie in bed at night, I have a terrible desire to feel my breasts and to listen to the quiet rhythmic beat of my heart.
>
> I already had these kinds of feelings subconsciously before I came here, because I remember one night when I slept with Jacque I could not contain myself, I was so curious to see her body . . . I asked Jacque whether as a proof of our friendship we might feel one another's breasts. Jacque refused. I also had a terrible desire to kiss Jacque and that I did. I go into ecstasies every time I see the naked figure of

a woman, such as Venus in the Springer History of Art. . . . It strikes me sometimes as so wonderful and exquisite that I have difficulty not letting the tears roll down my cheeks.

If only I had a girl friend!

But the diary is her girlfriend, and two days later, on January 7, she confides the history of her "boy friends," especially her passion for a boy called Peter, who was three years older.

> Once, when we spoke about sex, Daddy told me that I couldn't possibly understand the longing yet, I always knew that I did understand it and now I understand it fully. Nothing is so beloved to me as he, my Petel.
>
> I saw my face in the mirror and it looks quite different than at other times. My eyes look so clear and deep, my cheeks are pink — which they haven't been for weeks — my mouth is much softer; I look as if I am happy, and yet there is something so sad in my expression and my smile slips away from my lips as soon as it has come. I'm not happy because I should know that Petel's thoughts are not with me, and yet I still feel his wonderful eyes upon me and his cool, soft cheek against mine.

Anne is exquisitely conscious of her body, and at the first sign of spring weather she begins to feel that the world is almost a mirror for her longings. "Dear Kitty," she writes on February 12,

> The sun is shining, the sky is deep blue, there is a lovely breeze and I'm longing — so longing — for everything. . . .
>
> To talk, for freedom, for friends, to be alone. And I do so long . . . to cry! I feel as if I am going to burst, and I know it would get better with crying, but I can't. I'm restless, I go from one room to the other, breathe at the bottom of a window, feel my heart beating, as if it is saying, "Can't you satisfy my longings at last?" . . . — I believe that it's spring within me, I feel that spring is awakening, I feel it in my whole body and soul.
>
> I have to keep myself under control — time and again, I long for my Petel, I long for every boy. . . .

I feel completely confused, I don't know what to read, what to write, what to do, I only know that I am longing.

That day she felt a need to sign the entry "Anne Mary Frank," possibly to secure her sense of identity in the midst of all her confused longing. Later she conceives a passion for another Peter, the one who shares her hiding place. On March 22 she writes that "it is getting more and more wonderful here. I believe, Kitty, that we may have a real great love in the 'Secret Annexe.'" She goes on to describe how darling and good and handsome he is, but then writes, "I believe that what took him most by surprise about me was when he discovered that I'm not a bit the superficial worldly Anne that I appear, but just as dreamy a specimen, with just as many difficulties as he himself!"

Clearly she has a sense of her own identity. She seems so unlike a child that we have to remind ourselves that she is not yet fifteen. *I began to think of myself rather early on and to know that I am a person.* Similar thoughts occur to Nel, a character in Toni Morrison's novel *Sula*. Nel, who is only at the very earliest stage of puberty in this scene, has come home from a train trip with her mother, to attend a relative's funeral. On this trip she has experienced the most overt racism of her young life — it is 1920 — and the experience has changed her. Not the least of her problems, her mother who is part white is considered beautiful, and disdains Nel's more clearly African looks.

> It had been an exhilarating trip but a fearful one. She had been frightened of the soldiers' eyes on the train, the black wreath on the door . . . the feel of unknown streets and unknown people. But she had gone on a real trip, and now she was different. She got out of bed and lit the lamp to look in the mirror. There was her face, plain brown eyes, three braids and the nose her mother hated. She looked for a long time and suddenly a shiver ran through her.
>
> "I'm me," she whispered. "Me."
>
> Nel didn't know quite what she meant, but on the other hand she knew exactly what she meant.
>
> "I'm me. I'm not their daughter. I'm not Nel. I'm me. Me."
>
> Each time she said the word *me* there was a gathering in her like

power, like joy, like fear. Back in bed with her discovery, she stared out the window at the dark leaves of the horse chestnut.

"Me," she murmured. And then, sinking deeper into the quilts, "I want . . . I want to be . . . wonderful. Oh, Jesus, make me wonderful."

Nel's resolution, like Anne's, is superb. The bitterness, the brutality with which the world tries to rob them of their adolescence in the end only strengthens them — strengthens their resolve and their identity. *I'm me,* says Nel again and again. *Me.*

· · ·

At a clear risk of descending from the sublime to the ridiculous, I must say that my own adolescence, if less noble than these, was no less intense and confusing. I remember it as a bizarre amalgam of religiosity and priapism, of acting upright and just plain acting up. Early on, when I was already well along the path to Eagle Scout, a friend and I were caught scrawling profanities on the street, and we spent a couple of dismal hours scrubbing the tarmac. I was no 98-pound weakling; I was a 140-pound weakling. Still, in fantasy, I often carried a certain slightly older girl out of the burning school building as she swooned in my heroic arms.

But this alternated with fantasies of how I would change the world. At fifteen, when I was so scared of girls that the thought of taking one's arm or holding her hand on a date made me tremble all over, I had literal paroxysms of sexual longing on many nights — if not for my religious streak, they would have been much more frequent — and hoped against hope my mother wouldn't notice the stains on the sheets. I had inexplicable rages in which I threw furniture around, and I made holes with my fist and foot in several walls and doors. I also stood at the seaside in a storm, praying while the spray rose and soaked through my clothes.

Just before I became seventeen, I defied my parents' explicit orders and snuck out of the house to go to Washington for the 1963 civil rights march — a perfect blend of idealism and defiance. I slavered over the lingerie ads in the *New York Times Magazine,* dreaming of real-life thighs and breasts — but on the other hand it *was* the *New York Times Magazine.* The first time I had intercourse I was practically led by the hand, and I was so nervous I forgot to take my socks off. One night around that time I decided to test whether I could hold my liquor. I was a part-time busboy in a catering establishment, and I had three or four drinks there — among my first ever. When I got home at 4:00 A.M. I really got busy, raiding my parents' liquor cabinet. The last thing I remember was swaying in front of the dining room mirror, holding a four-ounce glass filled to the brim with scotch, telling my mirror-image that none of this had had much effect on me.

Blackout. I woke up many hours later in bed in my clothes. The bathroom door had a large hole in it where my parents had had to break through to drag my carcass out of there. (How I had managed to get from the dining room to the bathroom remains a mystery.) They had found me unconscious on the floor, a safety razor clutched in my hand, with shaving cream all over me, the walls, and the ceiling. Not long after that my father and I had a high-volume altercation over who would pick up my violin-music stand (he had knocked it over but I had left it in his path), which ended when he threw me out of the house. Over his fierce objections ("*Who do you think bought them for you?*"), I insisted on putting my pants on first. I spent the night sailing back and forth on the Staten Island Ferry, until dawn made life look a little brighter.

Given the importance I place on heredity, I think I can be forgiven for facing the forthcoming adolescent years of my own three children with an outlook amounting to something less than aplomb. If in the near future you hear a grown man yelling for help, there is a reasonable chance that I will be the source of the clamor. There is no need to call a rescue squad. Just tell me in soothing tones that someday it will be over.

• • •

"Think of your children as poisoned by hormones for five to ten years," said one amused psychiatrist I know — more or less giving up hope on a better theory of the teenage years. As all parents know, puberty can cause changes that make their children unrecognizable. For some kids, a new-born character seems to spring out of nowhere, complete with sulking, obstreperousness, unpredictability, secretiveness, peer-dependence, and temper tantrums that make the "terrible twos" look tame. The child who was at eleven a calm and dependable member of the family may become at thirteen a rebel who openly and proudly disrespects family and parental values in everything from fashion to politics. The testing of boundaries — bedtime, homecoming time, distance from home, money spent, and so on — becomes a way of life in some families with teenagers, who may go through it with a strong feeling of storm and stress.

Judy Blume, one of the world's most popular writers of books for teenagers, thought she might escape all this. Her kids "grew up hearing how lucky they were. 'Your mother is Judy Blume. You can tell her anything . . . right?' "

> Wrong. I hoped they would feel they could. But when the going got tough my daughter went to someone else. . . .
>
> At sixteen, my sweet daughter became angry, sullen, judgmental, emotionally closed to me. In other words, a typical adolescent. And even though I knew her rejection was necessary to prove she could survive without me, it hurt! . . .
>
> My son, Larry, who is two years younger . . . swore he would never act so stupid. Ha! Two years later it was his turn, and he made Randy's rebellion seem tame. . . . I felt alone and frightened. . . .
>
> How could this be happening? . . . After all, thousands of kids were writing to me every month. They trusted me. I knew how to listen without judging. . . . (Yes, but it's so much easier when they're not *your* kids. And it's so much easier for them to tell someone other than *their* parents.)

If it happened to Judy Blume, it's going to happen to you and me. But there is good news: "Most of us survive our children's adolescent years. . . . Somehow, with common sense and humor most of us manage to muddle through. And on the other side is a reward. A new relationship with adult children." The key insight seems to be, *I knew her rejection was necessary to prove she could survive without me.* How can any youngster loosen the tight bonds to parents that are made during childhood without anger, confusion, and sullenness? These feelings are crucial to their adaptation to life.

And this applies to many average children. When we look at the extremes, we find disaster: promiscuity, sexually transmitted disease, pregnancy, drug abuse, alcohol abuse, reckless driving, even homicide and suicide. These outcomes loom like secret terrors in the night for every parent of a teenager — so much so that many parents have to conceptualize the whole process of child-rearing as a way to avert them. Today this problem is particularly acute for black families. The eldest of Anita Gholston's three children, Benjamin, is only seven, but she must already anticipate their future risks:

> I hope that they are able to be what it is they want to be, and that they feel free enough to live the kind of lives they want to live. It's very scary to me, particularly for my boys, but certainly for Avery too, that they're growing up in this time when so many young men, particularly boys, are being turned off . . . of the mainstream of things. They don't feel like they're valued at all.
>
> I don't want my sons to go through that. I don't want my daughter to go through that. I want them to feel like special and important people.
>
> This society doesn't look favorably on black children. And it's even worse for them as they get older. The black teenager is an endangered species and there's a lot of very scary, life-threatening things waiting for my children.

The Gholstons, who are superb parents, worry about this every day. The statistics are worst for blacks, but teenagers face these scary outcomes in every ethnic group. And most of them are becoming more frequent as the closing decades of the century roll by.

Just poisoned by hormones? We can ultimately do better than that. First, for many, maybe most adolescents, parents' fears are never borne out. The fears, along with some theories, are belied by a growing sense of responsibility and even idealism in many teenagers. It can also be fun for them — a surprising number remember it as the best time of their lives. The first time I taught human development to college students, I thought it would be clever to begin the lectures on the teenage years by asking the students to raise their hands if they had had a happy adolescence. I expected to see maybe a sprinkling of hands, but two-thirds or so of the four hundred students raised their hands, and I was thrown off stride in my neat lecture. This poses a paradox for a biological theory: If adolescent storm and stress is driven by hormones, how can so many escape it? The answer is partly individual differences, and partly the welter of cultural forces that contribute as much to adolescent behavior as hormones do.

But hormones are certainly where we need to start. Puberty is first a powerful biological event, a legacy from our evolutionary past. All animals that reproduce by sex must become capable of sex, and of parenting, but no higher animal is born sexual. All develop sexual lives according to their species' genetic plan. For small mammals like mice and rats, development seems a headlong plunge from birth to maturity, a mere six weeks punctuated halfway by weaning. The *speed* of growth rises steadily from birth onward, starting to fall only shortly before sexual maturation occurs. Then growth slows until full adult size is reached at an age of three to four months.

In us, as in monkeys and apes, there are two peaks of growth, not the single peak of lower mammals. The first occurs in the womb. After birth, growth rate falls steadily in humans, except for a brief small increase around age six to eight, one of the features of the five-seven shift. Then, at about age eleven in girls and twelve in boys, a speed-up of growth begins in earnest. (These are *averages,* and there are *years* of normal variation on both sides of these numbers.) In both sexes this growth spurt is one of the earliest outward signs that puberty has begun.

It is the first sign in girls, but breast buds — the first, small step in breast development — are seen soon afterward, followed by the appearance of short, downy pubic hair. The peak speed of growth occurs about a year and a half after the spurt starts. Then, the growth rate drops. Pubic hair is fully adult by about this time, breasts within a year or so. About halfway between the peak and the end of the growth spurt, just before age thirteen, the average girl has her first menstrual period — a stunning event technically known as menarche, from Greek roots for "moon" and "beginning." Nowadays, growth is completed for girls at around age sixteen.

We will return to the meaning of that "nowadays." For now, keep in mind that these numbers are averages and most individuals defy them — a fact as true for boys as it is for girls. Boys, though, lag behind girls about two years in the growth spurt and to a lesser degree in sexual puberty as well — an evolutionary legacy that causes no end of embarrassment in junior high. In boys the speed-up of growth begins only at age twelve and is not the first event — the start of growth in the testes is. These tender, olive-shaped manufacturers of sperm and male hormones begin to enlarge after age eleven. Light pubic hair begins to show next, followed by the lengthening of the unaroused penis.

The growth spurt in boys peaks at fourteen, with slowing growth until eighteen, each milestone two years behind the same one in girls. The added time for growth is part of what helps give boys their size edge as adults. It is difficult to find, in boys, an event in puberty as impressive as a girl's first menstrual flow; but one that has been proposed is the first conscious ejaculation. *Conscious* here denotes simply awareness; it may be deliberate masturbation, which almost all boys do sooner or later, or it may be merely a nocturnal emission — a "wet dream" — that has been noticed by the boy. There may well have been prior unnoticed ones, highly unlikely in the case of menstruation. Yet although it is less precise, ejaculation seems a logical first sign of a coming readiness to reproduce one's kind.

Alfred Kinsey and his colleagues, studying thousands of American men, found that this milestone occurred on average at thirteen. This was confirmed by a recent study in Israel conducted by Zvi Laron and others at Tel Aviv University. That places first ejaculation during the acceleration of growth, while first menstruation is in the slowing phase. But both events are tied to the curve of physical growth.

There are many other changes. Boys add great muscle mass. Girls keep more of their "baby fat," concentrating it in the hips, buttocks, breasts, and upper arms — thus the more rounded look of women's bodies. Yet loss of fat in either sex can give some teenagers a gangly, string-bean look. Male hormones lengthen the slender muscles in the "voice box" just as they do the rest of the body's muscles; but here the result is a "cracking" and deepening of boys' voices. In both sexes the feet grow faster than the rest, which doesn't make it easier to avoid feeling awkward.

Again, there is tremendous variation. Most of these milestones can occur two-and-a-half or three years on either side of the averages and still be normal. Also, they mostly refer to the United States and England in recent years. Travel backward in time, or around the world to different cultures, and you will find that numerical bets are off.

• • •

But this is a dry rendition of very powerful changes. It doesn't hint at the meaning of moving through them — or at the emotions, ranging from pleasure and excitement through self-absorption and haughtiness to anger and despair, that may accompany these changes. Puberty is as close as any human can get to metamorphosis — the process by which a caterpillar turns into a butterfly. Yet to hear some pubescent children talk — and to measure their emotions — you'd think that a butterfly was changing into a caterpillar. According to some good studies, puberty increases depressive moods in both sexes, at least during the transformation itself. For girls, as shown by Carol Gilligan of the Harvard School of Education, among others, self-esteem appears to decline as they go through adolescence, while for boys self-esteem rises.

Before we can sort out these effects, we need to understand something about the ebb, flow, and occasional riptide of hormones. The first change comes long before puberty, during the five-seven shift, when the adrenal glands — small, pyramid-shaped hormone factories sitting atop each kidney — begin to make more androgens. These are male sex hormones, but at this stage they increase equally, and very gradually, in both sexes. They produce pubic hair in girls and, added to the much larger amount from the testes, help govern the whole course of puberty in boys.

But the main events of puberty are independent of these early ones, and have to do with three well-coordinated hormone-making centers. The first, the hypothalamus, is really part of the base of the brain; but it governs the hormonal climate of the body. It is the area most influenced by sex hormones *before* birth, which prepare it for its pivotal role in puberty.

Part two, the pituitary — sometimes called the master gland — is a chemical production plant that literally hangs from the brain by a channel of tiny blood vessels. This means the hypothalamus can signal the pituitary to make *its* hormones and dump them into the bloodstream. These hormones, known as FSH and LH, govern the sex organs in both men and women. Signaled by them, after the long trek from pituitary to pelvis, the testes produce androgens, mainly testosterone ("T" for short) and the ovaries produce both estrogen ("E") and progesterone ("P"). The gonads complete the triumvirate that governs puberty.

Why doesn't puberty happen sooner than it does? The current answer is that the hypothalamus is highly sensitive to what is called negative feedback, which works much like a thermostat in a home. Very low levels of sex hormones from the gonads are enough to suppress it — as if the thermostat were set at a low temperature, keeping the furnace turned off.

So the gonads receive little stimulation, and continue to release only tiny amounts of sex hormones. Yet these small amounts still suppress the system, keeping all hormones at a very low ebb.

That remains the story throughout early and middle childhood. Then, for unknown reasons, the hypothalamus gradually becomes less sensitive to feedback from the sex hormones. Could it be that the sensitivity of the "thermostat" just wears down after a decade or so? In any case the low levels that suppressed it in childhood no longer work; the system breaks away. The hypothalamus can no longer be turned way down; it sends *stronger* signals to the pituitary. The pituitary, in turn, stimulates the gonads to greater growth, faster production of hormones.

These changes are not small. T levels rise about eighteenfold in boys and twofold in girls, leaving boys with about ten times as much as girls in the end. E levels rise eightfold in girls and twofold in boys. And the changes are not slow either: a given boy's enormous rise in testosterone may occur in one year. Yet girls, despite their much lower levels, seem to be more sensitive to T; paradoxically, small increases may affect them as much as large increases affect boys.

The sex hormones produce most of the body's changes. In boys, the strongest hormone — driving genital size, pubic hair, and total body growth — is testosterone. In girls, estrogen, progesterone, and androgens all make important contributions. But there are other hormones involved, and we do not have the total picture. We do know that T or E, given by a physician, can accelerate puberty in children whose growth is delayed. But the same hormones that speed up growth eventually stop it, first stimulating and then shutting down cell-making centers in the bones.

Yet these events do not have to be tied together in lockstep fashion. Carol Worthman, a biological anthropologist then at Harvard University, did an important study of puberty among the Kikuyu in Kenya. Not only did they experience much later menarche — just under age sixteen — but they also had a different order of events. In contrast to England and the United States, Kikuyu boys actually entered puberty earlier than girls, with genital development, but apparently got off to a very slow start. Girls are first in growth, and so are taller for two years. But initiation ceremonies in this culture, as well as separate housing for boys, are tied to physical changes, not age. This increases the power of puberty as subjectively experienced. While boys and girls may be "out of synch" with each other, the Kikuyu have better synchrony of culture and biology than in our society, where keen awareness of chronological age heightens anxiety over the pace of bodily change.

· · ·

Do the hormones of puberty also produce behavioral and psychological changes? The evidence points toward a "yes," but it is hard to tease out direct hormone effects. However, when we look at adults and lab animals, where external body changes do not confound the issue, we find unmistakable direct effects. For instance, T is involved in aggression, and in particular a rise in T following a "win," whether in a college wrestling match, a !Kung San hunt, a tennis match, completing basic training in the military, or even some successes that have no obvious aggressive component, such as medical school graduation day. It also stimulates sexual desire in *both* sexes.

So it is not surprising that recent studies link T to these behaviors in adolescent boys. Dan Olweus, a psychologist at the University of Oslo, has for many years systematically studied the bullies in Norway's schools, as well as their victims. The overwhelming majority of bullies are boys — mostly a small percentage of boys who keep at it all through their teens. Olweus also found a strong relationship between T level and bullying behavior. This confirmed earlier studies, by psychiatrist Robert Rose and his colleagues, then at Boston University, who showed that in male convicts the age at first arrest, usually in the teenage years, was related to T; the higher their current level, the earlier they'd gotten in trouble with the law.

More detailed studies have been going on during the past few years. Richard Udry and Luther Talbert, of the University of North Carolina at Chapel Hill, studied hormones, personality, and sex in adolescents — two hundred boys and girls in the eighth to tenth grades. They used an Adjective Check List; the teenagers were asked to check which of three hundred adjectives were applicable to them. Higher-testosterone boys tended to check *ambitious, cynical, dominant, original, persistent, pessimistic, robust, sarcastic, severe, showoff, spontaneous, stingy, temperamental,* and *uninhibited.* High-T girls tended to check a list that was similar but not the same: *charming, cynical, discreet, disorderly, dominant, enterprising, frivolous, initiative, original,* and *pleasant.* Finally, combining the boys and girls led to five more choices: *outgoing, self-centered, sensitive, sexy,* and *understanding.* It's hard to find a label that would summarize all these words, but "intense and egotistical" comes to mind. Neither the child's age nor the level of development helped predict the adjectives, once the T level was known.

Finally, one fact surprised the investigators: progesterone helped explain some of the girls' personality tendencies. The level of P in the first half of the menstrual cycle — at its monthly low — was associated with a factor including the following adjectives: *boastful, foresighted, obnoxious, quitting, showoff, stern, tough,* and *unrealistic.* The list seems strange for a hormone that, at higher levels, helps maintain pregnancy, although *boastful, foresighted, showoff, tough,* and *unrealistic* might be adaptive then. But it may have different effects at lower levels.

Another study in which hormones seemed more important than age or stage of puberty was conducted by Michelle Warren and Jeanne Brooks-Gunn, and focused exclusively on girls — one hundred girls from fairly privileged homes and schools, ranging in age from ten to thirteen. Five hormones were measured, and the girls answered three different questionnaires. The Youth Behavior Profile tapped into depression, aggression, delinquency, and immature hyperactive behavior. The Self Image Questionnaire had seventy-eight sentences like "I feel nervous most of the time" and "I am a leader in school"; the girls were asked how true each one was of her. A similar scale measured sports involvement. Also, mothers were interviewed about their daughters' moods, and the girls were seen by a physician who assessed pubertal stage.

By using E as their main hormone, Warren and Brooks-Gunn showed some impressive trends in the girls' Youth Behavior Profiles. All the trends were U-shaped, with either a peak or a trough in the middle. Impulse control first dropped as E rose and then reversed direction and climbed again steadily. Depression, aggression, and psychopathology all rose first and then fell. Visible pubertal change, including breast development, did not predict the psychological changes; hormones did.

Yet common sense suggests that the outward transformations of puberty will make their impact on the child's mind in ways that have nothing directly to do with hormones. The body is changing shape. These changes are reflected both in the mirror and in the behavior of peers.

Elissa Koff, of Wellesley College, and her colleagues did an elegant study of the impact of pubertal timing, especially first menstruation, on how girls draw a person. Three groups were studied. Each girl made drawings twice, six months apart, and all three groups were the same average age.

But the groups differed in pubertal change despite their similar ages. One group had not yet reached menarche by the time of the second drawing, the second group reached the milestone between the two drawings, and the third was past menarche for both drawings. This proved a brilliant research plan: Menstrual status, not age, was the best predictor of what the girls drew. First, girls who had passed menarche between the two drawings increased in their tendency to draw a female figure first — an open choice, although all girls were eventually asked to draw both sexes. More important, all the drawings were scored for sex development — for example, the presence of breasts and rounded hips in the female figures. Girls who had not passed first menstruation by the time of the second drawing tended to draw pictures of prepubertal girls, with straight, boylike bodies. Girls who were past menarche both times tended to show the curving hips and narrowing waist of a woman, as well as marking the lower curves of the breasts.

Neither the "pre-pre" group nor the "post-post" group changed the way they drew between the first and second efforts. But the third group — the girls who went through menarche between the two drawings — increased their sex-development scores from the first to the second drawing. Here was one of the clearest demonstrations ever of the effect of first menstruation on body image. And it had another effect: Girls felt more satisfied with female aspects of the body after menarche than before.

Koff has done other studies of how both girls and women see this event. They confirm that menarche makes a large mental impact on girls — even in our culture, where little is done to mark it — and add that the impact is usually negative. Girls who have in one way or another been prepared for menarche have an easier time with it than girls who come upon it unexpectedly. But in general in our culture, it is experienced and remembered unfavorably. Koff's group found some positive reactions to menarche because of its association with greater maturity — reactions reminiscent of Anne Frank's "sweet secret." But these are outweighed by negative feelings "as girls become increasingly self-conscious, embarrassed, and secretive."

We can't completely separate the effects of menarche from those of hormones, since it is caused by them; negative feelings come partly from a rising tide of these hormones. But the way a girl draws a person is unlikely to reflect any direct hormonal influence that can reasonably be imagined. More plausible here is the explanation that must play a key role in any conception of pubertal change: Regardless of hormonal flux, the child, girl or boy, is an increasingly intelligent and knowledgeable spirit with a complex awareness of this great physical change.

In her *Memoirs of a Dutiful Daughter,* French author Simone de Beauvoir recounted this experience:

> We were staying with friends. . . . I awoke horror-stricken one morning: I had soiled my nightdress. I washed it and got dressed: again I soiled my underclothes. I had forgotten Madeleine's vague prophecies, and I wondered what shameful malady I was suffering from. Worried and feeling somehow guilty, I had to take my mother into my confidence: she explained to me that I had now become "a big girl," and bundled me up in a very inconvenient manner. I felt a strong sense of relief when I learned that it had happened through no fault of my own; and as always when something important happened to me, I even felt my heart swell with a sort of pride. I didn't mind too much when I heard my mother whispering about it to her friends. But that evening when we joined my father in the Rue de Rennes, he jokingly made reference to my condition: I was consumed with shame. I had imagined that the monstrous regiment of women kept its blemish a secret from the male fraternity. . . . I felt as if I could never hold up my head again.

There can be great physical as well as social discomfort. Many girls experience a sense of bloating premenstrually, or painful cramps — even, some women report in retrospect, as painful as contractions during labor — sending them to bed for a day or more each month. There may be a sense of pride in the development of feminine body contours, but if the girl places extreme emphasis on slimness, she may actually resist or reject the change in shape, which results largely from the laying down of fat. Boys tend to be happier with the changes they go through, since the ideal form changes less from boyhood to manhood; they just wish they had more muscles, and they get them.

But of course, muscles are not distributed equally, and some boys (me included) certainly feel outclassed because of their lack of development, just as some girls do. Consider this passage by English historian and novelist H. G. Wells, from his *Experiment in Autobiography*:

> To me, in my hidden thoughts, the realization that my own body was thin and ugly was almost insupportable — as I suppose it would be to most young men or women. In the secret places of my heart I wanted a beautiful body and I wanted it because I wanted to make love with it, and all the derision and humour with which I treated my personal appearance in my talking and writing to my friends, my caricatures of my leanness and my unkempt shabbiness, did not affect the profundity of that unconfessed mortification. Each year I was becoming more positively and urgently sexual and the desire to be physically strong and attractive was intense.

Religious or very sensitive boys may be deeply embarrassed by erections, nocturnal emissions, and the temptation to masturbate, even as they revel in the undeniable pleasure. This reaction was once much more common than it is now, as recorded in *Life and Confessions of a Psychologist*, by G. Stanley Hall, who later placed adolescent psychology on a scientific footing. The events he writes of took place around 1860.

> So great was my dread of natural phenomena that in the earliest teens I rigged an apparatus and applied bandages to prevent [ejaculation] while I slept, which very likely only augmented the trouble. If I yielded to any kind of temptation to experimentation upon myself I suffered intense remorse and fear, and sent up many a secret and most fervent prayer that I might never again break my resolve. At one time I feared I was abnormal and found occasion to consult a physician in a neighboring town who did not know me. He examined me and took my dollar, and laughed at me, but also told me what consequences would ensue if I became unchaste. What an untold anguish of soul would have been saved me if some one had told me that certain experiences while I slept were as normal for boys in their teens as are the monthly phenomena for girls. [I] thought myself secretly and exceptionally corrupt and not quite worthy to associate with girls.

Clearly, the mind is alive and aware; it is not just a brain bathed in hormones, but a fiercely attentive observer of the changes in the body. Much of the psychological change at puberty is a reaction of that mind to those bodily changes; and, indirectly, to the reactions of parents, other adults, siblings, and peers to these same metamorphoses of the body.

• • •

But we know that there are crucial historical and cultural differences in this process. Ample evidence shows that there has been a decline in the average age at puberty over the past one hundred fifty years in Europe and the United States. James Tanner of the Institute of Child Health in London, a leading authority on growth, summarized the evidence and thought that a drop as large as four or five years might have occurred. Grace Wyshak and Rose Frisch, of the Department of Population Sciences at Harvard, reviewed a substantially larger body of evidence in 1982, strongly supporting Tanner's basic hypothesis, though with a considerably smaller drop.

Today a very conservative estimate of the minimum drop in the age of puberty — as measured by the age at first menstruation — would be two years, with three years quite possible. The drop occurred at an average rate of two to three months per decade between the middle of the last century and the middle of this one. It stopped some time ago in the most economically well-off populations, and has stabilized at around age thirteen in Norway and England and around twelve years eight months in the United States.

The point is immediately raised: Couldn't those girls of a hundred years ago have been squeamish or frightened about reporting first menstruation, and so concealed it as long as they could? But this objection is easily disposed of. Menarche is tied to overall growth rate. And body size — especially height — is something directly determined with a measuring stick, a procedure done perfectly well in the nineteenth century. Children have long been measured for height, and records, summarized for example by Howard Meredith of the University of South Carolina, show that at every age they have become taller in succeeding generations. This includes adults — a fact often noted by visitors to medieval castles in Europe, surprised that they would be unable to fit into the suits of armor worn by the most dauntless and chivalrous knights.

But put it another way and it is even more striking: Pick a given height for a child — say, 4 feet 10 inches — and you will find that the age at which that height is reached during growth has been dropping over the past century or more at the same rate estimated for the drop in the age at menarche: two to three months per decade. So there is no getting around it; growth has accelerated, adult size is greater, and the age at puberty has substantially dropped. Overall, the historical process is known as the "secular" trend — from the Latin word for an era or generation.

We also have present-day comparisons of urban with rural populations throughout the developing world. Our folklore deems rural people more robust, but there is almost always a rural lag in growth. Phyllis Eveleth of the National Institutes of Health and James Tanner showed that rural girls experience first menstruation one to two years later than do urban girls in most developing countries. Some also suggest that the secular trend is continuing in some of them. In any case, one of the strongest historical trends is urbanization; given the rural-urban difference, movement into cities may have helped lower the age at puberty.

• • •

It also begins to hint at an explanation. What could it be about urban life that might make kids grow faster? The most believable answers are nutrition, health, and exercise. Indeed, urbanization is probably a stand-in for the whole process of modernization, which usually includes improved nutrition, improved health, and *decreased* exercise.

We have known for centuries that eating more, all other things being equal, enhances growth. About slowly growing teenagers, pediatricians say, "If you can't pinch an inch of skinfold, the treatment is meat and potatoes." Starvation stops growth for a time, but resuming adequate nourishment leads to a "catch-up growth" phase — growth actually speeds up to make up for lost time. But undernutrition can persist so long that catch-up is impossible. Although pediatricians used to be taught — and in turn taught parents — that bigger is better, the resulting overnutrition and obesity in American children has now convinced them that there is a point of diminishing returns to this philosophy.

This ideal caloric input will not be agreed on soon, but the relationship between food, growth, and puberty is clear. The same is true of the link between disease and growth. Children in other times and places have borne a much larger burden of infectious disease — measles and small-pox, for example — than our children do now. As with food shortage, periods of infection can halt growth; the body wisely recognizes that the cost of fighting the infection is so high that growth, also costly, must be suspended. These stoppages too are followed by catch-up growth, and if a child has only one or two such experiences, an ultimate change in adult size is unlikely. But if the burden of illness makes infection chronic — that is, the child is battling one onslaught of microbes or another almost constantly throughout development — then catch-up may be impossible.

Rose Frisch, who helped to demonstrate the secular trend, has also helped explain it, uncovering two ways the environment can affect puberty. At first she focused on fatness; a certain weight-for-height had to be reached by a girl during puberty before she would begin to menstruate. This helped to explain why girls had menarche some time after the peak of the growth spurt: Height settles down a bit while weight continues to increase fast, until a threshold is crossed in weight-for-height and first menstruation is triggered.

Further research showed that it was not just any weight, but fat that counted. Girls were laying down fat during puberty on their way toward womanly roundedness, and the key seemed to be the ratio of fat to the lean body mass. Once both could be accurately measured, it became clear that building up muscle would not trigger menarche. It had to be done by laying down a certain amount of fat in proportion to muscle, bone, and other body tissues. Strong support for Frisch's idea also came from laboratory experiments conducted by others. These showed that fat cells are able to make the female hormone estrogen — ironically perhaps, from their relatively sparse male hormones.

But Frisch went on to discover another key determinant: exercise. It may also work through body fat, by converting fat to muscle; but it is an effect separate from diet. Ballet dancers, especially ultra-thin ones, had late menarche compared with other girls, and continued to have irregular or infrequent menstrual cycles as they grew. Even more interesting was a study of college swimmers and runners, some of whom had begun their training before menarche, some after. Both groups had some menstrual irregularity in college, but only the ones who had trained *before* menarche postponed it. In fact, they reached it more than two years later, at just over age fifteen, as compared with the athletes who had begun training after menarche *and* the nonathletes; both these groups averaged under age thirteen.

One woman had begun swim training at seven and a half; her first menstruation came at fifteen and a half. In college, her periods were infrequent. She was extremely lean — about 83 percent of the medically "ideal" weight for her height, and about four and a half pounds below Frisch's "critical" weight for triggering menarche. She decided to load up on calories to see if she would have a period. After gaining five pounds, she had one. But she soon lost the same amount and her periods stopped again. It is difficult to separate training from diet effects, but either way, these studies help explain the secular trend. Over the past century or more, children have increased their food intake and decreased their exercise. Add a reduced burden of illness in childhood — resulting from improved sanitary conditions and, later, vaccination — and we have solved the puzzle of earlier puberty.

• • •

But what about the aspects of puberty parents fear? Consider two of them — school-age pregnancy and juvenile violence — as representative. They are certainly scary enough. And both are close to the heart of pubertal change, since throughout evolution the capacity for both reproduction and mature, effective aggression has been part of what maturation was for.

One way to track teen pregnancy is to look at early motherhood. A 1990 report of the National Center for Health Statistics showed that an eighteen-year, very slow decline in births to fifteen- to seventeen-year-olds was reversed in 1987, and in 1988 rose again, with 168,000 births in that age group. There are thousands of births each year to girls *under* fifteen. About a million American teenagers become pregnant each year, and just under half end up with births. More than 10 percent of them occur to the youngest teens. "Last year 125,000 junior high students flunked this simple test," says a recent Children's Defense Fund poster, above a photograph of a pregnancy test kit.

Sexual activity, of course, helps to explain all this. According to the Centers for Disease Control, the proportion of teenage girls and women who have had intercourse has increased very steadily between 1970 and 1988. In 1970 under 5 percent of *fifteen*-year-olds said they had had premarital intercourse; but the figure was 17 percent for 1980 and had risen to 26 percent in 1990 — in a decade in which headlines highlighted epidemics of AIDS, herpes, syphilis, gonorrhea, and other sexually transmitted diseases, not to mention school-age pregnancy.

By age nineteen, three-fourths of girls — up from two-thirds in 1980 and just under half in 1970 — had had premarital sexual intercourse. Other studies show that boys are always ahead — a lead made more impressive by the fact that boys lag behind girls in development. Casual sex is common — "scamming" and "scooping" are two of the least objectionable terms teens have for it — and in some circles intercourse is expected early in a dating relationship.

As for *safe* sex, according to the Guttmacher Institute's surveys, there isn't much of it. Five out of six teen pregnancies are unwanted. Only half of teenage girls and women claim to have used a contraceptive the first time they had intercourse. Roughly four out of ten pregnant teenagers terminate pregnancy, accounting for over a fourth of all U.S. abortions. Seemingly, hundreds of thousands of teenagers each year are essentially resorting to abortion as a contraceptive method — something even most supporters of abortion rights would be unlikely to approve.

Some think that early motherhood is merely a return to a more primitive condition of our species, but historical and anthropological evidence make this unlikely. In *Romeo and Juliet* the heroine is not yet fourteen, but when she calls marriage "an honour that I dream not of," her mother says,

> *Well, think of marriage now; younger than you*
> *Here in Verona, ladies of esteem,*
> *Are made already mothers. By my count,*
> *I was your mother much upon these years*
> *That you are now a maid.*

But Lady Capulet, persuaded as she is, is no demographer, and even her own story is most likely wrong. The literary source from which Shakespeare lifted the plot places Juliet's age at eighteen; he gained dramatic tension from dropping the age, but sacrificed accuracy. Careful studies by Peter Laslett and his colleagues at Cambridge University, using church, family, and other records, have proven that early teenage childbearing was almost nonexistent in England in the sixteenth through nineteenth centuries, and similar evidence exists for continental Europe and the United States.

Yet it is unlikely that this was mainly because of sexual restraint. Phillips Cutright, a sociologist at the University of Chicago, has studied out-of-wedlock births in the United States since the turn of the twentieth century; he believes that we have succumbed to "the myth of an abstinent past." Teenage births began to rise as early as 1940, but had been extremely low at the turn of the century. Yet sexual activity was common. Pubertal age resolves the paradox: If girls were having first menstruation at age fifteen, and then experiencing some degree of irregularity, sexual activity could have occurred with a very low birth rate. Maris Vinovskis, an authority on marriage and the family among the New England Puritans, argues that sexual activity and even premarital pregnancies were more common in the eighteenth than in the nineteenth century — a puzzling finding, given how "puritanical" the Puritans were. Nevertheless, *their* births did not occur until the *late* teenage years.

• • •

As for small-scale societies, much of the evidence points to late menarche there too — as late as age eighteen among the traditional people of highland New Guinea, for example. True, many of these societies performed marriages early, but that does not mean that the girls (and boys) entering the marriages were in any sense mature.

Take for example the !Kung: Demographer Nancy Howell of the University of Toronto found their first menstruation to be at sixteen on average, their first birth at nineteen. Yet we know that girls and boys engage in sex-play right through childhood, and that this gradually or abruptly changes to real adult sex — often *before* the first menstruation. Yet early and mid-teenage pregnancies do not occur among the !Kung, because of adolescent infertility. This general phenomenon was first proven by anthropologist Ashley Montagu, who carefully demonstrated the infrequency of births in most cultures, as well as in monkeys and apes, during the first few years after menarche.

Nisa, the !Kung woman whose life Marjorie Shostak studied, described a more or less continual experience with childhood sexuality, in play with other children. In her early to mid-teens she had two brief arranged marriages to older men. Both were soon dissolved — the first because her husband had sex with a woman his own age in the marriage hut, while the much younger Nisa was thought to be sleeping; the second because the young man fell out with Nisa's father.

Dissolution of these relationships was easy. In both she resisted her husband's sexual advances; despite extensive sex-play in childhood, reportedly including sexual intercourse with penetration, her first encounters with adult men were awkward and unwelcome. She was married for the third time through yet another arrangement by her parents, about one year before her first menstruation. She ran away from this husband many times, too, before settling down to married life with him.

She finally agreed to have sex with him once, but subsequently refused because of the pain this had caused her. It took years before their relationship actually assumed an adult cast:

> We lived and lived, the two of us together, and after a while I started to really like him, and then to love him. I had finally grown up and learned how to love. I thought, "A man has sex with you. Yes, that's what a man does. I had thought that perhaps he didn't" . . . I thought that, and gave myself to him, gave and gave. We lay with each other and my breasts were very large. I was becoming a woman.

The years from first menstruation to age nineteen, the age at first birth — a delay due mainly to adolescent subfertility — are important ones for the young !Kung woman. It is as though time were temporarily suspended; she is sexually mature but has no significant responsibility. She can ease gradually into adult roles and adult sexuality without having to deal with early motherhood. She has years — some before menarche, some after — to determine whether she is compatible with her husband. As long as she has not yet become pregnant, divorce is not very difficult.

Married or not, the primary responsibility for feeding herself and her husband is deferred, and borne by her mother and father. Even after her first birth, her need to remain near her mother is recognized, and it is not until the second child that she may be expected to move, with her family, to her husband's parents' village-camp. At that time — when she is twenty-three or twenty-four years old — she is essentially on her own, with the full responsibilities of motherhood. Still, she is never quite "on her own" in the sense that many young American mothers are; she remains in a context dense with her own or her husband's kin, and it is unusual for a marriage to be dissolved after it has produced living children.

• • •

It is against this broad cross-cultural background that adolescence in our own society must be seen. One hundred fifty years ago, a young woman menstruating at age fifteen and becoming a mother at eighteen could take her place as an adult in a society designed to support her with institutions of marriage, family, and a broader network of kin. Today, a girl menstruating at twelve and becoming a mother at fifteen, often unmarried and likely to remain so, is a schoolchild at sea in a grown-up world that is much more complex and unforgiving. Even if all of growth is compressed, so that today's fifteen-year-old has the body and even the brain of the eighteen-year-old of the past, there is no way for her to compensate for the three years of lost experience, or to struggle successfully in a complex society in which maturity, education, and experience are increasingly at a premium.

Whatever the causes, the secular trend is a profound change in human biology, with implications for psychology, education, and law. It's not that recent changes in rates of teen pregnancy are the simple result of changes in growth. Many other factors have intervened, and in fact England and Scandinavia, after similar secular trends, still have much lower rates of teen pregnancy, partly because of different sexual activity and partly because of birth control.

But it is clear that no rise in early teenage pregnancies could have occurred when they were physically impossible. We do not have to imagine a tight historical coupling between the secular trend and the pregnancy rate. The sexual activity of adolescents — and, even more so, our sexual mores — could be expected to resist change for a time during the slow biological transformation, and then perhaps to change quite rapidly as the difficulty of continued restraint came home to more and more adolescents.

Many demand restraint from teenagers, reasoning that loose morals explain their pregnancies. The call for restraint, common in Europe and the United States in recent centuries, arose for complex reasons. Most societies have not traditionally had such expectations. Equally important, they had a different biological reality. We may be tempted to imagine that if by legal or religious fiat exposure of teenagers to sexual ideas and stimuli could be drastically reduced, teenage sex would revert to the patterns of thirty years ago. No doubt this theory has some merit. But cause and effect may be much more complex, and indeed may be weighted in the other direction. Teenagers have been *producers* of changing mores in recent decades, not just passive recipients of adult liberality. It is plausible that faster maturation led them to seek earlier sex, and this striving may have affected adult mores more than it was affected *by* them.

Infancy and adolescence are both sensitive periods of growth. An early teenage birth affects two growing children, one in each period. Fetuses and infants are resilient, but with limits, and it is doubtful that a young teenager could provide an environment for optimal development, even with optimal support and care for the mother. Young teenage mothers, for their part, are completing the most rapid growth they have known since infancy, and are in the midst of a hormonal, emotional, and social turmoil on the threshold of adulthood. To bring a baby into this turmoil is to pit two children against each other — children with needs that may be incompatible.

"Childhood" series observer Marian Wright Edelman traveled to impoverished Elkins, West Virginia, an old lumbering and railroad town that has many teen mothers. The kids there are bright and lively enough, but they just don't see much of a future that might make avoiding pregnancy really worth the trouble. Edelman interviewed April, a sixteen-year-old mother of two-month-old twins. April lived with her mother, whose husband, April's stepfather, was only there sometimes. The gas had been cut off in the house. April was baby-sitting for her sister's child to earn money for diapers. There was no other visible means of support in this disrupted family. Youth Health Services, an Elkins agency that receives federal grants, brings tutoring to April; evidence shows that continuing education is key to bringing school-age mothers into productive work. But it is a steep uphill fight every step of the way.

It is doubtful that we can turn back the clock on teenage sexual activity. Although this kind of reversal may have occurred before in our history, we are now in a different circumstance. Current sexual activity is partly caused by media influence, but it also follows changes in the pace of maturation that have been going on for more than a century. To expect today's teenagers to live up to moral standards inherited from centuries past is to fail to recognize that teenagers are biologically different.

Under the circumstances it is perhaps not too strong to say that to withhold information about contraception from a young teenager who may be sexually active, and then to deny her the possibility of therapeutic termination of her pregnancy, may in itself be a form of child abuse. Whatever our opinions of the complex moral issues involved, we could act with a larger measure of compassion for the plight of today's teenager, caught between a mature body and immature, inexperienced emotions. The same logic by which we protect young delinquents from adult punishment would presumably apply to the protection of young teenagers from the consequences of their own sexual indiscretions. Referring to even the youngest teenagers as women rather than girls, simply *because* they have managed to achieve pregnancy or parenthood, only helps to rob them of their childhood.

Many changes have taken place in the behavior of young teenagers besides more sex, including a rise in school-age homicide, suicide, alcoholism, and drug abuse. Despite their complexity, these trends must be seen against the background of the prior profound historical change in the pace of growth. Its implications, for teenagers specifically and for changes in our culture more widely, are only now being explored.

• • •

To understand adolescent aggression, we need to recall the process of becoming male or female, since puberty takes it such a great step forward. Recall that the plan of the embryo is female. A Y chromosome must send a chemical signal to the budding gonads, to suppress the female organs and allow the male to flower. If the male organs grow, the testes will produce testosterone, abundant in males before birth. Experiments show that in many mammals this hormone influences the brain in the womb.

Sex hormones damp down to negligible levels after infancy. The sex differences that can be measured at this stage are subtle — small differences in muscle strength or reactivity. But what is not small is the difference in treatment accorded to the two sexes, from the moment of birth. *Is it a boy or a girl?* is the question we ask immediately, since we need the answer to guide our feelings and conduct. Pink and blue nurseries are only the start of cradle-to-grave training. Dress, decor, expectations, role models, games, toys, schooling, rules — almost every aspect of learning and experience gives the world a chance to shape the sexes differently, and most cultures take that chance and run with it. If in fact the sexes come into being with slightly different brains, then it is still up to culture to exaggerate that difference, reduce it, or leave it alone.

Margaret Mead's most indispensable contribution was her wide-ranging study of sex roles. Throughout an energetic career she returned to the South Pacific time and again — to seven different cultures in all. Beginning with the Samoa study that made her famous, she often focused on sex roles. For example, among the Tchambuli, on the shores of one of New Guinea's most beautiful lakes, "women, brisk, unadorned, managing and industrious, fish and go to market; the men, decorative and adorned, carve and paint and practice dance-steps, their headhunting tradition replaced by the simpler tradition of buying victims to validate their manhood." With their businesslike women and prissy, cosmetically obsessed men, they seemed to reverse classic American sex roles. But with the Mundugumor, riverside cannibals in another part of New Guinea, she found that "the women are as assertive and vigorous as the men; they detest bearing and rearing children, and provide most of the food, leaving the men free to plot and fight."

Reports like these helped Mead convince many that their cherished beliefs about "natural" roles for men and women were subject to great cultural variation. Women were supposed to be nurturing, gossipy, emotional homebodies intensely concerned about clothes and makeup and unprepared to shoulder real responsibility; men were their down-to-earth, practical counterparts, taking care of business and unconcerned about frivolities like fashion, cosmetics, and the arts. Mead's popular books helped edge our society toward a far more flexible concept of what is natural for men and women, and shaped very favorably the options we present to boys and girls.

Alice Schlegel and Herbert Barry III, in their 1991 book, *Adolescence: An Anthropological Inquiry* — a landmark cross-cultural study of this phase of life — carry Mead's work forward by making a broad comparison of 186 different cultures. Although there is much variety, just as

Mead had said, there are also great consistencies in the way boys and girls move through adolescence. Girls in the majority of cultures are found closer to home than boys are, and girls have extensive contact with their mothers and other adult female role models. Boys do *not* have comparable contact with their fathers, or in fact with adults of either sex. So they gravitate after puberty to other boys, forming all-male youth groups that take them farther from home and draw them into competition and aggression.

Schlegel and Barry see this as an evolutionary adaptation of our species, like that in monkeys and apes, designed to prevent incest, which might bring out genetic defects. Lionel Tiger of Rutgers University, in *Men in Groups*, attributed to adolescent male bands a primarily aggressive and political function. And Beatrice and John Whiting found that "fraternal associations" of adolescent males are significantly more likely to occur in societies that emphasize military glory — martial prowess, heroism, death in battle, and the like. In this view, peer groups separate boys from girls and women, and from their identification with women, the better to make them warriors. There is also evidence that when *non*-belligerent hunting-and-gathering people — like the Eskimo and the !Kung — become settled, and live at larger population densities, adolescent boys aggregate into gangs with a potentially destructive effect.

We pride ourselves on equal treatment of boys and girls. Yet advanced industrial cultures, ours included, increase the natural biological divergence between the sexes during development. Consider Karuna Nakayama, fourteen, and Megumi Hijikata, thirteen, Japanese girls of two "Childhood" families who study dance. Their society at large has firm traditions separating the roles of women and men; for centuries these assured male supremacy. Although this has softened, it remains a cultural pressure. Karuna takes modern dance; but Megumi, who takes classical ballet, adds to Japan's traditions a Western aesthetic model that also tends to maximize sex differences. In class she learns to maintain an exquisite but costly feminine poise — an effortful pretense of perfect grace. True, male dancers are seen as effeminate by some, but it is women who rise on point, wear ultrafeminine costumes, and fall swooning into the arms of the men. In the central event in classical ballet, the romantic pas de deux, the man stands firm and must be muscular enough to lift the woman easily. She must seem weightless, floating through the air on the strength of the man's arm.

Of course, every important cultural practice has complex effects. We know ballet training, if intensive, may also delay puberty — in a sense postponing the time when the girl becomes a woman. Yet Megumi feels mature in the dance class, where she learns adult values of self-discipline and hard work. Finally, her study of a European dance tradition contributes to westernization, which has been going on in Japan for generations. But meanwhile, amid all this complexity, it is sending a simple, powerful message through her young mind and body: Women have roles in life quite distinct from those of men.

At puberty, biology makes its largest impact on sex differences since before birth, when hormones may have helped shape the brain. Now drastic increases in hormone levels in both sexes send them off in different directions again, most obviously with changes in shape, strength, and voice. But hormones also directly affect behavior — most likely through the brain, which, although largely finished growing, still responds to hormones. How all this helps shape sex roles is controversial; but at the current pace of research we may soon have some answers. Meanwhile, whatever the impact of biology, our culture provides models, rewards, punishments, symbols, language, and beliefs that all tend to increase the divergence.

There are further biological divergences in store, but these are partly matters of choice. The woman who becomes pregnant is subjected to new hormonal effects no man will ever experience. The woman who breast-feeds her baby as recommended causes another cascade of hormonal changes. On the other hand, a woman who trains intensively in swimming or running will disrupt the female hormonal cycle, eliminating one biological difference between her and men. In fact, Rose Frisch has suggested that widespread athletic training for girls from age eight or nine would help to prevent teenage pregnancy by postponing fertile cycling.

But more important, almost certainly, are the social effects of these life choices — and the enormous impact of the cultural context on the individual. Throughout life, learning and maturation turn and pass and move and change in a complex, subtle procession that makes men and women take the course they do. Biology makes a strong wind, and to ignore it is to decrease our chance of compensating for it. But culture is the landscape across which we must walk, the atmosphere we move through and breathe. The more deliberately we shape culture, the more surely we control our journey.

• • •

One of the ways in which not only men and women, but boys and girls of every age differ is that males are more prone to physical violence. This is true in all cultures that have been studied — even the ones that impressed Margaret Mead as having a reversal of classic Western sex roles. The lake-dwelling Tchambuli men, doing their hair and practicing dance-steps while their wives earned a living, also had a long headhunting tradition and bought victims "to validate their manhood." Among the river-valley Mundugumor, women stick to earning a living, but they do it so as to leave the men "free to plot and fight."

In fact, male predominance in physical violence is a cross-cultural universal. Mead's first study was of Samoan teenagers, who seemed to have sexual freedom and a minimum of the "storm and stress" common in Western societies. Anthropologists have long said that traditional cultures give teenagers little to rebel about, since their futures are secure, and little to precipitate a crisis of identity, since there are few paths they can follow to enter adult roles. But Mead underestimated the conflict felt by Samoan girls and boys as they go through puberty. Later studies showed that virginity is prized for girls, so sex is hardly without conflict for them, and they have to resist or compromise with importuning boys. As for rebellion, a steep rise in delinquency occurs in Samoan boys after puberty, resembling the rise in industrial states.

The sex difference in aggression runs about as deep in the course of development as does aggression itself. At one year of age, as shown by Susan Goldberg and Michael Lewis, boys are more likely than girls to attack and break down a physical barrier separating them from a desired toy. A little later, hitting and other overt aggression occur with parents, siblings, and peers. Throughout early childhood, most studies find more male than female physical aggression, whether the aggression is playful (with smiling, chasing, and wrestling) or serious (hitting, kicking, and biting). After the five-seven shift, aggression is less frequent and more internalized. Verbal aggression may substitute, and in this there is no male excess — there may even be more in girls.

In middle childhood, there is less overt physical aggression, but there is still a male preponderance. At puberty, a further decrease in fighting occurs. But what there is is much more serious. Knives and guns come more into play; crime, violent or not, becomes more likely. Here males predominate again, and their excess increases through adolescence. Most crime in all countries is committed by young males.

Victims of violent crime are also mostly young males, except for the crime of rape. One of the valuable contributions of feminist social science has been to show how male violence against women — from date rape through beatings and torture to homicide — works to suppress all women and limit the options they see in life. Male violence directed against women is part of the environment that shapes girls as they move through the teenage years and assess the world around them. Fear of boys and men may lead to a sense of inferiority, lack of ambition, and a submissive approach to life. It may also lead them to play the strongest card they hold — sex — in a pragmatic, even cynical way, to increase their chances in a hostile and dangerous male-run world.

Still, the overwhelming majority of victims of homicide in the United States are young males, just as are the perpetrators. The number of fire-arms murders alone by offenders under eighteen has risen steadily from 444 in 1984 to 952 in 1989. The number of homicide victims ages fifteen to nineteen rose from 1,022 in 1984 to 1,641 in 1988. And as Anita Gholston said, this victimization is *not* equally distributed by race; the firearms death rate for black teenage boys is eleven times the white rate. In fact, the leading cause of death in young black males is homicide. More black young men died violent deaths in American cities during the hundred hours of the Gulf War than died from all causes in the gulf. Those who went to war were safer than those who stayed home.

• • •

With homicide, suicide, sexually transmitted disease, and birth rates to teenagers rising, and with other disasters like drug and alcohol abuse still very widespread, parents can be forgiven for feeling afraid as their children peer over the pubertal brink. Love, not strictness, generates this fear. But recent research shows that:

- *most* teenagers subjectively experience the course of adolescence overall as a positive experience, not a negative one;

- in *most* adolescents, conflict with parents, as well as impulsive behavior, depression, and aggression, increase in early adolescence
  during the pubertal peak itself, but soon begin to decline, and by
  late adolescence are better than at prepubertal levels;
- only a minority of adolescents end in what parents rightly see as
  disasters of the age group: unwanted parenthood, sexually transmitted disease, suicide, homicide, drug or alcohol dependence, or
  even accidental death.

So how can we reconcile the rising or at least high rates of disasters
with the overall picture of healthy, only mildly conflictful adolescence
headed toward a stable, healthy adulthood?

In all likelihood adolescence is a time of divergence, not just between
the sexes but between those youngsters who may be heading toward disaster and those who are either happy or just somehow keeping it all
together. This is the view of Anne Petersen, a psychologist at Pennsylvania State University who is a leading investigator in this field. She estimates from her research that "about 11 percent of young adolescents
have serious chronic difficulties, 32 percent have more intermittent and
probably situational difficulties, while 57 percent have basically positive,
healthy development during early adolescence." However, other studies
suggest that by the late teens the majority have experienced at least some
difficulty; perhaps some of those with early intermittent difficulties have
become chronically maladjusted.

There may be a continuum of vulnerability, with determinants we are
only beginning to understand. Genes certainly play a role, as do exposure
to alcohol and drugs while in the womb, and head trauma, accidental or
not, during childhood. But at least equally important are the cultural
factors: Young teenagers who are continually exposed to sex, violence,
and alcohol and drug abuse will have a much greater likelihood of experiencing a developmental crisis. For them, the conflicts of the pubertal
peak can begin a slide toward more serious problems, rather than being
a transient rough period to be gotten through.

Television and movies, unfortunate as their content often is, have not
been proven to play a major role in this. Children can tell the difference
between TV and real life. Television also provides many models of functioning families, including single-parent families; information about a

world that may be different from and better than the one they live in; the vicarious experience of solving many minor conflicts and problems; and the lesson that crime doesn't pay. In some neighborhoods television serves a positive function just by keeping children off the street.

But what is crucial is that some children are exposed to violence, to abusive or irresponsible sex, and to drug abuse — not in fiction but in their real lives. It is what they see in their families, on the street outside their homes, and among their friends that may make the difference between a stabilizing resolution of their pubertal conflicts and problems and a transformation of those problems into catastrophe.

• • •

Two recent studies throw light on this process. Cathy Spatz Widom, of Indiana University at Bloomington, studied children who had been abused or neglected in childhood, according to the court conviction records of a single county in a midwestern city, for 1967 to 1971. She found controls for 667 of these children, using very stringent matching criteria: For children abused before school age, she matched sex, race, date of birth (within one week), and hospital of birth; for those abused later, the criteria were sex, race, date of birth (within six months), same class in same elementary school, and home address within a five-block radius of the mistreated child.

Her question was: What percentage of the abused children would have criminal records twenty years later, compared to the matched controls? She found a juvenile delinquency record for 26 percent of the abused and neglected children but only 17 percent of the controls. Furthermore, the abused and neglected children had significantly more offenses per person, an earlier average age at first offense, and almost twice as many chronic offenders — those with five or more offenses (17 versus 9 percent). They also had significantly larger criminal records as adults, and more records for *violent* crime specifically.

Although the impact of having been abused was similar in both sexes, the crime rate, as in other studies, was always much higher in males than in females. For violent crime, the difference was extreme: at least five violent males for every violent female in both the abused/neglected *and* the control groups. The excess associated with abuse or neglect, although much smaller than the sex difference, was also consistent. Looking at all violent crime regardless of age, 16 percent of those who had suffered physical abuse and 12½ percent of those with neglect had records for such crimes, while only 8 percent of the controls did. Interestingly, those who had been sexually abused did not exceed the controls in violent crime, suggesting that the effect may have been specific to the type of abuse.

The interpretation of this study is not completely straightforward — for example, if the children were abused or neglected by genetic relatives, then a biological explanation could account for some of the association. If a violently abusive mother has a son who grows up to commit violent crime, perhaps they are both constitutionally violence-prone. But the association of teenage violence with earlier neglect would be harder to explain in this way. This ingenious study strongly suggests that abuse in childhood can direct the developmental process toward crime and violence after puberty.

The second study is more specific in asking how social context and biology interact to produce problem behavior during puberty itself. Working with Udry and Morris, Edward A. Smith of Johns Hopkins University studied the effect of close friends *and* hormones on the sexual behavior of boys and girls between ages twelve and seventeen. Interviews determined the stage of puberty, with the aid of drawings to show the standard growth of pubic hair, genital size in males, breast development, and so on. Subjects were also asked to rank themselves on a scale of sexual activity from kissing to intercourse, and a similar interview was given to a friend of each subject. The results showed how both biological and social forces act on adolescent sexuality. For boys, the subject's own pubertal development had the largest impact on sexual activity, but the sexual behavior of the close friend had a distinct additional influence. The two together predicted substantially more about the subject's sexual activity than did either alone.

For girls, distinguishing pubertal changes according to different hormones proved important. Pubic hair stage, reflecting androgens, had a strong relation to sexual activity, while other measures of puberty, such as breast development, reflecting estrogen, had a less strong, separate effect. This is consistent with a paradoxical but established finding from many studies: Women's sexual motivation is strongly influenced by androgens — the male hormones that they have at a fraction of male levels.

As with the boys, pubertal development alone did not predict girls' sexual activity nearly as well as when the influence of close friends was added. But the girls showed an even more intriguing pattern. While in the boys the biological and social forces could be simply added to enhance the prediction, in the girls the two forces created what is called an interaction, or colloquially, a multiplier effect. That is, they enhanced each other in a way that was surprising — *more* than additive. If you were a low-androgen girl even a sexy friend had little influence on you, while if you were a high-androgen girl, the friend had a powerful influence. Your internal, hormonally guided motivation would not come out if your friend was sexually inactive, but an advanced friend might have a big effect, making you much more overtly sexual. The biological and social forces formed for the girls an unexpectedly potent blend.

It must be said that all the factors taken together in this study did not predict sexual activity *really* well for either sex. This is partly because there are other factors — parental attitudes, family structure, religious beliefs, exposure to media, history of sexual abuse, physical attractiveness, popularity, and more — that influence sexuality. Still, this study blazes a path toward a new understanding of adolescent behavior which takes both biological development and social context into account.

It is naïve to think that social influences are so important that biological factors can be ignored; genetic studies prove that puberty and adolescent problem behavior are heavily influenced by genes. For example, identical twins are more alike in the age at peak velocity of growth in height, the age at first sexual intercourse, and the amount of delinquent behavior than are nonidentical twins. Despite the great transformations of puberty, correlations between identical twins, or between adopted children and their biological mothers, hold steady or increase. Experienced pediatricians know that the pacing of puberty often runs in families. These and other sources of evidence make it foolish to think that the influence of genes and biochemistry is trivial.

But it is also naïve to think, "Just poisoned by hormones." This abdicates moral responsibility for the social and cultural situations that motivate adolescent problem behavior. It is likely that the crucial contexts differ for different children. And it is likely that the received wisdom about which situations and influences are most important is far off the mark. Fortunately, the pace of research on adolescents has picked up to the point at which some of these questions may gradually be resolved.

• • •

In many societies, culture has taken a much stronger hand with adolescents than it does in ours today. We say, sometimes only tacitly, to young teens: In a few years, you are out of here and on your own. You have control of your destiny. Anything is open to you. But whatever you decide to do, you will soon have to take care of yourself. The little boat of the family that has held you above water all these years will soon either ease you or toss you overboard, and you will sink or swim according to what you have learned and what you can do. Yourself.

This withdrawal of support, this freedom of choice, can be terrifying to some children. But in any case few adolescents fail to get the message that it is coming. In traditional societies, specific expectations may be greater, and options are fewer. But you know you will have a place in the same world in which you grew up — that it, in at least some senses, will always take care of you. The culture says, explicitly: Here is what you will do; you have no choice. It is difficult, and you will have to be brave and work hard. But if you pull your weight — and you will — you will always have a place with us.

These cultures provide a cradle throughout life; although the individual cannot remain passive, neither will he or she ever be abandoned. But traditional cultures do make demands, and some of these are made through ritual. Such cultures often mark some of life's major transitions — birth, marriage, parenthood, death — with ancient, symbolic practices designed to impress upon members of the culture that these events are not merely biological; that there are right and wrong ways for a human being to go through them. In fact, for each transition in each culture there is usually only one right way. These transition rituals are called rites of passage, and many societies have particularly impressive ones for the life cycle phases of puberty and adolescence. Schlegel and Barry, in their broad cross-cultural study, show that 68 percent of societies in the World Cultural Sample have adolescent initiations for boys, 79 percent for girls.

Consider a !Kung girl who is experiencing her first menstruation at age sixteen. Wherever she is, whatever time of day or night, as soon as she notices the trace of blood she must sit down, keep absolute silence, and wait. This may occur while she is gathering wild foods in the bush, and it can be dangerous; while waiting, she may attract a lion, hyena, or wild dogs, especially with the smell of fresh blood. Nevertheless she sits and waits until it is noticed that she is missing. Knowing that she has been ripe for this transition, the women in her village — most of whom are her relatives — will go in search of her, leaving the men strictly out of it.

Being expert trackers, they find her relatively quickly, and when they come upon her in the bush her situation confirms what they have suspected. They go to her, lift her up — her feet are not allowed to touch the ground — and carry her all the way back to the vicinity of the village. There they build a tiny grass seclusion hut for her — it may only take an hour — and place her inside it. Soon a dance begins, strictly for women only. All the adult women in the village take part in it and, as the day, the night, and the next day wear on, the dance becomes a raucous and ribald one indeed. Women shed all articles of clothing except a small leather pubic apron or loincloth. And they toss it wildly around as they dance, even pulling it up to show off their genitals. These displays provoke uproarious laughter. Singing, dancing, and clapping go on continuously. No men are allowed anywhere near the place. Meanwhile, the menstruating girl sits alone and sober-faced in the nearby seclusion hut, not allowed to laugh or speak, only to watch and listen. The message cannot be lost on her; this is an uninhibited celebration of womanhood.

Baka tooth-chipping is harsher by comparison. Teeth filed to a point are considered handsome, and the child past eleven or twelve may elect to have the procedure or to forgo it — an analog, perhaps, of braces. Since it is very painful, filed teeth are also a symbol of endurance and maturity. Sakala, about twelve, has asked for them without adult prodding. He lies still on the ground while Babu, a relative skilled at this, takes a chisel to the boy's front teeth. Sakala bites into a piece of wood to help control the pain; when he whimpers, Babu applies warm plantain skin to soothe him, and another boy who has been through the ceremony assists. Other children walk in a circle around them, and tease Sakala by leaning down to squeeze his upper lip gently. He is not the most stoical of children, so his teeth are not quite filed to a point. But the experience qualifies him as sufficiently brave and mature.

Also among the Nuer, a cattle-herding, warrior people of the Sudan, the boy's readiness is what brings the ritual about. Knowing what is in store for him, he asks his father for *gar,* the ceremonial scars on his forehead that will make him a man. If his father agrees he is ready, his head is shaved by one of his sisters. At the appointed time he lies naked, his arms folded across his chest and hands holding his shoulders, surrounded by singing, dancing adult male warriors brandishing their spears. He lies perfectly still while a male relative takes a sharp blade to his forehead.

The cuts are as deep as they can be — they are said to leave marks on the skull — and begin behind the forehead over one ear, extending across the brow to a point above the other ear. There are four parallel lines that are left to bleed and form scars without being pressed or bound together. The resulting bands of scar tissue are thick, prominent, and lifelong — the unmistakable mark of a Nuer warrior. They have been earned by a boy who has shown his great courage, neither speaking nor weeping nor crying out throughout this painful public operation. Finally he is given a new name — a name that can be used only by a grown man.

There are many other pubertal rites. Throughout northern Africa millions of adolescent girls have the clitoris wholly or partly removed in a ritual designed to make them less sexual. They also may have their labia partly cut and then sewn together, to prevent premarital penetration. Considered mutilating by all health authorities, including those of the countries where this surgery is practiced, it is nevertheless held on to with fierce tenacity by women in traditional north African cultures. They consider it essential for their daughters and granddaughters in making the transition from girlhood to womanhood.

Among the traditional Australian aborigines, pubescent boys are brought into manhood by both circumcision and a subsequent, more extensive operation, subincision. In both the boy is laid over a rock and held down by male relatives. In the first rite, circumcision, one of them takes a sharp stone and removes his foreskin; the boy must be stoical. But a few years later, in the second stage, the underside of the penis is slit open from base to tip, also with a stone blade. The deep cut is allowed to form a thick scar, which can interfere with urination; but the scar is said to enhance women's pleasure in sexual intercourse. Again, the pain must be borne stoically. While healing, the boy is taught for several weeks by the men; this is a time for the culture to make a very firm impression on him.

By these standards, the vision quest of the North American Indians seems tame. In the buffalo-hunting cultures of the Great Plains, a boy had to purify himself in the sweat lodge and paint his body with white clay. Then he was sent out alone and naked to an isolated place to be close to the spirits for a few days. He ate nothing during this time, and did nothing but focus on his singular goal: an altered state of consciousness that would give him his vision. Essentially, he had to become delirious from hunger, thirst, exposure to the elements, and the fear of what might befall him — from mountain lions and bears to enemy war parties. The vision he sought was a private one; a spirit came to him *personally,* in the form of an animal, plant, ancestor, even a storm that became his guardian spirit. The result was a new identity — a sense of himself as being beyond boyhood.

Pubertal rites in Western cultures are very mild by comparison. One that is nevertheless interesting for its symbolic function is the Jewish bar mitzvah, in which a boy becomes, in religious terms, a man, at age thirteen. "Bar" means "son of" and "mitzvah," "commandment" or "good deed." The occasion was traditionally marked by being the first time the boy was called to the Torah during Sabbath services. The boy said a blessing before and after the Torah portion was read, and his parents said a blessing thanking God that they were no longer responsible for his sins. In this very public way the boy was made to know that he was now mature enough to perform blessings and rituals, and to be responsible for his own sins.

In every case these rites of passage serve a triple purpose: First, they put children through something — always fear, often pain — that gives them a stronger subjective purchase on adulthood; "Adults can take it, now I can take it, so I must no longer be a child." It is not correct linear logic, but in the deeper emotional logic of symbolic ritual, it is airtight. In the language of the cynical German philosopher Friedrich Nietzsche, "Whatever doesn't kill me makes me stronger"; or, we might add, more grown-up.

Second, as with the hazing routines of college fraternities, these initiation rituals, once completed, make you feel a part of something. That something is the culture, the larger community in which you have been maturing. There are those who are in, and there are those who belong to other groups, other cultures, who are out. They are to be disdained or pitied — there is chauvinism here. To some extent these memberships are arbitrary. But now that you have completed the initiation process, you are unmistakably *in*.

Third, the heightened subjective state of the child both before and after the main event is made use of for the transmission of culture. Direct, formal instruction is often a part of initiation — even in cultures where there is very little formal instruction otherwise. The child's eyes are wide with fear, possibly pain, and later exhilaration. All nerve endings are blazing. What better time to say explicitly: "This is what it means to be a Sioux man, a !Kung woman. This is what you will have to do. This is the custom. This is the law." These lessons are not merely made more memorable by the initiation ritual. They are laid down at a deeper level of mental and emotional life, sinking far below the crust of conscious understanding, down, down to a place where the future adult really lives.

• • •

In our culture, partly because of its size and diversity, we have the paradox of divergence in adolescence; the bad and the good seem to increase simultaneously. It is claimed that there are no bad kids, but there are certainly kids who consistently do bad things, and they, along with a larger number who do bad things occasionally, justify the concept of adolescence as fraught with problem behavior. But kids in this same phase of life also often involve themselves in one or another high ideal. Charity, patriotism, religiosity, music, scouting, athletics, conservation, pacifism, military discipline, racial integration — any of these and more are capable of catching the imagination of adolescents; not to mention the more specific ambitions that get some teenagers seriously in their grip, setting them on the long path to achievement as doctors, dancers, or soldiers.

Certainly there is this divergence among individuals at puberty, due to some blend of biology, upbringing, and circumstance. But even more paradoxical is the fact that — in many if not most pubescent children — bad and good, problem behavior and high ideals, rebelliousness and idealism increase simultaneously. This is exemplified by an informal survey of teens' heroes by Charles Leehrsen of *Newsweek* magazine. At the Immaculate Conception School in the South Bronx, New York, he asked eighth graders to write down the names of two heroes.

Michelle Graham, 13, said fashion model Elle MacPherson and Bart Simpson ("because I wish I could get away with treating my parents that way"); Shauneille Parker, 13, picked God and Arsenio Hall; Jose Centeno, 15, chose Michelangelo and Larry Bird; Nicole Howel, 14, picked New York Mayor David Dinkins and Public Enemy.

Many surveys of young teens' heroes show such a paradoxical mix; for example, in a 1965 survey the names John F. Kennedy, Martin Luther King, Jr., Elvis Presley, and James Dean all came up. But it was an inspired idea to ask *each* child for *two* heroes. The result, in all the above cases, was evidence of an inner split. Each child chose one more serious role model who would have warmed the hearts of parents and teachers alike; and one "bad" model, someone from the popular culture or even the counterculture, someone who represented at least some departure from parental and school values.

This duality exists in the hearts of most adolescents. We know that the rebellious strain comes from an interaction of hormonal and social factors. But what of the idealistic strain? We understand less about it, but in industrial cultures at least, there are advances in cognitive and moral development after puberty that are best summarized as a new capacity for abstract reasoning. Piaget and his colleague Bärbel Inhelder pioneered the study of those advances, and they proposed a phase of mental life called *formal operations,* the next after concrete operations, which dominate from the five-seven shift until puberty. Formal operations are highly abstract processes of reasoning — for example, probability problems, and the science of physical and chemical phenomena. These are beyond the capacity of prepubertal children.

However, they also prove to be beyond the capacity of teenagers who had not had quite good high-school educations, especially in math and science. More than any other phase of development in Piaget's theory, formal operations proved to be schooling-dependent, and psychologists now think that many adults of normal intellect never attain it. However, it is possible that we have not been ingenious enough in setting tasks that might show formal operations in unschooled people, even in nonliterate societies.

In any case, adolescent thinking is characterized by the ability to reason about possibilities that cannot be directly observed; by a kind of thought-experiment that mentally tries out different solutions to a problem; by thinking beyond conventional limits; and by second-order thinking — the ability to reflect on one's own thought processes. All of these abilities can be seen in younger children, but they are more characteristic of adolescents, and probably are widely true of many different cultures.

Certainly, the adolescent's impassioned embrace of causes and ideals beyond his or her own limited self appears to be a cross-cultural universal. Historically, young people have played a key role in rebellions and revolutions, not just because they naïvely accept radical theories but because their status as late-adolescents makes them fiercely — sometimes unreasonably but admirably even so — idealistic and unconventional. They can now imagine a future better than the present, but lack the experience that tempers imagination; and their aggressive impulses may lead them to take strong action to bring about the future they have imagined.

But, of course, transcendence of the self need not take political forms, and its manifestations may not be devoid of biological influence or purpose. Falling in love, for example, provides a potent blend of abstraction and animal impulse, biological selfishness and exquisite self-transcendance. It is about basic needs, of course; but since it can also produce a lifetime of devotion, and establish the base on which a family is founded, some cultures have understandably seen it as sacred. Consider the following, from James Joyce's novel *A Portrait of the Artist as a Young Man*. Stephen Daedalus, a youth fresh out of Catholic school, musing intensely on whether he truly has a vocation for the priesthood, sees a young woman wading at the seaside.

> A girl stood before him in midstream, alone and still, gazing out to sea. She seemed like one whom magic had changed into the likeness of a strange and beautiful seabird. Her long slender bare legs were as delicate as a crane's and pure save where an emerald trail of seaweed had fashioned itself as a sign upon the flesh. Her thighs, fuller and softhued as ivory, were bared almost to the hips where the white fringes of her drawers were like featherings of soft white down. . . .
>
> She was alone and still, gazing out to sea; and when she felt his presence and the worship of his eyes her eyes turned to him in quiet sufferance of his gaze, without shame or wantonness. Long, long she

suffered his gaze and then quietly withdrew her eyes from his and bent them towards the stream, gently stirring the water with her foot hither and thither. The first faint noise of gently moving water broke the silence, low and faint and whispering, faint as the bells of sleep; hither and thither, hither and thither: and a faint flame trembled on her cheek.

— Heavenly God! cried Stephen's soul, in an outburst of profane joy.

He turned away from her suddenly and set off across the strand. His cheeks were aflame; his body was aglow; his limbs were trembling. On and on and on and on he strode, far out over the sands, singing wildly to the sea, crying to greet the advent of the life that had cried to him.

Her image had passed into his soul for ever and no word had broken the holy silence of his ecstasy. Her eyes had called him and his soul had leaped at the call. To live, to err, to fall, to triumph, to recreate life out of life!

There could hardly be a better instance of how adolescence joins the most instinctual to the most sacred parts of life. Stephen realizes on this fateful evening that he is called to the holiness of the things of *this* world, not another. This new calling, for the writer he represents, will produce one of the greatest collections of fiction in modern literature.

So we leave this last, partly tumultuous phase of childhood with a sense of paradox and hope. It is a time of biological turmoil and metamorphosis; to worry over the outcome is natural. It is also a time of social convulsion. Adolescents are facing the fact that we will not take care of them always, and they know that taking care of themselves will involve hard work and hard choices. Understandably, they resent this. Yet somehow most children sail the rough seas of adolescence without running aground or going under. With a steady wind behind them in the form of a nurturing childhood, and some adult help in charting a safe course through the teenage years, only a small minority should founder. But this sea is unforgiving and the dangers are grave ones; we are losing far too many as it is, and we need to become more serious about preventing those losses.

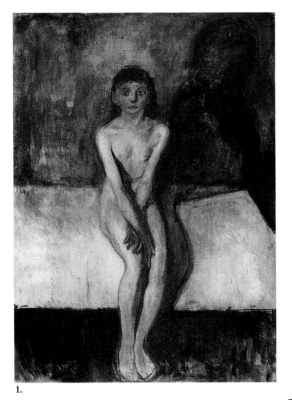

1.

3. A fourteen-year-old !Kung girl adds flowers to her beadwork during the brief rainy season in the Kalahari Desert, Botswana.

Adolescence alters images of the self.

1. *Puberty,* by the twentieth-century Expressionist painter Edvard Munch.

2. Pokot girls of Kenya are painted, shrouded in leather, confined, and instructed by older women as they heal from ritual removal of the clitoris — surgery still done on many thousands of girls each year in Africa.

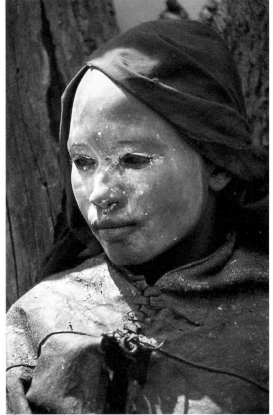

2.

3.

4.

4. This fourteen-year-old boy in Nepal is considered the sixth holiest Buddhist in the world.

5. Albrecht Dürer, self-portrait at age thirteen.

6. Simone Oliveira, fourteen, primps for carnival, São Paulo, Brazil, 1991.

7, 8. Young lady, or as in Baghdad, Iraq, young solider? A girl can apparently be either.

5.

6.

7.

8.

9.

9. Friendships in the schoolyard…

10. …or in the police station. Young prostitutes in Manila, the Philippines, one of the "sex capitals" of Asia.

11. Peering out a window of the detention unit of a boys' school, Wyoming.

10.

12.

From disdain...

...to discovery.

12. An uninviting glance at a Dorchester wedding in Boston.

13. A Vancouver boy asking a girl to go steady.

14. A New York couple kissing in a schoolyard.

A woman takes a man into her embrace...and the story of childhood begins again.

13.

14.

The House of Tomorrow

And they brought young children to him, that he should touch them; and his disciples rebuked those that brought them.

But when Jesus saw it he was much displeased, and said unto them, Suffer the little children to come unto me, and forbid them not; for of such is the Kingdom of God. . . .

And he took them up in his arms, put his hands upon them, and blessed them.

— *The Gospel According to St. Mark 10:13*

⸻

MARGARET WOODS, the thoughtful English mother we have heard from before, wrote to a friend in 1777: "I am now sitting with my dear little cares, watching them in their evening's repose. They (as thou justly observest) attach us strongly to life; and without a guard over ourselves, we are in danger of centring too much of our happiness in them."

The danger Woods spoke of was the ever-present possibility of loss. But from other things she wrote we know that she was also skeptical of how much one could bend a child to one's will. So she was aware of the more modern danger of getting our ambitions and dreams tangled up in our children. The thought is expressed more insistently, even archly, by the Lebanese philosopher-poet Kahlil Gibran:

Your children are not your children.
They are the sons and daughters of Life's longing for itself.
They come through you but not from you.
And though they are with you yet they belong not to you.

You may give them your love but not your thoughts,
For they have their own thoughts.

You may house their bodies but not their souls,
For their souls dwell in the house of tomorrow, which you cannot
visit, not even in your dreams.
You may strive to be like them, but seek not to make them like you.
For life goes not backward nor tarries with yesterday.

Kahlil Gibran's works contain many easy, even kitschy thoughts, but this passage holds some real wisdom. It lights a strong warning beacon against one of the greatest risks of parenthood. It even has a sort of Darwinian ring to it: "Life's longing for itself" recalls the sociobiological dictum that a child is only a gene's way of making another gene. Although this is far too cynical as a philosophy of parenthood, it does give us a necessary anchor-point in the theory of evolution. The child's fundamental, biological interests differ from those of the parents, and so Darwinian theory — as developed, for example, by Robert Trivers, of the University of California at Santa Cruz — strongly predicts parent-offspring conflict not as incidental friction but as the result of a fundamental difference of goals.

In the terms of modern molecular genetics, the shuffling of about a hundred thousand human genes after the momentary heat of sexual union creates each time a combination that never existed before. And in the last three decades, psychology has finally recognized this fact by giving the child's influence on the parent a significant place beside the parent's influence on the child. No parent who has had two children — and inevitably noted their individuality from the outset — takes seriously the notion that training and education can completely control a child's destiny.

And yet, of course, the Gibran passage is only partly true. If we did not seek to make them like us, and if we were not at least a little bit successful, there would be no such things as culture, tradition, language, or religion. There would be no stability to techniques from cooking to bridge-building or ideas like charity and democracy. Of course we try to make them like us, and to some extent are successful. And we can at least *try* to visit the future in our dreams; indeed, it would be a poor parent who didn't try. But when we attempt to make their dreams match ours, when we try to live our own lives vicariously through them, then we are treading on very shaky moral and psychological ground.

So what we wonder about, perhaps more than anything, is where to draw the line between legitimate, even necessary influence, and stifling our children's independence and individuality. And within the boundaries of what we see as legitimate influence we constantly ask how we can best exert it. The answer to that one is partly in the realm of research on childhood, which continues to ask, however haltingly, about the influence of things we do as parents on the ultimate outcomes for our children.

But the fact is that people have different goals for their children. One parent's happiness is another's laziness; one's neurosis, another's discipline; one's independence, another's rebellion; one's well-roundedness, another's dilettantism; one's dedication, another's guilt; one's strength, another's brutishness; one's ambition, another's greed; one's religion, another's conformity; one's taste, another's snobbery. A key reason discussions of what we should do with children grow so confusing is that we often tend to discuss the goal and the method of reaching the goal simultaneously. Either question is terribly difficult, but only the second is a scientific issue. After you have set your goals, then you can ask about what methods may help get you there. But if every dispute about methods hides a confusion or even a clash over goals, no resolution will be possible.

And there is yet another quandary. We still do not know how and how much the things we do with and for and against our children live on in their memories and destinies. When I was a young man just starting out, and trying to get an intellectual foothold, I was deeply influenced by the temper of the times, which combined the antiadult stance of the youth counterculture with the antiparent stance of pop psychotherapy. I was convinced that all the secrets of life lay in childhood, above all in the kind of parenting given in early childhood.

I was also influenced by most of the "Childhood" series observers, long before any of them knew who I was. Robert Hinde had done the most elegant and subtle studies of the mother-infant relationship in monkeys; together with experiments of Harlow and others, these proved to my satisfaction that seemingly minor perturbations of the infant's social relationships could have strong and lasting effects. Urie Bronfenbrenner had done his landmark study of Soviet and American child training, and was shaping the way American policymakers saw young children. His outlook, which he called an ecological view of childhood, emphasized the ways in which the cultural environment directs the child's mental and emotional growth.

I was fortunate enough to know Jerome Kagan personally and to study with him. He did his first cross-cultural study while I was writing my doctoral thesis. He had spent the first fifteen years of his career trying to discover and demonstrate continuities between early childhood and adulthood, and between infancy and later childhood. He was frustrated by this experience, which had produced mainly low and unimpressive correlations. Then in San Marcos, a little isolated Mayan village near a lake high in the hills of Guatemala, he found children who had experienced considerable cognitive deprivation in infancy. Yet their mental development later in childhood and adolescence, while slower than that of more advantaged children, eventually caught up on a number of different tests — suggesting that early deprivation did not have lasting effects.

This conclusion was criticized by many, including me. But I gradually realized that Kagan had a piece of the truth. Together with other evidence — including the then-new demonstration by Stephen Suomi and Harlow that even monkeys raised in isolation could have their abnormal behavior corrected — his research had convincingly shown *not* that there were *no* long-term effects of early experience, but that we did not yet know what they were or how they worked. Thousands of psychologists, psychiatrists, anthropologists, and educators had exaggerated the impact of early experience, and held strong, sometimes contradictory convictions about just how that experience works — convictions that were not really supported by the evidence.

After that I was prepared to accept the idea that some major aspects of human development were universal in all cultures — so strongly "canalized" that it was very difficult to derail them from their biologically destined course of growth. But what I still had not come to terms with was the possibility that *within* a given culture, individual differences are also partly based on an internally developing genetic program. Of this, Sandra Scarr had become convinced over a decade ago. Her own research and that of others like Robert Plomin were showing that the science of behavior genetics, long established in the explanation of animal behavior, was also a powerful paradigm for understanding the behavior, personality, and competence of developing children.

This evidence eventually forced me to concede that not just cross-cultural universals of development, but also individuality, had an important biological — or, more specifically, genetic — component. I did not find this particular change of mind to be comfortable or enjoyable. But eventually I became persuaded of two things: First, to deny completely the genetic background to children's differences is really to deny a major source of human individuality; second, to recognize the biological foundations of development is to gain greatly in our ability to influence its course.

I stumble along like any other parent, inventing solutions to child-rearing problems every day. Sure, I know more about research on childhood than do most parents, and that knowledge helps a lot. I know what they are likely to be capable of at a given age — whether in the realm of creativity or self-control or learning — and I know something about how to stretch their capabilities, when I choose to do that. I even know how to help them have fun. I know that it is neither possible nor desirable to protect them from every stress, and I try to help them develop tools to deal with the unavoidable ones. At the very least, I can almost always sympathize. Finally, I know about individuality — both the genetic and developmental kinds — and I usually don't fail to take it into account. It leads to a crucial paradox: In order to be treated fairly and equally, children have to be treated differently.

But academic knowledge only goes so far. Frequently common sense takes over; there is even a role for what some might call instinct. And of course there is the rule that what they see is more important than what we say — the effect we have on them just through being who we are. Like most parents with an egalitarian concept of sex roles, I have tried hard to keep my children from marching in well-trod gender paths. And, like many, I have been dismayed to see that to some extent they follow those paths anyway. Sarah, now four, loves frilly dresses and changing her hairdo. Of course, I know she is in that phase of early childhood when a child's identity as a boy or girl is still settling in, and as she becomes more comfortable with it she will probably be less relentlessly feminine.

But as far as parental influence goes, I could talk myself blue in the face about equality and not produce the kind of insight she had on a recent evening. I was lying beside her singing her to sleep when she began, like many a four-year-old, to talk about her marriage plans. "I'm gonna marry Chrissy," she said of a favorite five-year-old boy. "I'm gonna be the mommy and Chrissy's gonna be the daddy." Since she had often told me that she was planning to be a doctor, I said, "I guess you're gonna be a mommy *and* a doctor?" "Yeah," she said definitively. "I'm gonna go to work and Chrissy's gonna stay home and take care of the children." And then, after a thoughtful pause, she added matter-of-factly: "Just like you're doing now."

• • •

While childhood is significant to many of us as parents, it has universal importance as part of every human being's past. Not only what we do as parents, but what we do in every aspect of our lives is inevitably colored by what we experienced as children, whether we remember it or not. In the twentieth century the Freudian paradigm has so heightened this coloring that some people spend their lives blaming their parents, with ever-increasing analytic specificity and forcefulness, never grasping the fact that they must transcend childhood, leave it behind, in order to have adult lives that are useful and make sense. A character in *More Die of Heartbreak,* a novel by Nobel laureate Saul Bellow, puts it this way:

> "I meet people of eighty who are furious over their toilet training, or because their dad wouldn't take them to the ball game. Imagine such an infantile life! Such bondage to papa and mama. A whole life of caca-pipi! No self-respecting person would submit."

Recollections of childhood experiences play a great role in our concepts of ourselves, and psychotherapy, psychoanalysis, autobiographical writing, or just plain friendship can facilitate remembering and understanding those experiences. But the notion of discrete trauma tied to extraordinary occurrences is a very limited one, which has misled many into simplistic views of their lives.

Perhaps the greatest of Freud's contributions — despite my carping, I admire him greatly — was the development of a method of self-examination, a way of fulfilling the injunction implied in Socrates's saying, "The unexamined life is not worth living." Dostoevski wrote before Freud that "Some people appear not to think of their memories of childhood, but all the same preserve such memories unconsciously. They may be grave, bitter, but the suffering we have lived through may turn in the end into sacred things for the soul." Freud himself quoted Goethe as saying specifically, "When we try to remember what happened to us in early childhood, we often confuse what others have told us with our own directly perceived experiences." Freud believed that psychoanalysis gave him the key to retrieving those Dostoevskian memories from the unconscious, to teasing apart the real from the merely perceived in Goethe's observation.

But does it give us the key? Or is it merely that we piece together a story that makes increasing sense, as we develop a theory of who we are and why? Recent research into autobiographical memory, by Ulric Neisser and Michael Ross, among others, has marked some boundaries around the country of the unconscious. For one thing, we clearly do not record everything around us, but apparently we record a lot. Second, our ability to remember, either spontaneously or with effort, hinges as much or more on mechanisms of retrieval as it does on what has been put in storage. Third, memories of childhood are relatively few and far between during most of our adult lives, a phenomenon called childhood amnesia. Still, people differ markedly and somewhat consistently in the number and vividness of the memories of their lives. Finally, after the age of fifty — as long as we are mentally sound — our recollections of childhood become more numerous and dense, a phase known as reminiscence.

Whether childhood amnesia results from the sort of effortful forgetting that Freud called repression, and whether seemingly trivial memories of childhood always stand for something emotional and important, remain as questions for future research. But we do know that Goethe's observation is true. Experiments have shown that a person's memory of an event can become distorted later if deliberately misleading accounts are given by others. Studies have also shown that people misremember their previous attitudes in ways that make the past seem more consistent with the present. In addition, memories consistent with one's current beliefs are more readily retrieved than memories that are inconsistent. However, if people hold a theory of a particular kind of change over the life-span, they will distort memories in that domain to make the change they have undergone seem more impressive than it was.

One of the distortions in the bias toward consistency has to do with self-esteem. Nietzsche put it this way in 1886:

"I have done that," says my memory. "I cannot have done that," says
my pride, and remains inexorable. Eventually, memory yields.

But some people have low self-esteem, and remember selectively the clumsy, ignorant, and bad things they have done. Finally, there is the impact of narrative, perhaps the most important and general of all distorters of memory.

In our idle musings, in our conversations with lovers and friends, in public or private writing, in religious confessions, in psychotherapy — even in the way we present ourselves to our children — we often develop a story of our lives that we want to believe in. It can be almost any kind of story: a story of early deprivation and pain overcome, or one of a perfect childhood setting the stage for a disappointing life; a story of straying from a desired path and then being born again, or a story of a steady climb, essentially unswerving; a story of early talent precisely prefiguring the present, or a story of late development of an ability no one could possibly have predicted.

As these narratives take their form in our adult minds — and of course, they may change from decade to decade — we seem to remember selectively the experiences that fit into the narrative. André Maurois, a modern French novelist and essayist, put it this way:

Memory is a great artist. For every man and every woman it makes
the recollection of his or her life a work of art and an unfaithful
record.

But Maurois does not really find the unfaithfulness of memory to be terribly crucial or disappointing. There is an admiration here for the artistry of memory that seems to transcend its admitted inaccuracy.

It would seem that psychologists, the scientists of memory, would react very differently to the news that we do not remember veridically. But some of them too have decided that building a coherent narrative of our lives is so important that it outweighs the disadvantages of selectivity and even of inaccuracy. On this view, psychotherapy, journal-keeping, friend-ship, and confession do not have to produce a true story of our lives; they only have to produce a meaningful one. If we can construct a story that makes good sense to us, the story itself will have healing power, regardless of how well it reflects the absolute, factual truth.

As I review my own childhood, I am not really impressed by the impact of specific events, or convinced of the authenticity and indelibility of cer-tain memories. Perhaps this is because I was fortunate in being spared major psychological trauma, in spite of my parents' deafness. But what I am impressed with in retrospect is the tone of certain aspects of my child-hood, the daily consistencies in certain relationships and activities that continued in a steady way for years.

I remember my mother's sweetness, warmth, and basic acceptance of me, and my father's involvement in work. I remember frequent conflicts with them over missed communications, and being told often to speak more loudly. I remember being rather poor but not uncomfortable or afraid. I remember getting a sense of strength from school, and yet being too shy to raise my hand for most of junior high school and high school. I remember affection between my little brother and me, but also a lot of wrestling matches, and being threatened with a strap by our mother for fighting. I remember feeling burdened by my parents' expectation that I would help them to parent my brother. I remember many unpleasant telephone conversations that had to go through me. And I remember feeling guilty that I could hear.

But however valuable it may sometimes be to delve into the childhood sources of our current difficulties, sooner or later we have to stop delving and start living, stop blaming our parents and start taking more or less full responsibility for what happens in our own lives.

Poignantly, that often becomes possible when we become parents our-selves. Only then do we begin to see how difficult being a parent is, to appreciate the many and various forces that act on people raising chil-dren. Sympathy for the constraints on our parents, and for the choices they made, begins subtly but surely to release us from the stance of ac-cusation that may otherwise trap us in the concerns of our own child-hoods. Mary Catherine Bateson, a distinguished anthropologist who is the daughter of Margaret Mead, wrote an affecting memoir of her mother and father. Both women had studied other cultures. Mead had sometimes left her daughter with nannies while she went off to the South Seas, and had tried out many of her novel ideas of child rearing, derived from those faraway cultures, on Catherine. Her parents were divorced when she was eleven, and her mother subsequently was romantically involved with both women and men.

It seemed to the daughter in retrospect that "because so much of her thought was expressed in my upbringing, there is a sense in which my own happiness has had to carry the burden of proof for many of her ideas." Yet the memoir is very loving, and the daughter is full of gratitude for her mother's spirited emotional and intellectual legacy. Of the results of all this she speaks very wisely:

> There is no way finally that I can evaluate the extent of my own difference or how much this is related to infant experience. For it seems to me that all of us share to some degree in the experience of unintelligibility, sometimes feeling less than we might have been, or uncomfortable in our own skins and alien from those around us. I have always tended to look to the special circumstances of my childhood whenever I felt unhappy or lacking in confidence, and yet it is not reasonable to attribute a degree of estrangement that is part of the general human condition to a particular idiosyncratic experience. There is no form of human child rearing that does not leave an occasional residue of fear and yearning.

And as we release our parents from blame for our own existential discomfort, at the same time, of course, we release ourselves from the future accusatory glare of our own children grown up. Unless we are guilty of abuse or neglect, we can begin to take comfort in the fact that we are doing the best we can. We know that parenthood is not really a crime, population explosion and psychoanalysis notwithstanding. We hope that our children will not end up accusing us. But if, in the throes of adolescence and young adulthood, they do point a stiff, blaming finger in our direction, we can also hope that they go on to have children themselves; because in that day their self-righteousness will be undermined, just as ours was with them.

• • •

Psychology and biology alike predict that we will be preoccupied with ourselves and our own children, but their future and ours may hinge on how well we can transcend those preoccupations — on how much, in effect, we can care about other people's children. It may help to notice that other people's children will constitute the environment in which our children spend most of their lives, our grandchildren grow up, and we ourselves spend our declining years. If they are healthy, educated, and optimistic about their future, they will create one kind of environment; if they are sick, ignorant, and enraged, another.

At present in the United States our attitude toward children can be described fairly generously as one of unconcern. One-fifth of the nation's children — around thirteen million — live below the poverty line. Approximately one hundred thousand of these are homeless. Contrary to some beliefs, only a small fraction — around a tenth — of children in poverty live in inner-city areas that are pervasively poor. Although there are certainly regional differences, the great majority of the nation's poor children are distributed surprisingly evenly among our communities.

Thirty percent live in rural areas, another 28 percent in suburban areas. The majority are whites, and more than 40 percent are non-Hispanic whites. Despite a dramatic rise in the number of single-mother households, more than a third of poor children still belong to two-parent families. It's convenient, morally, to think of the poor as distant, sequestered, and very different from us in every way. But they are just around the corner or over the next hill; and, to paraphrase Ernest Hemingway, the main difference between us and most of them is that we have more money.

The United States ranked twenty-second among nations in control of infant mortality for 1990; among the places that have a lower percentage of infants dying are Spain, Austria, East Germany, Hong Kong, and Singapore. During the 1980s, a historically steady decline in our infant mortality rate slowed markedly for the first time in decades. This was but one indicator of the worsening of American children's situation in the last decade. While the elderly, avid voters, steadily emerged from poverty, children became the single largest American poverty group. The gap between rich and poor widened steadily, and the numbers of the completely homeless reached record levels.

To take just one example of our general moral failure in our obligation to children, immunization would seem to be a very high priority. But immunization levels in U.S. preschool children actually dropped between 1980 and 1985. At that time the administration — cagily from its own viewpoint but tragically for children — stopped its health agencies from collecting data on immunization rates, so that now we have no way of knowing just how bad the situation has become. But it is estimated that fully a third of poor children are now not vaccinated against common major diseases. We also know that severalfold increases in the rates of measles, mumps, and rubella in 1990 and 1991 have allowed American children to slide back two decades in their fight against these diseases. And when they do get sick, one-sixth of all American children are unprotected by health insurance. We are the only industrial nation other than South Africa that does not have a national health insurance plan.

In late 1989 the House Select Committee on Children, Youth and Families issued a bipartisan report stating that childhood had become "far more precarious and less safe for millions of America's children." Commenting on the report the committee's chair, Representative George Miller, Democrat of California, attributed the worsening of children's lives to the economic policies of the Reagan administration, which he said were "a massive social experiment on our children during the 1980s consisting of major changes in the economy and work force with cutbacks in public support." Or in the words of the *bi*partisan, published report itself, "The combined effects of persistently high rates of poverty, declining earnings, underemployment, and single parenting have made childhood far more precarious and less safe for millions of America's children." Since at this writing we are in the midst of a recession long predicted by critics of Reaganomics, the situation of poor children must now surely be worsening.

In a touching irony José Navarro, interviewed near his home in an East Los Angeles slum at the time the report was issued, said that he wanted to grow up to be a genetic engineer. The reason? "Because maybe I could change the facts of the world." At twelve, he had already given up on more conventional methods of raising the hopes and chances of people in his community. Actually, not only is his environment likely to hold him back from fulfilling this dream, but it is surprisingly likely to deal him a deadly blow in the form of homicide. And if he were black, the chance would be greater still. Black males fifteen to nineteen years old die at others' hands at a rate five times higher than that for white males, and the black male rate doubles for the next five-year age group, twenty to twenty-four. Louis Sullivan, M.D., the Secretary of Health and Human Services, called this pattern "appalling and heartrending." Referring to the fact that the Gulf War was safer for black young men than the same hundred hours at home, he asked poignantly, "Where are the yellow ribbons of hope and remembrance for our youth dying in the streets?"

According to T. Berry Brazelton, a leading pediatrician who has cared for twenty-five thousand children over forty years, and who serves on the National Commission on Children appointed by the White House and Congress, "We are the least family-oriented society in the civilized world." He based this conclusion not just on statistics, but on personal examination of families in both rural and urban poverty, of teenage boys in prison for homicide, and of teenage mothers and their crack-addicted premature babies. Everywhere he saw the potential for salvaging children and families, but little or no action to save them. Of the crack mothers and infants he said, "If this isn't addressed as a national emergency, the country will throw away two generations."

We have already considered in previous chapters the American rates of prematurity, low birth weight, illegitimacy, divorce, single-parenting with inadequate support, child neglect, child abuse both physical and sexual, inadequacies of education, school-dropout rates, the failure of those who stay in school to compete with their international counterparts, and rising rates of teenage sexual activity, pregnancy, and parenthood. These statistics give America a report card that would probably put its Founding Fathers (and, certainly, Mothers) into a rage. They ordained and established their new kind of government to "promote the general Welfare, and secure the Blessings of Liberty to ourselves and our Posterity," among other reasons; it is doubtful that they could be proud of the way we treat our children.

• • •

Child-development research, as we have seen again and again, underscores the needs of children, without which they will probably not develop normally, much less optimally:

- prenatal nutrition and care, including protection from illness and drug abuse, in a critical period for the formation of body and brain;
- appropriate stimulation and care for the newborn baby;
- the ability to form at least one close attachment during the first years of life — in plain English, to love and to be loved;
- support for the family under pressure from an uncaring world, including care for children whose parent or parents must work;
- protection of children from and in illness, through good nutrition, sanitation, immunization, and medical care;
- complete freedom from physical and sexual abuse;
- adults and playmates who can provide the support needed by children at risk, enhancing their natural resilience in the face of risk;
- respect for each child's individuality, and the presentation of challenges to a level and in a way that draws the child slowly but surely toward competence;
- schooling that is safe, orderly, nurturing, and challenging, and that helps the family and school work closely together;
- an adolescence that is free of pressure to grow up too fast, yet respectful of natural biological transformations, somehow giving the child extra room to experience a welter of new emotions;
- protection of the child from a premature parenthood that pits two children against each other in a crucial stage in the development of each, setting the course for another generation of hurt and failure.

These are some simple goals that parents, teachers, doctors, and child-development experts with many different perspectives can fairly well agree on. As long as they remain as far from fulfillment as they are in the United States today, we will continue to see those who care about children wringing their hands in dismay. And if we look beyond their familiar liberal urgings, we will see the statistics, continually worsening, that justify their dismay. It is said that a civilized person is one who can look at a page of numbers and weep. But — supposing ourselves to be civilized — after the weeping, what? We have been wringing our hands for decades. Didn't the 1960s and 1970s teach us that nothing can be done? That pouring money and effort into these kinds of problems is like pouring good wine into the drain?

• • •

That was the supposed wisdom of the 1980s. It was certainly applied by the federal government during that decade; people in Washington sent all these failures, all responsibility for decent treatment of children, back to hopelessly impoverished state and local governments. And predictably, most things got steadily worse for children. So it is very ironic that just at the moment when our culture and government were giving up on finding solutions, experiments in the eighties were proving that the right interventions could change things dramatically. Many people think that we have tried practically everything and that everything has failed. The fact is that we have tried very few things, and we back them with very little will; yet some of those things, in a fashion appropriate to the scale of the interventions, have succeeded very well indeed.

That was the message of an aptly titled 1988 book by Lisbeth and Daniel Schorr, *Within Our Reach: Breaking the Cycle of Disadvantage and Despair*. It details the evidence that our dinner-party despair about the impossibility of changing the lives of poor children is not well founded. And that evidence, expanded since 1988 as new programs have proved themselves, appears at every stage of childhood.

Piedmont, or "Pee-Dee," an impoverished region in the hills of northwest South Carolina, had the highest teenage pregnancy rate in the state and the highest infant mortality rate in the nation. But these dismal statistics did not daunt Marie Meglen, a nurse-midwife who founded Resource Mothers. She believed that pregnancy is a "teachable moment" in the life of a woman, or even of a teenage girl — something like the teachable moment provided in traditional cultures by rites of passage. And she began sending women who had become mothers themselves — often as teenagers — out *looking* for pregnant adolescents. They found them and befriended them, teaching them much about birth control, nutrition, and parenting. They followed them through their pregnancies as helpful friends, not experts. And they set an example of recovery and successful adaptation after the life-changing burdens of teen motherhood.

Pregnant teenagers in the Resource Mothers program had half the number of low birth weight babies as did others outside the program, and less than a fourth the number of very low birth weight babies. The Resource Mothers program cost about a thousand dollars a baby. Medical care for a very low birth weight baby costs fifty to a hundred times that much. So now who is wasting the taxpayers' money?

Or consider The Family Place, founded in 1981 by Maria Elena Orrega and Dr. Ann Barnett in the Mount Pleasant/Adams Morgan section of Washington, D.C. Every year, for 450 or more families with children under three, The Family Place provides a crucial link to information and psychological support. Groups of fifteen to twenty mothers, mostly Spanish-speaking, meet daily for twelve weeks. They discuss everything from AIDS and wife-beating to immunization schedules and ways to discipline toddlers without physical punishment. They are encouraged to learn and speak English, but what is mainly purveyed at The Family Place is an end to isolation and a beginning of self-esteem.

The results of this inexpensive self-help program? Young children in a crucial stage of development are nourished better, protected from illness, nurtured more, and abused less. Given what we know of the later consequences of deprivation in the first three years of life, how much money is that support worth to us?

Or take Homebuilders in Tacoma, Washington, and the Bronx, founded by the Catholic Children's Services, and described as a social version of the medical intensive care unit. Within twenty-four hours of referral they converge on a family that is about to have a child taken away because of abuse or neglect. Each team member cares for only three families, spending up to a hundred hours or more with each. They offer counseling, of course, but also plain old help — navigating the juvenile-services bureaucracy, driving family members to the market, obtaining basic home furnishings, helping get rid of the rats. In the first six years of the Tacoma program, 849 children — 92 percent of the target children, every one of whom had been destined for foster care or institutional placement — were kept with their families. Years later, on reevaluation, placement had still not been necessary for 90 percent of the children.

Now, the average cost of the Homebuilders program in 1985 was $2,600 per family. Foster care costs $3,600 per child, group care $19,500, and institutional care $67,500. *Every one of the Homebuilders children had been legally destined for one of those three options at time of contact.* Only one in ten ended up being so placed. The specific calculated savings on these more than eight hundred children was three and a half times the cost. So the question is not whether other communities can afford to imitate Tacoma's Homebuilders. The question is: Can they afford not to?

Or how about the Perry Preschool Program of Ypsilanti, Michigan? Perry is perhaps the most famous preschool experiment and a model for Project Head Start, the nationwide program that followed. Begun by psychologist David Weikart in 1962 and followed up for more than twenty years, Perry recruited three- and four-year-old children from low-income black families on the south side of town — one of the most congested slums in Michigan. Children were randomly — *randomly* — assigned to be in the program or the control group. All were below the poverty line and had IQs measured between 60 and 90. Fewer than 20 percent of their parents had completed high school. The program children had sessions of two and a half hours a day for two school years, with only five or six children per adult. They received a preschool education designed to prepare them for school. Each child was also visited at home by a teacher for one and a half hours every week.

Skeptics in the early years of programs like this one — and the later, larger effort involved in Head Start — predicted that the effects on the children would be transient, washing out when they went on to other, inferior schools. But at nineteen years of age the children who had experienced the Perry preschool program so many years before had a high-school graduation rate one-third higher, a pregnancy rate 42 percent lower, and an arrest rate 40 percent lower than their counterparts in the control group. Twice as many of the former Perry children were employed, attending college, or receiving further training as was the case for their matched counterparts who had not been in the program. The effects of one well-planned intervention had lasted for fifteen years.

The Perry program cost $5,000 per child. An economic analysis based on the differences at age nineteen estimated that each $5,000 spent on the program later saved $3,000 due to lower crime rates, $5,000 in special education costs, and $16,000 in public assistance, and yielded $5,000 in additional taxes paid by the Perry children as adults — a return of $5.90 for each dollar spent. Not surprisingly, a 1985 report of the Campaign for Economic Development called this "an extraordinary economic buy." Yet in the fifteen years preceding that report federal funding for the

Head Start program, for which Perry was a model, increased only 19 percent while enrollment nearly doubled, squeezing budgets so tightly that quality was compromised. Today, only a minority of the estimated two million children who need Head Start are getting it. Somebody in accounting should go over the figures with the leaders of our government, since it is plain to see that our failure to fund Head Start more fully is simply fiscal irresponsibility.

Last but not least, we should look at schools that work. We have already seen, in the cases of Thelma Peeples and Madeline Cartwright, how a dedicated, optimistic principal with high standards can turn a desperate and failing school around. This kind of effort has also been successful in several schools in New Haven, Connecticut, where child psychiatrist James Comer has spent almost twenty-five years reviving ailing schools. Comer himself came from a poor black family in East Chicago, Indiana. His father was a steelworker, his mother a domestic. He believes he succeeded where others around him failed because his parents had faith in education and in him. Yet he came to view schools as "the final common pathway in our society . . . more accessible to systematic change than the family." And he gave up the chance for a lucrative clinical practice to throw himself, body and soul, into the struggle against school failure.

He sees his work more as a process than a program. The guiding principles are to enhance knowledge of child development among teachers and parents; to establish a School Planning and Management Team including the principal and a dozen or so teachers, teacher's aides, and parents; and to set up as well a professional team consisting of the school social worker, the psychologist, the counselor, and the special-education teacher. The goal is "to interrupt the forces of confusion and conflict and to establish an orderly, effective process of education in the building." Comer emphasizes that the process takes a different course in different schools. But in any case he must be doing something right. The two schools he started with in 1968 continue to function far above the level of schools in comparable neighborhoods equally devastated by poverty.

Ten more New Haven schools have been added, and the "Comer School Development Program" in Prince George's County, Maryland, has applied the model in fourteen schools there. All received supplementary funds for additional teachers, teacher training, counseling, and equipment. Principals, teachers, counselors, and parents went to New Haven to consult with Comer. He told them the New Haven success story, but he also told them that their program would have to be different; near the heart of the program was its local responsiveness and flexibility.

Changes in Maryland were rapid. At the Columbia Park School, student suspensions went down from an average of 20 to 30 percent a year to 4 percent in the first "Comer year" and 1 percent in the second. One sixth-grade teacher who had been there for ten years said that the reduction of discipline problems had been the greatest change, in terms of improving teacher morale. He added that "Teachers can now spend their time teaching." They were also working nights and weekends, high on a new enthusiasm for their work. At the Green Valley School, children scored above the national average on standardized achievement tests for the first time in memory.

· · ·

But the world of childhood does not end at the borders of one country. The same logic that persuades us that our own children's safety requires us to care about the children of our fellow citizens also forces us to care about children around the world. Even if an isolationist stance were morally justifiable, in the future it will be practically impossible. In our own interest, we have to pay attention.

We have grown accustomed to the images on the evening news, or on those late-night programs designed to pull our heartstrings: every day, children are starving somewhere in the world. We begin to feel hopeless. We even wonder if we have done some countries a favor in curing or preventing childhood illnesses, thus aggravating their population burden. *Perhaps,* we think for just a moment, *they would be better off if . . .*

In Vietnam, a generation of children came to maturity without ever experiencing peace. In Beirut, relentless daily shelling, from the mid-1970s to the 1990s, has shattered the world of childhood. In Belfast, some children learn to hate before they learn to play. Throughout the developing world, from Afghanistan to Nicaragua, boys and girls in their early to mid-teens bear arms and march off to battle. And the Iran of the mullahs, in their war with Iraq, for years sent poorly armed pubescent boys to certain death in sacrificial waves.

These are only the "crisis" situations. They occur against the background of ongoing, routine, avoidable crises that cripple and kill children every day throughout the world. In September 1990, the United Nations convened more than seventy heads of state, along with high-level representatives from all other countries, to assess the state of the world's children. Here is what the data show:

- Almost 15 million children age five and under die each year; millions more become brain-damaged, physically disabled, weakened, and chronically racked by pain.
- Almost two-thirds of the deaths are caused by conditions easily remedied: diarrhea treatable with inexpensive oral rehydration therapy; respiratory infections treatable with easily available antibiotics; and whooping cough, measles, and newborn tetanus, all preventable with vaccination; another 7 percent are caused by malaria, usually treatable with quininelike drugs.
- About 40 percent — 150 million — of the children under five in the developing world are clinically malnourished; vitamin A deficiency, which blinds a quarter-million a year, can be prevented with a two-cent (U.S.) capsule twice a *year;* iodine deficiency, which damages millions of children's brains, can be prevented with a few cents' worth of iodized salt.
- Almost 100 million primary-school-age children have no access to schools or other educational programs; the amount spent per pupil is actually declining in more than half of one hundred developing countries; and there are almost one billion adults who cannot read or write.
- An estimated 100 million children live on their own on the streets of the world's cities; they are all neglected by definition, but in addition millions are physically and sexually abused, exploited as slaves, bonded laborers, and child prostitutes, and forced or drawn into the drug trade.

It is not only because these problems are so anguishing, nor even because we see them as intractable, that we tend to turn our attention away. It is also because we are not quite sure that solving them is a good idea. The Malthusian engine of population expansion has been building up steam for centuries. Death rates have dropped faster than birth rates in the world as a whole and in all individual developing countries. In much of Africa, Asia, and Latin America today, some indexes of modernization have not only stopped rising but have fallen in the last generation. The most likely explanation for this drop is that population growth has "eaten up" the gains of modernization as the number of people needing food, clothing, shelter, and services has far outpaced developing nations' ability to provide them.

These facts make us wonder, reasonably enough, if we are not merely sowing the seeds of future disaster when we act to save children's lives. And even if we decide to help feed them, political savagery and cynicism take their daily toll, withholding or diverting desperately needed food and medicine. As for education, we may be led to wonder what it can be for in a place where modernization has stagnated, so that even high-school graduates are overqualified for the kind of work, if any, that is available.

Paradoxically, modernization helps to solve the Malthusian dilemma. The demographic transition has taken a basically similar form in every country that has modernized. First there is a drop in death rates and an increase in life expectancy that causes population to expand exponentially for several generations. Then the birth rate begins to fall, until deaths balance births and expansion stops. In several industrialized countries today, births do not quite balance deaths, and therefore population is slowly declining. Although there are no guarantees, current trends lead population experts to predict that shortly before the year 2000 the total number of births in the world will begin to decline for the first time in history, and that world population will stabilize some time in the twenty-first century, at two or three times its present size.

Yet there can be no complacency, since grave social dislocations result from the demographic transition, and since population expansion has already more than absorbed the gains of modernization in many developing countries. In addition, rising expectations of people throughout the world assure a continuing environmental crisis even if population were to stabilize very soon. Still, we can recognize that modernization leads to population control, even when the control is not planned. China experienced both an enormous increase in birth rate and decrease in death rate in the late 1950s and early 1960s, after which birth rate began to drop. The population growth rate was halved between 1970 and 1976, *before* the draconian post-Mao measures that began to enforce the one-child family. Japan, with no severe measures, has cut its birth rate by two-thirds since the late 1940s, and its population-growth rate (births minus deaths) by more than half. Both countries began with higher growth rates than the world as a whole has now.

Extensive research has provided several explanations for the second phase of the demographic transition. Modernization brings at least four elements that tend to make birth rates fall. First, the assurance that your children will live makes it unnecessary to guarantee heirs through excess births. Second, realistic and rising expectations for your own and your children's futures lead you to want to invest more in the quality of life and development for each child. Third, increasingly available methods and knowledge of birth control reduce the number of unplanned and unwanted babies. Fourth, the education and rising status of women specifically leads to a lower *desired* family size as well as to greater knowledge of how to prevent unwanted births.

So we can say with some confidence that programs to improve the health, nutrition, and quality of life of children around the world will in the long run help solve the population problem, and improve the quality of the resulting adults' satisfaction and adaptation. This will make the world safer even for the self-centered goals of people in developed countries and their children. This is before we even mention the humanitarian imperative that constrains all decent people to support such programs.

• • •

But will the programs work? As with those directed at disadvantaged children in the United States, one of the greatest enemies of progress is the myth that nothing works.

Some things work. They need to be identified and emulated.

China, during the same period that it was dramatically curtailing population growth — both before and after the one-child family was stringently imposed — was also experiencing one of the greatest improvements in child survival and health so far seen in the developing world. Life expectancy at birth in China today is seventy, as compared with an average of less than sixty in the rest of the developing world — fifty-eight in India, for example, and sixty-five in Brazil. Overall life expectancy in the United States is seventy-six, but in New York City it is seventy-three for whites and seventy for nonwhites, while in the equally crowded Shanghai it is seventy-five and a half. Infant mortality in China is about 3 percent, as compared with a developing-country average around 8 percent — just under 10 percent in India, 6 percent in Brazil. The U.S. figure is just below 1 percent, but again the New York City figure is worse than Shanghai's.

This success comes from a major investment of effort, but not much money, in preventive medicine, health education, and primary health care. If you need a heart bypass operation, a transplant, kidney dialysis, or a neonatal intensive care unit, you will probably not get it in China. But if you are a pregnant woman, you will get a dense schedule of prenatal checkups, and if you are a baby you will be immunized against six major killing and crippling infections: whooping cough, diphtheria, tetanus, tuberculosis, measles, and polio. If you are a three-year-old with diarrhea or pneumonia, you will not die. Shanghai spends an average of $38 (U.S.) per person per year on health care; the corresponding figure for the United States as a whole is $2,100. Even in remote villages in China, basic primary care and preventive measures are available.

Indonesia has not had the success that China has had, but it is doing better in major health indicators than most comparably poor countries. More important, it is changing fast. In the 1970s the Family Welfare Movement set up child-weighing posts in villages around the country. These evolved into integrated health services outposts, called *posyandus*, each the focus of a lively monthly neighborhood gathering of mothers, pregnant women, and children under five. They meet in village halls and private homes for a social occasion and a primary-care encounter with one of 800,000 *kaders* — women volunteers now working in 57,000 of the country's 68,000 villages. In 1986, Indonesia's President Suharto announced the start of a "Decade for Children," and in the subsequent four years the number of outposts doubled to 217,000.

The monthly activities of these informal posts include monitoring of growth on a chart kept by the mother, referral of malnourished children for treatment, distribution of vitamin A capsules, immunization, oral rehydration therapy for diarrhea, prenatal examinations by midwives, supplementation of pregnant women with iron and folate, breast-feeding advice, and family-planning education and supplies. What cannot be accomplished by the volunteers, whose training is very brief, is done by visiting personnel from the nearest local health center. The results are impressive. Measles immunization coverage rose from 2 percent in 1980 to 50 percent in 1987. The diarrhea case fatality rate fell by 70 percent in the first half of the 1980s. Volunteers are being trained and retrained constantly; access to outpost gatherings is expected to reach 100 percent in 1991.

In Egypt in 1984 the Ministry of Health, assisted by USAID, launched a program to implement oral rehydration therapy (ORT) and continued breast-feeding for children with diarrhea. Forty thousand health care personnel were trained in ORT, and they distribute the rehydration salts free of charge. Local factory production of these salts doubled, reaching five million liters in 1987, and facilities for training parents in ORT were established in 3,200 centers around the country. Surveys have shown that more than 80 percent of Egyptian mothers can now mix the salts correctly, and at least half the childhood diarrhea cases are treated, up from 10 or 20 percent in 1983.

In the other major prong of Egypt's child-health thrust, 80 percent of all young children were immunized against the six major vaccine-preventable diseases. But in mid-1988 only 12 percent of pregnant women were immunized with the two doses of tetanus toxoid needed to protect the newborn. A nationwide, television-centered campaign was mounted, featuring famous entertainers and first lady Suzanne Mubarak, with Girl Guides, government workers, and traditional birth attendants doing the footwork and inoculations. In the closing months of 1988, the campaign covered over 820,000 pregnant women with two doses of toxoid, and another 270,000 with one dose. By the end of the year, 82 percent of all pregnant women were fully immunized.

The government of Zimbabwe gained its independence in 1980, and pledged to provide universal free primary education — to a population in which fewer than half the children were enrolled, and only a third were completing the seventh grade. Within five years every child — 2.3 million in all — was starting school, and three out of four were completing the seven-year course. By the end of the 1980s, education comprised 22 percent of the national budget — the fifth highest proportion in the world, more than the defense and health budgets put together. In addition, most schools have a building fund for expansion, and parents contribute cash or bricks. Mothers also have sewing cooperatives to make school uniforms.

Zimbabwean teachers have good salaries and benefits compared with those in other developing countries, and the government has instituted an innovative teacher-training program, as well as a new curriculum — the old British-based version has been changed to adapt it to the country's needs. The teaching of science, agriculture, and technical subjects integrates theory and practice. In a school at Tafara, children dug a fishpond in the shape of a world map, and proceeded to use it to study subjects ranging from fish-farming to geography to control of water-borne diseases. A school in Manicaland earns $500 a year for its programs from the sale of produce from its vegetable gardens. Where resources are scarce, teachers invent them. There are no Cuisiniere rods or calculators, but it turns out arithmetic can be taught quite well with stones. There may be no art supplies, but children can exercise their creativity making compositions from mud and leaves.

Underdevelopment is like a war. People, including children, are dying needless deaths; oppression is great, confusion and stress are ubiquitous. Some people — including some government ministers — take advantage of the opportunity to aggrandize themselves. Others give up the fight in exhaustion. But many are prepared to sacrifice a great deal for the good of their countries. Millions throughout the world are fighting fiercely every day. And in some places, like China, Indonesia, Egypt, and Zimbabwe, the war against underdevelopment is slowly being won.

The United States and its coalition partners spent billions of U.S. dollars every week of the Gulf War. A small fraction of that would provide the $1.4 billion needed to mount a global immunization program that in five years could protect almost all the world's children against the six major vaccine-preventable diseases, saving a million lives a year. The cost of operating a single B-1B bomber for a single hour, not counting bombs and other ordnance, could provide community-based maternal health care to ten African villages, reducing maternal deaths by half in one decade. UNICEF has called the 1990s the *Decade for Doing the Obvious*. All that needs to be added is that compared to the cost of the rest of our foreign policy — or even, for that matter, the cost of our entertainments — the obvious is available at bargain-basement prices. Obviously, we should do it.

• • •

The philosopher Jean-Jacques Rousseau, famed for his concern for children, set down in *Emile* a philosophy of child care:

> Your first duty is to be humane. Love childhood. Look with friendly eyes on its games, its pleasures, its amiable dispositions. Which of you does not sometimes look back regretfully on the age when laughter was ever on the lips and the heart free of care? Why steal from the little innocents the enjoyment of a time that passes all too quickly?

I have on my desk photographs of two courageous boys who together have a lesson to teach about the human species. The first is of a teenager who used to live in southern Italy, in a valley linking the Tyrrhenian and Ionian seas, approximately 11,150 years ago, give or take a couple of centuries. It's a photograph of his bones, actually, but they tell his life story. In those days the Italians — who were certainly known by some other name — used to hunt and gather for a living. In this particular region they lived in and around caves, and in one of these caves, near a place called Riparo del Romito, a team of Italian paleontologists in the mid-1960s disturbed the boy's eleven-millennium rest.

Here is what his bones said: He was about seventeen years old when he died of undetermined causes. He was buried together with an elderly woman in a very special cave, one of the few in Italy with prehistoric paintings on the walls. The fusion of the centers at the ends of his long bones showed that he had completed his growth. But he was only a little over one meter tall — not much more than half the average height for men of that Paleolithic era. In addition, he could extend his arms at the elbow only a little more than halfway, and his skull and face were not normally shaped. In fact, he had every skeletal sign of a form of genetically caused dwarfism that is rare in any human population.

It is possible, though far from certain, that he was the product of an incestuous mating. In any case, his distinctive and deformed shape must have been evident at birth. Since hunters and gatherers, as well as many other small-scale societies, traditionally often killed deformed infants at birth, somebody made a conscious decision to let this baby live. And not only was he allowed to live, but he was cared for throughout childhood and grew up with this deformity in a setting where mortality was probably 50 percent before age fifteen *without* a genetic abnormality. It is difficult to imagine this young man hunting with a pair of arms that could not be stretched at the elbows. In addition, judging from present-day victims of the same syndrome, he probably had impaired mobility and tired easily. That means that at the time of his death at seventeen, someone was still hunting for him and feeding him. Then, at his death, someone thought to bury him in a privileged place, with an older woman perhaps still believed to be taking care of him after death.

The second photograph is of David, known as "the bubble boy," talking with his doctor and his mother in the Texas Children's Hospital in Houston. Between him and them is the shiny cocoon of plastic film that has surrounded the boy for twelve years, and that made him the oldest survivor of severe combined immunodeficiency disease — a rare genetic defect that devastates the immune system, leading to death from any number of infections before age two. David had so far beaten the odds by staying in the bubble, which protected him from a world full of, to him, deadly microbes.

But he suffered from symptoms like nausea, diarrhea, and fever anyway, and it was deemed necessary to remove him from the bubble to be treated. After a new technique allowed him to get some of his fifteen-year-old sister Katherine's protective bone marrow, he was released from the bubble. His mother hugged and kissed him for the first time in his life. She expressed surprise at the thickness of his hair. His first request was for his very first Coke.

Although they were eleven thousand years apart and at opposite ends of the scale of technology, David seemed to me to mirror the experience of the handicapped boy at Romito. And what the two boys say about us is this: *We are the species that takes care of children.* Jane Lancaster, an anthropologist at the University of New Mexico, has pointed out that while all species of primates, indeed all mammals, feed their infants, only humans keep feeding children at least through puberty. Advanced apes like chimpanzees let their offspring hang around, but only in human societies do adults forage *for* children of all ages. In addition, only humans "feed" their young educationally; apes have merely the most rudimentary kind of teaching. Humans make a career out of it, realizing that to survive as a person, children must take in a great deal of knowledge — so much that they cannot get it on their own. So along with food and love they are given large and steady doses of culture.

It seems as if we could start taking our uniqueness more seriously. If by eleven thousand years ago we were already going to such great lengths to help a child survive, then we might as well realize that we were not built to feel quite comfortable with ourselves while children are visibly suffering around us. Television has brought them all into our living rooms; the world, we know, is a global village. They cannot see us through the television screen, but neither can we hide from their wide, penetrating, expectant eyes. Sometimes they almost seem to combine with the eyes of our children, or of ourselves as children, beset with so many hopes, so many needs.

Children are living messages we send into the future, a future that we will not see. We understand enough about them now to have a fairly good idea of what they need. In effect we are building the house of to-morrow day by day, not out of bricks or steel, but out of the stuff of children's bodies, hearts, and minds. As we age, we will reminisce more and more about our early lives, and ponder our reflections in the children who play around us, trying to grow up. Perhaps we will feel increasingly the kinship of similitude.

But in any case, as we nod and doze in our rocking chairs, we will probably visit the house of tomorrow in our dreams. Only we can act to insure that those dreams will not be nightmares, in which the house goes up in flames or crumbles under its own weight. Only we can dream dreams of the future in which we take a child — any child — by the hand and walk up to the threshold where we, of necessity, stop. Only we can send the child forward into the house with a sure step that speaks of health, poise, and strength, a voice full of warmth and intelligence, a hand that is skillful and steady, and eyes that glisten candidly with confidence and hope.

Bibliography/
Reading List

CHAPTER ONE

Burn, Barbara, and Alvin Grossman. *Metropolitan Children*. New York: Harry N. Abrams, 1984.

Cohn, Anna R., et al. *Generations*. New York: Pantheon Books, 1987.

Cole, Michael, and Sheila R. Cole. *The Development of Children*. New York: W. H. Freeman, 1989.

Kagan, Jerome. *The Nature of the Child*. New York: Basic Books, 1984.

Konner, Melvin. *The Tangled Wing: Biological Constraints on the Human Spirit*. New York: Henry Holt, 1990.

Rousseau, Jean-Jacques. *Emile*. New York: Teachers College Press, 1956.

Scarr, Sandra, et al. *Understanding Development*. New York: Harcourt Brace Jovanovich, 1986.

Zelazo, Philip, and Ronald Barr. *Challenges to Developmental Paradigms: Implications for Theory, Assessment and Treatment*. Hillsdale, NJ: Lawrence Erlbaum, 1989.

CHAPTER TWO

Brazelton, T. Berry. *Infants and Mothers*. New York: Delacorte Press, 1969.

Gibson, Kathleen, and Anne Petersen, eds. *Brain Maturation and Cognitive Development: Comparative and Cross-Cultural Perspectives*. New York: Aldine de Gruyter, 1991.

Lamb, Michael E., and Marc H. Bornstein. *Development in Infancy: An Introduction*. New York: Random House, 1987.

Maurer, Daphne, and Charles Maurer. *The World of the Newborn*. New York: Basic Books, 1989.

Meltzer, David. *Birth: An Anthology of Ancient Texts, Songs, Prayers and Stories*. San Francisco: North Point Press, 1981.

Nilsson, Lennart. *A Child Is Born*. New York: Delacorte Press, 1990.

Stern, Daniel N. *Diary of a Baby: What Your Child Sees, Feels and Experiences*. New York: Basic Books, 1990.

———. *The Interpersonal World of the Infant: A View from Psychoanalysis and Developmental Psychology*. New York: Basic Books, 1985.

Trevathen, Wenda. *Human Birth*. New York: Aldine de Gruyter, 1987.

Wertz, Richard, and Dorothy Wertz. *Lying In: A History of Childbirth in America*. New York: Free Press, 1977.

CHAPTER THREE

Bowlby, John. *Attachment: 3 Volumes*. New York: Basic Books, 1969–1980.

Kagan, Jerome. *Unstable Ideas: Temperament, Cognition and Self*. Cambridge: Harvard University Press, 1989.

Ladd-Taylor, Molly. *Raising a Baby the Government's Way: Mothers' Letters to the Children's Bureau 1915–1932*. New Brunswick, NJ: Rutgers University Press, 1986.

Mintz, Steven, and Susan Kellogg. *Domestic Revolutions*. New York: Free Press, 1988.

Piaget, Jean. *The Origins of Intelligence in Children*. New York: W. W. Norton, 1963.

Scarr, Sandra. *Mother Care — Other Care*. New York: Basic Books, 1984.

Spock, Benjamin, and Michael Rothenberg. *Dr. Spock's Baby and Child Care.* New York: Simon & Schuster, 1985.

Stone, Lawrence. *The Family, Sex & Marriage in England 1500–1800.* New York: Harper & Row, 1980.

Zigler, Edward, and Mary Lang. *Child Care Choices.* New York: Free Press, 1991.

CHAPTER FOUR

Bettelheim, Bruno. *The Uses of Enchantment.* New York: Vintage Books, 1977.

Brown, Roger. *A First Language.* Cambridge: Harvard University Press, 1973.

Dally, Ann. *Inventing Motherhood.* New York: Schocken Books, 1983.

Dunn, Judy, and Robert Plomin. *Separate Lives: Why Siblings Are So Different.* New York: Basic Books, 1990.

Hardyment, Christina. *Dream Babies: Three Centuries of Good Advice on Child Care.* New York: Harper & Row, 1983.

Hawes, Joseph M., and N. Ray Hiner. *Children in Historical and Comparative Perspective: An International Handbook and Research Guide.* New York: Greenwood Press, 1991.

Kagan, Jerome. *The Second Year.* Cambridge: Harvard University Press, 1981.

Lenneberg, Eric. *Biological Foundations of Language.* New York: John Wiley and Sons, 1967.

Piaget, Jean. *Play, Dreams and Imitation in Childhood.* New York: W. W. Norton, 1962.

Pollock, Linda. *A Lasting Relationship: Parents and Children Over Three Centuries.* New York: Cambridge University Press, 1987.

————. *Forgotten Children: Parent-Child Relations from 1500 to 1900.* New York: Cambridge University Press, 1984.

Sacks, Oliver. *Seeing Voices: A Journey Into the World of the Deaf.* New York: HarperCollins, 1990.

Zipes, Jack. *Beauties, Beasts and Enchantment.* New York: New American Library, 1989.

CHAPTER FIVE

Aptekar, Lewis. *Street Children of Cali.* Durham: Duke University Press, 1988.

Ariès, Philippe. *Centuries of Childhood.* New York: Vintage Books, 1962.

Boswell, John. *The Kindness of Strangers.* New York: Pantheon Books, 1988.

Crewdson, John. *By Silence Betrayed: Sexual Abuse of Children in America.* Boston: Little, Brown, 1988.

Elder, Glen H., Jr. *Children of the Great Depression: Social Change in the Life Course.* Chicago: University of Chicago Press, 1985.

Emery, Robert E. *Marriage, Divorce and Children's Adjustment.* London: Sage Publications, 1988.

Harlow, Harry F. *Learning to Love.* San Francisco: Albion Publishing, 1971.

Keller, Helen. *The Story of My Life.* New York: Grosset and Dunlap, 1904.

Lane, Harlan. *The Wild Boy of Aveyron.* Boston: Harvard University Press, 1976.

Ohlin, Lloyd, and Michael Tonry, eds. *Family Violence.* Chicago: University of Chicago Press, 1989.

Shahar, Shulamith. *Childhood in the Middle Ages.* London: Routledge, 1990.

Vaillant, George. *Adaptation to Life.* Boston: Little, Brown, 1977.

Werner, Emmy E., et al. *Vulnerable But Invincible: A Longitudinal Study of Resilient Children and Youth.* New York: Adams Bannister Cox, 1989.

CHAPTER SIX

Bernhard, J. Gary. *Primates in the Classroom.* Amherst: University of Massachusetts Press, 1988.

Chernoff, John Miller. "Music Making Children of Africa." *Natural History* 88, November 1989, p. 9.

Coe, Richard N. *When the Grass Was Taller: Autobiography and the Experience of Childhood.* New Haven: Yale University Press, 1984.

Gardner, Howard. *Frames of Mind: The Theory of Multiple Intelligences.* New York: Basic Books, 1983.

Goodlad, John I. *A Place Called School.* New York: McGraw-Hill, 1984.

Irvine, Jacqueline Jordan. *Black Students and School Failure: Policies, Practices and Prescriptions.* New York: Greenwood Press, 1990.

Kidder, Tracy. *Among Schoolchildren.* New York: Houghton Mifflin, 1989.

McGuinness, Diane. *When Children Don't Learn: Understanding the Biology and Psychology of Learning Disabilities.* New York, Basic Books, 1985.

Piaget, Jean. *Play, Dreams, and Imitation.* New York: W. W. Norton, 1962.

Sommerville, John. *The Rise and Fall of Childhood.* New York: Vintage, 1990.

Stevenson, Harold W. "America's Math Problems." *Educational Leadership,* October 1987, pp. 4–10.

———. "The Asian Advantage: The Case of Mathematics." *American Educator,* Summer 1987, pp. 26–31.

Tobin, Joseph J. *Preschool in Three Cultures: Japan, China and the United States.* New Haven: Yale University Press, 1989.

Ulich, Robert. *Three Thousand Years of Educational Wisdom: Selections from Great Documents.* Cambridge: Harvard University Press, 1975.

CHAPTER SEVEN

Coles, Robert. *The Spiritual Life of Children.* Boston: Houghton Mifflin, 1990.

Demos, John. *Past, Present and Personal.* New York: Oxford University Press, 1986.

Greven, Philip. *Spare the Child: The Religious Roots of Punishment and the Psychological Impact of Physical Abuse.* New York: Random House, 1990.

Hechinger, Fred M., and Grace Hechinger. *Growing Up in America.* New York: McGraw-Hill, 1975.

Huizinga, Johann. *Homo Ludens.* Boston: Beacon Press, 1955.

Opie, Iona, and Peter Opie. *The Lore and Language of Schoolchildren.* New York: Oxford University Press, 1987.

———. *The Oxford Dictionary of Nursery Rhymes.* New York: Oxford University Press, 1951.

Piaget, Jean. *The Moral Judgement of the Child.* New York: Free Press, 1965.

Smith, Robert Paul. *"Where Did You Go?" "Out." "What Did You Do?" "Nothing."* New York: W. W. Norton, 1957.

Sutton-Smith, Brian. *Toys As Culture.* New York: Gardner Press, 1986.

Whiting, Beatrice, and Carolyn Pope Edwards. *Children of Different Worlds: The Formation of Social Behavior.* Cambridge: Harvard University Press, 1988.

Whiting, Beatrice, and John Whiting. *Children of Six Cultures.* Cambridge: Harvard University Press, 1975.

Zborowski, Mark, and Elizabeth Herzog. *Life Is with People: The Culture of the Shtetl.* New York: Schocken Books, 1962.

CHAPTER EIGHT

Buckley, Thomas, and Alma Gottlieb. *Blood Magic: The Anthropology of Menstruation.* Berkeley: University of California Press, 1988.

Csikszentmihalyi, Mihaly. *Being Adolescent: Conflict and Growth in the Teenage Years.* New York: Basic Books, 1984.

Gilligan, Carol, et al. *Mapping the Moral Domain.* Cambridge: Harvard University Press, 1990.

Katchadurian, Herant. *The Biology of Adolescence.* San Francisco: W. H. Freeman, 1977.

Lancaster, Jane, and Beatrix Hamburg, eds. *School-Age Pregnancy and Parenthood.* New York: Aldine de Gruyter, 1986.

Mead, Margaret. *Coming of Age in Samoa.* New York: Morrow, 1961.

Postman, Neil. *The Disappearance of Childhood.* New York: Dell Books, 1982.

Schlegel, Alice, and Herbert Barry III. *Adolescence: An Anthropological Inquiry.* New York: Free Press, 1991.

Shostak, Marjorie. *Nisa: The Life and Words of a !Kung Woman.* New York: Random House, 1982.

Steinberg, Laurence. *Adolescence.* New York: Alfred A. Knopf, 1989.

EPILOGUE

Bronfenbrenner, Urie. *The Ecology of Human Development: Experiments by Nature and Design.* Cambridge: Harvard University Press, 1979.

———. *Two Worlds of Childhood — US & USSR.* New York: Touchstone Books, 1972.

Children's Defense Fund. *S.O.S. America! A Children's Defense Budget.* Washington, DC: Children's Defense Fund, 1990.

Comer, James. *School Power: Implications for an Intervention Project.* New York: Free Press, 1980.

Erikson, Erik H. *Childhood and Society.* New York: W. W. Norton, 1963.

Hewlett, Sylvia Ann. *When the Bough Breaks: The Cost of Neglecting Our Children.* New York: Basic Books, 1991.

Hinde, Robert A. *Biological Bases of Human Social Behavior.* New York: McGraw-Hill, 1974.

————. *Individuals, Relationships and Culture.* Cambridge: Cambridge University Press, 1987.

National Center for Children in Poverty. *Five Million Children: A Statistical Profile of Our Poorest Young Citizens.* New York: Columbia University, 1990.

Neisser, Ulric. *Memory Observed.* San Francisco: W. H. Freeman, 1982.

Schorr, Lisbeth B. *Within Our Reach: Breaking the Cycle of Disadvantage and Despair.* New York: Doubleday, 1988.

United Nations Children's Fund (UNICEF). *The State of the World's Children, 1990.* New York: Oxford University Press, 1990.

Text and Illustration Credits

TEXT CREDITS

Grateful acknowledgment is made to the following for permission to quote from copyrighted material:

"DO ME!" Words and music by Carl Bourelly, Michael Bivins, Ricky Bell and Ronnie DeVoe. Copyright © 1990 by Willesden Music/Bourelly Music, Inc. (administered by Willesden Music), Unicity Music, Inc., Baledat Music, Low Key Music, and Slick Star Music. Rights of Unicity Music, Inc., Baledat Music, Low Key Music and Slick Star Music administered by MCA Music Publishing, A Division of MCA Inc., New York, NY 10019. LYRICS USED BY PERMISSION. ALL RIGHTS RESERVED.

Excerpts from *The Spiritual Life of Children* by Robert Coles. Copyright © 1990 by Robert Coles. Reprinted with permission of Houghton Mifflin Company.

"Incident" from *On These I Stand* by Countee Cullen. Copyright 1925 by Harper & Brothers. Copyright renewed 1953 by Ida M. Cullen. Reprinted with permission of GRM Associates, Inc., Agents for the Estate of Ida M. Cullen.

Excerpts from *Anne Frank: The Diary of a Young Girl* by Anne Frank. Copyright 1952 by Otto H. Frank. Reprinted with permission of Doubleday, a Division of Bantam Doubleday Dell Publishing Group, Inc., and Vallentine Mitchell & Co., Ltd., London.

Excerpts from *The Prophet* by Kahlil Gibran. Copyright 1923 by Kahlil Gibran. Copyright renewed 1951 by Administrators C.T.A. of Kahlil Gibran Estate and Mary G. Gibran. Reprinted with permission of Alfred A. Knopf, Inc.

"Rendezvous" from *Mink Coat* by Jill Hoffman. Copyright © 1969, 1970, 1971, 1972, 1973 by Jill Hoffman. Reprinted with permission of Henry Holt and Company, Inc.

Excerpts from *Nisa: The Life and Words of a !Kung Woman* by Marjorie Shostak, Cambridge, Mass.: Harvard University Press. Copyright © 1981 by Marjorie Shostak. Reprinted with permission of the publisher.

Excerpts from *Baby and Child Care* by Benjamin Spock, M.D. Copyright 1945, 1946, © 1957, 1968, 1976 by Benjamin Spock, M.D. Reprinted with permission of Pocket Books, a Division of Simon & Schuster, Inc.

ILLUSTRATION CREDITS

Following page 21:

1. Museum fur Volkerkunde Staatliche Museen
2. Courtesy of the Department of Library Services, American Museum of Natural History
3. Courtesy of Biblioteca Apostolica Vaticana
4. Museum fur Volkerkunde Staatliche Museen
5. © Patrick Guis/Sygma
6. © Petit Format/Nestle/Science Source/Photo Researchers, Inc.
7. © Eugene Richards/Magnum
8. © Petit Format/Nestle/Science Source/Photo Researchers, Inc.
9. © Eugene Richards/Magnum
10. Courtesy of Gordon E. Mestler, Emeritus Scientist, Department of Anatomy, State University of New York Health Science Center, Brooklyn, New York
11. © 1984 Susie Fitzhugh
12. National Library of Medicine, Print and Photographs Collection
13. Courtesy of Gordon E. Mestler, Emeritus Scientist, Department of Anatomy, State University of New York Health Science Center, Brooklyn, New York
14. Marjorie Shostak/Anthro Photo
15. Marjorie Shostak/Anthro Photo
16. Spencer Grant/Science Source/Photo Researchers, Inc.
17. © Ray Ellis/Photo Researchers, Inc.
18. © Ed Lettau/Photo Researchers, Inc.
19. © Morris/ACC-Coll/Photo Researchers, Inc.
20. A. N. Meltzoff and M. K. Moore, "Imitation of facial and manual gestures by human neonates," *Science* 1977, *198:* 75–78
21. © Abraham Menashe
22. © Paul Fusco/Magnum

Following page 71:

1. © Ken Heyman/Black Star
2. Kavaler/Art Resource, NY
3. Courtesy of the Library of Congress
4. Dean Conger © 1985 National Geographic Society
5. James Chisholm/Anthro Photo

6. Courtesy of the Deparmtent of Library Services, American Museum of Natural History. By Rodman Wanamaker.
7. © Abbas/Magnum
8. Courtesy of the Gesell Institute of Human Development
9. The Johns Hopkins Medical Institutions. The Alan Mason Chesney Medical Archives.
10. © George Zimbel/Monkmeyer Press
11. © George Zimbel/Monkmeyer Press
12. The Metropolitan Museum of Art, Bequest of Michael Friedsam, 1931. The Friedsam Collection.
13. Virginia Museum of Fine Arts, Richmond. Gift of an anonymous donor.
14. Vyacheslav Remin
15. Vyacheslav Remin
16. Courtesy of Carolyn Rovee-Collier
17. The Metropolitan Museum of Art, Gift of Mortimer L. Schiff, 1918. (18.57.4)
18. Melvin Konner/Anthro Photo
19. New York Public Library: Astor, Lenox and Tilden Foundations
20. Marjorie Shostak/Anthro Photo

Following page 125:
1. Melvin Konner/Anthro Photo
2. © Ursula Marcus/Photo Researchers, Inc.
3. © Joel Sackett
4. © Laura Dwight/Black Star
5. © Mariette Pathy Allen/Visions
6. © David Sassoon
7. Joel Halpern/Anthro Photo
8. Scala/Art Resource, NY
9. The Children's Aid Society
10. Rudy Gaskins
11. Napoleon Chagnon/Anthro Photo
12. Melvin Konner/Anthro Photo
13. © Ken Heyman/Black Star
14. © Ken Keyman/Black Star
15. © Christian Simonpietri/Sygma
16. Vyacheslav Remin
17. © Joel Sackett
18. The Metropolitan Museum of Art, Rogers Fund, 1921. (21.35.2)
19. Richard Lee/Anthro Photo
20. © Stephen Shames/Matrix
21. © Ken Heyman/Black Star

Following page 179:
1. © Lisa Silcock/Dja River Films, Ltd.
2. Raghu Murthy
3. © Angela Fisher/Robert Estall Photo Library
4. Bernardo Magalhaes
5. "Riding brother on his back (Battle with the Slum)" Jacob A. Riis Collection, #358 Museum of the City of New York

6. © Ken Heyman/Black Star
7. Marjorie Shostak/Anthro Photo
8. Raghu Murthy
9. © Wayne Miller/Magnum
10. © Ken Heyman/Black Star
11. The Metropolitan Museum of Art, Purchase, Rogers Fund and the Kevorkian Foundation Gift, 1955
12. © Ursula Bellugi, The Salk Institute for Biological Studies, reprinted with permission.
13. Picture from *The Treasures of Childhood* by Iona Opie, Robert Opie, and Brian Alderson published by Arcade Publishing (US) and Pavilion books (UK)
14. Courtesy of Saxton Freymann
15. Courtesy of Saxton Freymann
16. Picture from *The Treasures of Childhood* by Iona Opie, Robert Opie, and Brian Alderson published by Arcade Publishing (US) and Pavilion Books (UK)
17. "The Far Side" cartoon by Gary Larson is reprinted by permission of Chronicle Features, San Francisco, CA.
18. Scala/Art Resource, NY
19. Scala/Art Resource, NY
20. Courtesy of The Simon Wiesenthal Center Archives, Los Angeles, CA
21. Courtesy The Strong Museum, Rochester, New York
22. © Andy Hernandez/Sygma

Following page 227:
1. Courtesy of the Fogg Art Museum, Harvard University, Cambridge, MA, Gift of Philip Hofer, no. M4325
2. © Sebastaio Salgado/Magnum
3. Courtesy of *The Atlantic*. Artwork accompanied the article "Growing Up Scared" by Karl Zinsmeister.
4. © Bart Bartholomew/Black Star
5. Harlow Primate Laboratory, University of Wisconsin
6. Harlow Primate Laboratory, University of Wisconsin
7. Harlow Primate Laboratory, University of Wisconsin
8. Harlow Primate Laboratory, University of Wisconsin
9. © Jerry Cooke, Inc. 1985
10. © Arturo Robles/JB Pictures Ltd.
11. © Abraham Menashe
12. © Abraham Menashe
13. Rudy Gaskins
14. Vyacheslav Remin
15. Courtesy of Sheldon Greenfield
16. © Cornell Capa/Magnum
17. © Arthur Tress/Magnum
18. © Abbas/Magnum
19. The Metropolitan Museum of Art, Gift of Alexander Smith Cochran, 1913

20. Courtesy of the Library of Congress
21. Special Collections, Milbank Memorial Library, Teachers College, Columbia University
22. © J. P. Laffont/Sygma

Following page 279:
1. © David Hurn/Magnum
2. From Saxe, G. B. "Body Parts of Numerials," *Child Development,* vol. 52, 1981, pp. 306–316. 1981.
3. Picture from *The Treasures of Childhood* by Iona Opie, Robert Opie, and Brian Alderson published by Arcade Publishing (US) and Pavilion Books (UK)
4. Raghu Murthy
5. From *Nadia: A Case of Extraordinary Drawing Ability in an Autistic Child* by Lorna Selfe with permission from Academic Press, 1977
6. Reprinted with permission from *Young Children and Their Drawings* by Joseph DiLeo published by Brunner/Mazel, Inc. 1970
7. Courtesy of Rhoda Kellogg, *Analyzing Children's Art* by permission of Mayfield Publishing Co. © 1969, 1970 Rhoda Kellogg
8. Reprinted with permission from *Young Children and Their Drawings* by Joseph DiLeo published by Brunner/Mazel, Inc. 1970
9. Alexander Allard Jr. Collection
10. "Pietro Learning to Make an English Letter" Jacob A. Riis Collection, #160 Museum of the City of New York
11. © David Seymour/Magnum
12. National Archives: 16-G-162-S-11401C
13. Courtesy of the Library of Congress
14. © J. P. Laffont/Sygma
15. Scala/Art Resource, NY
16. Foto Marburg/Art Resource, NY
17. © Alex Webb/Magnum
18. The Cleveland Museum of Art, Purchase from the J. H. Wade Fund
19. © Henri Cartier-Bresson/Magnum
20. © Steve McCurry/Magnum
21. Bridgeman/Art Resource, NY
22. Bridgeman/Art Resource, NY

Following page 331:
1. © K. C. Bailey
2. © Stephen Shames/Matrix
2a. © Arthur Tress/Magnum
3. © Stephen Shames/Matrix
4. © Stephen Shames/Matrix
5. © Bruno Barbey/Magnum
6. © Elliot Erwitt/Magnum
7. Marjorie Shostak/Anthro Photo
8. © Joseph Rodriguez/Black Star
9. © Mariette Pathy Allen/Visions

Index

Abandonados (street children), 316–318
Abortion, 367, 372
Abuse, 10, 70–71, 203, 204, 206–207, 211
    child, 202–203, 204–206
    infant, 69–70, 203–204
    personality effects of, 379–380
    sexual, 70, 71, 205, 206, 207–210
    spousal, 203
    transgenerational, 205–206
"Acting out." *See* Conduct disorders
Adamson, Lauren, 63, 196
Adolescence. *See* Puberty
Adolescence: An Anthropological Inquiry (Schlegel and Barry), 373
Aggression
    adolescent, 17, 358, 372
    cultural differences, 196, 358
    fantasy and, 177
    gender differences, 162, 163, 376–377
    physical abuse and, 204
Ainsworth, Mary, 87, 90–91, 92
Alcohol (fetal alcohol effects), 9, 40–41, 52, 58
Ali, 10
Als, Heidelise, 63
American Pediatric Association, 110
American Sign Language, 152
Among School Children (Kidder), 272
Anemia, 42
Anxiety, 88, 90
Ariès, Phillipe, 193, 194
Arsenian, Jean, 87

Attachment
    day-care and, 117
    infant, 86, 87, 90, 91, 92
    insecure, 93
    multiple, 116
    separation and, 118–119
Attention deficit disorder, 248, 249, 250–251
Attunement. *See* "Bonding" and relationships
Autism, 212, 248, 254
Avoidance behavior, 90, 92

Baby and Child Care (Spock), 68, 110
Baillargeon, Renée, 64, 96
Bakeman, Ronald, 196
Balanchine, George, 256
Barlett, Peggy, 309
Barnett, Ann, 416
Barr, Roger, 62, 196
Barry, Herbert, III, 113, 373–374
Bates, Elizabeth, 151
Bateson, Mary Catherine, 409–410
Behavior (general discussion)
    cultural differences, 307–310
    gender differences, 311
Bellow, Saul, 406
Belsky, Jay, 117
Bernhard, J. Gary, 271
Berrigan, Kevin, 151–152
Berrigan, Krystle, 152
Berrigan, Sheryl, 151–152
Berrigan, Terry, 152

Bettelheim, Bruno, 18, 179
Birth
    control, 370, 372
    defects, 39–40
    order, 166–167, 172
    rates, 366, 421–422
    see also Childbirth
Blake, William, 256
Block, Jack, 219
Block, Jeanne, 219
Blume, Judy, 352
Blurton Jones, Nicholas, 67, 104, 162
"Bonding" and relationships
    emotional, 84, 87, 101
    father/infant, 86
    mother/infant, 66, 85–86, 87, 89, 90–
        91, 100–103
    prenatal, 38, 52–53, 103
Bowlby, John, 18, 87, 90, 117
Bradstreet, Anne, 43–44, 45
Brain, 35–37, 42, 57–62
    behavior and, 165–166
    early childhood and, 138
    experience and, 120
    language acquisition and, 149, 153
    learning abilities and, 239–240, 254,
        270
    mental development, 59, 63, 97, 98,
        153, 241
    physical development, 93–96
    size, 93
Brazelton, T. Berry, 19, 63, 413
Breast-feeding, 67, 68, 87, 103, 110
    cessation of, 137
    cultural differences, 196
Breuer, Joseph, 207
Bronfenbrenner, Urie, 12, 69, 170, 171,
        174
    peer group study, 318–319, 320, 403–
        404
    television study, 323
Brooks, Jeanne, 121
Brooks-Gunn, Jeanne, 359
Brown, Ann, 271
Bruner, Jerome, 148, 154
Byrd, William, 201

Canalization, 214
Carraher, Terezhina, 246, 247
Cartwright, Madeline, 275–276, 418
Case, Robbie, 59
Cassem, Edward, 327
Castration fear, 158–160
Cat in the Hat, The, 56, 58

Caudill, William, 113
Changeux, Jean-Pierre, 36
Chen, Chuansheng, 277
Cherlin, Alfred, 219
Child, Irvin, 196
Childbirth, 13, 43–50, 53–54
    mortality rates, 43–46, 195
    natural, 13, 47–49, 50, 51, 53
Child-care theories, 325–326
    brutal treatment, 193–195
    cultural differences, 106–110, 111–112
    spoiling, 119
    strict schedules, 110, 111
Child development
    cultural differences, 419–428
    policies, 411–419
    see also Fetal development
Childhood amnesia, 407–410
Childhood and Society (Erikson), 176
Childhood in the Middle Ages (Shahar),
        194
Children of Different Worlds: The Forma-
        tion of Social Behavior (Whiting and
        Edwards), 310
Children's Bureau, The, 106–107, 112
Childs, Carla, 244
Chisholm, James, 11
Chomsky, Noam, 141, 144–146, 148,
        149, 150, 151
Clarke-Stewart, Alison, 117, 118
Cocaine. See Drugs
Coles, Robert, 328–329, 330, 331
Comer, James, 418–419
Coming of Age in Samoa (Mead), 108
Competence motivation, 121
Competent Infant, The, 55
Competition, 314–317, 358
Conduct disorders, 10, 218, 249
Conservation of quantity, 241–242
Control needs in infants, 64–65, 66, 88
Crying
    by children, 294
    by infants, 62–63, 65, 70–71, 88–89,
        196
    separation and, 118–119, 120
Cutright, Phillips, 368

Daly, Martin, 206
Damon, William, 300
Darwin, Charles, 11, 63, 139, 206, 402
Davidson, Richard, 99
Day-care, 9, 68, 92, 114–118
Deafness, 145, 149, 151, 152–153
Death, 326–327, 331. See also Mortality
        rates

De Beauvoir, Simone, 361
De Mause, Lloyd, 193, 194
Demos, John, 194
Dependency, 9, 103–106
Depression, 10, 218, 249
DeVore, Irven, 19
Dewey, John, 18, 277
Diary of a Young Girl (Frank), 226–227
Diamond, Adele, 96–98
Dickens, Charles, 221–222, 225
Diet and nutrition, 41–42, 195, 364
Discipline, 14, 71, 196, 204–205
Disease and infection, 87, 195, 197, 200,
    427
  day-care and, 117
  growth rate and, 364–365
  health policy and, 412
  sexual, 367
Divorce, 216, 217–221
Dostoevski, Feodor, 406–407
Down's syndrome, 257
Draper, Patricia, 306
Drugs
  childbirth, 47
  fetus affected by maternal use of, 39–
    40, 41, 42, 52, 58, 191, 224, 253,
    413
Drug therapy, 8, 249, 250
Dunn, Judy, 167–168
Dyslexia, 250, 251, 253

Edelman, Marian Wright, 42, 371
Education
  book learning, 258–259
  philosophy and cultural differences,
    261–270, 271, 274–279
  school environment, 257–258, 259–
    261, 266–267, 273–274
Edwards, Carolyn Pope, 162, 310, 311–
    312
Egeland, Byron, 205
Ehrhardt, Anke, 163
Eibl-Eibesfeldt, Irenäus, 139–140
Eimas, Peter, 56
Elder, Glen, 224, 309
Elias, Marjorie, 11, 113, 114
Ember, Carol, 309
Emotion, 138, 154
Environment, 166, 253. *See also* Educa-
    tion: school environment
Erikson, Erik, 18, 19, 90, 176
Erskine, James, 303
Eveleth, Phyllis, 364
Exercise, 365

Experiment in Autobiography (Wells),
    362

Facial expressions, 140
Fairy tales and nursery rhymes, 178–179,
    197–198, 292
Family
  cultural differences, 319–320
  extended, 103, 216–217
  resilience of, 14–15
  single-parent, 217, 411
Family Bed, The (Thevenin), 114
Family Place, The, 416
Fantasy, 123, 154, 174–179. *See also*
    Fairy tales and nursery rhymes
Farming societies, 308–310
Farrar, Michael, 149
Fauber, Robert, 218, 219
Featherstone, Joseph, 262
Fetal development, 34–39, 52
  alcohol and, 9, 40–41, 52, 58
  brain damage, 42
  diet and malnutrition and, 41–43
  drug effects and, 39–40, 41, 42, 52, 58,
    191, 224, 253, 413
  low birth weight, 41–42
  psychological influences on, 52, 58
  sexual, 163
  smoking and, 163
Flavell, John, 241
Fox, Nathan, 99
*Frames of Mind: The Theory of Multiple
    Intelligences* (Gardner), 255
Frank, Anne, 226–227, 257, 347–349,
    350, 360
Free-time activities, 320–323. *See also*
    Television
Freud, Sigmund, 18, 88, 110, 124, 160,
    207, 406–407
  emotional development theory, 138
  fantasy study, 176
  Oedipus complex, 110, 159, 242
  penis envy theory, 158
  repression theory, 407
  trauma theory, 210
  sexual abuse studies, 207–208, 209
Frisch, Rose, 363, 365, 375
Furstenberg, Frank, 219

Galaburda, Albert, 251
Games. *See* Play and games
Gardner, Howard, 255, 256
Garmezy, Norman, 222

Gender
  behavior differences, 311
  identification, 160–164
  See also Sex roles
Genes/genetics, 33, 34, 36, 37, 98, 405
  brain development and, 58, 95
  I.Q. and, 253
  personality and, 164, 166
  of twins, 164, 167
Gesell, Arnold, 13
Gewirtz, Jacob, 61
Gholston, Anita, 170–171, 353, 377
Gholston, Avery, 10, 116, 124, 169, 171
Gholston, Benjamin, 10, 169, 170–171,
  353
Gholston, Felton, 170, 171
Gholston, Malcolm, 169, 170–171
Gibran, Kahlil, 401–402
Gilligan, Carol, 356
Goethe, Johann Wolfgang von, 406–407
Goldberg, Susan, 376
Goldfrank, Esther, 329–330
Golding, William, 316
Goldin-Meadow, Susan, 152–153
Goodlad, John, 273
Greenfield, Patricia Marks, 244
Greven, Philip, 204
Grossman, Klaus, 92
Growing Up in New Guinea (Mead), 109

Haith, Marshall, 55–56
Hall, G. Stanley, 362
Hamburg, Beatrix, 323
Harlow, Harry, 16, 102, 214–215, 403,
  404
Hartup, Willard, 175
Head Start program, 417–418
Herzog, Elizabeth, 259
Hetherington, Mavis, 218, 219
Hijikata, Megumi, 374–375
Hinde, Robert, 67, 102, 103, 110, 403
Hine, Lewis, 308
Hiner, Ray, 194
History of childhood, 192–195
Holt, John, 257, 272, 273–274
Homebuilders, 416–417
Homicide, 69, 70, 202, 206, 377, 413
Homo ludens (Huizinga), 313
Homosexuality, 10
Hormones, 10
  adolescence and, 351, 353–354, 356–
    357, 380–381
  aggression and, 17, 372
  estrogen ("E"), 356–357, 359, 365

pregnancy and, 375
  progesterone ("P"), 356
  sex roles and, 375
  testosterone ("T"), 356–357, 358, 359
How Children Fail (Holt), 272
Howell, Nancy, 368
Hubley, Penelope, 100
Huizinga, Johann, 313
Hyperactivity, 8, 41, 249, 250–251

Identity. See Self-concept
Incest, 209
Independence, 382, 402
Infant care, 67, 68–69, 89, 92, 93
  cultural differences, 103–104
Infant development, 93–95
Infection. See Disease and infection
Inhelder, Bärbel, 387
Interpersonal World of the Infant, The
  (Stern), 123
Intelligence classifications, 255–257
Intelligence quotient (I.Q.), 251–253,
  256, 257
Intersubjectivity, 100–101, 119
Irritability, 10, 52
Itard, Jean-Marc, 212

Joceline, Elizabeth, 43, 44–45
Joyce, James, 388

Kagan, Jerome, 19, 64, 85, 94, 404
  object-permanence test, 97
  self-awareness studies, 122, 123
  timidity studies, 165, 166, 167
Kalugin, Natasha, 84
Kalugin, Vera, 84, 112
Kamala (Baka baby), 10
Katz, Mary Maxwell, 122
Kaufman, Barbara, 50–51, 52, 53, 68
Kaufman, David, 50–51, 52, 53, 68
Kaufman, Michelle, 10, 50–51, 53, 55,
  68
Kaye, Herbert, 56
Keller, Helen, 255–256
Kempe, C. Henry, 203
Kennell, John, 53
Kidder, Tracy, 272
King, Truby, 110–111
Kinsey, Alfred, 355
Kirkpatrick, Kelly Ann, 324
Kirkpatrick, Michael, 324–325
Kirkpatrick, Nancy, 324–325
Kirkpatrick, Shannon, 10, 324–325

Klaus, Marshall, 53
Koff, Elissa, 360
Konner, Adam, 11, 123, 142–144, 173–174, 241
Konner, Sarah, 11, 123, 156–157, 179, 239, 241, 242, 326–327, 405
Konner, Susanna, 11, 142, 239
Korner, Annelise, 39
Krilov, Anya, 10, 320, 345–346
Kruger, Ann Cale, 150, 299–301

La Leche League, 68, 113–114
Lancaster, Jane, 427
Lane, Harlan, 211
Language
  deprivation, 211–212
  scaffolding concept, 148, 150, 151, 154, 271
  universal, 13, 145
Language Acquisition Device (L.A.D.), 145, 146, 148, 153
Language development, 121, 138–139
  cultural differences, 150–151, 154
  first words, 146
  learning patterns, 141–148
  nonverbal interaction, 148
  parental role, 149–150
  preverbal patterns, 148
  self-concept and, 87, 124–125, 155–156
Laron, Zvi, 355
Laslett, Peter, 367
Latency, 242
Lathrop, Julia, 107
Learning, 239–244
  apprenticeships, 244–246
  disorders, 248–249, 250, 253
  informal, 246–248
  postnatal, 53–57
Lee, Shin-Ying, 264, 268
Leehrsen, Charles, 386
Leiderman, Gloria, 115–116
Leiderman, Herbert, 115–116
Lenneberg, Eric, 141, 144, 145–146, 149
LeVine, Robert, 312
Lewis, Michael, 65, 121, 139, 376
Life and Confessions of a Psychologist (Hall), 362
Life expectancy, 422–423
Likano (father of Ali), 10
Limbic system, 99, 138, 165
Lipsitt, Lewis, 56
Lissak, Louis, 51
Literacy, 258

Locke, John, 204
Long, Nicholas, 219
Lord of the Flies (Golding), 316
Low birth weight, 41–42
Lozoff, Betsy, 113

Maccoby, Eleanor, 92, 161, 162
MacFarlane, Jean, 221
McGraw, Myrtle, 13
McKenna, James, 68
Main, Mary, 92
Malthus, Thomas Robert, 420, 421
Machi, Maria, 199–200
Marriage, 216–217, 219
  cultural differences, 368–370
Marshall, Lorna, 262–263
Mascall, Elizabeth, 302, 304
Mason, William, 215
Masturbation, 159, 196, 355, 362
Mather, Cotton, 200–201
Mather, Katherine, 200
Mather, Samuel, 302–303
Maurois, André, 408
Mead, Margaret, 108–110, 147, 158, 194, 409
  sex roles study, 373–374, 376
Medrich, Elliott, 321
Meggitt, Mervyn, 262
Meglen, Marie, 415
Memoirs of a Dutiful Daughter (de Beauvoir), 361
Memory, 63–64, 66, 407–410
Men in Groups (Tiger), 374
Menstruation/menarche, 354, 355, 357, 360–361, 363
  body weight and, 365–366
  cultural differences, 368, 382–383
  sexual activity and, 368
Mental development, 59, 63, 97, 98, 153, 241
Mental retardation, 251, 254
Meredith, Howard, 363
Midwifery, 48–49, 50
Miller, George, 412
Miracle Worker, The, 225
Montagu, Ashley, 368
Morality and fairness, 297–304, 325–326
Moral Judgement of the Child, The (Piaget), 298, 300
More Die of Heartbreak (Bellow), 406
Morelli, Gilda, 115
Moretti, Vanessa, 191–192
Moro reflex, 54
Morozov, Pavlik, 319, 320

Morrison, Toni, 349
Mortality rates
    child, 195, 197, 199
    cultural differences, 420–421
    infant, 51, 69, 195, 197–201, 411
    mothers in childbirth, 43–46, 195
Mubarak, Suzanne, 424
Multiple caretaking, 85, 115
Multiple intelligences, 255–257
Munroe, Robert, 310
Munroe, Ruth, 310
Murray, Lynne, 63
Mylander, Carolyn, 153

Nakayama, Chizuka, 10, 259
Nakayama, Karuna, 374
National Incidence Study, 204–205
Natural childbirth, 13, 47–49, 50, 51, 53
Nauta, Walle, 138
Navarro, José, 412–413
Neglect. *See* Abuse and neglect
Neill, A. S., 262
Neisser, Ulric, 252, 407
Nelson, Katherine, 146
Neuropsychology, 13–14
Neville, Helen, 153
Nietzsche, Friedrich, 385, 408
Nighttime Parenting (Sears), 114
Night-waking, 112
*Nisa: The Life and Words of a !Kung
    Woman* (Shostak), 306–307
Nonverbal communication, 100, 139–141
Nouhata, Kenzaburo, 10, 84, 88, 169
Nouhata, Koichiro, 112, 169
Nouhata, Mikiko, 84, 112, 160
Nouhata, Yojiro, 113, 169
Nursery rhymes. *See* Fairy tales and nurs-
    ery rhymes
Nussbaum, Hedda, 203
Nutrition. *See* Diet and nutrition

Object permanence, 64, 66, 96–99
Ochs, Eleanor, 150
Oedipus complex, 110, 159, 242
Oliveira, Maria, 51, 198–199, 257
Oliveira, Manoel, 51, 198–199, 257
Oliveira, Sandra, 345
Oliveira, Sergio, 345
Oliveira, Simone, 344–345
Oliveira, Suellen, 345
Oliveira, Sydney, 10, 51, 53, 257
Olweus, Dan, 358
Opie, Iona, 292, 294

Opie, Peter, 292, 294
Orrega, Maria Elena, 416

Pain sensitivity, 9
Palincsar, Annemarie Sullivan, 271
Parenting styles, 106–110, 196–197
Pavlov, Ivan, 242
Paxson, L. M., 113
Peekaboo game, 88
Peeples, Thelma, 275, 418
Peer groups
    competition in, 314–317
    cultural differences, 318–320
    day-care and, 171
    interaction in, 171–172
    mixed age/mixed sex, 172–173
    same age/same sex, 16, 173, 315
    solidarity in, 317–318
Penis envy, 158–159
Perry, Michelle, 266–267
Perry Preschool Program, 417–418
Personality development, 164–166
Petersen, Anne, 378
Physical contact. *See* "Bonding" and rela-
    tionships: mother/infant
Piaget, Jacqueline, 175
Piaget, Jean, 11, 18, 64, 120
    child-development theory, 305
    on fantasy, 175, 176
    genetic theory, 98
    mental-development theory, 148, 241,
        242, 387
    on object permanence, 96–97
    on rules and children, 298, 300, 301
Place Called School, A (Goodlad), 273
Play, Dreams, and Imitation in Childhood
    (Piaget), 175
Play and games, 16–17, 138, 157
    animals and, 305
    child culture and rituals in, 291–295
    cultural differences, 296–297
    fantasy in, 123, 154, 174–177
    gender divisions in, 311
    group participation, 313–315
    hide-and-seek, 295–296
    peekaboo, 88
    rules, 297–299
    sexual, 196, 242
    social, 172
    sports, 312–313, 365–366
    therapeutic, 176
    warlike, 313
Playmates, 138, 161, 172–173
Plomin, Robert, 166, 404

Poetry, 155
Pollock, Linda, 194
Popov, Larissa, 168
Popov, Mikhail, 169
Popov, Stas, 168–169
Popov, Vera, 10
Popov, Vitaly, 51, 53, 95, 168, 169
Portrait of the Artist as a Young Man
    (Joyce), 388–389
Poussaint, Alvin, 221
Poverty, 211, 411
    /child abuse ratios, 205
    fertility and, 199
    learning disorders and, 249
    mother/infant bonding and, 91, 103
Prechtl, Heinz, 54
Pregnancy, 17
    age statistics, 367–368
    health of fetus, 39–43
    hormonal changes, 375
    mortality rates, 43–46
    teen, 366, 367–368, 370–371
Prenatal care, 51–52
Primates in the Classroom: An Evolution-
    ary Perspective on Children's Educa-
    tion (Bernhard), 271
Problem-solving, 121
Project Head Start, 417–418
Prostitution, child, 317–318
Psychological deprivation, 211–214, 222–
    223
Puberty, 17, 240, 350, 386–389
    age at onset, 363
    cultural differences (rites of passage),
    357–358, 363–364, 370, 382–386
Punishment. *See* Discipline
Purcell, Linda, 271

Rapid-eye-movement, 61
Reading skills, 270–271, 276
Reagan, Ronald, 412
Regev, Eli, 105–106
Reinisch, June, 163
Religion and spirituality, 301–303, 325–
    326, 327
    cultural differences, 328–331
Reproduction, 33–39
Resiliency of children, 221–224
Resistant behavior, 90, 92
Resource Mothers program, 415–416
Robbers Cave Experiment, 315–316, 328
Rogoff, Barbara, 243, 271
Rose, Robert, 358
Rosenblum, Leonard, 214

Roskies, Diane, 259
Ross, Michael, 407
Rothenberg, Michael, 112
Rouge-spot experiment, 121–122, 125
Rousseau, Jean-Jacques, 312, 320, 426
Rovee-Collier, Carolyn, 64–65, 139

Scaffolding concept, 148, 150, 151, 154,
    271
Scarr, Sandra, 85, 114, 117, 404
Scheper-Hughes, Nancy, 198, 199
Schieffelin, Bambi, 150
Schlegel, Alice, 373–374
Schools Where Children Learn (Feather-
    stone), 262
Schorr, Daniel, 415
Schorr, Lisbeth, 415
Sears, William, 114
Self-concept, 17, 121–125
    language and, 87, 124–125, 155–156
    separation and, 87
Selfe, Lorna, 254
Self-reliance, 118–120
Selye, Hans, 225
Sendak, Maurice, 178
Separation
    attachment and, 118–119
    day-care and, 117
    fear of, 86–87, 88, 89
    mother/infant bonding and, 102
    object permanence and, 98–99
    reunion behavior, 89–90, 91–92, 93
    self-concept and, 87
Sewall, Samuel, 303
Sex roles, 110, 373–375, 376
Sexual abuse. *See* Abuse: sexual
Sexual activity, 366–367, 368, 371–372
    cultural differences, 368–369, 370
    hormones and, 380–381
    violent personality traits and, 380
Sexual development, 158–160, 358
    gender identification and, 160–164
    play and games, 196, 242
Shahar, Shulamith, 194, 200
Shaul, Dvora Ben, 67
Shaw, George Bernard, 204
Sherif, Muzafer, 315–316
Sherrod, Lonnie, 162
Shlyapnikov, Igor, 346
Shlyapnikov, Seryozha, 259, 320
Shostak, Marjorie, 11, 306, 368–369
Sibling rivalry, 167–171, 173, 323–325.
    See also Competition
Sign language, 145, 152, 226

Six Cultures Project, 307–310
Skinner, B. F., 18
Skuse, David, 213
Sleeping
    bed-sharing, 67, 68, 71, 103, 112–114, 196
    night-waking, 112
Slobin, Dan, 151
Smiling, 61, 62, 70, 88, 89, 139
Smith, Edward A., 380
Smith, Robert Paul, 321, 323
Smoking, 41, 52
Snow, Catherine, 146
Social development
    cultural differences, 310–312
    of infants, 61, 62, 65, 70, 85, 96, 100–101
Social/sexual development, 343–351
    emotional changes, 355–356
    physical changes, 354–355, 356–357, 358, 359, 361–362, 363–365
Social isolation, 211–216
Social referencing, 101, 119–120, 140
Spare the Child: The Religious Roots of Punishment and the Psychological Impact of Physical Abuse (Greven), 204
Spiritual Life of Children, The (Coles), 328
Spock, Benjamin, 18, 68, 70, 110–112, 114
Sports, 312–313, 365–366
Sroufe, Alan, 92
Steinberg, Joel, 203
Steinschneider, Alfred, 56
Stepparents, 206
Stern, Daniel, 66, 123–124
Stevenson, Harold, 264, 266, 268, 276–277
Stigler, James, 266–267
Strangers, fear of, 86–87, 88, 89
Strange Situation test, 87, 89–90, 91, 93, 102
    cultural differences, 118–119
    day-care centers and, 115, 117
Stress
    adaptation, 224–225
    fetal, 52
    infant, 52, 89
    resistance, 222
Stress of Life, The (Selye), 225
Sucking reflex, 54–55, 56
Sula (Morrison), 349
Sullivan, Annie, 225–226

Sullivan, Louis, 413
Summerhill (Neill), 262
Suomi, Stephen, 215, 404
Super, Charles, 64

Talbert, Luther, 358
Tanner, James, 363, 364
Task assignment, 243–244, 305–307, 309
    child-care duties, 314
    gender divisions in, 311
    family chores, 15–16, 193, 195
Television, 161–162, 164, 322–323, 378–379, 428
Temperament, 89–93, 164–165, 169
Thalidomide, 39–40, 58
Thevenin, Tine, 114
Tiger, Lionel, 374
Timidity, 9, 14, 165, 166–167
Tolstoy, Leo, 45
Tomasello, Michael, 149–150
Touching. See "Bonding" and relationships: mother/infant
Trivers, Robert, 402
Tronick, Edward, 63, 115
Trust relationships, 90
Tulkin, Steven, 113
Twins, 164, 166, 167, 381
Two Worlds of Childhood (Bronfenbrenner), 318–319

Udry, Richard, 358, 380
Universal grammar, 145
Unwed mothers, 191. See also Pregnancy: teen
Uses of Enchantment, The (Bettelheim), 178
Uttal, David, 277

Vaillant, George, 221, 225
Violence
    childhood abuse and, 379–380
    gender differences, 376–377
    juvenile, 366, 377–378
    homicide, 69, 70, 202, 206, 377, 413
Vision, infant, 55–56, 62, 65
Vulnerable But Invincible (Werner), 224
Vygotsky, Lev, 148, 242, 271

Wallerstein, Judith, 217–218
Warren, Michelle, 359
Watson, John S., 64–65, 66, 107–108, 110
Wells, H. G., 362

Werner, Emmy, 222, 224
Wertsch, James, 271
Wesley, Susanna, 204
Where Did You Go? Out. What Did You Do? Nothing. (Smith), 321
Where the Wild Things Are (Sendak), 178
White, Merry, 268
White, Sheldon, 239
Whiting, Beatrice, 19, 162, 307–308, 310, 311–312, 374
Whiting, John, 19, 162, 196, 307–308, 374
Widom, Cathy Spatz, 379
Wiesner, Thomas, 173
Wild Boy of Aveyron (Victor), 211–212, 213–214
Wilson, Margo, 206

Within Our Reach: Breaking the Cycle of Disadvantage and Despair (Schorr and Schorr), 415
Wong, Eugene, 204
Wong, Mary, 204
Woods, Margaret, 303–304, 401
Wordsworth, William, 201
Worthman, Carol, 357
Wyshak, Grace, 363

Young, Mikal, 42

Zajac, Chris, 272–273
Zametkin, Alan, 250–251
Zborowski, Mark, 259